Dodging Bullets

Dodging Bullets

Changing U.S. Corporate Capital Structure in the 1980s and 1990s

Robert N. McCauley, Judith S. Ruud, and Frank Iacono

MIT Press
Cambridge, Massachusetts
London, England

© 1999 Massachusetts Institute of Technology

This book was set in Stone Serif and Stone Sans by Achorn Graphic Services, Inc. Printed and bound in the United States of America.

Library of Congress Cataloging-in-Publication Data

McCauley, Robert N.
  Dodging bullets : changing U.S. corporate capital structure in the 1980s and
  1990s / Robert N. McCauley, Judith S. Ruud, and Frank Iacono.
  p.   cm.
  Includes bibliographical references and index.
  ISBN 0-262-13351-2 (hc : alk. paper)
  1. Leveraged buyouts—United States—History—20th century. 2. Consolidation
and merger of corporations—United States—History—20th century. 3. Corporations—United States—Finance—History—20th century. I. Ruud, Judith S.
II. Iacono, Frank. III. Title.
HD2746.55.U5M35   1999
338.8'0973—dc21   **3 2280 00746 4712**   99-32604
                                                                               CIP

Contents

About the Authors

Robert N. McCauley is a Senior Economic and Financial Representative at the Representative Office for Asia and the Pacific of the Bank for International Settlements in Hong Kong.

Judith S. Ruud serves as an economist covering financial markets and institutions at the Congressional Budget Office in Washington, D.C.

Frank Iacono trades credit derivatives with Chase Securities in New York City.

The views expressed in this book are those of the authors and should not be interpreted as those of the Bank for International Settlements, the Congressional Budget Office, or Chase Securities.

Preface

What is this book about? How does this book relate to other books on the same subject? For whom is it written? This preface answers these questions with quotations, at times paraphrased, of the reviewers who examined the book at the behest of the publisher.

This book offers an entertaining and careful summary of the trends in U.S. corporate financial policy in the past decade and a half. It addresses three major questions: Why did corporate leverage rise in the 1980s? Why did the leverage wave come to an end? And, how and why did companies deleverage in the early 1990s? The chronological organization makes sense, because one cannot understand why companies deleveraged in the 1990s without understanding the leverage wave of the 1980s. The last part of the book focuses on public policy, and the recommendations in these chapters are supported by the research in the early chapters. Readers who did not follow the financial press closely over the past 15 years could pick up this book and understand why leveraged buyouts occurred in the 1980s and why they have been reversed in the 1990s.

This book fills a void on the subject of capital structure. Whereas the subject of chapter 2, the rise and fall of the leverage wave, has been covered extensively in the popular press and in some academic work, the deleveraging of the 1990s has received much less attention. During the 1980s takeover wave, publishers had a ready audience for tales of greed and power struggles. Although deleveraging is not sexy, the authors' account is carefully researched and written in a style to hold the reader's attention. The treatment is objective without being too academic.

The book covers a wider range of material than most serious treatments of corporate finance. One of its strengths is its style of writing. Unlike some economists, the authors do not torture the reader. The authors use sound theoretical arguments, supported by careful analysis of data, but avoid the technical details and heavy academic jargon. The Minsky-Kindleberger paradigm is an ingenious stylistic device that holds the book together. This book fits between the broadest market for books on corporate finance and the scholarly market for treatises on the theory of corporate behavior.

This book thus addresses itself to two audiences. First, it can supplement a corporate finance text for advanced undergraduates in business curricula or for students in master's in business administration programs. For these, the book provides a lively complement to textbooks and journal article treatments of corporate finance. Standard textbooks rarely analyze manias and bubbles. Even when the possibility of manias is allowed, the standard analysis can be smug and dry. Away from the academic community, nearly everyone in the finance business does not question the existence of manias. Finance school students need to learn the details of models that are based on strict rational optimization. But they also need some exposure to this type of careful analysis, which recognizes that security markets in the United States may not conform to the standard model of rational markets run by participants with full information.

Second, the book addresses a wide audience in the business and finance community. Very few analysts at investment banks have a big-picture perspective on corporate finance. This book can go a long way toward bridging that gap. Likewise, many people currently working in corporate treasuries were either not in the field in the 1980s or have dim memories of corporate capital structure issues. Anyone associated with corporate finance should read this book.

Acknowledgments

The core of this book developed as a series of briefings that took place a day or two before Federal Open Market Committee meetings at the Federal Reserve Bank of New York, mostly in 1991–92, but also as late as 1994. Looking back, we benefited from the need of policy makers to make sense of developments in corporate finance in real time. We wish to thank our colleagues there and then, especially Eli Remolona and Edward J. Frydl. We would also like to thank Elizabeth Berko and Kevin Cole for excellent research assistance, and Rose Carafalo for secretarial assistance. We thank current and former economists of the Capital Markets Section of the Federal Reserve Board: Lee Crabbe, Jean Helwege, Nellie Liang, Steve Oliner, Wayne Passmore, Margaret Pickering, and John Rea.

We thank Charles P. Kindleberger for inspiration; his work is the North Star for this book. We also thank Robert Z. Aliber for his encouragement. One cannot hope for better teachers. We are grateful to Reiner Kraakman for his reading of chapter 3, and we appreciate the hard work of several anonymous reviewers.

Closer to home, we thank Clark R. McCauley for his editorial help on most of the chapters and Paul E. Ruud for his tireless efforts to get the manuscript shipshape and ready for publication.

Finally, we wish to thank E. Gerald Corrigan for his gruff intonation of the last line of this book.

1   *Introduction*

The end of the 1980s brought big news in U.S. corporate finance no less than in international affairs. Yet while the television cameras followed the party atop the Berlin Wall, no cameras captured the change in how U.S. firms financed themselves.

An editor might splice together the following film clips to introduce a viewer to how the 1980s yielded to the 1990s in U.S. corporate finance. *Scene One: Late 1988.* F. Ross Johnson, chief executive officer of RJR-Nabisco, says into the telephone, "What makes you think Peter [Cohen of Shearson Lehman] can go any higher than we have? Jesus, Jim [Robinson, head of American Express], these numbers are giving me nosebleed already." *Scene Two: January 1990.* RJR-Nabisco's treasurer is called out of a meeting with Robert Rubin, co-head of Goldman Sachs, and returns to report, slack-faced, "You're not going to believe this, but our bonds have been downgraded by Moody's"; the meeting breaks up as Rubin excuses himself and Lou Gerstner, chief executive of RJR, huddles with other executives around a computer monitor to watch the prices of RJR's bonds tumble. *Scene Three: February 1990.* Fred Joseph, head of Drexel Burnham Lambert, hangs up the telephone after talking to regulators at the Securities Exchange Commission and Federal Reserve, turns to an aide and says, "I've just been told by the most powerful men in America to put this company into bankruptcy—

immediately." *Scene Four: February 1990.* The camera pans over the Phoenician, the extravagant Arizona resort built by Charles Keating, and then zooms into the hotel ballroom, where Henry Kravis promises a roomful of skeptical junk bond buyers that he will restore the value of their bonds, and warns: "Financial panics are almost always the result of a herd mentality run amok."[1]

These four clips represent the broad reshaping of U.S. corporate finance. The 1980s featured pitched takeover battles that culminated in the debt-financed bidding for RJR-Nabisco. It is noteworthy that Home Box Office made a movie of the RJR-Nabisco takeover even though it could earn its "R" rating only by virtue of the saltiness of the takeover generals' language rather than for any sex or violence. The later downgrading of RJR-Nabisco's bonds sent the junk bond market into a panic. Shortly after, Drexel Burnham Lambert, which had risen to the top rank of U.S. securities firms by selling junk bonds to finance takeovers, filed for bankruptcy—an act that resulted from, and contributed to, distress in the market for low-rated bonds. The junk bond market recovered only after Henry Kravis, who had beaten Ross Johnson in the bidding for RJR, made good on his promise to the holders of the firm's bonds by buying them back with the proceeds of freshly issued equity. The substitution of debt for equity in the 1980s turned into the substitution of equity for debt in the 1990s.

This book addresses a number of substantive issues in the course of chronicling U.S. corporations' return to equity in the 1990s. Why did the 1980s' substitution of the fixed obligations of debt for the less-demanding claim of equity give way to its opposite in the 1990s? In particular, what happened to the firm that went private in the biggest leveraging transaction of the 1980s but has since proved the biggest deleveraging firm of the 1990s? What kind of firms, spurred by what forces, sold equity? How important was the return to equity in relation to the fortuitously falling trend of short-term interest rates from 1989 through 1993 in relieving U.S. corporations of the burden of their debts? How did investors fare who bought into the archetypal transactions that reduced debt with equity? How did the return to equity affect the ability of young high-tech firms to finance themselves without selling out to foreign firms? Is the booming mergers and acquisition market of the 1990s a return to the deal making of the 1980s? What lessons are there for policy makers in the fate of the leveraging business?

This book is divided into three parts. The first part addresses the question of why the leveraging business of the late 1980s fell apart. The second part addresses the return to equity in the 1990s. The third part draws lessons from corporate leveraging and its aftermath.

1.1   The End of the 1980s

Chapters 2 and 3 examine competing answers to the question of why the 1980s ended. The former argues for a market process, albeit one not found in textbooks; the latter considers arguments for a political process, arguments that threaten to become the conventional wisdom on the basis more of repetition than of evidence.

Chapter 2 interprets the leveraging wave of the 1980s as a financial market mania. This interpretation goes beyond a merely negative claim that the main movements in U.S. corporate finance in the 1980s cannot be explained within a narrow range of models of house-trained *homo economicus*. Instead, following Minsky and Kindleberger, we identify what set off the infatuation with debt, how the debt euphoria expressed and propagated itself, what shook the shared presumptions of those engaged in promoting debt, how they panicked, and what factors conspired to prevent a spectacular crash. This chapter does not intend to test formally the Minsky-Kindleberger model against the evidence of the 1980s; rather we use their model to organize the experience of the 1980s around themes and sequences common to financial market excesses of the past. The value of the model emerges as the leveraging wave of the 1980s loses its surprising or anomalous appearance.

Chapter 3 offers a competing interpretation. Whereas chapter 2 argues that U.S. financial markets in the 1980s went through a cycle of excess, chapter 3 weighs the claims that political and legal forces brought an otherwise successful series of market adaptations to an early and untimely end. This chapter reviews a series of legal and regulatory changes at the close of the decade, discusses how each is asserted to have undermined the leveraging business, and then confronts such assertions with the available evidence. The legal and regulatory changes cover a wide range, from Delaware case law to state anti-takeover statutes, to the congressional prohibition on savings and loans' holding junk bonds, to tax law changes that limited the deductibility of interest on junk bonds, to bank regulators' treatment of bank loans to leveraged firms, to state insurance regulators' capital rules. This interdisciplinary chapter not only gathers in one place the scattered assertions about the impact of regulatory and legal changes, but more importantly assesses the timing of these changes and weighs their several effects on the leveraging business. We find little support for the variety of assertions that judges, lawmakers, and regulators killed the leveraging business.

Chapter 4 examines the case of RJR-Nabisco, which exemplifies the transition from the 1980s to the 1990s. The 1988 bidding contest and the 1989 closing of the $22 billion buyout made the deal the largest and most-remarked-upon transaction among the 1980's acquisitions. Despite RJR's operating more or less according to plan, however, by 1990 the company faced a serious risk of bankruptcy. Only a timely replacement of some of the equity that had so recently been drained from the company, raised from both investors already involved and outside investors, kept the company's finances from imploding. In these transactions, RJR-Nabisco again epitomized a larger movement, this time in the contrary direction of retiring debt with equity and refinancing higher coupon debt with bonds issued in a less-demanding bond market. Chapter 4 shows how near RJR came to falling without a net and documents how the firm instead eased its way down to the ground. The chapter also exploits the natural experiment that occurred among tobacco companies in late 1988: Tobacco giant Philip Morris bought Kraft Foods while tobacco giant cum food company RJR-Nabisco undertook a leveraged buyout. To determine what difference the buyout made, we contrast the evolution of the market value and the cash thrown off by RJR with those from Philip Morris. We also examine direct measures on the performance of RJR and Philip Morris, including profit margins, overheads, capital spending, and labor productivity and layoffs at the two companies. The buyout of RJR-Nabisco emerges as neither the spectacular success of early reports nor as the big loser it is now generally thought to have been.

1.2 The Return to Equity in the 1990s

Chapter 5 returns from the particular to the general and documents the turnaround in corporate finance in the 1990s from net equity retirement to net equity issuance. The aggressively leveraged deals of the 1980s became almost impossible in the early 1990s. Moreover, mergers and acquisition activity more generally slowed, and what activity remained changed in its nature from relying on debt to relying on equity. The rally in the stock market after the Gulf War permitted U.S. corporations to return to Wall Street for unprecedented billions of equity capital. Likewise, a rally in the bond market presented U.S. firms with the opportunity to call their bonds and to refinance them with new paper bearing less-burdensome rates of interest.

Chapter 6 shows that all the activity of corporate treasurers outlined in chapter 5 did not amount to much compared to the effect of short-term interest rates. The effect of corporate refinancing in 1991–93— selling equity, calling bonds, and selling new bonds—was mostly to reduce the burden of interest payments on corporate cash flows. Quite apart from the activity of corporate treasurers and their Wall Street advisors in the securities markets, another factor was at work in the early 1990s to relieve the burden of interest payments on corporate cash flows. That is, the downward trend of short-term interest rates all by itself worked through short-term corporate liabilities directly to reduce corporate interest payments. Chapter 6 decomposes the decline in the interest–to–cash flow ratio for the U.S. nonfinancial corporate sector into the portion attributable to corporate refinancing and that attributable to lower short-term interest rates. Relative to corporate refinancing, lower short-term interest rates turn out to have been surprisingly potent in relieving corporate cash flows of the burden of debt service.

Chapter 7 focuses on the equity offerings in the early 1990s that eased firms down from the high wire of debt. Companies involved in the big leveraged deals of the 1980s were able to slough off some of the burden of debt undertaken by making what came to be known as reverse leveraged-buyout initial public offerings (reverse LBO IPOs). If the LBO was the characteristic deal of the 1980s, the reverse LBO IPO became the characteristic deal of the early 1990s. We examine the evidence bearing on the question of how the investors fared in buying into reverse LBO IPOs. Did the market prices of these offerings reward investors, not only on the days immediately following the offerings, but over longer periods as well? Observers have argued that the issuers of IPOs and their Wall Street advisors intentionally leave money on the table, which shows up in the form of initially high returns to IPO investors. Reverse LBO IPOs provide interesting evidence in that the sellers may be presumed to be very knowledgeable. More importantly, how did investors do over the year or two after the issue? Could it be that precisely the equity capital that did most to prevent a crash of leveraged companies into bankruptcy offered weak returns to the investors? Chapter 7 investigates the short- and long-term returns on the largest reverse LBO IPOs of 1991–93.

Chapter 8 highlights an international dimension of the return to equity in the 1990s. The hot equity market in the 1990s not only permitted leveraged companies to bring their debt service into better balance with their cash flow but also afforded high-technology companies access to public equity at a surprisingly early stage of their development. The willingness of public equity investors to buy into what they hoped would prove the next Microsoft meant that high-technology firms were much less likely in the 1990s than in the 1980s to look to foreign firms for buy-ins. The evidence on the substitution of the U.S. equity market for foreign investment in U.S. high-technology sectors should be of interest to those observers who have expressed concern about such investment.

Chapter 9 profiles the mergers and acquisition market of the 1990s. In general, mergers in the 1990s have featured an exchange of equity so that they have not served to flush cash out of corporate America or to mortgage future operational strength to making heavy interest payments. Exceptions to this generalization in defense and pharmaceuticals point to a more discriminating merger market than that of the 1980s. Whether all the mergers in media and telecommunications (not to mention finance) will prove boons to shareholders is an interesting question, but one with less policy salience than the macroeconomic and banking risks posed by the 1980s leveraging business on Wall Street. At the same time, under pressure from increasingly vocal shareholders, major corporations have been splitting themselves up, so that the regrouping of corporate divisions into more coherent firms continues without much assistance from leveraged buyouts.

1.3 Lessons

Chapter 10 draws policy lessons from the experience of corporate leveraging and its aftermath. One conclusion that should not be drawn is that monetary policy in the 1980s should have been tighter. Interest rates remained high enough in the latter part of the 1980s to keep inflation in check. Whereas money was fairly tight, credit got very loose in the late 1980s.

Chapter 10 pays more serious attention to policies to tighten credit in the face of increased leveraging. One such policy was in fact adopted, namely, the required disclosure of banks' exposure to the leveraging business. This market-friendly approach had much to recommend it, for it permitted stock market buyers to distinguish banks with a relatively risky lending strategy. We urge policies to restrain credit availability, including limits on leverage applied to mergers and increases in required capital for financial institutions. In the extreme, reserve requirements could have in effect put a tax on rapid growth in loans. In considering these policies, we provide examples of where central banks have in fact adopted such measures.

Chapter 10 also considers more mainstream policy responses to the leveraging business. Long-standing incentives for firms to finance themselves with debt can hardly be blamed for suddenly causing corporations to leverage up in the 1980s. Nevertheless, a recasting of tax policy to make it neutral in the choice between equity and debt makes a great deal of sense, and we consider revenue-neutral means to approach such neutrality. Finally, we take seriously the claims of the proponents of leverage that it served to discipline managers not otherwise accountable for their stewardship. We urge policy changes to accelerate the momentum toward institutional investors' taking a larger role in corporate governance.

Chapter 11 concludes our profile of corporate financing in the 1990s. We highlight the main themes from chapters 2 through 10. Then we emphasize how serendipitous were the market conditions that permitted the fragile capital structures built in the 1980s to be reinforced before they collapsed. Falling short-term rates not only helped highly leveraged firms directly but also induced American savers to switch from bank deposits to mutual funds, which in turn bought the equities and bonds from refinancing corporations. If market conditions had not permitted short-term rates to fall so far and remain so low, the corporate leveraging crash might not have been averted. We consider what might have been the policy response to the distress of scores of major corporations in the event such private equity had not been available: Instead of private equity, public equity might have been injected into the distressed firms.

All this argumentation would amount to a merely historical exercise if one could not imagine a revival of the leveraging business. A downturn in the long bull equity market that has marked the 1990s would put corporate valuations within reach of the leveraged-buyout firms that are sitting on substantial sums of private equity. Such a downturn would be accompanied by a decline in the flow of savings into the equity mutual funds that have done so much to support the corporate sector's return to equity. The banking system's return to profitability and ongoing consolidation leave it, in the late 1990s primed to make leveraged loans again. The waning memory of the averted disaster risks leaving the impression that the high-wire experiment with debt was a near success that bears repetition. We close by urging the adoption of policies to restrain another outbreak of the corporate leveraging mania.

The rescue in 1998 of the persuasively named and highly leveraged hedge fund Long-Term Capital Management offers a reminder: The leveraging business can show up not only in the market for whole companies but also in the usually boring bond markets. Those asking what should be done about the leveraging business of the 1990s might wish to consult the lessons of the leveraging business of the 1980s.

I The End of the 1980s

2   *Why the 1980s Stopped: Leveraging as a Mania*

Observers have offered at least two different explanations for why U.S. corporations stopped leveraging their finances by substituting debt for equity as the 1980s yielded to the 1990s. Both recognize that the leveraging business slowed well before the economy entered recession in 1990, so that the normal movement of mergers with the business cycle cannot offer a satisfying explanation. The first account sees the participants in U.S. corporate leveraging as swept up in a mania until the panic of 1989–90 and the barely avoided crash thereafter. The second holds that a defensive coalition of entrenched managers and unionized workers used politics and regulation to restrict credit and otherwise to handicap outside bidders for corporations. The first account points to a playing out of a market phenomenon that has much in common with other manias. The second points to the interruption of a market innovation by politics.

This chapter argues that U.S. corporate leveraging in the 1980s and its reversal fit the archetype of financial excess as described by Minsky and Kindleberger. Chapter 3 critically examines the alternative political account of the turn in U.S. corporate financing in the late 1980s.

Kindleberger drew on the work of Minsky to construct a schema that organizes historical experience of an unstable credit system in a way that emphasizes the common elements across such excesses.[1]

According to this schema, a full-blown mania goes through five stages, which we will first define and then use to tell the story of corporate leveraging in the 1980s and its reversal in the 1990s.[2]

In stage 1, a *displacement* occurs at the outset of a mania and signals to market participants a new source of profit. Examples include not only such classic disturbances as wars and harvests but also strictly financial events such as the refinancing of government debt at lower interest rates and a prominent and oversubscribed issue of securities. Suddenly a new way of making money comes compellingly into view.

Stage 2, *euphoria,* can succeed the displacement. Credit expands faster than nominal output, pushing up prices of real and financial assets. Such asset price inflation need not entail general inflation: Japan in the late 1980s experienced the former but not the latter. A widening circle of traders buy assets with the prospect of selling them rather than reaping income from them. Lenders relax standards and require lower down payments, less-secure coverage of interest payments, and less of a track record in managing debt. Easy credit and high asset prices typically spur investment and consumption spending, which stimulates economic activity. Contrary to academic models of a bubble in the price of a single asset, experience suggests that trading and capital gains in one market, for example, Japanese equities, feed on and stimulate trading and capital gains in another market, for example, Japanese real estate. Moreover, such market interaction rarely confines itself within national borders. Toward the end of euphoria, swindles and scandals come to light.

Distress, stage 3, characterizes the transition from euphoria to panic. Price or transaction records may continue to be set, but deals get harder to close. Shrewd market participants may begin to hedge their bets. Liquidity begins to dry up, and market participants may consider for the first time the possibility of being stuck with their current holdings.

Panic ensues in stage 4 when the crowd runs for the door. The favored assets find only sellers and few buyers. Prices of the heretofore favored assets plummet.

Finally, in stage 5, a *crash* brings down the structures of credit that have been erected around the objects of speculation. Bankruptcy spreads from the fringe players toward the center as the difficulties of the lesser players cast doubt on the assets of the central players.

This, then, is the Minsky-Kindleberger schema. It provides the structure of our interpretation of corporate leveraging in the 1980s as a financial mania (table 2.1).

2.1 Displacement

A mania starts with an event that signals a new opportunity for profit, such as war, harvest, or a prominent transaction. In the case of the leveraging wave of the 1980s, the standout deal involved the company that owns the hip cartoon cat Garfield:

> In 1982 an investment group led by William Simon, a former treasury secretary, took private a Cincinnati company, Gibson Greetings, for $80 million, using only a million dollars of its own money. When Simon took Gibson public eighteen months later, it sold for $290 million. Simon's $330,000 investment was suddenly worth $66 million in cash and securities.
>
> It was a fluke, an accident of timing, but it turned heads on Wall Street. Gibson Greetings became its equivalent of gold at Sutter's mill. Suddenly everyone wanted to try this "LBO thing," even though few knew how it worked. And try it they did.[3]

William Simon's 10,000 percent return in 18 months drew attention to a business that had already been broadened from its traditional venue. This venue on Main Street was far from the floor of the New York Stock Exchange on Wall Street. When a founder of a firm approached retirement with no heir, a leveraged buyout could cash out the founder and permit a new manager to lever his own modest resources into ownership of the business. From such humble beginnings, the leveraged buyout came into use as a means of financing a division sold off by a conglomerate. Some partnerships in the buyout business

Table 2.1
Kindleberger's model of euphoria

Key feature of Kindleberger model	Relevance of recent U.S. corporate experience	Comment
Displacement Exogenous shock that changes profit opportunities significantly.	Gibson Greetings buyout at $80 million in 1982 and subsequent public offering at $290 million.	Former Treasury Secretary William Simon earns $66 million or 10,000% in 18 months.
Expansion of credit Fuels investment boom related to restructuring and triggers asset price rises.	Credit to nonfinancial corporate business grows much faster than nominal GDP. Price of companies and pieces of companies rises.	No real investment boom.
Speculative trading Purchase of real and financial assets for resale rather than income.	Firms are increasingly bought to be resold in pieces.	Many companies are recycled through Wall Street leveraging business two or three times.
Excessive leverage Lax lending practices permit speculative purchases with cash requirements that are low relative to prevailing asset prices and possible price fluctuations.	Junk bonds allow corporate raiders to bootstrap into boardroom.	Campeau finances purchase of Federated Department Stores with 97 percent debt.
Positive economic feedback Expansion of credit supports large wealth increases, increased effective demand and investment.	Increased demand for investment bankers, lawyers, and accountants stimulates office building.	Cutbacks in capital expenditure and research and development by leveraged firms limit economic feedback.

Table 2.1   (continued)

Key feature of Kindleberger model	Relevance of recent U.S. corporate experience	Comment
Market interconnections— intranational		
At least two objects of speculation are involved, with speculative price increases in one market fueling increases in related market.	Markets for LBO funds, corporate divisions, stocks, junk bonds, and leveraged bank loans all stimulate each other's prices and liquidity.	Collapse of leveraging business in 1989–90 points to key role of credit: bank debt and junk bonds.
Market interconnections— international		
"Overtrading" historically tends to spread from one country to another through capital flows.	Foreign firms acquire U.S. firms, divisions, real estate. Rapid expansion of foreign, especially Japanese, banks in the United States eases syndication and trading of leveraged bank loans.	In peak year, foreign firms account for nearly a third of acquisitions. Foreign banks take half of RJR loan.
Swindles, scandals		
"The making known of malfeasances" is an important signal that the euphoria has been excessive.	Scandals range from insider trading to fraud and violations of fiduciary duty by mutual fund managers to reckless overinvestment in junk by semicaptive insurance companies and savings and loans.	Levine, Boesky, Milken, Keating spend time in jail.

have continued to focus consistently on buyouts of divisions, the "stepchildren" of large, diversified firms.[4]

But other firms in the leveraged-buyout business grew and began to target entire firms and indeed larger and larger firms traded on the New York Stock Exchange. To finance ever larger transactions, the buyout firms raised equity from institutional investors. The equity committed would flow through blind equity pools, so named because the investors would not see any transactions until after funds were committed.

2.2   Euphoria

The history of fund-raising by what proved to be the largest arranger of leveraged buyouts, Kohlberg, Kravis, Roberts (KKR), offers an idea of the surge of interest in leveraged deals among equity investors. The firm had started in 1976 with $120,000 of the three partners' money. The first investors in 1976 included Kravis's father, Kohlberg's cousin, a Pittsburgh venture capitalist, First Chicago's venture capital subsidiary, and four other individual backers. The next round of investment in 1978 raised $30 million from such institutional investors as Allstate and Teachers Insurance as well as the venture capital subsidiaries of such banks as Citicorp, Continental Illinois, and Security Pacific. In 1980 the partners hit the road again and raised $75 million from banks and insurance companies. In 1982 KKR raised $316 million from, among others, the state employee pension plans of Oregon, Washington, and Michigan, as well as from Metropolitan Life and the endowments of Harvard University and Swarthmore College. Those running the state employee plans felt a thrill in dealing with the likes of the KKR partners and counted themselves privileged to be invited to participate in ventures with such high prospective returns.[5] The partners raised $980 million in 1984 and $1.8 billion in 1986, eventually sign-

Billions of dollars

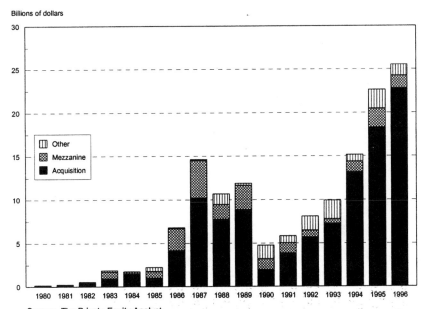

Source: The Private Equity Analyst.
Note: "Other" includes distressed debt and other funds. Distressed debt accounted for $320 million of the "Other" category in 1991 and $1 billion in both 1992 and 1993. KKR's fund is included in 1991-92 when it raised the funds. KKR promised not to use the funds until its 1987 fund was fully invested.

Figure 2.1
Commitments to private equity funds

ing up even such corporate pension funds as those of Coca Cola, Hughes Aircraft and Avon. In 1987 KKR raised no less than $5.6 billion.[6] Stepping back, successive funds assembled two years apart showed a doubling in size, until the 1987 fund, which showed a tripling in one year.

KKR was not alone in roping in investors into such private equity funds (figure 2.1). Commitments to all private equity funds accelerated from near 0 in 1980 to more than $14 billion in the peak year of KKR's 1987 blockbuster fund. But blind pools continued to draw institutional investment at a rate of about $10 billion per year through 1989.

Fund organizers promised returns in excess of those available on ordinary stock market investments and tied their own compensation to

Table 2.2
Washington State Investment Board's investment in KKR's funds

Partnership fund	Investment ($ millions)	Total value at December 31, 1993 ($ millions)	Rate of return* (percent)	Management fees paid to KKR ($ millions)
KKR 1982 fund	13.0	38.9	36.8	0.3
KKR 1984 fund	127.1	544.2	32.0	3.1
KKR 1986 fund	168.0	348.5	22.4	9.2
KKR 1987 fund	1,035.6	1,434.4	11.6	40.6
KKR 1993 fund	5.9	5.9	0	0
Total	1,349.6	2,371.9	20.5	53.2

Source: Brinson Partners, Inc., Chicago, *Executive Summary of Investment Performance as of December 31, 1993: Alternative Investments*, report prepared for the State of Washington State Investment Board, May 1994, Appendix on KKR Portfolio, p. 6.
* These average annual returns for February 1983 to December 1993 are net of management fees (i.e., management fees paid directly to KKR are included as a cash flow in computing the return for each fund).

the realization of those promises. Typically, fund organizers charged a flat management fee on committed funds and an incentive fee, namely, some substantial fraction of fund profits. In particular, KKR charged a 2.5 percent management fee payable on the total of funds committed, whether invested or not, and 20 percent of all profits as an incentive fee.

The few investors who bought into KKR's early funds did very well. Results as of late 1993 must be regarded as interim, since KKR expected a commitment of 12 to 18 years from investors. Nevertheless, investments in the 1982 and 1984 funds were showing returns of more than 30 percent, and investment in the 1986 fund was showing gains of more than 20 percent (table 2.2). The many investors who bought into KKR's 1987 fund were faring poorly; that is, they would have done better buying the Standard and Poor's 500 shares and borne less risk from leveraged positions as well. Chapter 4 discusses the reasons for this lackluster performance.

Expansion of Credit

Leveraging passed from handicraft to manufacturing with the motive power of junk bonds. Like leveraged buyouts, junk bonds predated the 1980s but were pressed into service in very different circumstances in the 1980s. Junk bonds are bonds that the rating agencies rate below "investment grade," that is, Baa (Moody's) or BBB (Standard & Poor's). Before the 1980s, junk bonds were born almost entirely by accident, by virtue of the decline in the fortunes of a firm that had originally issued investment grade debt. Because of the way they came about, back then below–investment grade bonds were known as "fallen angels." In the 1980s junk bonds came to be bred intentionally. Public junk bond issuance rose from $8 billion in 1983 to $34 billion in 1986 (figure 2.2). Public junk bonds outstanding climbed to about $225 billion by the end of 1989, fully one-fifth of the corporate bond market (figure 2.3).

Junk's early propaganda always focused on such fast-growing issuers as MCI Telecommunications, but the junk bond market came to draw its dynamism in the 1980s from another kind of firm: mature firms just acquired or engaged in mergers and acquisitions. As late as September 1985, Congress could be reassured that most junk bonds were issued by small firms uninvolved in mergers and acquisitions and that mergers and acquisitions drew little financing from junk bonds.[7] But already in 1985, one-third of the proceeds of all junk bond issues went to finance mergers and acquisitions (figure 2.2).[8] In 1986–89 the bulk of funds raised in the junk bond market financed acquisitions. In sum, although not themselves new, junk bonds found a new use in takeovers. Thus junk bonds represented not a product innovation but rather a process innovation.[9]

Michael Milken deserves the credit for this innovation. Into the mid-1980s Milken and his employer, Drexel Burnham Lambert, dominated the junk bond business. Many of the issuers had manifold relations with Drexel: sellers of securities, buyers of securities, buyers of

Billions of dollars

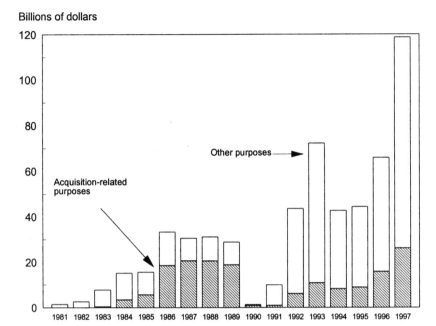

Source: Merrill Lynch.
Note: Includes nonconvertible, corporate debt rated below investment grade by Moody's or Standard & Poor's.Excludes mortgage- and asset-backed issues, as well as non-144a private placements.

Figure 2.2
Issuance of junk bonds by purpose

assets, bidders in takeovers, and so on. An outside investor, such as an insurer or mutual fund, buying a junk bond was in some respects blindly funding a loose connection of companies.[10] Thus, KKR's blind equity pool in some respects found a parallel in the Drexel blind debt pool.

After Gibson Greeting had exposed the glint of a new way to get rich and Drexel had brought junk bonds to bear on financing takeovers, mainline securities firms sought to challenge Drexel's hold on the business. Well-established Wall Street firms had considerable incentives to try to muscle into Drexel's niche. In 1985, for instance, Salomon Brothers, First Boston, and Goldman Sachs took win, place, and show, respectively, in the race to underwrite corporate debt.[11] Yet Drexel, a

Billions of dollars

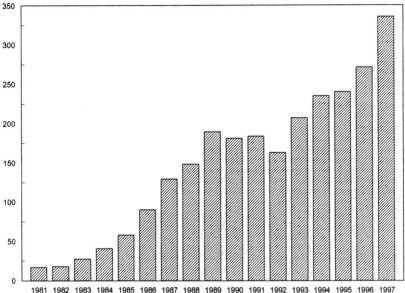

Source: Edward I. Altman, as cited in Merrill Lynch *Extra Credit*.
Note: Par value of straight debt issues only, excluding defaulted issues.

Figure 2.3
Junk bonds outstanding

slow fourth in the underwriter race, took in more underwriting fees, $280 million, than Salomon Brothers, at $193 million. With fees for investment grade corporate bonds at 0.65 percent but fees for junk bonds at 3 percent, the incentive for even the most genteel securities firm to get into junk bonds was nearly irresistible.[12]

Junk bonds created a massive and apparently lucrative new business line for banks. The immediate and initial effect of junk bonds was actually negative: The evidence is clear that junk bonds displaced bank credit in buyouts. The substitution of junk for bank credit is evident in the contrasting composition of early deals like Gibson's, for which banks provided the overwhelming bulk of the credit, and later deals like the buyout of RJR-Nabisco, for which banks provided just over half the credit. In each deal junk bonds substituted for bank credit. But junk bonds helped to push so many firms into taking on debt that banks expanded the volume of loans to leveraged firms very rapidly notwithstanding their reduced deal-by-deal role.

Broadly viewed, then, banks complemented the credit newly available in the junk bond market with their own credit to corporations going deeply into debt. For banks, lending to firms just taken over or borrowing to avoid a takeover represented in many cases a return to a spurned lending relation. By the early 1980s, large, well-capitalized firms came to rely on banks to extend credit lines to backstop sale of commercial paper, to effect foreign exchange transactions, and to provide other services, but such firms' fund-raising had shifted to bond markets and commercial paper markets. So in the leveraging business, banks welcomed back to their balance sheets borrowers who were suddenly needy because they were suddenly highly indebted. The bank nerds took their revenge on corporate treasurers.

Leveraged bank loans to large corporations got so large that they were spread around dozens of banks through syndication. The arrangers of a large loan enlist other banks into a syndicate in order to spread the credit risk widely. Syndicated loans for leveraged U.S. firms shot up from modest amounts in the early 1980s to almost $200 billion per year in the peak year 1989 (figure 2.4).

The syndicated loan brought with it a fee structure that some have pointed to as a cause of weakened credit analysis and excessive lending. Within the syndicate, a hierarchy of underwriting and distribution developed. At the top the agent bank negotiated pricing, set the distribution strategy, and signed up the lead managers. Lead managers guaranteed the availability of the loan by taking on a sizeable piece of a loan—as much as $100 million, $200 million, or even $500 million— and selling off pieces to manager and participant banks. The return on a loan varied with a bank's position in the hierarchy. The agent bank received several basis points on the whole loan amount, whereas lead managers received a front-end fee on a smaller base equal to the

Billions of dollars

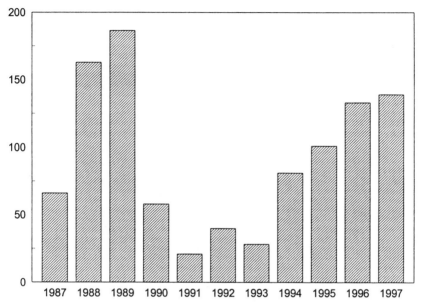

Source: Loan Pricing Corporation and same source as reported in Steven Miller, "Not Your Father's Commercial Loan Market," Merrill Lynch *Extra Credit*, July/August 1997, p. 25.
Note: 1997 datum is annualized first-half activity. Leverage refers to LBO, recapitalization, and acquisition.

Figure 2.4
Value of syndicated loans for leveraged corporations

amount that they underwrote. A mere manager or participant bank received a front-end fee on only the amount that it lent.

With such a fee structure, a bank reaped the highest return by taking on large risks briefly and selling down its actual holdings to as small a sum as possible. There were limits, however, on how far this logic could be carried in the initial syndication of a loan. It would look odd if the agent bank retained no more credit than a lowly participant were allocated.

John Reed, chief executive officer of Citicorp, whose Citibank was one of the largest agent banks for syndicated leveraged loans, later described how the fees bent the credit process:

We were becoming deal junkies. I got a memo on the Campeau deal that told me we had big fees before it described the transaction. All of Wall Street had the same attitude, of course, and it was hard for me to tell if I was just getting too old for this, that the world was changing in ways I didn't like, or if something was out of kilter.[13]

In this market, competition among lead managers for fees, and even for inflated titles, could be keen:

The consummate stampede by eager lenders occurred one morning in February 1987, at the Park Lane Hotel in New York. Packed into the hotel's red-carpeted ballroom were about thirty major bankers, ready to hear about the virtues of Owens-Illinois Inc., America's largest glass container company. This would be KKR's latest conquest—a buyout that required more than $3 billion in new bank loans. Objectively, it was a riskier proposition than the Beatrice or Safeway deal. The company's interest-coverage ratios would be skimpier after the buyout, and its business was much more vulne rable to the economic cycle. . . .

To the astonishment of Owens-Illinois's top executives, bankers hardly listened to each fact-filled talk. Instead, as one witness would recall, "a cat fight broke out" in the audience as bankers scrambled to collect an early-bird special being offered by KKR's Jamie Greene. The first seven bankers who agreed to lend $400 million had been promised the title of "agent bank," and an extra $1.25 million fee. As word got out that four of those slots had already been snapped up, gung-ho bankers bolted from their chairs partway through the Owens-Illinois talks, elbowed other bankers aside, and tried to claim slots five through seven. Agile bankers from Continental Illinois, Bank of America, and Chemical Bank got the prize. One of them, in fact, later won a "Carl Lewis Award" from his peers for racing so fast to KKR.

Hot behind the first seven bankers, another seven piled in with $400 million loan pledges in the next few days. Desperate to win special fees, these second-round bankers pleaded with Greene until he relented and dubbed them "agent banks" as well. All told, the Owens-Illinois buyout attracted more than $7 billion in loan pledges from the most powerful banks in the United States, Japan, Canada, and Europe.[14]

Speculative Trading

Purchase of assets for resale marks speculative trading. Whatever else an LBO might do or be, it is certainly a speculative trade. Indeed, one can interpret the LBO as the culmination of developments in the U.S. securities industry, whence came most of the LBO sponsors, toward taking larger and longer trading risks. In the early 1970s, modestly capitalized securities firms—still partnerships—mostly bought and sold securities for a commission, but by the late 1970s some firms' capital could support large "block trades" in equities to accommodate sales by large customers such as pension funds. This ability to take on large risks was applied in the early 1980s to underwriting new issues, as large syndicates to spread risk gave way to so-called bought deals in which one or two underwriters took on all the risk. As the Gibson Greeting deal illustrated, a successful LBO could amount to a block trade stretched out over 18 months that bridged the buyout on one side and an "initial" public offering of shares on the other side.

Repeated LBOs of the same firms or divisions disclose another aspect of speculative trading in the LBO wave. Consider the example of Houdaille, a machine tool maker. In the ten years from 1979 to 1989, the firm went through a KKR buyout (1979), closed down a division, purchased John Crane (1981), went through a KKR recapitalization (1986), was sold to a British company (1987), and reemerged without John Crane as a third KKR LBO (1988),[15] namely IDEX. The second and third LBOs helped justify the first LBO by providing good returns to the investors. The 1986 recapitalization, in which an earlier KKR partnership sold the firm to a later KKR partnership, became a point at issue between Kohlberg on the one side and his two partners on the other. Kohlberg's suit argued that the recapitalization unfairly reduced his stake in Houdaille: The second deal was really the same as the first deal. Whatever the merits of the suit, it highlighted the churning of the same assets across the partnerships of even the same LBO sponsor. At a larger level, the LBO market as a whole recycled many firms and divisions through the leveraging business, with the risks of the later deal providing the returns that justified the risks on the earlier deals.

Purchases of corporate assets became more and more speculative as the price paid increasingly depended on the purchaser's ability to sell some or all of the assets at a higher price. By the late 1980s, buyouts frequently required more cash interest and amortization of debt than the firm's underlying cash flows could hope to support.

Excessive Leverage

Evidence of excessive leverage in the late 1980s abounds: Leveraged buyouts got larger, their pricing and capital structure got stretched, and junk bonds got demonstrably junkier. Buyers of junk bonds among mutual funds, insurance companies, pension funds, and savings and loans failed to claim wider spreads over the yields of safe bonds to compensate for the decline of credit quality. In the face of market developments, questions arose over the stability of the standards of the rating agencies and the acuity of the Securities and Exchange Commission's disclosure standards for mutual funds. Despite their enthusiasm, banks managed to protect themselves to some extent, not by the obvious expedient of avoiding more leveraged deals, but rather by tightening their claim on the property, plant, and equipment of leveraged companies by demanding more security and earlier repayment.

Leveraged buyouts boomed into 1989 (figure 2.5). These deals joined private equity to public debt, namely junk bonds, and private debt— generally bank loans, but also bonds privately placed with insurance companies and loans from some finance companies. A prototypical leveraged buyout would start with a thin layer of equity at the bottom, add a middling layer of junk bond debt, and then pile on a thick top layer of bank debt. The bank creditors at the top would enjoy the best security, with their loans secured with corporate assets including land, buildings, and machinery. In theory, junk bond holders in the middle were to get paid off only after the banks.

As activity heated up, the prices for leveraged buyouts rose and the resulting companies' already high leverage rose as well. Leveraged deals got more expensive relative to the stock market: The exit premium— the excess (over 1) of the final price paid for shares divided by the

Billions of dollars

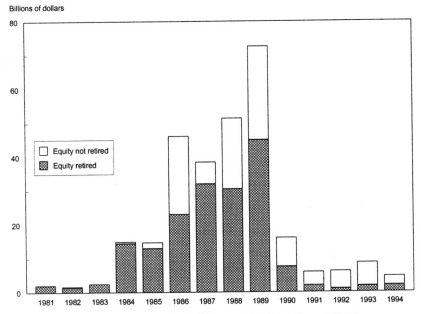

Sources: Securities Data Corporation; Board of Governors of the Federal Reserve System.
Note: 1994 figure is annualized.

Figure 2.5
Equity retired through leveraged buyouts

market value of the shares observed two months before—rose from one-quarter in 1985 to one-half in 1988. In the extreme case of RJR-Nabisco (see chapter 4), shareholders receive more than $100 of cash and securities for a share of stock that had traded in the 50s mere months before, for an exit premium verging on 1.

The capital structures of LBOs piled even more debt on equity in the course of the 1980s. In 1983–85, $5 of debt rested on each dollar of equity. In 1986–89, $10 of debt rested on each dollar of equity.[16] In an extreme case like the Campeau purchase of Federated Department Stores, $33 of debt rested precariously on each dollar of equity. Wrote one astute observer in 1987: "We haven't seen such leveraged companies—a debt-to-equity ratio of 100:1 in Metromedia—since the pyramidal holding companies of the 1920s."[17]

Buyers of junk bonds bought bonds of demonstrably lower quality with the passage of time. One can measure the declining quality of junk bonds by the rising burden of interest payments on the cash flow of junk bond issuers. Consider the broadest measure of cash flow, earnings before interest, taxes, depreciation, and amortization. Such operating earnings reflect the excess of sales revenue over current costs, such as wages and the cost of inputs. Note that this balance is struck before any allowance is made to replace worn-out machines, to pay interest, or to pay taxes or dividends. At 100 percent, interest costs are eating up all available funds, and the business, starved of even replacement investment, must run down. At a comfortable ratio of one-sixth or one-fifth, a firm enjoys considerable financial flexibility.

The burden of interest payments on the cash flow of junk bond issuers doubled over the 1980s even in the face of declining interest rates (figure 2.6). As the 1980s progressed, less cushion was left to deal with disappointing revenues or unexpected costs. Because junk bonds were unsecured and often subordinated, the buyers stood to lose in any untoward event.

Having committed so much to their creditors, the firms created by leveraged buyouts had less and less room to maneuver. In one sample of leveraged buyouts, the ratio of interest to cash flow rose from 80 percent in 1985 to 90 percent in 1988 and, perhaps more importantly, the ratio of cash interest payments plus required debt repayment to cash flow lurched ominously from 90 percent to 110 percent.[18] In short, the deals of the late 1980s tended to promise more cash in the near term than they had any prospect of realizing from ongoing operations.

Even higher-risk bonds might have made sense if they offered investors higher returns. But the spread of junk bond yields over Treasury bond yields, the promised compensation for the junk bond buyer's bearing higher risk, did not increase systematically (figure 2.7). Commented a close observer:

Risk premiums in the non–investment grade [junk] market displayed an ambiguous pattern during 1985–88. The differential between the Merrill Lynch High

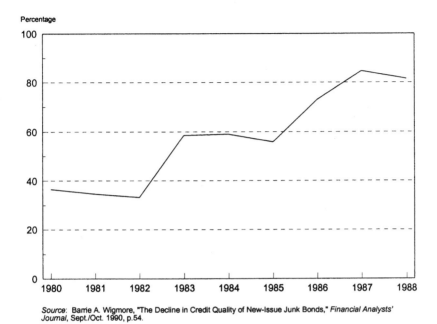

Percentage

Source: Barrie A. Wigmore, "The Decline in Credit Quality of New-Issue Junk Bonds," *Financial Analysts' Journal*, Sept./Oct. 1990, p.54.

Figure 2.6
Burden of interest on cash flows of junk bond issuers

Yield Master Index and ten-year Treasuries varied from 284 basis points (February 1985) to 530 basis points (August 1986). Even though the spread was narrowest near the beginning of the period, it is not safe to conclude that risk premiums increased as the credit quality of new issues deteriorated in 1987–1988. For one thing, the spread declined sharply following the August 1986 peak, getting as low as 342 basis points in August 1987—18 basis points less than the initial (January 1985) level of 360. On the whole, it would be difficult to argue that risk premiums increased in direct response to the observed decline in new-issue credit quality.[19]

The elasticity of credit standards over the 1980s has led observers to ask: Where were the rating agencies, supposed gatekeepers of credit? By one measure, at least, they gave ground to arguments that U.S. firms could operate safely and more efficiently with higher leverage. The burden of interest on the cash flows of firms of a given junk rating got heavier over the 1980s (figure 2.8).

Percentage points

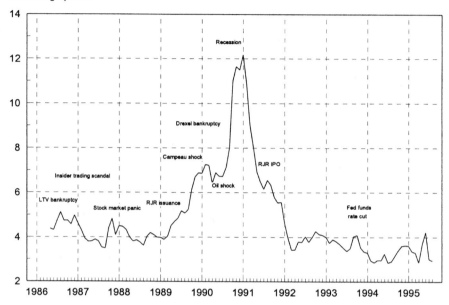

Source: Morgan Stanley

Figure 2.7
Junk bond yields: spread over U.S. treasury

One junk bond professional has taken issue with the seeming implication of the evidence of a higher burden of interest payments on
B-rated companies' cash flows, arguing that the implication suffers
from the fallacy of composition:

> Neglecting the subdivisions of the Single-B category, however, obscures the fact
> that both Moody's and Standard & Poor's rated an increasing percentage of
> the Single-Bs in the lowest portion of that category as the decade progressed.
> . . . we find that in aggregate for the three-year periods [1983–85 and 1986–
> 88], the percentage rated in the lowest part of the Single-B category rose from
> 32.3% to 36.8% at Moody's and from 48.3% to 56.6% at Standard & Poor's.[20]

Whether this small shift in the mix of B-rated debt fully balances the
aggregate rise in the interest burden on cash flows of B-rated bonds

Percent

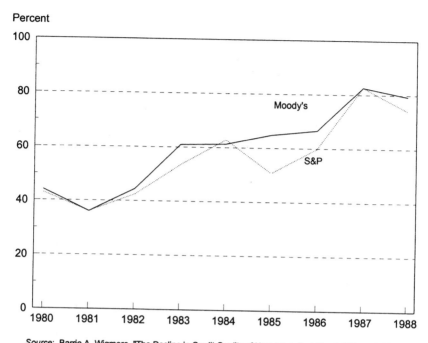

Source: Barrie A. Wigmore, "The Decline in Credit Quality of New-Issue Junk Bonds," *Financial Analysts Journal*, September/October 1990, p. 58.

Figure 2.8
Interest burden on cash flow of firms issuing B-rated bonds

remains to be demonstrated. More importantly, all are agreed that junk bonds became junkier in the 1980s.

Another alleged lapse in standards that permitted excessive leverage centered on junk bonds that paid no cash interest. Two innovations of the 1980s made it easier for a time for junk bond issuers to carry a heavy burden of interest: payment-in-kind bonds and zero-coupon bonds. Payment-in-kind (PIK) bonds, or bunny bonds, reproduced themselves instead of paying cash interest. That is, bondholders received what used to be called scrip—more paper IOUs—instead of cash, twice a year. Zero-coupon bonds, first issued by high-quality firms in the early 1980s, were sold at a discount to face value. Interest on such bonds takes the form of the rise in the value of the bond until it hits the face value. Such bonds that do not pay cash interest for a time or at all, often derided as Chinese paper or wampum, temporarily relieved the burden of high interest payments on cash flows.

These cash-saving innovations can best be understood as the means of squaring the circle in particularly leveraged deals. Because the argument was often made that the virtue of leverage lay precisely in its tying the hands of management—leaving no funds for grandiose investments or slack operations—it might seem strange that junk bonds appeared that deferred the burden of interest on cash flows. But research has shown that the payment-in-kind and zero-coupon bonds were associated with deals in which the burden of interest on cash flows was particularly high.[21] The mutation of high-interest junk bonds into bonds not paying any cash interest therefore signaled that buyout pricing had cut loose from the underlying cash flows of the actual businesses.

The ability of PIK bonds and zero-coupon bonds to magnify the cash actually thrown off by an operating company raised questions about the appropriate disclosure of returns on mutual funds holding junk bonds. At least one observer criticized the Securities and Exchange Commission for permitting junk bond mutual funds to include non-cash interest in their reported returns. Such funds, holding approximately one-third of outstanding junk bonds, appealed to investors looking for yield. Writing in 1989 in *Barron's*, Louis Lowenstein argued that deferred interest bonds manufactured the desired yield for uninformed mutual fund shareholders:

Assume that you own all of Federated Department Stores, with no debt at all. You would be earning almost $400 million a year before taxes. That's not bad, but it's all you earn. But because Federated has promised to pay interest at the rate of $600 million a year, the accountants are allowing mutual funds and other institutional investors to tell the world that they are earning *from Federated 50 percent more than Federated itself is earning*. A dollar there is turned into a dollar and a half here.[22]

Positive Economic Feedback

The typical financial mania spills over into the real economy by stimulating a spending boom of some kind. The bubble in Japanese land and share prices in the late 1980s certainly fit this general pattern. Japanese firms found themselves able to sell equity at very favorable prices and to borrow against their land holdings readily. With the proceeds, Japanese firms cranked up their capital spending to a share of Japanese output not seen for a generation. A debate still rages over how much of the added capacity could be economically rationalized either at the time or since, but the gleaming new factories and dormitories were enough to tell even a visiting Martian in the 1990s that something happened in Japan in the 1980s.

The leveraging wave of the late 1980s in the United States, by contrast, left behind little for that visiting Martian. The brigades of investment bankers and lawyers hired to complete the deals increased demand for office floor space and thereby encouraged the simultaneous mania for construction of prime urban office buildings. But not much else was built thanks to the leveraging business. The leveraging wave of the 1980s contradicts the Minsky-Kindleberger model in the handcuffs it put on the investment spending by the firms most immediately involved.

A variety of studies have sought to measure the effect of higher leverage on corporate investment. The basic reasoning is that firms invest most readily out of their own cash flow, funds that they do not have to raise from outside the firm. But higher leverage mortgages this cash flow to creditors. Moreover, high leverage puts a lien on collateral, such as land, machinery, and brand names, leaving the firm less scope to borrow to finance investment that cannot be paid for with internal cash flows.

One group of studies has compared capital spending before and after firms underwent LBOs. One study found that, in a sample of more than 900 LBOs at the divisional level in the 1980s, capital spending in relation to sales fell by 9 percent in the year after an LBO.[23] Another study measured a median decline of 38 percent in the ratio of capital spending to sales in the first year of an LBO.[24] A study of 24 large recapitalizations in the late 1980s—leveraging transactions by incumbent managers in response to a hostile bid or to forestall one—found that capital expenditures as a fraction of sales fell by 15 percent in the first year after the recap and by a like percentage in the second year.[25] Several studies have documented how newly leveraged firms shelved research and development (R & D) spending plans.[26]

These findings for LBOs are not surprising because broad cross sections of firms show strong effects of cash flow on investment spending. One study can be interpreted as showing that every additional million dollars in interest payments—and thus lower net cash flow—reduces investment demand by $230,000.[27] Another study found that, compared to less-leveraged firms, more-leveraged firms increase (decrease) investment spending more in relation to a given increase (decline) in cash flow.[28]

Taken together, these studies suggest that the leveraging wave of the 1980s tended to lower capital spending. Indeed, this unusual link between a euphoric development in the financial markets and the real economy is not debated. Instead, defenders of the leveraging wave argue that the investment not undertaken had no reasonable prospect of earning its required return.[29] Therefore, they argue, society was well served by debt service working to flush funds out of the firms that earned them into the hands of investors who might finance smaller or newer firms with better investment prospects.

Market Interconnections—Domestic

Kindleberger observes that financial excess gathers force by a contagion of markets: Buoyant prices and activity in one market stimulate prices and activity in another market. Contrary to economists' neat models of so-called rational bubbles, as a general rule a financial market gets carried away not in isolation but in interaction with other markets, both within a country and across national frontiers. These interactions are typically not one-way affairs but dynamics of reciprocal influence.

Observers have described three different ways in which financial markets involved in the 1980s leveraging influenced other domestic markets. The junk bond market, as a process innovation, has been identified as the stimulant of activity and pricing in U.S. equity markets and debt markets. Other observers have pointed to the greater liquidity of the market for corporate assets as a stimulant for acquisitions, including leveraged ones, and of the junk bond market and other debt markets. Finally, leveraged bank loans stimulated the development of sales of loans by banks to banks and, eventually, other investors as well. Kindleberger leads us to expect that activity and pricing in each interconnected market reinforces activity and pricing in the others.

Junk Bonds as Stimulant

With money raised in the junk bond market, managers and financiers increased turnover and prices on the New York Stock Exchange (B→F in figure 2.9). After (if not before) Drexel issued its famous letter, claiming to be "highly confident" that it could sell junk bonds to finance a buyout, market participants would bid up the shares of the target company. Other securities firms sought to wrest business from Drexel by extending bridge loans to a buyer, in substitution for Drexel's highly confident letter. In this case, market participants would also bid up the shares of the target company, this time in anticipation of a payment out of the capital of the securities firm, which was to be repaid with the proceeds of a junk bond issue.

Junk bond–backed bids also encouraged so-called arbitrageurs to accumulate publicly traded stock on the possibility, rumor, or probability of the launching of a bid. At any one time billions or tens of billions of dollars' worth of shares might rest uneasily in the hands of the "arbs," financed largely with borrowed money. The most famous arb was Ivan

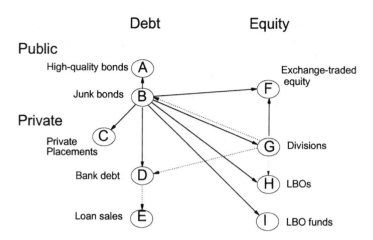

Figure 2.9
Market interconnections in the corporate leveraging wave of the 1980s

Boesky, who was portrayed by the press as presiding over a vast quantitative research effort to identify likely targets until prosecutors charged
him with more old-fashioned if not legally sanctioned methods. Some
measure of the importance of such activity may be inferred from the
setback suffered when the United Air Lines deal fell apart in October
1989. As the likelihood of further deals was reestimated downward,
selling by the arb contributed to the one-day 7 percent decline in the
Dow-Jones average.

   Junk bonds also stimulated the private equity markets. The availability of junk finance helped enliven bidding for whole divisions (B→G
in the figure). As noted above, the market's acceptance of junkier junk
made for higher prices on LBOs in relation to underlying cash flows
(B→H). And the ability to leverage deals up to 9:1 or even 19:1 with
the help of junk permitted LBO fund organizers to promise institutional investors high returns on subscriptions to private equity funds
(B→I), even though the funds were intended to buy companies the
institutional investors already collectively owned.

   Although bond finance and bank finance are often viewed as substitutes, as argued above, leveraged bank lending received a stimulus from

the junk bond market (B→D). Junk bonds only partly replaced bank credit in deal structures, so that sufficient expansion of the junk bond–financed deals resulted in the observed expansion of leveraged lending. Thus, activity in public, junk debt markets stimulated activity in private, bank debt markets.

Moreover, the threat of junk-financed takeovers induced incumbent managers to leverage up to avert a takeover, and the extra demand for debt showed up both in the bond market and in the bank loan market. The debt markets that served acquirers of firms also came to be used by managers defending themselves against the threat of a takeover. Companies like CBS, Kroger, Newmont Mining, Phillips Petroleum, Santa Fe Pacific, and Unocal all repurchased a large fraction of their shares or paid special dividends.[30] The $100-per-share dividend paid by Santa Fe did wonders for shareholder returns—the stock had been trading at well less than $100 before the announcement. Transactions such as these put cash into public shareholders' hands (B→F, again) but reduced the difference between investment grade yields and junk bond yields.

Junk bonds used to take over highly rated companies encouraged other such companies to borrow more through a process familiar to participants in the used car market.[31] When RJR's managers put the company into play in late 1988, for example, holders of its theretofore highly rated bonds awoke to find themselves holding junk bonds. Buyers of bonds of other highly rated firms had to factor this possibility, termed "event risk," into the price that they were willing to offer for such high-rated bonds. As a result, bond buyers would pay less, or equivalently, charge a higher rate of interest, to highly rated issuers. Just as a prospective buyer cannot know whether the car on the used car salesman's lot is a lemon, so a bond buyer could not know the intentions of the manager of the firm selling the bonds. Therefore, just as the used car buyer offers a lower price than he would if he knew precisely what the deal was, so too bond buyers came to offer less for first-rate bonds.

But under these conditions, highly rated corporations end up paying for the possibility of leverage. For those already partly paying for higher leverage, actually leveraging up became less costly at the margin. So junk bonds encouraged investment grade bond issuance (B→A).

One analyst has provided evidence for the interpretation that junk bonds stimulated leverage in the aggregate.[32] A variety of macroeconomic and financial variables were found to track changes in the ratio of debt to assets and the growth of debt for U.S. firms before the 1980s. But these factors did not explain corporate debt in the 1980s without the inclusion of a measure of the junk bond market size as an explanatory variable.

Liquidity of Corporate Assets as a Stimulant

Another perspective on market interconnections in the corporate leveraging wave of the 1980s puts the spotlight on the market for pieces or divisions of companies.[33] This perspective argues that the market for divisions enjoyed extraordinary liquidity in the 1980s, in the sense that a price could be realized in fairly short order that reflected the most valuable use of the assets, typically in the hands of a firm already in the business. Behind this liquidity lay not only a cyclically normal strengthening of corporate cash flows in a business upswing but also the coincidental relaxation of antitrust constraints and foreign firms' strong appetite for takeovers of U.S. firms.

Readily salable corporate assets stimulated debt-financed acquisitions (G→F) predicated on asset sales. One public firm could buy another with a view to selling off unwanted divisions readily. One study found that hostile acquirers sold 30 percent of the acquired assets in the 1980s. Asset sales were often essential to LBO game plans, and fully 40 percent of LBO assets were sold.[34] KKR could buy Beatrice, a conglomerate marketing not only foods—Tropicana juice, Hunt's tomato paste, Wesson oil, Swift meats, Coca Cola—but also rental cars (Avis), Samsonite luggage, and Playtex underwear, and sell off the pieces to industry buyers. Thus Seagram (a Canadian company) bought Tropicana, so that it could offer both freshly squeezed orange juice and vodka, ConAgra bought most of the foods, Coca Cola bought the Los Angeles bottler of its product and American Brands bought most of the nonfood businesses.[35] RJR-Nabisco's financiers could not have been surprised to learn that the French food company BSN had bought Nabisco's European operations shortly after the buyout closed. Ready salability of assets also encouraged foreign acquirers, as when the Anglo-American conglomerate Hanson bought SCM Corporation, sold off all the businesses save the namesake Smith Corona typewriters, and essentially kept the latter for nothing.

Increased liquidity of corporate assets over the 1980s also encouraged banks to make leveraged loans (G→D). In making loans secured on those assets, banks must evaluate what price they can realize if the borrower defaults. A more liquid market for divisions means that the assets can be sold speedily at a price close to their best-use value, so banks are willing to lend more against given collateral.

It has been pointed out, moreover, that banks depended on asset sales as part of their defense against the increasingly high prices paid in buyouts in the late 1980s. Banks shortened the maturity of their leveraged loans over the 1980s with striking results. In the early 1980s cash interest and required debt repayments claimed about 90 cents of every dollar of cash flow. In the latter part of the 1980s, cash interest and debt repayments claimed $1.10 or $1.20 of every dollar of cash flow.[36] Banks scheduled loan repayments to force asset sales and thereby to reinforce their senior status. The liquidity of the market for corporate assets gave plausibility to the banks' strategy of shortening their leveraged loan maturities to protect against the rising leverage.

Greater liquidity of corporate assets also stimulated activity and pricing in junk bonds (G→B). Again, the notion is that greater liquidity of corporate assets raises the amount of debt that they can support. A manager of a firm that had sold junk could always peddle pieces of a firm to service debt, so a smaller yield premium on junk seemed appropriate.

It would be a mistake not to recognize the reciprocal nature of the influence of the liquidity of the market for divisions in spurring buyout activity and leverage. Buoyant LBO, junk bond, and bank loan markets contributed to the liquidity of the market for corporate assets such as divisions (one could add H→G, B→G, D→G). LBO funds were willing to buy a division, seek to improve its performance, and sell it to an industry buyer or to the public. A buoyant junk bond market meant that an already debt-laden company could buy another company in the same industry with long-term financing free of the kind of restrictive covenants that banks or insurance companies might write into bank loans or private placements. For instance, cable companies' access to junk bond finance made it easier to sell cable properties.

Leveraged Lending as a Stimulant to Loan Sales

A market interconnection that has received less notice than it should occurred within the bank loan market. Leveraged loans flowed so strongly into the banking system that banks created a secondary market for loans.[37] Data on the quarterly flow of loan sales clearly show a rise and fall with the leveraged lending business (figure 2.10). In this market, large New York, Chicago, and West Coast banks that served as agents or lead managers in syndicates sold loans to regional and foreign banks. The seller and buyer usually agreed to a price of par, or face value, but sometimes the selling bank could "skim" some interest spread. For example, if a loan carried an interest rate of 2.5 percent above the London interbank offered rate (LIBOR), the selling bank might find a buyer willing to accept a 2.25 percent spread. In this case, the selling bank could keep the front-end fees and .25 percent interest over the life of the sale.

The loan sales market resulted from a convergence of needs on the part of large U.S. banks and foreign banks in the United States. Major U.S. banks could maximize their returns on leveraged loans by underwriting them and selling them off, retaining the front-end fees. Foreign banks were looking to build assets quickly. In pursuing this market

Billions of dollars

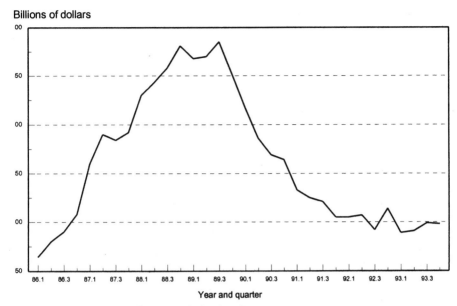

Year and quarter

Source: Federal Financial Institutions Examination Council.
Note: U.S. banks are all insured domestic banks.

Figure 2.10
Loan sales by U.S. banks

share strategy, major foreign banks enjoyed a cost-of-capital advantage over U.S. banks. That is, foreign banks could target a lower return on assets than U.S. banks and still satisfy their shareholders.[38] Thus, the loan sale market allowed U.S. banks to specialize in origination, based on their skills in arranging and distributing loans, and at the same time allowed foreign banks to specialize in holding loans, based on their lower required rates of return.

The development of the loan sales market helped relax a constraint that otherwise might have checked the leveraged-lending wave sooner. Above, we noted how the agent or lead manager bank in a leveraged-loan syndicate could hardly sell down all of its share of the loan in the initial syndication. But such a bank could flush much of its final allocation out into the market through its loan sale desk. As a result, the large bank was able to continue to take on large underwriting positions without piling up leveraged loans on its books. In short, the loan sales market helped make leveraged lending a throughput business rather than a warehousing business. Even following the strategy of selling loans in the secondary market, large banks let their highly leveraged loans reach 87 percent of equity capital in 1989—in effect, betting the bank.[39] Without the vent of the loan sales market, banks' internal limits on such loans could have crimped the leveraged-lending business.

Market Interconnections—International

Kindleberger emphasizes that the interaction of markets across international boundaries regularly reinforces financial excesses. The leveraging wave of U.S. corporate finances in the 1980s certainly drew strength from an extremely strong acquisition wave by foreign firms. Figure 2.11 shows that acquisitions of U.S. companies by foreign firms surged to more than $60 billion per year in the late 1980s.

This foreign buying stimulated U.S. equity markets, both public and private. Foreign companies joined U.S. companies in putting cash in the hands of holders of New York Stock Exchange–traded shares and thereby helped drive stock market prices higher. Foreign firms also bought divisions of U.S. firms and thereby contributed to the greater liquidity of the market for U.S. corporate assets. The ability of foreign companies to buy U.S. companies in short order encouraged organizers of leveraged buyouts in the belief that they could pay down debt if necessary by selling off assets to foreigners.

These foreign acquisitions drew on strong equity markets abroad. British firms had long been the largest foreign buyers of U.S. companies, but the robust performance of the London stock market around the Big Bang liberalization in 1986 allowed British firms to outbid U.S. firms in auctions of U.S. firms. More strikingly, the vertiginous heights reached by the Tokyo stock market signaled to Japanese firms that they

Billions of dollars

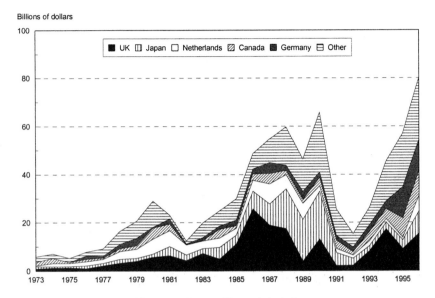

Source: U.S. Department of Commerce, Bureau of Economic Analysis.
Note : Negative net inflows are depicted as 0.

Figure 2.11
Acquisitions of U.S. firms by foreign firms

could afford to pay a high price for a U.S. firm in relation to that firm's earnings. A statistical analysis of the determinants of foreign acquisitions in the United States in the 1980s shows that equity prices abroad and in the United States are the most important determinants of the variation over time in the strength of foreign acquisitions.[40]

Foreign acquisitions not only stimulated the leveraging wave in U.S. corporate finance in the late 1980s, they also participated in it to some extent. British firms buying into the United States, particularly after the crash of 1987, often financed their acquisitions with debt and even relied on U.S. investment and commercial banks for financing. Whereas British firms buying U.S. firms in 1985–86 often relied on equity finance and had price-earnings ratios close to those of their targets, British firms buying in 1987–88 more often relied on debt and often had price-earnings ratios below those of their targets.[41]

Swindles, Scandals

A final feature of euphoria Kindleberger highlights is the revelation of scandals. Certainly the closing phase of the Tokyo bubble had its share of unlikely financiers and less-likely deals. British firms buying U.S. firms in the late 1980s had their share of financial scandal. The underwriting of the stock of Blue Arrow, which staged a hostile takeover of the U.S. temporary firm Manpower, gave rise to charges of parking of securities to avoid disclosure of the extent of an underwriting flop. The U.K. defense firm Ferranti collapsed after it learned belatedly that many of the sales contracts of its target, ISC, a Pennsylvania defense firm, were bogus. Maxwell extended himself buying the publishers Macmillan and Official Airlines Guide, misappropriated the assets of his British firms' pension funds, and apparently drowned. The founder of the U.K. firm Polly Peck, which bought Del Monte's fresh fruit business, became a fugitive from British justice. Manpower's original American management was brought back in, Ferranti's shareholders were offered a penny a share, Maxwell's bank debt fell to 34¢ on the dollar, and Polly Peck's debt fell to 4 or 5¢ on the dollar.[42]

The leveraging wave of the 1980s in the United States provided a succession of shady characters: Dennis Levine, Ivan Boesky, Michael Milken. It is sometimes said in surprising places that Milken pleaded guilty to "six comparatively technical felonies."[43] Milken pled guilty to six felonies: "conspiracy with Boesky; aiding and abetting the filing of false statements in connection with the Fischbach scheme [in which Boesky ostensibly bought shares but Milken bore the risk]; aiding and abetting the evasion of net capital rules; securities fraud for concealing the ownership of MCA stock; mail fraud for defrauding investors in [a mutual fund,] Finsburg; and assisting the filing of a false tax return."[44] The latter two crimes involved a mutual fund manager exchanging favors with Milken at the expense of fund shareholders and taxpayers. The common element of the felonies was a blurring of the line between

Milken and his associates working on Wall Street or with institutional investors.

These "comparatively technical" felonies hardly exhaust the seduction of fiduciaries. Consider the case of the distribution of warrants in Storer, a cable TV company acquired by KKR, for which Drexel underwrote junk bonds carrying with them a detachable equity kicker, namely warrants or long-term stock options. A manager of junk bond investments for Fidelity, the largest mutual fund sponsor, was convicted of personally accepting the warrants rather than demanding them for the mutual fund shareholders. The judge said at the sentencing:

> It is perfectly obvious from what [Milken] said that he was giving [the interest in the Storer warrants] to Mrs. Ostrander because he wanted to have a nice relationship with her. . . . The underlying problem is that this fund officer was entrusted with billions and billions of dollars of the public's money to invest, and . . . [the warrants] put her in a position of obligation to Milken. She had to know that . . . and that's a subversion of the duty of trust that had been imposed on her.[45]

2.3   Distress

Metaphors for distress vary. Meteorology: The barometer has dropped off, although the storm has yet to arrive. Geology: The ground has begun to shift. Cartoons: The character has run off the cliff but has yet to look down.

The market for corporate leveraging became distressed in the course of 1989, a year before the economy entered a recession. Opinion had begun to shift, perhaps after the prolonged spectacle of the bidding contest for RJR-Nabisco. Some earlier buyouts had come a cropper:

> The first eight months of 1989 saw $4 billion worth of junk-bond defaults and debt moratoriums, the most spectacular being the troubles of Canadian entrepreneur Robert Campeau's retail empire.[46]

Already by early summer, corporate executives responded to a business school professor's survey in a manner that suggested that the leverage fever was cooling.

The survey concerned what is termed "creating shareholder value," or in plain English, boosting the share price. Whereas a year before, executives had responded to a similar survey by opting for leveraging transaction in substantial numbers, by summer 1989 many fewer were persuaded that more debt meant more value. In particular, 118 respondents from firms with revenues in excess of $1 billion were asked to choose among strategies for creating shareholder value in three categories, both for strategies the firms had pursued in the past and strategies they were currently contemplating. In the capital structure category, 66 *had* chosen to "expand utilization of debt in capital structure" but, going forward, only 45 contemplated so doing. Similar reactions to "inaugurate/expand a share repurchase program" were recorded: 63 *had* pursued this course but only 46 foresaw so doing. The author of the survey concluded, "surprisingly, interest in reducing the cost of capital through expanding the use of leverage is waning. And less reliance is being placed on stock repurchase programs as a future avenue to enhance value."[47] The record of defaults makes the change of attitude on the part of corporate treasurers unsurprising.

The first clear sign that the assumptions built into so many deals might prove wrong came in September 1989. Campeau's inability to make a scheduled interest payment caused the stocks of leveraged firms to drop by about 2 percent[48] and sent junk bond prices down. Junk bond spreads widened from 500 to 700 basis points, and one of the principal sources of fresh flows of funds into the junk bond market started to flow the wrong way. Gross inflows into junk bond mutual funds sagged and redemptions spiked in September and after (figure 2.12). Net redemptions in September and October 1989 mounted to 5 percent of the outstandings in junk bond funds.

The second sign that the buyout business would not soar to new heights came just one month later, in October 1989. As recently as

Billions of dollars

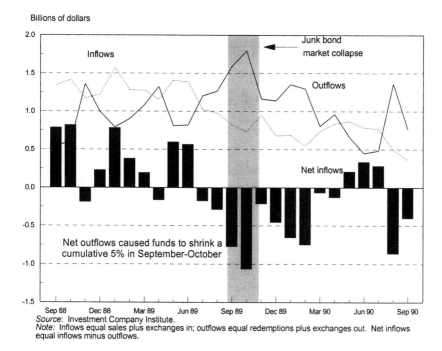

Source: Investment Company Institute.
Note: Inflows equal sales plus exchanges in; outflows equal redemptions plus exchanges out. Net inflows equal inflows minus outflows.

Figure 2.12
Flows into junk bond mutual funds around September 1989

summer, banks had thrice oversubscribed the $11 billion loan for War-ner Communications' acquisition of Time Incorporated by commit-ting $30 billion. Emboldened by such willingness to lend, United Air Lines' chief executive, Stephen Wolf, sought to take UAL private with $7.2 billion in bank financing. A more unlikely candidate for an LBO would be hard to imagine. Instead of predictable cash flows, an airline can encounter wind shears as oil prices rise, competitors cut fares, pas-sengers take fright, or recession leaves seats empty. Instead of low re-quirements for investment, the firm's aging fleet needed expensive new planes. Still, Citibank and Chase undertook to provide almost half the needed funds and to raise the rest from other banks.

Even at this point it is hard to say why the banks failed to line up the necessary funds. Japanese banks reportedly had demurred for a range of reasons, ranging from Ministry of Finance guidance to reservations expressed by the Secretary of Transportation to the nonparticipation of UAL's machinist union. The trade press also pointed to the deal's "aggressive" terms. In particular, commitment fees amounted to only 1.25 instead of the "typical" 2 percent or the 2.24 percent that RJR paid on its buyout loan.[49] In any case, news that the loan could not be assembled shook the stock market. Risk arbitrageurs holding shares that they hoped would be leveraged out of their hands at fancy prices unloaded them in a rush. The Dow Jones Industrial Average, theretofore supported by the prospect of deals, plunged 197 points, or 7 percent.

The shares of borrowers and lenders in the leveraging business did worse. A sample of 29 leveraged firms saw their shares marked down by 3 percent more than one would expect from their usual relation to broad market movements.[50] The shares of the large banks that had been most deeply involved in leveraged lending fell by 10 percent or more:

The announcement dealt a heavy blow to bank issues. Bankers Trust New York Corp., one of the most exposed to leveraged lending, dropped $6.375 to $50.25. Citicorp was down $3.875 to $30.63; Chase Manhattan Corp., $3.875 to $39.75 and Wells Fargo Co., $3.25 to $83.50.[51]

2.4 Panic

Panic in the market for corporate leveraging set in around the turn of the year 1989–90. Defaults of low-grade issuers in the commercial paper market were not so large but served to cut off a source of funds to some leveraged firms at a time when alternative sources were scarce.

Events in January and February 1990, however, put the kibosh on the leverage enthusiasm. Campeau's department store empire, won just a year before, pitched into bankruptcy on January 15. At a single go, more than $10 billion of junk bonds and bank debt slipped from capital markets to courts. February brought the bankruptcy of Drexel Burnham Lambert, the firm that had held a predominant role in underwriting and trading junk bonds.[52] From January, the junk bond market closed to further issues.

2.5 Crash Averted

Kindleberger recognizes that not all cases of distress pass to panic and not all panics yield to crashes. Corporate leveraging in the 1980s could have crashed in the 1990s. A slew of leveraged companies could have entered bankruptcy leaving junk bond holders with larger losses, securities firms with even more illiquid investments in half-done deals, and banks with large slugs of illiquid claims of uncertain value.

To consider how things might have gone worse is not to imply that things went well. After the leveraging wave of the 1980s, many managers of large U.S. firms sought protection under Chapter 11 of the bankruptcy code. In 1990, the number of large company bankruptcies— that is, those involving more than $100 million in liabilities each— reached 24 and accounted for an aggregate of $27 billion in liabilities (table 2.3). The number of large filings rose in 1991 to 31, although total liabilities fell off to $21 billion. In 1992, the third year of extraordinary attrition of large companies, the number of large bankrupcies declined sharply but the debts involved edged down only slightly.

The right way to measure junk bond defaults became a matter of debate as defaults mounted.[53] One measure much used in promoting the sale of junk bonds simply took the ratio of junk bonds defaulting in a given year to the number or value of junk bonds outstanding. Another approach followed each cohort of bonds over its life. If junk bonds are less likely to default in the year or two after they are issued, the two approaches could give quite different impressions. That is, in

Table 2.3
Major U.S. corporate bankruptcies, 1990–1992

1990—24 major bankruptcies, total liabilities = $27.8 billion	
Company	Liabilities (in billions)
Allied/Federated Department Stores	$7.7
Continental Airlines	5.9
National Gypsum	2.3
Ames Department Stores	1.4
Integrated Resources	1.0
others	5.1
1990 major prepackaged bankruptcies	
Southland	3.4
Others	0.9

1991—31 major bankruptcies, total liabilities = $21.0 billion	
Company	Liabilities (in billions)
Pan American Airlines	$2.7
Columbia Gas	2.3
Carter Hawley Hale Stores	1.4
American West Airlines	1.3
Hills Department Stores	1.0
Others	8.6
1991 major prepackaged bankruptcies	
Interco	2.0
Others	1.8

1992—17 major bankruptcies, total liabilities = $18.8 billion	
Company	Liabilities (in billions)
R.H. Macy & Company	$5.3
Zale	2.2
Wang	2.1
El Paso Electric	1.2
Phar-Mor	1.1
Others	2.3
1992 major prepackaged bankruptcies	
Memorex Telex	2.4
Others	2.2

Percentage

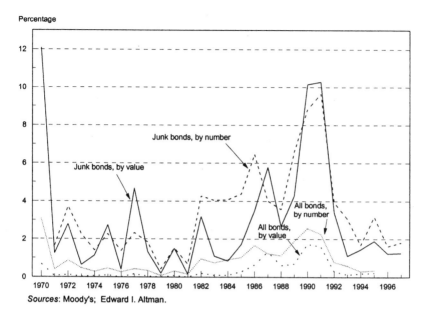

Sources: Moody's; Edward I. Altman.

Figure 2.13
Junk bond defaults

a fast-growing market, the disproportionate fraction of newborn or yearling junk could hold down the aggregate default rate.

However one looks at the question, junk bonds pitched into default at alarming rates in 1990 and 1991. Junk bond defaults measured as a share of value outstanding mounted to 10 percent by 1990; measured as a share of the number of junk bonds outstanding, results are not much better (figure 2.13).

From the perspective of this chapter, the argument over the right way to measure junk bond defaults is beside the point. As credit standards are loosened and asset prices rise in a financial mania, credits that might have gotten into trouble in a normal environment can instead get refinanced. As a result, observers will typically not get an early warning from defaults, however measured. For instance, right through 1981, international bankers could report fairly that their international

Percentage

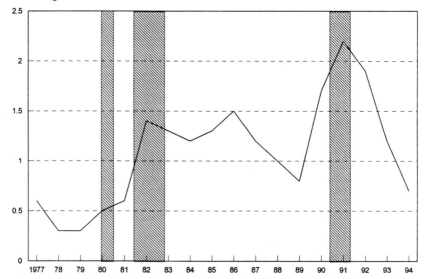

Sources: Dun & Bradstreet, Business Failure Record; First Boston, *High Yield Handbook* ; Board of Governors of the Federal System, Flow of Funds data; authors' estimates.
Notes: Estimates for 1994 annualizes first half data. Defaults combine Dun & Bradstreet "failure liabilities" and First Boston bond defaults by nonfinancial firms. For the years 1977-88, financial sector defaults are assumed constant at 5.1 percent of total bond defaults. Shaded areas indicate recession periods as designated by the National Bureau of Economic Research.

Figure 2.14
Nonfinancial corporated defaults as a share of total liabilities

loans had a better loss record than their domestic loans—and then the lending stopped, and the losses on international lending spiked. Loans against real estate in Tokyo must have looked quite safe up through the end of 1989, when land prices peaked.

Our attempt to piece together a comprehensive measure of default across the whole corporate sector shows an arresting departure from the difficulties corporations faced in the previous business cycle. In 1982 and 1983 corporate defaults on bonds, bank loans, finance company loans, and other liabilities reached the range of 1 to 1.5 percent of liabilities and stayed there through 1987 as recession rolled through the Farm Belt and oil fields (figure 2.14). But in 1991, the default rate rose well above its earlier peak, despite the shallowness of the 1990–91 recession compared to the earlier downturn.[54]

Stepping back, the new structures of debt proved more fragile than those who had put them into place imagined. The 1980s came to an end for the same reason that a house of cards falls down.

But as long as the casualty list was, it came very close to getting much longer. Leveraged deals came closer to crashing en masse than is now remembered. Had the largest LBO ever, namely RJR-Nabisco, gone to the wall, it would likely have swept others with it. Chapter 3 considers a competing answer to the question of why the 1980s stopped. Chapter 4 follows with the story of how disaster at RJR-Nabisco was averted and who made out in the deal.

Before we leave the interpretation of the 1980s as a financial mania, let us pause long enough to ask whether some kept their heads while all around them others were losing theirs. Let us ask whether there was any smart money in the 1980s leveraging boom.

2.6   Smart Money?

The view that there were identifiable pools of smart money in the 1980s leveraging mania takes a position midway between two more extreme interpretations. The rational-bubble interpretation sees an economy inhabited by people who collectively push asset prices up to unsustainable levels, but do so as knowing individuals.[55] No one is swept away; rather each hopes to get out before the collapse and demands a higher and higher risk premium for holding the asset subject to the bubble. This empirical prediction is hard to reconcile with the evidence of junk bond riskiness and reward reviewed above.

Kindleberger prefers the contrary interpretation that most participants in a mania buy into a story about why the activity and pricing they witness are reasonable. A social process draws people into the mania, and participation bends understanding in the direction of its popular rationale. The social propagating mechanism at work in a mania is more often condemned than understood: Often thought a private vice, "greed or, less pejoratively, appetite for income is highly infectious. Seeing one's neighbors or acquaintances get capital gains, if only on paper, tends to make one less careful."[56] And once less careful, one is open to stories that turn yesterday's lack of caution into today's good sense. In short, risk assessment under uncertainty is quintessentially a social construction subject to all conformity and consistency pressures studied by social psychologists.[57]

An intermediate position is that some participants—the smart money—know what is going on, whereas other participants—the dumb money—do not. Careful analysts of the 1980s leveraging have identified bankers, investment bankers, and LBO promoters as the smart money and buyers of junk bonds as the dumb money.[58] It is argued that bankers protected themselves from the price and leverage trend by shortening their maturities, offering smaller shares of the financing, and increasing their front-end fees, and that investment bankers and LBO promoters took more of their cut in fees that were unrelated to the performance of the deals they assembled.

Banks as Smart Money?

Let us examine each of these claims in turn. Admittedly, banks did shorten maturities, and this move reinforced the de jure seniority of bank loans over junk bonds. But how were the loans to be repaid? By planned asset sales, as described earlier. Is paying off loans through resale rather than with cash flow not an aspect of euphoria explored above? Also, shorter maturities had the effect of making deals more likely to falter, even if banks' senior status protected them well.

That banks offered a smaller share of the credit as the deal prices rose in relation to cash flows turns out to be a weak test of banks' smart-money status. In the face of rising prices, banks taking a smaller (senior) share is necessary but not sufficient for stable credit standards, defined as lending only a certain multiple of cash flow. Louis Lowenstein tells the story an LBO in which the banks expressed concern over their risk exposure. The investment bankers then came back with a proposal for the banks to put up the same money but enjoy the "protection" of a larger slice of subordinated debt, in effect to be given to the other investors in the deal, namely the equity holders. The banks dropped their objection. In this case, the revised deal would show the banks taking a smaller share but no smaller risk: The addition of more subordinated debt had hardly improved cash flows or raised asset values. In the late 1980s, additional junk debt appears to have been at the margin just raising acquisition prices, so banks may have derived a false sense of security from the decline in their share of deals.

Finally, banks' increasing their front-end fees is ambiguous evidence of banks' acting smart. The challenge to a bank's senior management is to maintain a discipline over promotion and compensation that does not reward loan officers for pulling in the front-end fees without regard to the ultimate fate of the residual credits that remain on the books. By this test, banks did not come out of the leveraged lending business very well; loan write-offs later swallowed their earnings from front-end fees and spreads. Consider Citicorp, the bank with the largest leveraged loan book (and, usefully for the present purpose, some of the most comprehensive shareholder disclosure). Its fees and spreads on leveraged loans looked good in 1988, but eventually loan write-offs caught up with what the bank had earned (table 2.4). The obvious question is whether the pursuit of the front-end fees had dulled the edge of the credit analysis.

Citi was able to break even on its leveraged lending only because the bank led lots of credits and retained relatively little on its own books. When asked what effect the regulatory initiatives (described in chapter 3) had on banks regarding leveraged lending, one deeply involved regulator cited the greater propensity of big banks to sell their leveraged loans. If so, Citi and other big banks came out as whole as they did

Table 2.4
Citibank's experience with highly leveraged lending

	1988	1989	1990	1991	1992	1993
HLT loans						
Senior—United States	4.200	5.600	5.000	3.700	2.400	1.500
Foreign	0.600	2.100	2.200	1.200	0.300	0.200
Senior—Subtotal	4.800	7.700	7.200	4.900	2.700	1.700
Subordinated	1.100	1.100	1.000	1.700	1.000	1.100
Total	5.900	8.800	8.200	6.600	3.700	2.800
Fees and interest income						
Fees	0.233	0.207	0.184	0.054	0.059	n.a.
Interest income*	0.118	0.166	0.138	0.103	0.062	0.052
Total income	0.351	0.373	0.322	0.157	0.121	0.052
Cumulated						
Total income	0.351	0.724	1.046	1.203	1.324	1.376
Write-offs						
United States**	0.021	0.101	0.162	0.137	0.089	0.032
Foreign	n.a.	0.004	0.034	0.208	0.070	n.a.
Total	0.021	0.105	0.196	0.345	0.159	0.032
Cumulated	0.021	0.126	0.322	0.667	0.826	0.858
Net income						
Income	0.330	0.268	0.126	−0.188	−0.038	0.020
Cumulated	0.330	0.598	0.724	0.536	0.498	0.518

Source: Annual reports.
Note: Figures presented are in billions of dollars.
* Interest is calculated as .02* (HLT loans less nonaccruals of $0 billion in 1988, $0.502 billion in 1989, $1.31 billion in 1990, $1.445 billion in 1991, $0.6 billion in 1992, and $0.2 billion in 1993).
** Figure for 1988 presented as a three-year average.

thanks to the regulatory pressure. The smaller banks to whom the loans were marketed had less reason to thank the regulators, however.

Overall, banks did not suffer losses of the scale experienced on their real estate loan books of the late 1980s or on their developing country loans of earlier years. The timing of the banks' sour leveraged loans and the associated write-offs proved extremely awkward, coming as they did when the real estate prices were crashing. If the banks broke even or earned the Treasury bill rate on the equity backing their leveraged loans, it was more good fortune than smart banking.

Securities Firms as Smart Money?

How about the investment bankers: Did they not pocket the front-end fees and generally come off looking like smart money? Recall that Drexel ended up in bankruptcy, because the collapse in junk bond prices drove down its net worth. It might be objected, however, that Drexel after Milken ceased being smart money, whereas Milken after Drexel still had his smart money. In addition to Drexel, Shearson Lehman and First Boston got stuck with bridge loans that could not be refinanced with junk bonds after the market's collapse. In each case, a rich parent came to the rescue—American Express and Credit Suisse, respectively—and absent that aid, the survival of each firm was in some doubt. Basically, Drexel, Shearson, and First Boston had gotten into the banking business (making bridge loans) to snag junk bond underwriting mandates, and their diversification strategies did not turn out well. It is worth noting that junk bonds underwritten by these firms went into default even more frequently than those underwritten by Drexel.[59] Again, the departure of First Boston's leading merger specialists in 1988 might be argued to have left the firm at a loss. But the larger point here is that it is difficult to sustain a characterization of Wall Street as the smart money, given the size and prominence of the two firms that might have collapsed if their parents had taken the same

hands-off approach as Banque Bruxelles Lambert did of its troubled
U.S. affiliate, Drexel Lambert.

LBO Promoters and Investors as Smart Money?

If banks and securities firms did not do very well, how about the former
investment bankers who put the deals together? The LBO promoters
may come off as the smart money in the corporate leveraging wave of
the 1980s. The Henry Kravis wing of the Metropolitan Museum of Art
suggests that the promoters took some money off of the table.

But the few promoters must be distinguished from their many investors. The investors in LBO funds might be thought smart money, but
this identification is not self-evident. Returns of 30 percent sound good
until one recognizes that a bet on the S & P 500 consisting of one part
equity and five or ten parts debt would have done even better, given
the trend of equity prices.[60] Institutional investors who are prepared
to sell their shareholdings in the market to LBO organizers who then
reap substantial fees from the same institutions for underperforming
a (leveraged) benchmark do not meet a minimal test of smart money.

The best defense of the institutional participation in LBO funds is
that it permitted pension funds in effect to raise their portfolio weight
on equity in a manner that the rules that they were operating under
would otherwise have made very difficult:

Paradoxically the situation is that pension funds own both the debt of LBOs
as well as the equities, although not in the same pension fund in the same
company. The equity holding in an LBO has the characteristic of offsetting the
characteristically very high debt positions that pension funds have. Thus the
holding of an equity position in the LBO that may be characterized by a 10 to
1 debt ratio within the LBO company amounts to the equivalent of nullifying
the stated debt position that is held by the pension fund. Thus a holding of
an LBO may be a way of changing the debt to equity relationship of a pension
fund without it appearing risky. If this is true, then it is an uneconomic way
to solve the problem that most pension funds hold substantially higher holdings of debt than make economic sense for their long-run assignment.[61]

There was scarcely any smart money to be found.

To conclude, as competition heated up, junk bonds got junkier, leveraged-buyout prices rose, equity financing got leaner and leaner, various markets reinforced each other, and deal makers and bankers grabbed more compensation up front. As in other euphorias, most market participants lost track of risks until the structures that they created fell of their own weight.

3   Why the 1980s Stopped: Did Judges, Lawmakers, and Regulators Kill the Leveraging Business?

In the late 1980s and early 1990s, the framers of many new laws and regulations sought explicitly to deter debt financing and leveraged and hostile acquisitions. Other legislation and new legal doctrines not explicitly crafted to impede such transactions were nevertheless predicted to have similar effects. Some argue that these measures and not the internal dynamics of the leveraging business brought this business to a halt in 1990. Those who have argued that politics and not economics stopped the leveraging business usefully remind us that financial market outcomes occur within a structure of corporate law and taxation as well as financial-firm regulation. Still the reader may be surprised at the cast of characters said to have ganged up on the leveraging business: Congress, federal judges, state legislators, state judges, national bank regulators, and state insurance regulators, a group covering all three branches of government and independent regulators, at both the federal and state levels.

This chapter examines legal developments related to leveraged acquisitions, with particular emphasis on those occurring in 1989 and 1990. Specifically, we discuss five legal developments: changes in state corporate law (*Paramount v. Time*'s statement of fiduciary standards for corporate directors, and the evolution of anti-takeover statutes); federal tax law (new treatment of original-issue discount bonds); bankruptcy law (the clarification of its treatment of bond exchanges); federal regulation of depository institutions (bank regulators' policies on leveraged bank loans and forced liquidation of junk bonds by savings and loans); and state insurance regulation (disclosure and capital rules for junk bond holdings). We ask whether these legal developments could have been fully, substantially, or even partially responsible for bringing an end to the leveraging business.

Generally, each of the five discussions is organized in three parts. First, we point out how the law governing certain transactions changed. In most cases this is relatively simple—a statute or regulation was enacted, clearly spelling out a new rule. But in some cases, particularly the *Time* decision, the change in the law is more subtle, and more discussion (in appendix 3.1) is required. In these cases, reasonable people can disagree as to how much the law really changed, or if it changed at all. Though acknowledging that other interpretations are possible, we try to make the best case for the law's having changed substantially. Next, we try to explain how the change in the law could have discouraged corporate acquisitions and/or leverage. This part of the discussion is generally theoretical or hypothetical, and in each instance we try to present the most reasonable argument for the most significant effect. The concluding part of most of the sections confronts the hypothesized effects with the evidence. Generally the data are incomplete, do not lend themselves to statistical hypothesis testing, and can be interpreted only with the help of further argumentation. For this reason, drawing definitive conclusions is difficult, and in no case do the data suffice to reject a prior view that the legal changes discussed either did or did not cause the observed declines in corporate leveraging.

Our conclusion is that the proponents of this political account of the end of the leveraging business have overstated the change in the law and exaggerated the effect of such changes that were made. At most, and this is by no means evident, the legislation requiring savings and loans to divest their junk bonds may have contributed to the seizing up of the junk bond market. The other legal developments tended to discourage leverage only marginally. Taken together, the legal changes may have been cumulatively significant but cannot convincingly bear much responsibility for the end of the leveraging business.

3.1 State Corporate Law

It has been argued that developments in state corporate law are at least partly responsible for the decline in hostile and highly leveraged acquisitions after 1989. In particular, observers point to the Delaware Supreme Court's 1989 decision in *Paramount Communications v. Time*[1] and the proliferation of various anti-takeover statutes in the late 1980s. In appendix 3.1, we analyze the *Time* decision at some length. Below we simply state the conclusions of this analysis. In the subsequent section we analyze the state anti-takeover statutes, then draw on the existing empirical studies to determine to what extent these legal developments could have been responsible for the decline in acquisition activity in the early 1990s. The existing evidence fails to support the claim that developments in corporate law caused the observed decline.

The Time *Decision*

The *Time* decision gave new weight to an incumbent board's business strategy and slightly broadened the range of an incumbent board's defenses against a hostile bid to include some mergers and acquisitions. As a result, hostile bids became less likely to succeed, and less profitable if they failed, because a hostile bidder became less likely to have a higher bid into which to tender shares already acquired. With the probability of success lower and a lower payoff in the event of loss, *Time* unambiguously lowered expected profits to a hostile bidder. We examine below the difficult question of how much the *Time* decision tilted the balance against hostile acquirers and how important it could have been to the observed slowdown in hostile bids.

State Anti-Takeover Statutes

In the middle and late 1980s, as takeovers proliferated, legislatures responded by enacting statutes designed to protect businesses incorporated in their states from the threat of hostile bids. The typical drama began with an outsider's tender offer for a corporation. While this bid was pending, the management of the target would then lobby the legislature in the corporation's home state for protection. Management would ask its representatives to enact into state law a provision that looked very much like amendments that their peers at other companies had placed in their own corporate charters. But here there was no time for a shareholder vote, and even if there were, the shareholders might not vote for the management-sponsored alternative. With little deliberation, the legislature would grant its constituents' request, making sure the scope of the provision would include the offending bid.

The political economy in Delaware, however, was different, because about half of all large U.S. corporations are incorporated there. Any other state could pass a law that would protect managers of locally incorporated firms while narrowing its own takeover options only marginally. Not so in Delaware, where takeover battles often involved a constituent target *and* bidder. Ultimately, though, Delaware legislators succumbed to the threat of losing Delaware's market share. They feared that if the gap between the protection that they offered and that offered by other states widened substantially, managers would reincorporate elsewhere, losing for Delaware tax revenues and legal and other administrative jobs.[2]

Figure 3.1 shows the level of state legislatures' anti-takeover activity in 1982 through 1991. These laws took three different forms, but the type with the broadest application, the "business combination freeze,"

Percentage share of corporate assets   Number of states

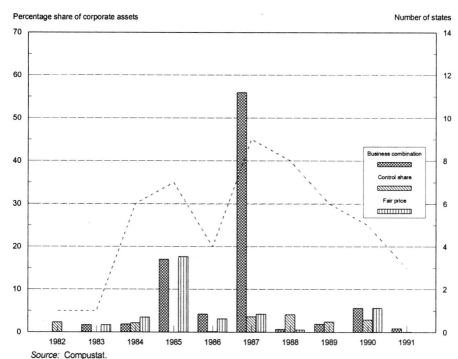

Source: Compustat.
Note: Bars represent assets in states adopting anti-takeover statutes each year (left scale). Dashed line represents number of states adopting such statutes in each year (right scale).

Figure 3.1
State anti-takeover statutes

prevented the holder of a substantial bloc of shares from merging with the target for some years. Delaware adopted such a statute in 1987, which accounts for the height of the charted bar that year. In addition, "fair price" laws required either that two-thirds of disinterested share-holders approve a merger or that the price offered be above that set by a prescribed formula. New York adopted both fair price and business combination freeze statutes in 1985. A third type of law, the "control share acquisition," stripped a would-be acquirer's shares of voting rights unless the rest of the shareholders voted their approval. The tim-ing of these changes is crucial to the argument: Whether one weights each state law change by the assets of the corporations incorporated there or simply counts the number of states adopting any of the three types of anti-takeover statute, 1987 stands out as the peak of activity. These laws all strengthened the franchise of existing shareholders to the benefit of incumbent management and thereby limited the power of a hostile bidder's money. Appendix 3.2 offers more detail on these laws and lays out the theoretical argument that these laws could slow acquisition activity. Most importantly, the business combination statute could keep an acquirer's hands, and those of its banker, off of the target's assets, which distance would raise risks for lenders and increase the cost of credit if it did not make it unavailable altogether. In Delaware, current shareholders and incumbent boards gained a better bargaining position to demand a better price. We now turn to the empirical evidence on the importance of changes in corporate law.

Changes in Corporate Law: The Empirical Evidence

As elaborated in appendixes 3.1 and 3.2, changes in corporate law occurring in the late 1980s could conceivably have deterred tender offers. The *Time* decision and business combination statutes could lower the probability of a given bid's success; any of the anti-takeover laws could lower the expected payoff from a successful bid; and the *Time* decision as well as some state laws (control share and fair price statutes) could lower the expected payoffs (or increase expected losses) from an unsuccessful bid.

However, some difficulties arise when these abstract arguments confront the observed decline in mergers and acquisition activity in the early 1990s. The first and most obvious problem is apparent upon a simultaneous inspection of figures 3.1 and 3.2. Together, they show that whereas anti-takeover legislation peaked in 1987, the acquisition market continued to boom through 1989. To list specific transactions discussed elsewhere in this book, after Delaware adopted its anti-takeover legislation, Paramount launched its hostile bid for *Time;* Kohlberg, Kravis, and Roberts launched their hostile bid for RJR-Nabisco;

Billions of dollars

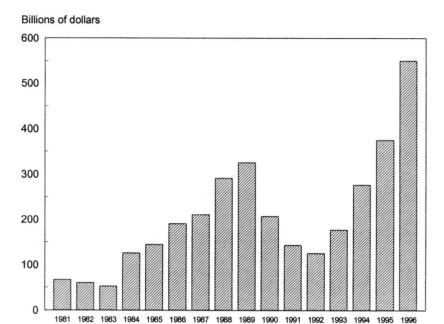

Sources: 1981-86: *Mergers and Acquisitions*, May/June 1987; 1987-96: *Mergers and Acquisitions*, March/April 1997.

Figure 3.2
Value of completed M&A

and Grand Met launched its hostile bid for Pillsbury. Such laws cannot explain the subsequent drop-off in activity. Moreover, none of these laws has prevented the subsequent rise of mergers and acquisition activity to levels well above those reached in the 1980s.

A review of some relevant empirical studies does not challenge this preliminary conclusion. It should be noted first, however, that some of these studies do find statistically significant effects. There is evidence that state anti-takeover statutes have resulted in a decrease in the stock prices of companies incorporated in those states.[3] Because the lower stock prices would at least in part reflect lower expected takeover premiums, it can be inferred from this evidence that anti-takeover statutes do in fact discourage takeovers. Moreover, direct studies of takeover activity reinforce these findings. Pound found that firms that adopted anti-takeover charter amendments between 1971 and 1979 experienced a significantly lower incidence of tender offers for their shares in subsequent years, as compared to other companies that did not have anti-takeover amendments.[4] And although they did not conduct a test of statistical significance, Hackl and Testani found that fair price statutes appear to result in fewer bids for companies affected by them.[5]

However, observed effects on activity, even statistically significant ones, do not by themselves support a claim that the statutes passed in the late 1980s really explain the drop-off in acquisition activity. It is also necessary to examine the coefficients that result from statistical calculations involving these effects to assess their potency as explanations. Hackl and Testani found that the "average" state adopting a fair price statute before 1986 experienced an adjusted decline in takeover attempts of between 3 and 10 percent.[6] Even the high end of this estimate is insufficient to explain much of the change in market behavior between 1988 and 1990, during which time the number of announced hostile tender offers for public companies declined from 46 to 8, or 83 percent.[7]

Moreover, interpreting Pound's evidence yields an ambiguous assessment of *Time*'s impact. In his sample, over the period 1974 to 1984, the following statistically significant differences appeared:

1. Whereas 38 percent of the companies with no anti-takeover amendments received takeover offers, only 28 percent of companies with anti-takeover amendments did: Anti-takeover amendments were associated with a one-third lower bid frequency.

2. Managements with anti-takeover amendments resisted bids more frequently (68 percent vs. 38 percent).

3. *Every* company that had an amendment *and* resisted a bid ultimately escaped a transfer of control. Without an amendment, resistance succeeded only 61 percent of the time.

In short, companies with anti-takeover amendments receive bids less frequently and are more likely to escape takeover. One might be tempted to interpret the *Time* decision as encouraging policies that would lead to fewer takeover threats.[8] However, the weakness in this interpretation is revealed when one observes that in Pound's sample, the will to resist and an anti-takeover policy (which presumably would follow from the will, given the ability of managements to put in place anti-takeover policies that did not require shareholder approval) sufficed to ensure independence. However, if *Time* had any impact at all, it could only have increased an independence-minded board's probability of staying independent.[9] Seen in this way, the *Time* decision gave corporate boards nothing they did not already have.

Pound's sample notwithstanding, for all U.S. companies, the probability of the independence-minded board armed with an anti-takeover amendment losing to a hostile bidder is not 0. What might safely be inferred from Pound's evidence is that this probability is low. *Time*'s impact, in that case, would boil down to a question of how much extra help the Delaware Supreme Court could have given boards that already wielded great power to resist a hostile bidder.[10]

The outcome of tender offers in the 1990s, compared to that in the 1980s, does not suggest that the *Time* decision stopped such bids. To begin with, *Time* and the other legal changes reviewed in this chapter did not prevent tender offers in 1996–98 from outnumbering those in 1986–88 (figure 3.3). Moreover, 1986–88 were chosen as the peak years of the last decade, while tender offers were accelerating in 1999. For the present purpose, the key question is whether the evidence suggests that the *Time* decision let incumbent managers "just say no" with substantially greater success. Here the evidence is quite clear. Contested tender offers leaving the target firm independent represented 4 percent of all offers in the late 1990s and 4 percent of all offers in the late 1980s. Viewing the same data from the other side, tender offers have ended favorably (in success or in acquisition by white knights to whom shares could be sold at a premium) in the same frequency

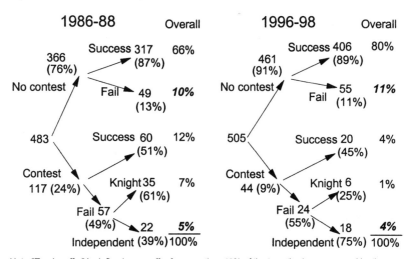

Note: "Tender offer" is defined as an offer for more than 10% of the target's share governed by the Williams Act. "Successful" offer is defined as one in which some shares are tendered and the suiter does not cancel the offer. ("White) knight" is defined as an acquirer accepted as friendly by the target.

Source: Houlihan Lokey Howard & Zukin Mergerstat Review, 1996-99.

Figure 3.3
Outcome of tender offers

(85 percent) in the late 1990s as the late 1980s. It is true that the frequency of contested tender offers remained lower through 1998 than in the corresponding years in the 1980s and that, given a contest, a target firm remained independent more frequently in the 1990s. Now one might argue that the *Time* decision forced would-be acquirers in the 1990s to make generous, "too good to refuse" bids, offering rich premia (albeit in the coin of their own shares). Or one might hold that the lesson was learned that the winner of a 1980s bidding war often turned out the loser. In either case, from the evidence of the 1990s, the *Time* decision cannot be held responsible for the sharp decline of mergers and acquisitions in general and leveraged mergers and acquisitions in particular.

In sum, although the *Time* decision appears to have given boards license to do almost anything in response to almost nothing, boards already had strong means of maintaining independence prior to the decision's being rendered. Thus, the practical effect of the *Time* decision is questionable. Notwithstanding the *Time* decision, firms receiving tender offers have remained independent in about the same fraction of cases in the mid-1990s as in the late 1980s. Moreover, although some state anti-takeover statutes have demonstrably slowed takeover activity since being enacted, they lack both the power and the timing to explain why the leveraging business of the 1980s stopped.

3.2 Federal Tax Law

As state legislators and judges were moving to slow takeovers, Congress changed the Internal Revenue Code to make it more difficult or expensive for leveraged firms to issue junk bonds. First, in the Omnibus Budget Reconciliation Act of 1989 (OBRA '89), Congress eliminated or deferred some interest deductions for junk bonds issued at large discounts to face value ("original-issue discount" or OID bonds[11]). A year later, as part of OBRA '90, Congress eliminated tax advantages for distressed debt exchanges by firms not operating under protection of the bankruptcy court.

Deferred Interest Junk Bonds

As described in chapter 2, the rising trend of leveraged buyout prices in relation to cash flows led to junkier and junkier junk bonds, as zero-coupon bonds and PIK bonds squared the circle between underlying cash flows and promised debt payments. After hearings that highlighted the possibility that leveraged deals were just exploiting the tax deductibility of interest and indeed that leveraged firms could take tax deductions for interest promised but unpaid, Congress took away the tax deductibility of certain high-yield, deferred-interest corporate bonds.[12] After describing the tax change, we estimate in box 3.1 an upper bound for the change's effect on the RJR-Nabisco deal, had it occurred after OBRA '89. This result and our consideration of stylized cases lead us to conclude that lobbyists on Capitol Hill succeeded in making sure that this tax change would do no more than pare some takeover premiums rather than block deal financing.

The Tax Change

After high-grade U.S. corporations started issuing zero-coupon bonds in the early 1980s, Congress legislated a *symmetric* treatment of corporate issuers of OID bonds (under section 163(e)) and taxable holders of such bonds. With zero-coupon bonds (or more generally, with bonds carrying coupons below the market rate), all (or some) of the return comes from the appreciation of the bond price from the original discount to face value. Congress opted for symmetry by allowing a borrower to deduct interest accrued (assuming constant yield to maturity under section 1272[13]) but unpaid interest while at the same time requiring a lender to pay tax on interest accrued but as yet unreceived.

The 1989 provisions shifted to an *asymmetric* treatment, reducing interest deductions for the issuers of high-yield, deferred-interest bonds while continuing to make holders pay taxes on accruing interest. For quite junky deferred-interest bonds—those paying more than a 5 percent spread over U.S. Treasury bonds[14]—the accruing but unpaid interest would be deductible only when actually paid. PIK or "bunny" bonds, as termed in chapter 2, would be treated as discount bonds for this purpose. Any accruing interest corresponding to a spread wider than 6 percent over U.S. Treasury bonds came in for worse treatment as a nondeductible return to equity.[15] This tax change, in short, deferred or even eliminated interest deductions for issuers of high-yield bonds with significant interest deferral while still requiring holders to pay current taxes on the unrealized income.

Box 3.1
The 1989 Tax Code Changes and the Leveraged Buyout of RJR-Nabisco

To assess the impact that OBRA '89 (sections 163(e) (5) and (i)) might have had in discouraging actual highly leveraged transactions, this box analyzes the largest leveraged buyout ever completed: RJR-Nabisco. The final phase of that transaction, the refinancing of the bridge facilities, occurred two months before the effective date of sections 163(e) (5) and (i). However, if the transaction had been subject to these provisions, they would have cost the parties at most $1.3 billion, about 5 percent of the $26 billion transaction or about 11 percent of the $12 billion acquisition premium. In all likelihood, the cost would have been much less. In light of the relatively small fraction of the acquisition premium absorbed in the counterfactual, it appears sections 163(e) (5) and (i) would not have broken the deal.

In the leveraged buyout of RJR, three bond issues would have been subject to the provisions. The adjustable-rate senior converting debenture[1] (the "convertible") maturing in 2009 and the 15 percent PIK bonds and zero-coupon bonds[2] maturing in 2001. The gross proceeds from these issues was about $1.8 billion, $2 billion, and $1 billion, respectively. The comparable U.S. Treasury yield ("applicable federal rate") was approximately 9.2 percent at the time of the issues (April and May 1989), so all three had a yield spread of more than 5 percent (but less than 6 percent). Moreover, each had significant deferred interest. The convertibles did not have to pay any cash interest for ten years, and the PIKs and zeros did not have to pay for five years.[3]

Because the yields to maturity of the issues did not exceed the applicable federal rate by more than 6 percent, there was no "disqualified portion" to be taxed as a return to equity, so the provisions would have bitten solely through the lost time value of money. To estimate the size of this effect, it is necessary to make assumptions about certain business factors: conversion, the appropriate discount rate, future profitability of RJR, subsequent repurchases of the bonds by RJR, and RJR's subsequent behavior toward its option to pay cash interest sooner than required on the PIKs and the convertibles. In addition, it is necessary to make assumptions about the disposition of two legal questions. As it turns out, the simplest assumptions all work to overstate the value that would have been lost to the parties by operation of the provisions, and in addition make disposition of the legal questions unnecessary.

In table 3.1, top panel, we assume the holders of the convertible do not convert.[4] The 15 percent yield to maturity on the bonds is used as the discount rate.[5] Next we allow for different assumptions about when RJR was expected first to produce taxable income. Once taxable income is generated, RJR is as-

Table 3.1
Transaction value that would have been lost to new OID rules, RJR-Nabisco leveraged buyout

Assuming no bond conversion
Years to profitability

0	1	2	3	4	5
1,340	1,330	1,290	1,220	1,130	1,030

Assuming bond conversion
Years to profitability

0	1	2	3	4	5
760	740	710	650	570	270

Note: Figures presented are in millions of dollars.

sumed to use net operating loss carry forwards created by the bonds to offset current taxable income.[6] Last, we assume that none of the bonds is retired within five years of issue[7] and that the PIKs and zeros never pay cash interest before 1994.[8] As the top panel of table 3.1 shows, under these assumptions, the value lost by the parties if sections 163(e) (5) and (i) had been in effect would have ranged from $1,340 million, in the case of immediate profitability, to $1,030 million, in the case of profitability only after five years.

In table 3.1, bottom panel, we assume that the holders of the convertible exercise their conversion option. This scenario raises two legal questions. The first is whether under the pre-1989 rules, RJR would have to amend its prior tax returns to remove deductions for OID that will never have to be paid. In a case involving the conversion of liquid-yield option notes (LYONs),[9] the Treasury originally took the position that the prior deductions should be disallowed. However, after the filing of the Tax Court petition, the Treasury abandoned its challenge.[10] Thus we assume that on conversion, the prior deductions stand. The second issue is whether the accrued OID is considered "paid" when the holder converts. If it is, RJR gets a large tax deduction on conversion under the post-1989 rules. If it is not, RJR loses the OID deductions forever. For simplicity, and in keeping with our practice of overstating the effect of the provisions, we assume the interest is not considered paid in this circumstance. As substantive justification, we point to section 163(i), which provides that interest paid in common stock is not deemed "paid." As table

3.1 shows, assuming conversion, the value extracted from the transaction ranges from $760 million, assuming immediate profitability, to $270 million, assuming profitability only after five years. The more successful the LBO, the more likely conversion, so the 1989 tax rules would have put up taxes less on a more successful LBO.

Moreover, the transaction could easily have been structured to lessen the impact of the provisions. A simple way to avoid classification is to have bonds pay cash interest from the beginning. However, it seems that this structure would have placed too much strain on the company in the first year or two after the LBO. During the first year alone, more than $600 million in fixed cash obligations would have come due. Given the company's tight cash situation at that time, this option would have been impractical.

As a less restrictive alternative, however, the bonds could have provided for the cash payment of all (or most) of the deferred interest exactly five years after their issue. Such a modification avoids a determination that a bond has "significant OID." At least one transaction that closed subsequent to the effective date of the provisions employed this very device.[11]

Whether or not this technique could have been used by the parties to prevent the diversion of value to the Treasury, $1.34 billion remains as an upper bound for the penalty that the provisions would have imposed. This is more than one-third of the proceeds of the issues and about 5 percent of the transaction value. Although this sum is by no means insignificant, it amounts to only about 11 percent of the total takeover premium of about $12 billion. Thus, it is probably safe to say that the 1989 tax changes could not by themselves have broken the RJR-Nabisco LBO. At most, they might have forced the bidding to stop at a price of $103 per share, instead of the actual $109.

Notes

1. These were issued in the back-end merger of April 1989.
2. These were sold pursuant to the refinancing of the bridge facilities in May 1989.
3. Although the convertibles and the PIKs left RJR the option of making interest payments in cash, the test under section 163(i) is whether or not the issuer is required to make cash payments.
4. By the terms of the debenture, a holder of the convertible had to elect to convert by April 1993 or lose the option forever.

5. It can be argued that a higher discount rate, corresponding to the cost of equity, should be used, since the value of the tax shield depends upon expected profits, which represent residual cash flows. Nonetheless, because the point here is to show that the provisions would not have extracted a large fraction of the takeover premium, we can afford to err on the side of producing a large estimate.

6. Further erring on the side of producing a large estimate, we assume that once RJR has a profitable year, its profits are immediately large enough to make use of all the net operating loss carry forwards associated with the bonds and that the tax law immediately allows RJR the full benefit of these deductions.

7. As it turned out, RJR periodically repurchased these issues on the open market. By the end of 1993, the convertibles had been called and less than $1.7 billion of the PIKs and zeros remained outstanding.

8. As it turned out, RJR did make cash payments on both these issues.

9. LYONs are similar to RJR's convertibles in that both are discount bonds convertible into common stock.

10. See Lee Sheppard, "IRS Stance in *Staley* Underscores Roaring Issues Raised by LYONs," 53 *Tax Notes* 1453, December 30, 1991; "Merrill Lynch Affirms Tax Status of LYONs after IRS Challenge," *Wall Street Journal*, December 23, 1991, p. B5; and Laura Jereski, "Super LYONs," *Forbes*, June 8, 1992, p. 44.

11. Lee Sheppard speculates that the Container Corporation of America employed this structure primarily so that its junk bonds could avoid being subject to the new provisions. See "Ring around the Interest Disallowance Rules," *Tax Notes Today*, vol. 20, December 20, 1989, pp. 254–5. See also Dale S. Collinson, "United States Tax Legislation Affects Junk Bonds and LBOs," 90 *Tax Notes Today* 38-20, January 31, 1989 (stating that escaping the new rules will "depend primarily on techniques for avoiding a determination that the debt is issued at a deep discount").

The Impact of the Tax Change

Box 3.1 demonstrates that the 1989 tax code changes would have had no more than a marginal impact on the RJR-Nabisco buyout had they been in effect at the time. If the financing of leveraged acquisitions generally relied on interest-deferred junk bonds more than the RJR-Nabisco transaction did, the impact of the 1989 provisions might have been more pronounced. As table 3.2 shows, for a plausible structure, a substantial portion of the transaction value *could* have been lost to the provisions. For example, a deal 50 percent financed by ten-year

Table 3.2
Percentage of LBO transaction value lost to OBRA '89 rules

Terms of AHYDOs (years)	Percentage of purchase price financed by AHYDOs							
	5	10	15	20	25	30	50	75
8	1.1	2.2	3.3	4.4	5.5	6.6	11	17
10	1.5	3.0	4.6	6.1	7.6	9.1	15	23
12	2	3.9	5.9	7.8	9.8	12	20	30
15	2.7	5.3	8	11	13	16	27	40

Note: Figures in the table assume that all applicable high-yield debt obligations (AHYDOs) are 18 percent zero-coupon bonds, the applicable federal rate is 8 percent, and all tax deductions are fully utilized as soon as they are available.

zeros loses 15 percent of its value, which would in fact have been enough to break a lot of leveraged buyouts. This figure, 15 percent of acquisition value, corresponds to about half of the average acquisition premium for management buyouts reported by Kaplan and Stein,[16] and by *Mergerstat Review*. It also represents roughly the 30th percentile acquisition premium in the late 1980s.[17]

In practice, the share of interest-deferred junk bonds in financing leveraged acquisitions prior to 1989 was generally too small for the 1989 tax changes to have had much impact. About 60 percent of management buyouts from Kaplan and Stein's sample from 1987 to 1989 used PIK and discount debt, and in these transactions, the average ratio of this debt to total capital was 16 percent. This ratio was fairly constant over the 1987–89 period and was considerably lower before, so it would appear that most LBOs would have been located in the left half of table 3.2, where the extra tax burden imposed by the 1989 changes would have claimed only 3 to 5 percent of transaction value. Given the order of magnitude difference between such fractions (which are themselves upwardly biased estimates) and observed takeover premiums over the same period, it is safe to conclude that although the tax hike on interest-deferred junk bonds may have forced down takeover premiums for LBOs, it is unlikely that it would have derailed many deals.

Table 3.3
Distressed debt exchange offers

Year	Amount
1985	2,152
1986	2,037
1987	684
1988	569
1989	1,662
1990	275
1991	185
1992	37
1993	711

Sources: Morgan Stanley, 1985–89; Moody's, 1990–93.
Note: Amounts presented are in millions of dollars.

Distressed Exchange Offers–OBRA '90

As discussed in chapter 2, one technique that Michael Milken pro-moted to avoid outright defaults of junk bond issuers was voluntary exchanges of bonds that the issuer could not service for bonds with easier terms that it might be able to service. Before 1990, exchange offers were a popular means of restructuring the debt of corporations in financial distress (table 3.3). Between 1986 and 1989, an average of about 0.8 to 0.9 percent of all high-yield bonds were exchanged an-nually.

In 1990, however, two legal developments raised the cost of out-of-bankruptcy exchange offers. The first was the Bankruptcy Court's January 1990 decision in the LTV case. The second was Con-gress's change in the tax treatment of out-of-bankruptcy debt ex-changes by solvent companies. The remainder of this section discusses this latter change. (A discussion of the impact of both these develop-ments is deferred until the discussion of the LTV case in the next section.)

The essential feature of a bond exchange for a distressed firm, namely that it reduce the firm's debt burden, poses a tax question. Although the new bond might pay as much as the old bond's face amount at maturity, the new bond typically sets lower interest payments. As a result, the issuer experiences a capital gain (or a capital loss on a liability, legally a "cancellation of indebtedness") at the time of the exchange. Tax law can encourage such exchanges, by not treating the capital gain as taxable income, or discourage them, by considering the gain as taxable income. As the tax code stood through 1989, Congress had encouraged such exchanges, generally recognized as a lower-cost alternative to bankruptcy.[18]

As part of OBRA '90, Congress removed this tax break for debt-for-debt exchanges outside of bankruptcy. In effect, debt relief is treated under the revised rules as income, reducing losses that can be carried forward to shelter any future income. An exception remains, however, if the exchange occurs when the issuer is in bankruptcy or is insolvent (defined as having liabilities in excess of assets). While the effect would be subtle, at the margin this tax change must have made distressed bond exchanges more difficult by removing a fiscal bonus for the involved parties to reach consensus.[19]

3.3 Federal Bankruptcy Law on Distressed Exchanges: The LTV Decision

The Bankruptcy Court Ruling

A 1990 ruling in the LTV bankruptcy case further discouraged distressed exchange offers.[20] The record indicates that in May 1986, the issuer, LTV, exchanged about $116 million of its 13⅞ cash interest paying–debentures (the "old bonds") for 15 percent bonds, which, despite the higher interest rate, were valued at a deep discount from par, having a face value of $116 million (the "new bonds") plus equity. Two months later, in July 1986, LTV filed for bankruptcy. The issue before the court was whether the holders of the new bonds would have a claim in bankruptcy equal to the face value of the new bonds, which was the same as the face value of the old bonds, or the fair market value of the new bonds at the time of the exchange (adjusted upward for the amortization of the discount accrued prior to the filing of the bankruptcy petition). Chapter 11 of the U.S. Bankruptcy Code provides that unsecured creditors are not allowed a claim for interest that accrues after the filing of bankruptcy.[21] Relying on this section, the court held that the new bond holders would not be allowed a claim for the full face value of the new bonds (or, equivalently, the old bonds tendered in May 1986).

Did LTV Say Anything New?

As a first principle, if an interpretation of existing law is to be viewed as suddenly causing a change in behavior, the new interpretation must somehow differ than from prevailing one, that is, the decision must come as news. It is hard to read the *LTV* decision as a surprise, however. The treatment of deeply discounted bonds in bankruptcy was a simple logical inference from explicit statutory language. In fact, the prospectus for LTV's new bonds in 1986 disclosed the possibility that the new bond holders' claims could be reduced. In view of this, how market participants could have talked themselves into an expectation of the opposite result in *LTV* is not clear, but we offer some conjectures.

First, this was not a simple case of a sale of new securities for cash, but rather an exchange of old securities for new ones. Perhaps the new bondholders hoped to persuade the judge that the exchange should not be treated as a new issue, but as a modification of an existing agreement. The problem with such an argument is that (unlike in a renegotiation of a loan or private placement) for public debt securities, compliance with the Trust Indenture Act as a practical matter requires that new bonds, governed by a new legal agreement, be exchanged for the old ones.

Second, perhaps market participants believed that Bankruptcy Court Judge Bernard Lifland would accept the new bondholders' argument that interpreting the law to reduce their claim would discourage future workouts. Perhaps market participants were not thinking wishfully that the judge would consider such a "policy" argument, since Judge Lifland expressed no sympathy for strict statutory construction (or "judicial conservatism"). As it turned out, however, the judge apparently did not find the policy argument compelling.

The Combined Effect of LTV and the Tax Law Change

In 1991, Jensen argued that the *LTV* decision, in combination with the taxation of debt-for-debt exchanges, had caused out-of-bankruptcy distressed exchange offers "to slow to a trickle," senselessly pushing some issuers into bankruptcy.[22] This section fleshes out Jensen's claim by going through the argument one step at a time. Next we review data that support the assertion that after 1989 voluntary debt exchanges became less prevalent, and bankruptcy more prevalent, as a means of reorganizing the finances of distressed firms. We then argue that there are a multitude of competing explanations for the drop-off in successful exchange offers. More important, we conclude by arguing that whatever the cause of the drop-off in voluntary exchange offers, it is very doubtful that it could have raised the ex ante costs of junk bond issuance substantially.

The Asserted Effect

The *LTV* decision and the repeal of the tax break for debt relief outside of bankruptcy could have raised the cost of voluntary debt exchanges, and thereby made them less likely, in two ways. First, the tax change reduced the net operating losses of distressed firms that make such exchanges, ultimately increasing the tax bite of any future profits in the event of recovery or acquisition. Firms could still enjoy the tax break by going into bankruptcy, however. Second, the *LTV* ruling allegedly discouraged bondholders from accepting voluntary exchanges. According to the *LTV* precedent, such acceptance would pose the risk of later going into a bankruptcy proceeding with a smaller claim than otherwise. Because about half of voluntary exchanges are followed by bankruptcy,[23] exchanging bondholders would understandably insist on higher yields or more cash interest in exchange offers to compensate for the increased risk they were undertaking. Thus, some offers that might have succeeded under the (presumed) old regime would no longer succeed, increasing the probability of bankruptcy.

Congress and the bankruptcy court both seemed to discourage private workouts and to push distressed firms into bankruptcy. If bankruptcy entails more dead-weight administrative and managerial costs and disrupts business relations to a greater extent than voluntary exchanges, then both discouraged the leveraging business by imposing costs on risky debt.

The Effect and Its Importance

Distressed debt exchanges short of bankruptcy certainly did become less frequent after 1989. The actual dollar amount of such exchanges dropped off, while the number of bankruptcies rose (table 3.3). These facts seem to support Jensen's claim that legal developments discouraged private workouts of the debts of firms in financial distress.

But a brief consideration of three other forces at work counsels caution in interpreting these data. Recession overtook an already faltering economic expansion in 1990. Recession reduces cash flows and immediate business prospects and may render bankruptcy, with its ability to impose a comprehensive debt restructuring, the preferred alternative for a firm in financial difficulty. Moreover, recession may increase the dispersion of creditor beliefs about a distressed firm's prospects, making agreement on a voluntary restructuring more difficult.

Second, the rise of vulture funds in the period may have tilted the balance toward bankruptcy. Such investment funds bought distressed junk bonds at deep discounts in sufficient quantity to command a seat at the table in any bankruptcy proceeding. These funds could plausibly earn more for their investors by forcing firms into bankruptcy and emerging as the new owners.

Third, the seizing up of the junk bond market could have scuppered debt exchanges. One promised advantage to participating in a debt exchange was the greater liquidity of the new as compared to the old bonds. An illiquid market undermined this incentive to participate.

Even if one accepts the notion that Congress and the bankruptcy court conspired to push firms into bankruptcy, the question remains open how much the rise in bankruptcy could have raised the ex ante cost of issuing junk bonds in a rational and forward-looking market. Although there is little evidence on the indirect costs of bankruptcy,[24] several studies of the direct costs have been conducted. In the most famous of these studies, Warner found that in a sample of 11 railroad company bankruptcies, the direct costs were about 5.3 percent of assets.[25] Since then, the bankruptcy code has been revised, arguably toward the end of facilitating reorganizations.

Whatever the costs of traditional bankruptcy, there is reason to believe that new, streamlined bankruptcy proceedings limited the direct costs of any extra bankruptcies generated by the actions of Congress and the bankruptcy court. So-called prepackaged bankruptcies arose as an outgrowth of attempted voluntary debt exchanges that could not achieve the critical mass of participation by creditors. Instead, simultaneously with a bankruptcy filing, management of the distressed firm would submit the failed voluntary restructuring plan, and in most cases the court and the required majority of creditors would accept the plan. As a result, prepackaged bankruptcies spent months rather than years in court, incurred lower fees, and yielded higher recovery values on the defaulted debt.[26]

Prepackaged bankruptcy very much responded to the difficulties en-countered in restructuring leveraged firms' debt. The first prepack occurred in 1986, but prepacks came into their own in 1990 when vol-untary debt exchanges foundered (table 3.3). LBOs unable to service their debt represented about half of prepackaged bankruptcies between 1986 and 1993.[27] Their increased use served to limit the costs of bank-ruptcy for financially distressed firms.

Our reading of the evidence is that market developments more than legal developments pushed distressed firms from voluntary renegotia-tion of debts to bankruptcy. But even if Congress and the bankruptcy court are to be blamed for the shift, the development of prepackaged bankruptcies minimized the cost of this shift. Moreover, it must be remembered that any extra cost is ex post, realized only in the event of financial distress. Junk bond pricing should discount any such extra costs to reflect their probability. It strains credulity to believe that the legal developments of 1990 substantially raised the ex ante cost of issu-ing junk bonds.

3.4 Federal Regulation of Depository Institutions

With this section we move from the rules on governance and taxation of leveraging firms to the regulation of financial firms involved in the leveraging business. Here we take up regulation of banks (senior lend-ing) and savings and loans (purchases of junk bonds); in the last section of this chapter we take up the regulation of insurance companies (pur-chases of junk bonds).

Bank Regulators' Polices toward Highly Leveraged Transactions

We saw in chapter 2 that banks typically provided more credit to LBOs than did junk bond buyers. More generally, even though the lev-eraging business drew on credit from new, nonbank sources, it still depended on bank credit, especially to finance acquisitions in short order and thus to provide a "bridge" to bond issues. So bank regulatory policies that chilled leveraged bank lending could quite plausibly have contributed to the decline of corporate leveraging at the end of the 1980s.

The Evolution of the Highly Leveraged Transaction Classification

The regulatory response to U.S. bank lending to leveraging U.S. corporations in the 1980s started quietly early in 1984 but became very public in 1986 and again in 1988 and 1989. In 1984 the Board of Governors of the Federal Reserve instructed Federal Reserve bank examiners to treat leveraged loans as a "potential concentration of credit," notwithstanding the variety of industries the borrowers represented. In other words, the common elements of the leveraged-buyout business were interpreted as imparting common risks to loans to firms in manufacturing or in services, in the United States or abroad. Examiners were told to pay particular attention to the relationship between a borrower's debt service requirements and cash flow and, in particular, the stability of its cash flows during the last recession. Examiners were to review banks to ensure "that credit-standards are not compromised in order to increase market share."[28] Substantial exposures to leveraging transactions were to be written up on the first page of examination reports, where directors would have a hard time missing them. In interviews, bank examiners suggest that their considering leveraged loans as a possible concentration may have led originating banks in the late 1980s to sell off more of the loans than they would have otherwise, which meant that when the market turned against leveraged lending the effect was more diffuse across the banking system.

The Federal Reserve attempted in mid-decade more directly to regulate the financing of leveraged acquisitions but retreated in the face of a firestorm of opposition directed by the Secretary of Treasury. As Paul Volcker, then Chairman of the Board of Governors of the Federal Reserve, has recalled the story in an interview, the target of a leveraged

buyout approached the Federal Reserve and argued for a novel application of the Federal Reserve's legal duty to set margin requirements.
Margin requirements limit the extent to which equities can be bought
on credit, to restrain the sort of stock speculation that preceded the
Great Crash of 1929. In 1986, however, a bidder in a prospective buyout planned to use the target's shares as collateral for debt, and the
target in question sought to limit the bidder's borrowing capacity by an
application of margin requirements. Volcker reports his contemporary
doubts about the feasibility of making the margin limits stick, given a
raider's ability to structure its borrowings in different ways:

> Nevertheless, we played around with making a ruling to apply the margin re-
> quirement to the extent we could. Don Regan, then the Secretary of the Trea-
> sury, got practically every agency in the government to write to us saying that
> such a ruling would destroy America. Even the State Department wrote to us.
> And what the hell did the State Department have to do with it?
>
> The administration didn't want us to interrupt the M&A boom. That was partly
> ideology, partly whatever. We circulated the proposed ruling for comment, and
> suddenly this very technical question was a highly distorted front-page story
> in *The New York Times*.[29]

In the event, the Federal Reserve drew its ruling narrowly against the
raider's borrowing so that the "market could find a way around it."
But the political lesson was clear. Asked if in retrospect there was any
way to avoid the overleveraged activity, Volcker responded:

> As a sheer political matter, I think it would have been almost impossible, even if
> you had had more conviction than I had. The intensity of the political pressure
> sometimes startled me.

Despite this pressure, the Federal Reserve revisited its bank regulations regarding leveraged lending two years later, by which time Volcker had left. As the market for leveraged loans heated up in the late
1980s, Federal Reserve bank examiners had difficulty with the variation
across banks in their definitions of leveraged loans. Banks with substantial exposures to cable TV companies, for instance, took the view
that despite their typically high leverage—as a result of their largely

intangible assets, namely subscribers—their cash flows justified their exclusion from leveraged loan totals. Other banks included loans to cable TV companies in their leveraged loan totals.[30] A bank examiner could either accept such differences or attempt a fresh and time-consuming aggregation while on site in the midst of an examination. In response to this problem, the three bank examination agencies, the Comptroller of the Currency, the Federal Deposit Insurance Corporation, and the Federal Reserve, attempted to arrive at a common definition in 1988.

Characteristically, the Comptroller put out its own proposed definition in late 1988,[31] and the Federal Reserve followed suit in February 1989. The Comptroller left the definition of and limits on leveraged loans to a bank's board of directors. The Federal Reserve definition subjected corporate loans to a dual test: A loan was considered leveraged in which credit is extended in connection with an acquisition by, or a restructuring of, a firm; and in which the debt–to–total assets ratio of the borrowing firm reaches 75 percent.[32] Eight months later, the three regulatory agencies had agreed to a joint definition, essentially a modification of the definition the Federal Reserve had issued in February.[33] The October regulations wove the net more finely than had the February rules, however, because the later rules also encompassed transactions that doubled a firm's leverage to a fraction over one-half (even if its overall debt-to-assets ratio remained less than three-quarters).

In late 1988, the Securities and Exchange Commission (SEC) shone its light on the obscure business of leveraged lending. As the RJR-Nabisco bidding contest proceeded, the SEC began to suggest that banks disclose their leveraged loans to their shareholders. This response by the SEC reflected no hostility to the buyout movement: Whereas Chairman Alan Greenspan of the Federal Reserve expressed a cautious view in October regarding bank involvement in leveraged buyouts, Chairman David Ruder said that the SEC is "not inclined to interfere" with the buyouts; that "those who want to throw a monkey wrench into the operations of the free market have the burden of proof"; and that LBOs bring vigor to sluggish firms.[34] In this latter claim, the SEC chair drew on the results of Chicago-school researchers at the SEC. The SEC chose to mandate disclosure not to slow leveraging but to slow the political forces demanding more drastic measures such as outright prohibitions of thrift and bank investments in leveraged buyouts. Thus in early November 1988, the specialist press quoted SEC staff as aiming for end-year clarification of expectations regarding banks' disclosure.[35] By mid-December, the press reported that "the SEC has spoken with banks informally on the matter," and that same month, Bankers Trust went public with its own definition of leveraged loans.[36]

The Securities and Exchange Commission thus played an important role in making the data defined by the banking regulators available to the market. U.S. banks' annual reports for 1988 disclosed leveraged loans outstanding where these were substantial, and at least in the case of major agent banks, information on the fees associated with the business and some information on write-offs of such loans as well.[37] Later the bank regulators required public disclosure of highly leveraged transaction (HLT) lending on a quarterly basis.

The banking regulators have since dropped the reporting requirement for HLT loans, but the SEC disclosure requirement continues. Responding to bankers' complaints about the HLT definition and to more general concerns about constraints on the supply of credit, the banking regulators revised the definition a bit in early 1992 and phased out the formal definition and discontinued the reporting requirement as of the reports of condition for June 1992.[38] The HLT remains a potential credit concentration in the bank examination process, however. The banking regulators' last formal definition in 1992 continues to shape the shareholder disclosure on HLTs the SEC still mandates.

The Effect of Enhanced Disclosure

Jensen has claimed that measures by the bank regulators to compel disclosures of HLTs put the kibosh on leveraged lending. In his account, the HLT regulations, among other measures, overrode a normal market correction of excesses. In conjunction with the rules imposed by the Financial Institutions Reform, Recovery and Enforcement Act on savings and loan holding of junk bonds and with "much tightened oversight by banking regulators," the HLT regulations, claims Jensen, "depressed high-yield bond prices further, raised the cost of high leverage, and made the adjustment to over-leveraged capital structures all the more difficult," and also contributed to the sharp increase in LBO defaults.[39]

What effect did the HLT definition have? As figure 2.4 shows, the value of leveraged loan syndications declined by more than two-thirds in 1990 to less than $60 billion from more than $180 billion one year earlier. This coincides with the publication of the joint definition in late 1989. The joint definition levied no extra capital charge against HLTs, however, and placed no limit on HLT loans in relation to capital. Bank examiners were not told to classify HLTs as substandard or doubtful for any reason different from those applied to other loans. The direct effect of defining HLT lending was at most to draw the attention of bank managers, bank directors, bank examiners, and last, but not least, bank stock investors to the risks.

Probably the most important effect of the HLT definition worked through the market for bank equity. While bank regulators refined their definitions, market participants responded to the RJR-Nabisco contest by inquiring which banks were more exposed to leveraged lending. In December 1988 Standard & Poor's published a qualitative study of bank exposures.[40] Several weeks later the *Wall Street Journal* surveyed senior bankers and published hard (if sometimes smoothed and variously defined) data.[41] If one includes the rating agencies and the business press in a broad notion of the market, a well-defined demand for information on banks' leveraged loans appears to have developed months before the banking regulators or the Securities Exchange Commission required any disclosure. To the extent that the definition of HLT became more comprehensive in 1989, the old figures and new figures were available to market participants and discussed thoroughly.[42] Thus it seems reasonable to conceive of the regulatory definition of HLTs and the disclosure of bank-by-bank exposures as, above all, official standard setting for a fundamentally market-generated process.

Equity market prices are hard to reconcile with the pure regulatory account of the HLT designation's effect. As noted in chapter 2, share prices of New York banks were hit hard in the minicrash that greeted the collapse of the UAL deal. More broadly, these share prices began to fall in October 1989 even as the Standard & Poor's average continued to rise unevenly through the third quarter of 1990. The timing of this underperformance has been ascribed to concerns about the HLT portfolios.[43] The small difference between the Comptroller's 1988 definition and the Federal Reserve's February 1989 definition, on the one hand, and the joint October 1989 definition, on the other, cannot plausibly explain either the stock market prices or the decline in HLT loan originations after 1989.[44] It remains for those who adopt the pure regulatory interpretation to explain this timing, considering all the regulatory action before that date.

The market-based interpretation is that investors in the shares of large banks became concerned in September 1989 when Campeau missed an interest payment, junk bond mutual fund investors took fright, and the junk bond market sold off sharply. Investors moved to selling in the following month when the United Air Lines deal fell apart.

Indeed, the best case that can be made for regulation's having brought HLT lending to a halt is a fairly indirect one centering on that event. When the $7.2 billion United Air Lines deal fell apart in October 1989, there was considerable market commentary that the deal failed because Japanese banks had decided to pass on the deal.[45] U.S. bank regulators recall repeated visits earlier in 1989 from Japanese Ministry of Finance officials who inquired about the HLT regulations. And the composition of the RJR-Nabisco loan syndicate in early 1989 makes it quite plausible that the reluctance of Japanese bankers to join in the later leveraged buyout of United Air Lines doomed the deal (table 3.4). In the crucial first two tiers of the RJR-Nabisco syndication (managing agents and underwriting agents), in which banks had to commit a minimum of $500 million, Japanese banks provided 48 percent of the $8.5 billion in credit while they provided no less than 42 percent of the overall initial syndication of the $13.75 billion loan.

Far from the asserted heavy-handed regulation in which banks were told not to make leveraged loans, U.S. bank regulators' dealt with the leveraging business with light hands. They imposed a common definition of leveraged loans—although one could argue for a definition based on cash flows—without which investors in banks could hardly compare different banks' exposures. The SEC's disclosure requirement allowed bank stock investors to signal to bank managers their perception of the low quality of earnings from the leveraging business. In effect, decentralized equity investors, not a cabal of regulators, told the banks to drop out of the leveraging business. We return to this model of regulation in chapter 10.

FIRREA

Whereas bank regulators are asserted to have discouraged lending to leveraged firms, Congress clearly removed savings and loans from the junk bond market. On August 9, 1989, President Bush signed into law the Financial Institutions Reform, Recovery and Enforcement Act (FIRREA). In short, this law overhauled the regulation of the savings and loan (S&L) industry by, among other things, setting up new guidelines designed to reduce the riskiness of S&Ls' portfolios. Two of these rules are discussed here: the mandatory liquidation of junk bonds and the imposition of risk-based capital standards. After a brief exposition, we present the generally accepted scenario linking the passage of these laws to a decline in the junk bond market. Finally, we assess the merits of these claims for linkage by using capital market data as well as data on junk bond holdings by S&Ls and selling by the Resolution Trust

Table 3.4

RJR-Nabisco loan syndicate, February 1989

	Amount ($ millions)	Share (percentage)
Managing agents	5,233.9	38.1
Chase Manhattan	682.1	5.0
Manufacturers Hanover Trust	682.1	5.0
Bankers Trust	552.8	4.0
Citibank	552.8	4.0
Dai-Ichi Kangyo	552.8	4.0
Fuji	552.8	4.0
LTCB	552.8	4.0
Sanwa	552.8	4.0
Security Pacific National	552.8	4.0
Japanese bank share of managing agents		42.2
Underwriting agents	3,291.4	23.9
Bank of New York	470.2	3.4
Bank of Nova Scotia	470.2	3.4
IBJ	470.2	3.4
Mitsubishi	470.2	3.4
Nippon Credit	470.2	3.4
Sumitomo	470.2	3.4
Toronto-Dominion	470.2	3.4
Japanese bank share of underwriting agents		57.1
Lead managers	2,053.1	14.9
Tokai	380.6	2.8
Credit Agricole	334.5	2.4
Midland Montagu	334.5	2.4
Mitsui Trust	334.5	2.4
Royal Bank of Canada	334.5	2.4
Societe Generale	334.5	2.4
Japanese bank share of lead managers		34.8
Managers	1,647.3	12.0
Continental Assurance	249.0	1.8
Bank of Tokyo	240.3	1.7
Banque National de Paris	193.0	1.4
CIC	193.0	1.4
Credit Lyonnais	193.0	1.4
Mitsubishi Trust	193.0	1.4
National Bank of North Carolina	193.0	1.4

Table 3.4   (continued)

	Amount ($ millions)	Share (percentage)
Taiyo Kobe	193.0	1.4
Japanese bank share of managers		38.0
Comanagers	1,527.0	11.1
First Wachovia	169.0	1.2
Arab Bank Ltd.	97.0	0.7
Banca Commerciale Italiana	97.0	0.7
Banque Paribas	97.0	0.7
Chemical Bank	97.0	0.7
Continental Bank	97.0	0.7
First Bank	97.0	0.7
First Interstate	97.0	0.7
First National Bank of Chicago	97.0	0.7
Hokkaido Takushoku	97.0	0.7
Kyowa	97.0	0.7
National Bank of Canada	97.0	0.7
Progressive Casualty Insurance	97.0	0.7
Saitama	97.0	0.7
Yasuda Trust & Banking	97.0	0.7
Japanese bank share of comanagers		25.4
Total	13,752.7	

Corporation (RTC), which took over the assets of failed savings and loans.

Forced Liquidation of S&L Junk Bond Portfolios

Section 1831e(d) of the U.S. Banking Code, which was added by FIRREA, states very clearly that "[n]o savings association may, directly or through a subsidiary, acquire or retain any corporate debt security not of investment grade."[46] Debt securities are of investment grade only if they are rated in one of the four highest rating classifications by at least one nationally recognized rating agency.[47] Thus, the statute used the commonly understood definition of high-yield or junk bonds. With respect to non–investment grade bonds held by S&Ls at the time FIRREA was enacted, the subsection required their divestiture "as quickly as can prudently be done, and in any event not later than July 1, 1994."[48]

Introduction of New Capital Standards

FIRREA also sought to strengthen the thrifts' finances by imposing three separate capital standards: a leverage limit, a tangible capital–to–assets test, and a capital–to–risk-based assets test.[49] The first required S&Ls to maintain core capital equal to at least 3 percent of assets;[50] the second required tangible capital—shareholders' equity less intangible assets like goodwill—equal to 1.5 percent of assets;[51] and the third mandated total capital of at least 8 percent of risk-weighted assets. Similar to the standards of the Basle Accord governing internationally active banks' capital, these weights generally range from 0 for government securities to 100 percent for most corporate debt instruments.[52]

Did FIRREA Kill the Junk Bond Market?

Figure 3.4 shows yield spreads on junk bonds from 1986 through early 1994. The spread, shown by the solid line, is calculated by subtracting the yield on 10-year Treasury bonds from the average yield on junk bonds, obtained from Morgan Stanley. As can readily be seen, yield spreads on junk bonds generally remained below 5 percent between mid-1986 and mid-1989. After the passage of FIRREA in August 1989, however, they began to spike upward, peaking at more than 12 percent in January 1991. This rise in yields corresponds to a 30 percent decline in the value of a hypothetical 10-year junk bond issued at par in August 1989.

Lest it be suggested that the problems in the junk bond market were related to coincident difficulties in the stock market in 1989 and 1990,[53] the figure also shows the dividend yield on the Standard & Poor's 500 stock market index.[54] The center dotted line represents the dividend yield multiplied by 1.25. The outer dotted lines represent the dividend yield multiplied by 1 and 1.5. As can be seen, from mid-1986

Percent

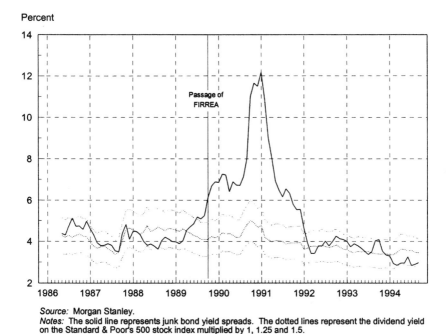

Source: Morgan Stanley.
Notes: The solid line represents junk bond yield spreads. The dotted lines represent the dividend yield on the Standard & Poor's 500 stock index multiplied by 1, 1.25 and 1.5.

Figure 3.4
Junk bond yield spreads and equity dividend yields

to mid-1989, the junk bond spread generally stayed within this range. However, shortly before the passage of FIRREA in 1989 it moved above this range and did not return until early 1992. The implication of this observation is that although equity yields and junk bond risk premia tend to move together, stock prices alone cannot explain the decline in the junk bond market between 1989 and 1991.

Thus, a decline in the junk bond market coincided with the passage of FIRREA, and this decline was larger than stock price movements would have suggested. Can a causal link be demonstrated? As table 3.5 shows, at the end of 1988, thrifts held more than $15.3 billion in junk bonds, or about 8 percent of the total junk outstandings of $188 billion. Within one year, their holdings of junk bonds had declined to about $10.7 billion, or less than 5 percent of the $227 billion market.[55]

Table 3.5
Savings and loan institutions' holdings of junk bonds

Year	Quarter	S&L holdings	Total junk bond market	S&Ls as a percentage of the market
1985	Q4	$6,023	$81,200	7.42
1986	Q1	5,993	91,700	6.54
1986	Q2	6,830	102,300	6.68
1986	Q3	7,531	112,800	6.68
1986	Q4	8,096	123,300	6.57
1987	Q1	9,114	132,000	6.90
1987	Q2	10,625	140,600	7.56
1987	Q3	11,691	149,300	7.83
1987	Q4	12,493	157,900	7.91
1988	Q1	12,635	165,500	7.63
1988	Q2	13,498	173,100	7.80
1988	Q3	13,595	180,700	7.52
1988	Q4	15,342	188,300	8.15
1989	Q1	14,698	197,800	7.43
1989	Q2	13,425	207,300	6.48
1989	Q3	13,612	216,700	6.28
1989	Q4	10,676	226,200	4.72
1990	Q1	7,570	226,400	3.34
1990	Q2	6,169	226,600	2.72
1990	Q3	5,371	226,800	2.37
1990	Q4	4,521	227,000	1.99
1991	Q1	2,545	225,300	1.13
1991	Q2	1,659	223,600	0.74
1991	Q3	300	221,900	0.14
1991	Q4	221	220,200	0.10

Note: Figures presented are in millions of dollars.

By the end of 1990, their holdings were less than 2 percent of the market. Although 6 percent of the market is not insubstantial, how can the sale of that amount over a two-year period be responsible for such a dramatic decline in the junk bond market? After all, the RJR-Nabisco deal increased the outstandings in the market by 6 percent without any such effect.[56]

The story is often told as follows. Because FIRREA's divestiture mandate precluded S&Ls from holding most of their junk bonds until maturity, generally accepted accounting principles (GAAP) required S&Ls to mark their holdings to market for reporting purposes. Owing to junk bonds' historical price volatility, a large portion of some S&Ls' balance sheets would potentially be subject to wide variation. This created the risk that S&Ls that were close to the line would not meet FIRREA's tough new capital standards. S&Ls were therefore forced to conduct hasty liquidations to mitigate this regulatory risk, even though the law gave them until 1994. Moreover, the RTC was given the mandate to seize unhealthy S&Ls and to liquidate their assets at a minimum risk and cost to the taxpayers. S&Ls might have feared that bureaucrats, feeling they had more to lose by taking the risks of holding seized junk bonds, would be inclined to sell indiscriminately. For these two reasons, some $15 billion worth of junk bonds was potentially subject to immediate sale by actors not behaving in an economically rational manner. In addition, there was a fear that prohibitive regulation of insurance company holdings of junk, which represented about 30 percent of the market, could follow the rules imposed by FIRREA.

These considerations made market participants doubt the liquidity of the junk bond market in the near term. To avoid the risk of being stuck with illiquid assets, many decided to bail out of junk bonds sooner rather than later. Through this mechanism, the fear of illiquidity became a self-fulfilling prophecy. To make matters worse, as selling pressure drove prices down, the inventory of Drexel Burnham Lambert, the leading and unusually dominant underwriter and market maker,

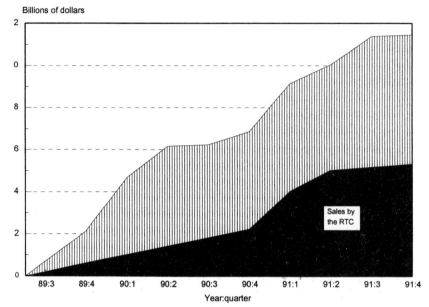

Sources: Federal Home Loan Bank Board and Office of Thrift Supervision call reports, and authors' estimates.
Note: Raw data adjusted for changes in holdings due to downgrades, retirements, and variations in market prices.

Figure 3.5
Savings and loan divestitures of junk bonds

began to erode in value.[57] Fears of Drexel's ultimate demise made the prospects for liquidity even dimmer, thereby inducing further selling. When Drexel finally did fail in early 1990, the market's principal source of liquidity disappeared.

The data seem to be consistent with this hypothesis. Yields began their upward movement in mid-1989 as it became clear that Congress was going to do something to discourage S&Ls' participation in the junk bond market.[58] A second surge followed in the months after FIRREA's passage. Then, as figure 3.5 shows, S&Ls began to remove junk bonds from their balance sheets at an accelerated pace in early 1990. However, most of this was not actual liquidation but the transfer of junk bonds to the RTC as institutions were seized. When the RTC finally stepped up its own selling of junk bonds in late 1990 and early 1991, junk bond yield spreads spiked a third time, rising to almost three times their long-term levels.

But once again market developments suggest that this reading may suffer from the post hoc ergo propter hoc fallacy. Individuals and institutions were not pouring money into junk bond mutual funds after FIRREA became law to take advantage of the forced selling by thrifts. Instead, they were redeeming their shares, without any instructions from any regulator, legislator, or judge. The timing of the spike in mutual fund redemptions in September points to the Campeau default.[59] In September and October 1989, net redemptions by junk bond mutual fund investors amounted to 5 percent of the outstanding value of such funds. Because such funds held about 30 percent of all junk, the unforced selling by these funds represented more than 1.5 percent of all junk bonds, more than a quarter of the sales by thrifts over a two-year period. The Campeau default and subsequent market turbulence also seem to have induced policyholder runs on insurers with heavy junk bond holdings: First Capital in California faced $404 million of redemptions in September through November 1989, 4 percent of its assets and 10 percent of its junk holdings.[60] The most reasonable view is that junk bond buyers were spooked by defaults in the absence of recession in 1989, spooked by the downgrading of RJR-Nabisco's bonds, as described in chapter 4, spooked by the bankruptcy of Drexel and then spooked again by war, the oil price rise, and ultimately recession in 1990.

3.5 State Insurance Regulation: NAIC Disclosure and Capital Standards

Although regulating insurance companies is primarily the responsibility of the states, a single organization, the National Association of Insurance Commissioners (NAIC), has taken the responsibility of establishing of uniform guidelines, which the state regulators generally follow. In response to a general concern about the riskiness of insurance company assets, the NAIC in June 1990 announced two changes in its guidelines that discouraged insurance companies from acquiring and retaining high-yield bonds.

The Regulatory Changes

The first change the NAIC made stepped up the disclosure required of insurers. Prior to 1990, the NAIC required insurers to report publicly their holdings of corporate bonds according to a schedule that designated the bonds by rating (table 3.6).[61] As can be seen, prior to 1990, bonds receiving the highest junk bond rating, BB/Ba, were placed into the same category as investment grade bonds. Thus, what insurers reported as their holdings in junk bonds was not really the total amount of such bonds held. In June 1990, the NAIC modified its disclosure rules to require more detailed reporting of bond holdings by rating. This change required insurers for the first time to disclose their holdings of the highest non–investment grade bonds (and the lowest investment grade bonds), and as a result disclosed junk bond holdings nearly doubled.[62]

Table 3.6
National Association of Insurance Commissioners bond ratings

Pre-1990		Post-1990	
Rating	NAIC designation	Rating	NAIC designation
AAA/Aaa to BB/Ba	Yes	AAA/Aaa to A/A	1
B/B	No*	BBB/Baa	2
CCC/Caa to C/C	No**	BB/Ba	3
D/D	No	B/B	4
		CCC/Caa to C/C	5
		D/D	6

The second change affected capital requirements. NAIC guidelines require insurance companies to hold mandatory security valuation reserves (MSVRs) for their investments. The required reserve for corporate bond investments is based on the NAIC's quality designation schedule described above. Prior to 1990, insurers were required to hold 2, 10, 20, and 20 percent reserves against bonds designated Yes, No*, No**, and No, respectively. Pursuant to the change announced in June 1990, insurers were required to hold 1, 2, 5, 10, 20, and 20 percent against bonds designated NAIC 1, 2, 3, 4, 5, and 6, respectively. This had the effect of requiring insurers to hold more reserves against BB/Ba rated bonds (5 percent versus 2 percent) than they previously had to, thus raising the regulatory capital cost of investing in junk bonds.

The Effect: Divestiture by Insurance Companies

Regarding these changes in disclosure and capital standards, Federal Reserve Board economists noted that

[w]hile both . . . changes could have lessened insurance companies' appetite for below–investment grade bonds, market participants appear to stress the former as the principal factor. The sudden appearance of a much-increased percentage of below–investment grade securities on life insurance company balance sheets apparently focused attention by buyers of life insurance company products on insurers' holdings of below–investment grade bonds. Indeed, many insurance companies report that buyers of GICs and life insurance policies have become much more sensitive to the apparent credit risk of insurance company assets. This has discouraged many insurance companies from purchasing lower quality credits (and even encouraged some selling of them) out of a fear that they may lose business to competitors with lower proportions of below–investment grade bonds in their portfolios.[63]

The mechanisms of market discipline ranged from the insurance product market, where policyholders cashed in policies and new policyholders took their business elsewhere, to the stock market. There, announcements of write-downs of junk portfolios by First Executive hit the stocks of other junk-heavy insurers, particularly those with potentially liquid deposit-like liabilities.[64]

Table 3.7

Below–investment grade bond holdings of 20 large U.S. insurance companies

Year	(A) Total bond holdings	(B) Rated "B" or below holdings	(C) Rated "BB" holdings	(D) (B)/(A)	(E) (C)/(A)
1987	$211,637	17,545	n.a.	8.3%	n.a.
1988	255,089	17,810	n.a.	7.0	n.a.
1989	281,881	19,604	n.a.	7.0	n.a.
1990	303,548	17,504	15,659	5.8	5.2%
1991	334,965	16,502	13,962	4.9	4.2
1992	350,186	15,523	13,330	4.4	3.8

Source: Conning and Company; authors' estimates.

Notes: Sample consists of the top 20 life insurance companies in terms of corporate bond holdings. Data for TIAA-CREF not available. Table does not include some companies with large holdings of low-rated bonds but relatively small total bond holdings, such as First Capital and Executive Life. "Total bond holdings" are in millions of dollars.

The data on junk bond holdings of the 20 largest holders of corporate bonds among life insurers suggest no more than a modest liquidation in the junk bond market's nightmare year. Table 3.7 shows that the largest insurance companies did reduce their holdings of junk bonds in 1990, from $19.6 billion at the beginning of the year, to $17.5 billion at the end. Given the sharp price decline in 1990, however, any asset revaluations or trading in junk bonds at these firms could have lowered the end-year holdings without net sales.

It is not safe, however, to conclude that the NAIC regulators substantially worsened the problems in the junk bond market—for two reasons. The first is timing: Insurers expanded their holdings in 1989, when junk bond prices took their first tumble, and did not become net sellers until 1990. Unfortunately, though, data on year-end holdings do not permit the timing issue to be settled: Insurers could have started selling in mid-1989 in anticipation of the rules adopted in June 1990.

The second, more fundamental problem lies in characterizing the change in disclosure rules as "regulatory." As noted above, policyholders staged a quiet run on a California insurer with heavy junk holdings and close links to Drexel in September through November 1989, before the new regulations took effect.[65] In the end, a better informed insurance product market, backed up by the stock market, rather than any heavy-handed capital regulation disciplined insurers' portfolio choice. Chapter 10 considers such market-based regulation through disclosure.

3.6 Conclusions

Our analysis is consistent with the theme of Mark Roe:[66] Incumbent managers, in an alliance with labor, operated in the three branches of government to erect barriers to outsiders' bootstrapping their way into running firms with borrowed money. State takeover laws, *Time,* the tax code changes and FIRREA were significant legal developments that all expressed hostility to hostile takeovers. Though it may be argued that FIRREA's prohibition of S&L junk bond investment was motivated by legitimate concern for the safety of federally insured institutions and not by a desire to put an end to leveraging, note that the legislation did not prohibit the activity that was primarily responsible for the savings and loan debacle, commercial real estate lending. This lends support to the claim that Congress was, in fact, out to get the junk bond market.

That there was a political reaction to the leveraging business and that it spurred significant legal developments do not imply that the legal developments killed the leveraging business. At most, FIRREA may have contributed to the demise of the leveraging business by eliminating one class of investors in junk bonds, savings and loans. But even this phased reduction in demand was no larger than the new supply that resulted from the RJR-Nabisco buyout. Direct efforts to stop takeovers through anti-takeover statutes were probably not pointed enough to explain the corpse. Nor were indirect efforts, such as the loosening of fiduciary standards in *Paramount v. Time,* the discouragement of distressed exchange offers though tax and bankruptcy law, and enhanced disclosure requirements for banks and insurance companies. It is possible to argue, however, that a number of legal and regulatory changes that individually appear quite marginal add up to a significant force.

A study that set out to show—and by the study's lights succeeded in showing—that regulatory changes accounted for most of the losses in stock market values of twenty-nine highly leveraged firms in 1989–91 helps put legal developments in a quantitative perspective.[67] The three biggest pieces of bad news, in chronological order, were the ban on thrift investment in junk bonds with the passage of FIRREA in July, the failure of Campeau to make an interest payment in September, and the collapse of the UAL deal in October 1989. True, the congressional ban on thrifts' junk investment came as bad news, inflicting losses, above and beyond what one would expect from general market movements, of 1.9 percent on the leveraged firms' equity holders. But more important were the collapse of the UAL deal and the failure of Campeau to make an interest payment, which were associated with unexpected losses equal to 3 percent and 2 percent, respectively. We would accept the identification of FIRREA as a political development, but not Campeau's default or the collapse of the UAL deal, which were market developments. The first cost investors in leveraged firms 2 percent, the latter two, 5 percent. By this measure, the corpse showed the wounds from five knives from market developments and two knives from Congress.

From a different perspective one could argue that it is a false dilemma to ask whether market developments or the law stopped the leveraging business. The revulsion phase of the Minsky-Kindleberger cycle entails a change in market participants' views of socially acceptable risk. The legal and regulatory changes reviewed in this chapter can to some extent be considered expressions of the same turnaround in social norms.

In any case, having reviewed the political account, we find that the leveraging business expired when it ran out of new creditors to accept new risks and when its own excessive risks thereby became manifest.

Appendix 3.1 Fiduciary Standards and Paramount v. Time

Corporate law generally imposes two types of fiduciary duties on the officers and directors of a corporation—the duties of care and loyalty. This appendix first introduces Delaware's law of fiduciary responsibility, then summarizes the two fiduciary standards that regulate a target board's conduct in the context of a hostile acquisition attempt.[68] The state of Delaware law on hostile acquisitions as it stood in the early part of 1989 is then presented. Next comes an examination the *Time* decision focused on whether the decision changed the law as it was previously understood. We argue that *Time* allowed an incumbent board of directors to hunker down into a defensive posture in a broader range of circumstances and permitted new weapons to be used in the defense. Whether this significant legal development brought hostile acquisitions to an end is an empirical question treated in the corpus of the chapter.

The Duties of Care and Loyalty

The *duty of care* is essentially a procedural requirement that corporate decision makers "exercise that degree of skill, diligence and care that a reasonably prudent person would exercise in similar circumstances."[69] The flip side of this requirement, the business judgment rule, holds that so long as the officers and directors of a corporation act "on an informed basis, in good faith and in the honest belief that the action taken is in the best interests of the company," they are shielded from liability even if their decisions turn out to be wrong.[70] Thus if fiduciaries meet the "procedural" requirements of obtaining information and acting in good faith, the courts do not second-guess their "substantive" business policies.

The *duty of loyalty* requires that fiduciaries act solely in the best interests of their corporation. Generally this standard is intended to regulate those occasions when a corporate decision maker has interests that are at least potentially in conflict with those of the corporation.[71] The law does so not by imposing flat prohibitions, but through procedural safeguards first, and then, if necessary, substantive fairness review by a court.[72]

Fiduciary Duties and Hostile Acquisitions

Both duties, care and loyalty, give rise to legal doctrines regulating the conduct of corporate directors in the face of a threatened acquisition. Generally, these duties acknowledge that when a company is the subject of a tender offer, corporate directors face a potential conflict of interest. Often, a corporate raider intends to replace existing management and the existing board of directors. Thus managers may be tempted to preserve their jobs by resisting the offer, even if doing so is not in their shareholders' interests. Even outside directors, such as lawyers and investment bankers, may face the same conflict to the extent that their business relationship with the corporation depends on the incumbency of the existing management. However, the courts view this conflict as somewhat less compelling than the classic cases (e.g., sale of corporate assets to officers and directors). Thus, although the duty at stake is mostly a duty of loyalty, some of the more flexible standards from the duty of care also apply.[73]

In the course of refereeing the proliferation of hostile and semi-hostile acquisitions in the early 1980s, the Delaware courts articulated two standards against which board conduct would be measured: the *Unocal* and *Revlon* standards. The first standard, which applies when a board takes defensive action[74] intended to preserve corporate independence, was stated in *Unocal v. Mesa Petroleum Co.*[75] Imposing a two-pronged test, it requires the board to show that (1) in good faith and after a reasonable investigation, it perceived a threat to corporate welfare, and (2) it acted reasonably in relation to the threat posed.[76] If the board fails to make both showings, its action is not protected by the business judgment rule, and the court is likely to reverse or prohibit that action.

The second standard, set out in *Revlon Inc. v. MacAndrews and Forbes Holdings*,[77] applies only when some board action clearly puts a company up "for sale," or renders its breakup imminent. When such a "trigger" event occurs, the existing shareholders no longer have a "continuing corporate entity or policy to threaten. Therefore, defensive tactics are impermissible as they can bear no relation to nonexistent threat."[78] At this stage, the board is transformed into an auctioneer, bearing the duty of "getting the best price for the shareholders at a sale of the company."[79]

As with most legal doctrines, this abstract statement of the law gains concrete meaning only when key words and phrases are defined. To understand the *Unocal* and *Revlon* duties it becomes necessary to analyze the following three questions:

1. What constitutes a threat to shareholder welfare?

2. When is an action "reasonable in relation to the threat posed"?

3. What constitutes a "sale" or "breakup" that triggers the *Revlon* duty?

The remainder of this appendix, relying largely on the work of Ronald Gilson and Rainier Kraakman, offers answers to these questions, as they were understood prior to *Time*, and explains how the *Time* decision might have changed those answers. In short, the *Time* decision appears to have granted directors new authority to resist hostile tender offers by (1) recognizing a new type of "threat" warranting defensive action, (2) easing the test of the reasonableness of a defensive tactic, and (3) narrowing the scope of *Revlon* by declaring an auction less readily.

The Law Prior to Time

The Unocal *Standard*

Just prior to the *Time* decision, Gilson and Kraakman observed that *Unocal* recognized three types of threats to the collective shareholder:

i. opportunity loss, or the . . . dilemma that a hostile offer might deprive target shareholders of the opportunity to select a superior alternative offered by target management;

ii. structural coercion, or the risk that disparate treatment of non-tendering shareholders might distort shareholder decisions; and, finally

iii. substantive coercion, or the risk that shareholders will mistakenly accept an underpriced offer because they disbelieve management's representation of intrinsic value.[80]

Regarding the second prong of the *Unocal* test, (i.e., the determination of whether a defensive maneuver was "reasonable in relation to the threat posed"), Gilson and Kraakman argued that courts would balance the response against the threat posed rather than taking a "no-holds-barred" approach to any threat crossing a threshold.[81]

The Revlon *Zone*

The *Revlon* case involved a hostile tender offer for Revlon's shares by Pantry Pride. The board responded by adopting several defenses, including granting a "lockup" option[82] to Forstmann Little & Co., in anticipation of consummating a transaction with that leveraged-buyout firm. The court held that by entering into this agreement, the board had put Revlon up for sale. At that point, its fiduciary role shifted from "defenders of the corporate bastion to auctioneers charged with getting the best price for the stockholders."[83] The court went on to hold that although lockups are not necessarily illegal even in the auction mode, the agreement with Forstmann served not to promote the auction, but to cut it short, and the agreement was therefore disallowed.

In *Revlon*, the board's action made it clear that the target company was for sale. For this reason, the real impact of the *Revlon* case lay in its setting a standard for conduct. Subsequent cases determined when that standard would be applied. In a paper written before the publication of the Delaware Supreme Court's opinion in *Time,* Gilson and Kraakman argued that Delaware courts had developed a "control block" rule, under which the *Revlon* duty was triggered when voting control shifted from "disaggregated public shareholders" to "an identifiable party or group".[84]

Time*'s Modification of the* Unocal *Standard and the* Revlon *Trigger*

The Facts of Time

Since as early as 1983, the board of Time had considered joining its businesses of publishing, pay television programming, and the operation of cable franchises to the actual production and ownership of the films and videos it provided through its cable operations. However, the board was also concerned with the maintenance of Time's independence and "corporate culture." Specifically, the latter term referred to a long-standing management commitment to preserve the company's journalistic integrity by keeping journalism separate from the company's business side.

Toward this end, Time began discussing a joint venture project with Warner in 1987. By 1988 the board had authorized management to negotiate a merger agreement contingent upon Time management's exercising control over the combined entity. Ultimately, the companies agreed to combine through a stock-for-stock merger: The shareholders of Warner would own 62 percent of the combined entity, but Time would survive and its CEO would ultimately run the new firm.

Before the transaction was put to a vote by Time's shareholders, as required by New York Stock Exchange rules, Paramount made an all-cash tender offer for Time's shares at $175 per share. Time's board formally rejected Paramount's offer and restructured the proposed transaction with Warner. The new structure, a debt-financed cash tender for Warner's shares, did not require the approval of Time's shareholders. This modification increased the premium for Warner's shareholders from 12 percent to 56 percent. Subsequently, Paramount increased its cash bid to $200 per share, which Time's board also rejected.

Paramount and a group of Time shareholders sued the board. The shareholders claimed that the proposed transaction amounted a sale of the company, and therefore the board had failed to meet its *Revlon* duty to get the best price Time could fetch. Paramount's claim, which the shareholders joined, alleged that the board's response was not reasonable in light of Paramount's all-cash tender offer, so that the board had failed to meet its duty under *Unocal*.

The *Revlon* Trigger

The Delaware Supreme Court held that the *Revlon* duty had not been triggered. In its decision, the court set two circumstances in which the *Revlon* duty may arise:

- when "active bidding," contemplating the "clear breakup of the company," begins, and

- when the target company "abandons its long-term strategy *and* seeks an alternative transaction involving the breakup of the company" [emphasis added].[85]

Although the result in the case was consistent with the "control block" rule in that Time's many public shareholders remained the owners of Time-Warner, the court's language allowed for the possibility that not all sales of effective control trigger the *Revlon* duty. Specifically, where the company maintains its "long-term strategy," the *Revlon* duty may be avoided even if a control block is transferred. Understood in this light, the *Time* decision arguably altered the marketplace's understanding of when the *Revlon* standard would be applied.

The Unocal *Standard*

Next, the court decided that the directors of Time had not violated their duties under *Unocal*. In its discussion of the first prong—a threat to shareholder interests—the court acknowledged that prior case law may have "suggested that an all-cash, all-shares offer, falling within a range of values that a shareholder might reasonably prefer, cannot constitute a legally recognized 'threat' to shareholder interests."[86] Relying on these holdings, Paramount argued that, since its offer was not front loaded,[87] the only conceivable threat was inadequate value. The court rejected this reasoning, quoting in a footnote the above passage from Gilson and Kraakman's article, emphasizing their concept of "substantive coercion."[88] The court went on to suggest that, apart from inadequate value, the possibility that "shareholders might elect to tender into Paramount's cash offer in ignorance or a mistaken belief of the strategic benefit which a business combination with Warner might produce" constituted a recognizable threat.

However, it is not clear that this "threat" from Paramount was in fact the "structural coercion" that Gilson and Kraakman had in mind.[89] They contemplated an "underpriced offer" and, at the very least, management's assertion that their policies will in fact ultimately generate higher stock prices.[90] Here no such assertion was made, nor did stock values seem to be of concern to the court.[91] Rather, the court was satisfied with the mere fact that a transaction with Paramount would cause a modification in Time's long-term corporate strategy, regardless of whether that strategy could maximize shareholder value. Thus, the *Time* case appears to have introduced a fourth type of threat that could satisfy the first prong of *Unocal:* the damage that a hostile bid could do to any "deliberately conceived corporate plan." By recognizing such a threat, the court in *Time* appears in effect to have broken off the first prong of *Unocal*. One can hardly imagine a case where a target board will not be able to articulate a corporate strategy and persuade a court that a hostile tender offer threatens to derail it in some way.

Finally, on the second prong of the *Unocal* standard (the proportionality test), the court found that because Paramount's offer was contingent on the nullification of the Time-Warner merger, the board's shift to a debt-financed merger was reasonable in relation to the threat posed. The court was apparently impressed that the board did not "cram down" the management alternative in that Paramount still had the option to make a bid for the combined entity or to remove termination of the merger as a precondition to its bid. Nonetheless, as Paramount asserted and some commentators have noted, the $7–10 billion in additional debt contemplated by the Time-Warner merger made a bid for the combined entity impossible as a practical matter.[92] For this reason, the *Time* decision filed the second prong of *Unocal* test down from proportional response to a weak threshold test. So long as there was some recognizable threat, the board could adopt any measure that did not logically preclude a competing tender offer.

How Paramount v. Time *Could Have Discouraged Hostile Offers*

In summary, the *Time* decision could have been seen as

1. Narrowing the scope of *Revlon* by allowing the board to sponsor a "change of control" transaction, which does not involve the abandonment of the company's long-term strategy, without triggering the duty of conducting an auction.

2. Stripping the *Unocal* standard of any substance by recognizing any tender offer that foils an articulable business strategy as a "threat" that authorizes a response by the board, and by allowing any response that does not logically preclude a tender offer, even if the response does so as a practical matter.

Could either or both of these have been expected to discourage the initiation of tender offers, and/or to reduce in the number of tender offers completed? The answer, it seems, is that both changes could have served both to discourage the initiation of tender offers and to decrease the probability of their success. Of the two changes, the erosion of the *Unocal* standard could have been expected to have a more pronounced effect than the narrowing of *Revlon*'s scope.

One can clarify the question by laying out the calculus of an acquisition bid. The preparation of a tender offer involves costs, which include identifying the target, analyzing its financial statements, studying its business, preparing the bid, obtaining legal advice, and preparing the Williams Act filing or any other statements required by law. If these costs did not exist, the changes effected by the *Time* decision could not have decreased the number of hostile tender offers initiated.[93] However, because these costs are real, a potential bidder must weigh the expectation of these costs (C) against his expected payoffs, which constitute the sum of

- the product of the probability of success $(P(s))$ and the expected gains accruing to him in the case that his bid is successful $(E(G|s))$, and

- the product of the probability of failure $(1 - P(s) = P(f))$ and the expected gains (or losses) in the case the bid fails $(E(G|f))$.

If this sum exceeds his costs, the potential bidder will initiate his search.[94] Assuming that expected payoffs are higher in the case of a win than in the case of a loss, it follows that when a change in the law lowers a bid's probability of success, expected payoffs become lower. Because fewer bids will then show expected payoffs in excess of costs, fewer will be initiated. How many fewer depends on how large is the cost of bidding, C. Lucian Bebchuk argued that these costs are not very large in relation to the expected returns involved.[95] If this is so, then the number of tenders initiated can be expected to change only marginally as a result of *Time*.

We are still left, however, with the assertion that the legal changes made by *Time* reduce the probability of an offer's success. This claim, if one accepts the above characterization of *Time*'s effect on the common understanding of Delaware law, should not meet with much resistance. Because *Time* arguably gave corporate boards much more discretion in resisting hostile tender offers, both by broadening slightly the range of defenses that do not trigger an auction and by making it easier for boards to "just say no" to all offers, it would seem that even if the number of bids does not decrease, fewer can be expected to succeed. Alternatively, in a new equilibrium, there might be fewer hostile offers but the same probability of success for each. This could occur if bidders refrain from conducting searches or initiating bids that they know in advance are likely to fail. In either event, however, the unambiguous effect will be fewer hostile acquisitions completed.

In addition, the narrowing of *Revlon* in *Time* can be seen as reducing the bidder's expected gains (or raising his expected losses) if he is not ultimately successful in acquiring the target. Bebchuk, in his case for open auctions of targets, argued that the ability to sell into the winning bid can encourage potential bidders to enter the fray by compensating them for a lower probability of success.[96] But because *Time* reduced the probability that a losing bidder would have lost by being outbid (as opposed to having the board "just say no"), it diminished the expected payoffs from initiating a hostile bid. This could be expected to reduce the number of hostile bids further.

It is unclear which of the two doctrinal changes annnounced in *Time* would have the greater impact. The narrowing of the *Revlon* zone expanded only slightly the range of defensive tactics boards could use safely. After *Time*, in addition to the familiar poison pills, self tenders, and so forth, boards seemingly had at their disposal a subset of "change of control" transactions that they previously lacked. But the narrowing of *Revlon* could also have reduced an important component of a bidder's expected payoffs: expected payoffs given failure of the bid. On the other hand, the new statement of the *Unocal* standard could have been interpreted as dramatically increasing the efficacy of all defensive actions intended to maintain the target's independence.

Appendix 3.2   State Anti-Takeover Statutes

This appendix provides a brief description of the Delaware and other state anti-takeover laws. It then discusses whether and how they may have deterred tender offers since their enactment.

Business combination freeze statutes generally restrict the ability of a so-called interested shareholder—defined in terms of percentage ownership—to enter into a business combination with the target for a specified period of time, sometimes called the "freeze" period. Delaware's business combination statute, less restrictive than many, went into effect in December 1987.[97] This statute prohibits an interested stockholder (defined as any entity holding more than 15 percent of the target's shares) from entering into a "business combination" with the target (defined broadly to include mergers and major asset sales) for three years after the acquisition of the stock. There are, however, three important exceptions to the general rule. Interested stock holders, under Delaware law, may enter into business combinations when

1. the target's board of directors approves the transaction before the interested shareholder purchases its stock;
2. the interested shareholder owns at least 85 percent of the target; or
3. the board and two-thirds of the disinterested shareholders approve the transaction after the interested shareholder purchases its stock.

Moreover, individual corporations can opt out of the provision in their original articles, or by a board amendment to the bylaws within 90 days of majority shareholder approval.

Wisconsin's business combinations statute[98] is among the most restrictive. It provides that no interested holder (defined as an entity holding more than 10 percent of the target) may enter into a business combination with the target for three years. The only exception occurs when there is prior approval by the board. There is no opt-out provision.[99] New York's statute is less restrictive than Wisconsin's insofar as it defines an interested holder as an entity holding more than 20 percent and that limited opt-out rules are provided, but more restrictive insofar as it sets a freeze period of five years.

Control share acquisition statutes provide that when an acquirer obtains more than a specified percentage of a company's shares, it cannot vote the shares in excess of the specified percentage unless a majority of disinterested holders give approval. *Fair price* statutes generally provide that business combinations must either be approved by the holders of statutorily defined supermajority (usually two-thirds) of the disinterested shares or occur at a price that is deemed "fair" according to a prescribed formula.

In her compilation of the laws, theories, and evidence respecting takeovers, Roberta Romano argues that these statutes can

raise the cost of some takeovers prohibitively, and thus chill some bids. Shares without voting rights are obviously of no value to acquirors seeking control to implement their own business plans, highly leveraged buyers need access to target assets to service the debt that makes their bids possible, and firms may not make toehold acquisitions, which may be crucial for a takeover's success, when they face a tax at 100%.[100]

In terms of the trade-off framework developed in appendix 3.1, the costs to which Romano refers are lower expected payoffs, ($P(s) \times E(g|s) + P(f) \times E(g|f)$) as elaborated below. Recall that these expected payoffs must exceed the cost of making a bid to encourage a bidder to proceed.

Business combination freeze statutes can in theory deter hostile bids by lowering the probability of a bid's success and/or lowering expected payoffs for winning bidders. These statutes, by restricting the bidder's access to the corporate assets, serve primarily to impair financing. Many leveraged acquisitions in the 1980s contemplated the sale of non–core business assets as a means of reducing the transaction debt. For the most part, senior "bridge" facilities[101] were refinanced through these divestitures. The promise of immediate repayment encouraged these private lenders to make credit available, and at modest spreads over the banks' wholesale cost of funds. Similarly, the promise of lower debt-to-asset ratios, with less senior debt, encouraged investors to buy the subordinated long-term debt, or junk bonds. In addition, all lenders received some comfort in the fact that, if the deal subsequently turned out badly, they could have claims against the company's assets.

Because the general principles of corporate law preclude even majority shareholders from disposing of corporate assets, so-called back-end mergers, in which the target company is united with an acquisition shell company, were necessary to assure all this. Business combination statutes, by inhibiting back-end mergers, could have deterred senior bridge lenders by lengthening the expected maturity of their loans, thus compounding their exposure to the company, and subordinated debt holders by leaving in place large claims that ranked above them. In addition, "structural subordination" could have further discouraged both types of lenders. Because their claims were against a shareholder of the corporation and not the corporation itself, in the event of bankruptcy, the corporation's shareholders would have to be paid in full (or almost in full) before the acquiror's creditors would see any part of the money owed to them.

Such considerations could have decreased the availability of credit and/or caused an increase in its price. With less financing available and/or higher anticipated interest costs, bidders would have had to reduce their premiums over market prices. In some cases, target shareholders would not be impressed, thus assuring a lower probability of success. And even if the bidder did win, he would be left with more expensive debt, thus lowering his expected payoff from the deal. In Delaware, with its extensive opt outs, the prospect of more expensive credit would strengthen the bargaining position of incumbent boards and thereby make acquisitions more expensive.

Control share statutes lower the bidder's expected payoff if he wins the bidding contest. With a control share statute in effect, the bidder runs the risk that he will not be able to use his votes to implement his business plans, which will often include a back-end, or "freeze-out" merger. Fair price statutes expose bidders to a similar risk. At first blush, however, it might appear that fair price statutes would be less chilling than control share statutes, because the bidder at least has the option to buy out the disinterested shareholders, albeit at a high price. But on the other hand, the typical two-thirds approval required in a fair price statute (as opposed to 50 percent in a control share statute) increases the likelihood of a holdout problem, enabling the disinterested shareholders to extract greater concessions from the bidder. Moreover, fair price statutes tend to be triggered sooner than control share statutes (generally at 10 percent versus 20 percent), so their scope is slightly larger.

If the costs of becoming an interested holder under a control share or fair price statute are perceived as too high, the bidder may opt not to make the purchases that would put him over the threshhold. In this case, the statute's effect would be to reduce the bidder's payoffs if he loses. In defending his position in favor of open auctions, Lucian Bebchuk argued that the ability to tender shares into the winning bid induces bidders to incur the costs of making their bids.[102] But if other factors discourage bidders from acquiring large blocks, this inducement is diminished.[103] Thus, it seems that the unambiguous effect of control share statutes and fair price statutes would be fewer hostile bids, by lowering payoffs in cases of both successful and unsuccessful bids. And it would appear that for the reasons stated above, fair price statutes discourage bids more than control share statutes.

4   RJR-Nabisco: A Case Study

In early 1989 shareholders received checks in the mail from the largest leveraged buyout ever. In February they received some $18 billion in cash and something less than a third of that sum in securities for their shares in RJR-Nabisco. The former managers, who in October 1988 had put the company into play by offering $75 per share, lost to a bid worth more than $100 per share.

The RJR-Nabisco deal was bigger than the deal that assembled U.S. Steel in 1901. The earlier deal remains much larger in relation to the U.S. economy of the time.[1] Nevertheless, the RJR deal ranks among the epochal deals of American business history.

Surely the RJR buyout warrants careful analysis. Not only is it the largest buyout ever, but it remains also the most talked about and perhaps the most notorious. Journalists have written not one but two books about the buyout itself[2] and another journalist has written a biography of the sponsoring partnership, KKR.[3] One book became a movie, *Barbarians at the Gate*, that must for its millions of viewers define the era of corporate leveraging.

These journalistic and film treatments uniformly sounded the themes of excess and greed. Yet opinion remains divided on the subject of the social usefulness of the transfer of control of the second largest tobacco-cum-food company in the United States. The first published study of the deal in the summer of 1990 concluded that the former shareholders scored big, the former bondholders lost a bit, and the new owners—KKR and KKR's institutional partners and managers—"may also turn out to be big winners."[4] A briefer but no less ebullient review a year later concluded that "the consequences to date of the RJR buyout for all investors, buying as well as selling, appear to be a remarkable $17 billion in added value."[5] Several years later, the RJR-Nabisco deal got bad press: " 'Deal of the Century'? Not for RJR Investors"; "KKR's Luster Dims as Fall in RJR Stock Hurts Investors' Take"; "How KKR Got Beaten at its Own Game."[6]

The RJR-Nabisco LBO recommends itself for special attention for reasons beyond its size and controversy, however. As suggested in chapter 2, RJR-Nabisco—and with it perhaps some more leveraged deals—came closer to default than is generally appreciated. The story of this near miss not only looks back to the outcome of the Minsky-Kindleberger credit cycle sketched in chapter 2 but also looks forward to the turn from debt to equity treated in the next chapter.

This chapter systematically profiles the leveraging and deleveraging of RJR-Nabisco, then draws two analytic comparisons of RJR-Nabisco to a very similar firm, Philip Morris. The profile shows how the buyout left $15 of debt resting precariously on every $1 of equity, focuses on the too clever financial engineering that turned into a time bomb in RJR-Nabisco's capital structure, traces the series of transactions by which the bomb was defused, and leaps ahead in time to the shock delivered by the outbreak of 1993's cigarette price war. The chapter then compares the trajectory of market value of RJR-Nabisco to that of Philip Morris and finds that the latter firm played tortoise to the former firm's hare. Finally, the chapter assesses, again by comparison to Philip Morris, what the buyout meant for profitability, overhead costs, and capital spending as well as for the workers at RJR-Nabisco, and finds that the more leveraged firm did cut spending and proportionately more jobs.

4.1   RJR-Nabisco's Leveraging and Deleveraging

For three years RJR-Nabisco busied more investment bankers and lawyers than any firm before or since. The buyout itself required two
stages, with bridge loans from two securities firms repaid out of the
junk bonds they underwrote some months later. The financial engineering that resulted in the near default was simple enough, but its
defusing required a deleveraging of RJR-Nabisco's finances that ran
through six stages.

The Biggest LBO Ever

The history of RJR-Nabisco up to the time of the LBO may be summa-
rized quickly for those who have not been exposed to its treatment in
any medium. The CEO of RJR, Ross Johnson, persuaded his board of
directors to accept a $75 per share bid from Shearson Lehman in Octo-
ber 1988, when the stock was trading in the mid-50s. Henry Kravis of
KKR, who had discussed the possibility of an LBO with Johnson, was
not amused that Johnson had in his campaign allied himself with
Shearson Lehman, and in effect, Shearson's parent, American Express,
and its CEO, Jim Robinson. After several rounds of bidding, the RJR
directors accepted the KKR bid of $108 per share, yielding a striking
100 percent premium on the price of the shares before the bidding.

The winning bid mixed a cash payment for three-quarters of RJR's
shares with a payment of so-called back-end paper for the remaining
quarter. The cash amounted to $18 billion and the paper amounted
to another $6 billion. The $6 billion of paper deserves special attention:
It turns out to have been booby-trapped.

The actual buyout took several steps. First came the cash payment
of $18 billion to tendering shareholders and another $0.8 billion in
fees in February 1989. This cash was raised through a $12 billion

syndicated loan, $5 billion of bridge debt privately placed by Drexel, $0.5 billion of debt to a KKR partnership, and $1.5 billion of equity, mostly from KKR, with some participation from Drexel and Merrill Lynch. Later the $6 billion of paper was exchanged for the remaining public equity, and another $0.3 billion in fees was paid out of an increase in bank debt and with RJR's cash. In May, $4 billion of the $5 billion bridge loan was refinanced with publicly issued junk bonds. By the end of July, RJR's balance sheet showed $30 billion of debt resting on $2 billion of equity (table 4.1).

Near Miss

The aspect of the RJR buyout that threatened to explode the firm's finances was a nice bit of financial engineering intended to turn junk into sure value. The so-called reset feature of the $6 billion back-end paper required that the coupon of 13.7 percent that applied in late 1989 be reset within two years of issue.[7] The new coupon would be set so as to leave the bond trading at par, or full value. In the language of the investment bankers: "The Fixed Interest Rate will be designed to result in the Senior Converting Debentures trading at par."[8]

This reset feature appealed to the investment bankers working for RJR's board, who in late November 1988 had advised KKR's competitors, Shearson in alliance with RJR's chief executive, to "[f]irm up [their] securities. Unlike the Kravis securities," explained Burrough and Helyar, "Shearson's had no 'reset' mechanisms that, in effect, guaranteed a security would trade at a certain number over time."[9]

The reset feature seemed innocent enough at the time; *Barbarians at the Gate* mentions the feature only in passing. To work, RJR would only have to be meeting its goals and repaying its debt; the reset might actually result in a lower coupon. Another risk to the feature required some imagination to call to mind in late 1988: a general drying up of liquidity in the junk bond market and consequently across-the-board weak prices for junk bonds. In other words, the value the RJR directors'

Table 4.1
RJR-Nabisco's capital structure, July 1989

Debt			29.975
Bank debt			13.175
Asset sale bridge facility		6.0	
Refinancing bridge facility		1.5	
Revolving credit and term loan		4.675	
Working capital facility		1.0	
Junk bonds			11.7
Bridge private placement			
Increasing rate notes—refinanced		1.0	
Back-end paper		6.4	
Senior converting debentures due 2009 (PIK, reset)	2.3		
Subordinated exchange debentures due 2007 (PIK, reset)	4.1		
Refinancing of bridge		3.8	
Subordinated discount debenture due 2001 (deferred interest)	1.9		
PIK subordinated debenture	1.0		
Subordinated debentures due 2001 at 13.5%	0.5		
Subordinated extendible reset debentures	0.2		
Subordinated floating rate notes due 1999	0.2		
KKR partnership debt (subordinated, Treasury yields plus 4%, then 5%)		0.5	
RJR bonds (originally investment grade)			5.1
Equity			2.0
Common equity			1.5
KKR		1.4	
Drexel & Merrill Lynch		0.1	
Warrants			0.5

Sources: Prospectuses of May 12, 1989, for RJR Holdings Capital Corp.: $1 billion 15% payment in kind subordinated debentures due 2001, $4.1 billion subordinated discount debentures due 2001, $250 million subordinated floating rate notes due 1999, $525 million subordinated debentures due 2001, $225 million subordinated extendible reset debentures, and RJR-Nabisco's 10-K for 1989.
Note: Amounts presented are in billions of dollars.

bankers attached to reset bonds expressed their faith in the untroubled future of a market that had barely existed in the previous recession. The events of January 1990 put a cloud over KKR's ability to make the now $7 billion of reset notes—not for nothing were PIK bonds often referred to as bunny bonds—trade again at par. In mid-January Campeau had entered bankruptcy, shocking the junk bond market with billions of dollars of junk defaults. As described in chapter 1, however, late January brought the bad news that sent RJR bonds, and the whole junk bond market with them, into a tailspin: the downgrading of RJR by Moody's Investors Service.[10] In the two days Friday and Monday, January 26 and 29, 1990, the biggest RJR bonds dropped from 72 cents on the dollar to 56 cents on the dollar.

At these prices, a reset would require a coupon so high that RJR's debt would explode. Reset at, say, a 25 or 30 percent coupon, the face value of the bonds would double in two-and-a-half to three years. The metaphor perforce shifts from rabbits' breeding to cancer's spreading or radioactive particles' reacting in a chain. By the time the bonds would start to pay cash interest in 1994, they would have imposed an impossible burden on RJR. As a result there threatened to be no coupon *high enough* to result in par pricing that would be *low enough* to be paid out of RJR-Nabisco's cash flows.

In the event, KKR's equity fund investors saved the day. Only their enthusiasm back in 1987 kept RJR from bankruptcy in 1990. So large was the 1987 fund—$5.6 billion—that KKR's $1.5 billion investment in RJR had not exhausted it. So large was the 1987 fund that investments in the grocery chain Stop & Shop, the battery maker Duracell, and various publications under the K-III rubric had not exhausted it. So enthusiastic had KKR's institutional investors been in 1987 that $3.2 billion of their funds were available to bail out their own investment in RJR in 1990, and KKR used more than half for that purpose. Such use of their funds required the approval of KKR's limited partners; they could have fought KKR in court if they were convinced that KKR was throwing good money after bad.[11] But the limited-partner institu-

Table 4.2
RJR-Nabisco's deleveraging transactions

Step	Amount ($ billions)	Source of funds	Use of funds
1	1.7	KKR's 1987 Fund injects equity.	Stronger balance sheet permits coupon to be set on reset bonds.
2	(1.7)	(KKR's 1987 Fund.)	RJR purchases of (reset) 17 percent bonds.
3	3.4	RJR sells preferred shares to raise $1.6 billion, borrows $1.8 billion from banks.	RJR retires $2.4 billion of 17 percent bonds, retires $1 billion Drexel private placement.
4	1.2	RJR exchanges $0.7 billion of equity and $0.5 billion of cash.	RJR retires $1.2 billion of 17 percent bonds.
5	2.8	IPO of $1.3 billion; junk bond issued at 10.5% in amount of $1.5 billion.	RJR retires $1.9 billion of 17 percent bonds and repays banks $0.5 billion.
Total	$9.1 billion		

tional investors sustained their prior commitment; their standing by after having written a blank check is not surprising. As a result, the same investors, putting in funds in the same proportions, could reinforce RJR's equity. Less enthusiasm in 1987 and thus the absence of previously committed funds would have left KKR with the nearly impossible challenge of getting all the investors to stump up in proportion to their 1987 investments.

RJR's Deleveraging

RJR reversed about half of the leveraging that it had undergone in the 1989 buyout in five steps from mid-1990 through spring 1991 (table 4.2). The unifying theme of the five steps was the substitution of

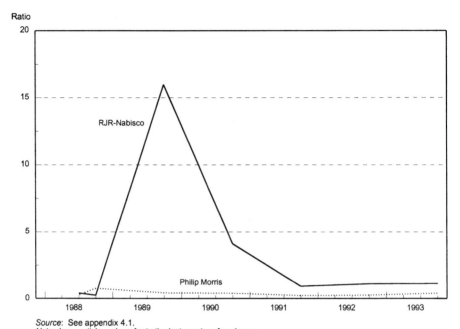

Source: See appendix 4.1.
Note: Longer tick marks refer to the last quarter of each year.

Figure 4.1
Ratio of debt to market value of equity for RJR-Nabisco and Philip Morris

equity for debt. The process started with an equity injection by KKR's 1987 fund and ended with a public offering—we will say an initial public offering—of RJR's stock to the public in April 1991. These transactions taken together did most of the job of bringing RJR's debt down from 94 percent of the firm's capital in July 1989 (table 4.1) to 75 percent at the end of 1990 and 50 percent at the end of 1991 (figure 4.1).

The first step, a key transaction, was the KKR 1987 fund's injection of $1.7 billion, which doubled the fund's investment. The prospect of this investment permitted rates of 17 percent to be fixed on the reset bonds. In the second step, most of the equity injected was used to purchase the 17 percent bonds. Thus, step one brought equity into RJR and step two used the proceeds to retire debt.

In step three, a combination of preferred equity and cash raised from banks was exchanged for more than $3 billion of junk bonds. Preferred shares in the amount of $1.6 billion retired a like amount of the 17 percent bonds. RJR also borrowed $1.8 billion from banks to retire another $0.8 billion of the 17 percent bonds and the $1 billion remaining of the junk bonds that Drexel had privately placed to finance the original acquisition.

Step four featured the exchange of common shares for still more of the 17 percent bonds. In particular, the company retired $1.2 billion of the bonds with equity and $0.5 billion of cash.

The last step in RJR's return to equity centered on its stock offering in April 1991. Underwriters sold 115 million shares at $11.25 per share to raise $1.29 billion. With no less than $4.6 billion of equity raised in ten months, RJR was able to return to the junk bond market for $1.5 billion of seven-year money at a mere 10.5 percent. Most of the proceeds served to retire $1.9 billion of the 17 percent junk bonds, and $0.5 billion in proceeds paid down bank debt.

Stepping back, KKR drew on private equity, preferred equity, bank debt, and the public equity market to infuse more than $6 billion of cash into the moribund junk bond market. Only after nine months of these massive transfusions did the junk bond market come to life. Had KKR not held unused commitments from its institutional investors, junk's flagship could very well have sunk.

Marlboro Friday

On Friday, April 2, 1993, RJR's managers and stockholders suddenly learned that RJR's largest competitor in the domestic tobacco business, Philip Morris, had shredded the presumptions that underlay their business plans and investments more finely than tobacco leaf on its way to a rolling machine. RJR's *Annual Report* told the tale as follows:

In April 1993, RJRT's [RJR Tobacco's] largest competitor announced a shift in strategy designed to gain share of market while sacrificing short-term profits.

The competitor's tactics included increased promotional spending and temporary price reductions on its largest cigarette brand [Marlboro], followed several
months later by list price reductions on all its full-price and mid-price brands.
RJRT defended its major full-price brands during the period of temporary price
reductions and, to remain competitive in the marketplace, also reduced list
prices on all its full-price and mid-price brands in August 1993. . . . depressed
margins are expected to continue until such time as the competitive environment improves and operating costs are further reduced.[12]

The outbreak of competition hit RJR's top and bottom lines. Net sales
for the domestic tobacco business fell 20 percent, and for the worldwide tobacco business, 10 percent. Leverage that was still quite high
amplified the effect of the decline in sales on the bottom line. Operating results (net income before restructuring expense and amortization of intangibles) for the domestic tobacco business fell by more than
40 percent, and for the world tobacco business, by more than 30 percent. RJR took a "restructuring charge" of $544 million "to streamline
both the domestic and international operations by the reduction of
personnel in administration, manufacturing and sales functions, as
well as rationalization of manufacturing and office facilities."[13] Note
that such economies were asserted to be possible after four years of
close oversight by those still the majority holders, the 1987 KKR
partnership.

Even before Marlboro Friday, returns from the RJR-Nabisco buyout
to the investors in KKR's 1987 fund were reported to have fallen behind
those that would have been generated by a comparable investment in
the Standard & Poor's 500.[14] After Marlboro Friday, KKR's investors'
dissatisfaction became public.[15] Of the $998 million that the Washing-
ton State Investment Board invested in the last fund, almost half, $418
million, went into RJR, where it was worth $358 million at the end
of September 1993. The executive director of the Washington public
pension, Basil Schwan, commented in 1994:

That certainly wasn't the expectation for RJR. KKR has to show the investors
that it can turn the company around. We make commitments to these guys,
and we're relying on them.[16]

The public shareholders who paid $11.25 a share in April 1991 for shares that now traded at less than $10 a share were no happier. But the fate of private or public equity holders cannot provide the measure of the success or failure of the RJR buyout. After all, the original shareholders of RJR-Nabisco made out well from the vertiginous bidding, and debt holders have collected interest payments on schedule. Taking the measure of the RJR-Nabisco buyout requires a careful choice of benchmark; a careful accounting of the value of not only equity values but also debt values; and a careful accounting of cash thrown off in dividends, repurchases, and interest payments.

4.2 Effect of the Buyout on Market Value: Contrast with Philip Morris

Any attempt to measure the effect of RJR's LBO on its market value immediately runs up against the need for some benchmark. We juxtapose observations on RJR-Nabisco with those for Philip Morris and ask how the owners and creditors of the two firms fared in the years after the buyout, and how accounted profits, administrative costs, investments, and employee head counts evolved. Our method of comparing the values the market attached to the two firms and the cash that they have thrown off requires some elaboration.

Advantages of a Comparative Approach

Benchmarking the performance of RJR-Nabisco against that of Philip Morris has much to recommend it over a before-and-after analysis of the type that has been repeatedly applied to Campeau's buyout of Federated Department Stores.[17] A before-and-after case study with no peer comparison, however, risks ascribing all change to the change of management and associated rise in leverage, courting the post hoc ergo propter hoc fallacy. An approach that implicitly ascribed the losses

Table 4.3
Business mix of RJR-Nabisco and Philip Morris

	1990		1991		1992		1993	
	RJR	Philip Morris	RJR	Philip Morris	RJR	Philip Morris	RJR	Philip Morris
Tobacco	77%	68%	75%	72%	74%	69%	65%	62%
Food	23	27	25	23	26	27	35	33
Beer	—	3	—	3	—	2	—	3
Financial services and real estate	—	2	—	2	—	2	—	3

Sources: RJR-Nabisco, *Annual Report*, 1993, p. 27; Philip Morris Companies, Inc., *Annual Report*, 1993, p. 20; Moody's *Industrial Manual*, 1994, vol. 2, p. 3395.

resulting from Philip Morris's new pricing strategy in April 1993 to the buyout four springs earlier would clearly be inappropriate. By using a control, general developments in the stock market or in the tobacco and food business should not tip the scales in our analysis.

As to the choice of firm for comparison, there can be little debate. After Philip Morris and RJR-Nabisco, the third largest tobacco firm is BAT, a British conglomerate engaged in insurance in the United States (Farmers) and in Britain (Eagle). Philip Morris bought Kraft Foods in 1988, so fortunately it spans tobacco and food as does RJR-Nabisco. Philip Morris is inevitably not a perfect match for RJR: It runs a moderate-sized finance company, for instance. Nevertheless, the two are reasonably comparable in the balance of business between tobacco and food sales (table 4.3).

The Comparative Valuation Exercise

Our first step is to measure each firm's market value as the sum of the market value of equity and the value of credit market debt on seven days—September 30, 1988, before any hint of a buyout of RJR-Nabisco,

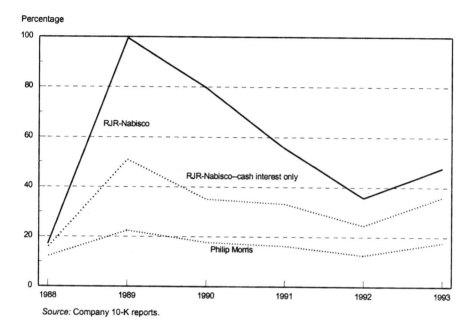

Percentage

Figure 4.2
Interest burden on cash flow for RJR-Nabisco and Philip Morris

and the last day of 1988, 1989, 1990, 1991, 1992, and 1993. But these market values do not tell the whole story, because the heavy debt loaded onto RJR forced the firm to pay out its cash flow while Philip Morris enjoyed the luxury of retaining its cash flow and growing its assets faster (figure 4.2). So we add to the market value of each firm the cumulated cash paid out to creditors and shareholders.

Determining Market Value

To the value of equity outstanding we add the value of debt outstanding, calculated as the sum of short-term (or floating-rate) debt valued at book and the market value of long-term debt (see appendix 4.1 for details). The market value of RJR-Nabisco jumped after the announcement of the buyout but has not shown much of trend since then (figure 4.3). In early October 1988, RJR traded in the mid-50s, but the $75 per

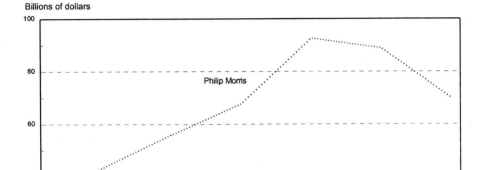

Source: Annual reports of RJR-Nabisco and Philip Morris.
Note: Longer tick marks refer to the last quarter of each year.

Figure 4.3
Market value of RJR-Nabisco and Philip Morris

share bid by management and the subsequent frenzied bidding took the price to about $100 per share by year's end. Bondholders' losses offset these shareholders' gains only to a very limited extent, so the company's total value overall rose from $19 billion on September 30, 1988, to $26 billion on December 31, 1988. The firm's value then edged down with 1989's distress in the junk bond market and suffered further from the 1990 downgrading of its junk bonds and the associated collapse of the junk bond market. In 1991 things turned up: The equity market recovered from the Gulf War and recession, the junk bond market stabilized, and RJR managed to refinance its debt, so the value of RJR-Nabisco surged. In 1993, the market value fell as Marlboro Friday gave U.S. smokers an unwonted whiff of price competition. Stepping back, RJR's total market capitalization, both debt and equity, rose but a little over the five years from September 1988 to December 1993.

By contrast, Philip Morris arrived at the end of 1993 worth about three-quarters more than what it was worth after the 1988 merger with Kraft (figure 4.3). The firm's value showed three years of strong gains, more than doubling by the end of 1991, before a moderate decline in 1992 and a sharp drop in 1993. By this partial comparison, Philip Morris bested RJR by a wide margin, and the buyout had little to show for itself.

Cumulating Cash Flows

Keep in mind, however, that a leveraged buyout puts its new managers under the gun to pay out more of its cash flow to creditors. As a result, despite the fact that RJR-Nabisco started out in September 1988 only half the size of its rival, in servicing its bonds RJR threw off about as much cash as Philip Morris (figure 4.4). Note also that despite its succession of refinancings, RJR's cash flows have been much more consistent than those of Philip Morris. In particular, Philip Morris has enjoyed the financial flexibility to draw in large sums from the securities market to fund asset growth.

We cumulate these cash flows as if their recipients reinvested them in comparable instruments. For instance, when Philip Morris paid a dividend or repurchased its shares, we let that cash payment grow as if it were plowed back into stocks as represented by the Standard & Poor's index. When RJR paid the $17 billion to its shareholders, we let that cash payment grow in a similar fashion. When Philip Morris paid interest to its commercial paper and bond holders, we let those cash payments grow with the A2/P2-rated commercial paper yield and with returns on A-rated bonds, respectively. When RJR paid interest on its bank debt and junk bonds, we let those cash payments grow with bank debt yields and B-rated junk bond returns.[18]

The comparison of cumulated cash thrown off by the two companies casts RJR-Nabisco in a very good light. If investors had reinvested cash

Billions of dollars

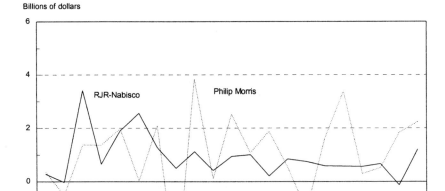

Year:Quarter

Sources: 10-Ks, 10-Qs, and Annual reports of RJR-Nabisco and Philip Morris.

Figure 4.4
Cash thrown off by RJR-Nabisco and Philip Morris

coming out of the firms in instruments similar to those giving rise to
the cash flow, they would have accumulated almost as much from RJR
as from the larger Philip Morris (figure 4.5). Because the appropriate
basis for the comparison is the market value of the two firms in September 1988, when Philip Morris was worth about $40 billion and RJR less
than $20 billion, the near parity in dollar value of their cumulated cash
flows is quite remarkable.

Adding Market Values and Cumulated Cash Payments
So far, each firm has corresponded to its stereotype: the less-leveraged
firm grew faster in market value, but the leveraged firm put relatively
more cash into the hands of investors. Now we draw the balance: It

Billions of dollars

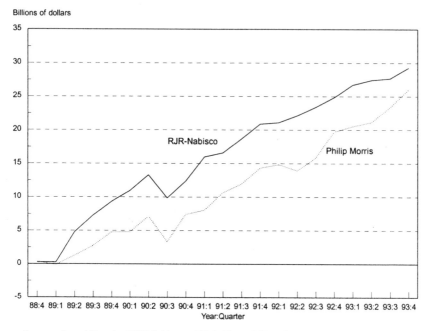

Sources: Annual Reports of RJR-Nabisco and Philip Morris; DRI-McGraw/Hill; USECON.

Figure 4.5
Cumulative value of cash thrown off by RJR-Nabisco and Philip Morris

appears that the sum of RJR's market value and cumulated cash flow has grown faster than the corresponding sum for Philip Morris (figures 4.6 and 4.7). RJR-Nabisco's adjusted market value rose from $19 billion to $52 billion, for a gain of 174 percent, while Philip Morris rose from $40 to $97 billion, for a gain of 143 percent.

But on an after-tax basis, the 1993 adjusted market values come very close indeed (figure 4.8). Taking into account taxes hurts the relative performance of RJR-Nabisco, because it is putting more cash into claimants' hands. In particular, we estimate that the initial payout to RJR-Nabisco's public shareholders of $24 billion of cash and back-end paper led to capital gains taxes of almost $3.5 billion (see appendix 4.1).

In summary, has the buyout of RJR-Nabisco made money as measured by the firm's value and the cash it has thrown off as compared

Billions of dollars

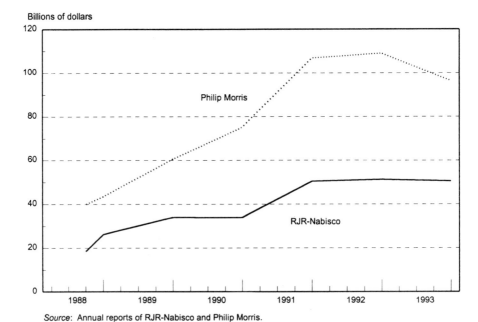

Source: Annual reports of RJR-Nabisco and Philip Morris.
Note: Longer tick marks refer to the last quarter of each year.

Figure 4.6
Adjusted market value of RJR-Nabisco and Philip Morris

to the same for Philip Morris? An observer from Missouri would not be persuaded that value had been created.

Breaking the Tie with Fees?

At this point, a reader may well wonder: Where do the above valuations leave the fees that RJR-Nabisco paid its investment bankers, commercial bankers, and lawyers? The authors confess having left them out of the calculus but beg the readers' assistance as to how to count them.

These fees amount to no small sum, even by the standards of a large U.S. corporation. Fees immediately associated with the buyout totaled at least $784 million, split among providers of bridge loans, bankers, and investment bankers, including the organizer/buyer, KKR (table 4.4, top line). Add the underwriters' fees for bringing the junk bonds

Index: 1988:3 = 100

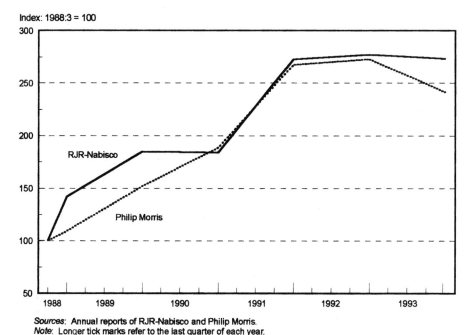

Sources: Annual reports of RJR-Nabisco and Philip Morris.
Note: Longer tick marks refer to the last quarter of each year.

Figure 4.7
Comparison of adjusted market value of RJR-Nabisco and Philip Morris

to market a few months later ($120 million) and KKR's charge to its 1987 fund investors for its efforts over the time from the commitment of their funds to the employment of their funds ($23 million), and the total reaches almost $1 billion ($927 million). Fees for selected refinancing operations and KKR's fee on the further investment of the 1987 fund brings the total up to $1.363 billion.

These sums make it evident that leveraged buyouts showered fees on Wall Street in amounts without postwar precedent. When Standard Oil of California acquired Gulf Oil in a $13.2 billion transaction, corporate managers paid no more than some $63 million in fees.[19] In other words, the Street received less than 0.5 percent of the transaction value. By contrast, $927 billion represents almost 4 percent of the RJR-Nabisco transaction value. Dollar for dollar, leveraged deals that put

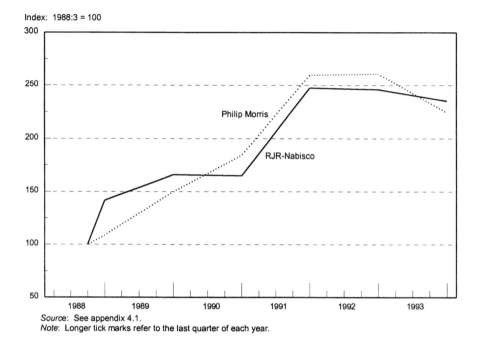

Index: 1988:3 = 100

Source: See appendix 4.1.
Note: Longer tick marks refer to the last quarter of each year.

Figure 4.8
Comparison of after-tax adjusted market value of RJR-Nabisco and Philip Morris

financiers in control yielded ten times as much to the Street as less-leveraged mergers that left the managers of one of the newly merged companies in control.

The popular view of these fees is that they are the scalps that Wall Street has taken from corporate America. An economist's translation of this view might be that the fees charged stood far above the opportunity cost of the efforts of those involved in the buyout. Another perspective is that the hotly contested bidding contest for RJR-Nabisco helped assure that the successful bidders no more than earned their keep. In other words, the fees covered only the marginal costs of those rendering the service.

This difference of views bears on the evaluation of the RJR-Nabisco buyout in a manner counter to our intuition. To the extent that the

Table 4.4
Fees paid by RJR-Nabisco and its private owners, 1989–93

Fees associated with the buyout	*$784*	*million*
Investment banking fee paid to KKR[1]	$75	million
Bridge loan fee paid to Drexel and Merrill Lynch ($227M to Drexel and $109M to Merrill Lynch)[2]	$336	million
Front-end fees paid to banks (2.5% · $13 billion)	$323	million
Investment banking fees ($25 million each to Morgan Stanley and Perella)	$50	million
Fees for underwriting the junk bonds to refinance ($4 billion · 3%)	*$120*	*million*
Fees for the refinancing in spring 1990[3]	*$250*	*million*
Banks for $2.25 billion credit and amendment fee	$200	million
Lawyers, printers, investment bankers	$50	million
Underwriting fees for April 1991 refinancings	*$123*	*million*
Public offering of equity ($1.3 billion · 6%)	$78	million
Junk bond issue ($1.5 billion · 3%)	$45	million
KKR management fee on 1987 fund commitments	*$86*	*million*
(1.5% yr.[4] · $1.5 billion · 1 yr.)	$22.5	million
(1.5% yr. · $1.7 billion · 2.5 yrs.)	$63.8	million
Total	$1,363	million

[1] Anders, *Merchants of Debt*, p. 216.
[2] Burrough and Helyar, *Barbarians at the Gate*, p. 510.
[3] Anders, pp. 266–8.
[4] Anders, p. 51.

fees represent real costs, they do not weigh in the comparison of RJR-Nabisco and Philip Morris. On this hypothesis, the transformation of the ownership and debt structure of RJR-Nabisco absorbed real resources—principally specialized and high-priced labor but also concentrated financial risk bearing—on which Philip Morris, with its stable, dispersed ownership and continued reliance on equity, made no demands. By contrast, to the extent that RJR-Nabisco's financiers paid themselves inflated fees, they help tip the balance of our comparison toward RJR-Nabisco. On this hypothesis, the transformation of the firm's ownership and debt structure provided the occasion for the diversion of shareholder funds that should be cumulated in our valuation exercise above. Thus as a technical matter, the bigger the rip off, the better the case that the RJR-Nabisco buyout created value, that is, was socially useful.

4.3 Buyout Effect on Accounting Profits, Overheads, Investment, and Employment

Money does not settle all the arguments that have swirled around the RJR buyout. Has new ownership and the pressure of debt service made RJR-Nabisco a more efficient company?[20]

Profitability

Gross profit margins for the two firms (figure 4.9) ranged between 16 and 20 percent in 1988 through 1992, then sank after Philip Morris cut its prices in the spring of 1993. Philip Morris shows a larger and more consistent improvement through 1992. Overall it is very hard to argue that RJR-Nabisco's new owners and higher leverage forced the firm to manage a sustained rise in operating profitability in relation to its competitor.

Corporate Overhead

Much of the public ridicule of RJR-Nabisco's former management focused on what was portrayed as egregious overhead it inflicted. The 10-jet RJR "air force," at times said to be put at the service of the CEO's dog, has passed into U.S. folklore as a symbol of U.S. managers' excessive spending. But there was more: celebrity golf outings, penthouse apartments, free cars, beach houses, maids, antiques, and $50,000-per-year pensions for directors.[21]

Percentage

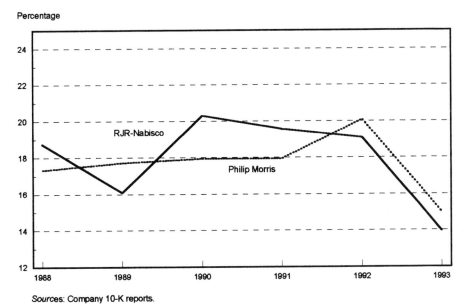

Sources: Company 10-K reports.

Figure 4.9
Operating earnings in relation to sales for RJR-Nabisco and Philip Morris

Is there any evidence that RJR's new owners and higher leverage forced the company to reduce overhead spending as a fraction of sales? Again the comparative evidence does not speak in favor of the buyout. Salary, advertising, administrative, and general expenses in relation to sales rose unevenly at RJR in 1988–92 (figure 4.10) while falling unevenly at Philip Morris. The disposal of the RJR air force may have trimmed overheads, but other such expenses seem to have crept up more than enough to offset the savings.

Capital Expenditure

The argument over capital spending at RJR-Nabisco has proceeded in such fashion as to leave the evidence subject to conflicting interpretations. The film of *Barbarians at the Gate* turned the smokeless cigarette,

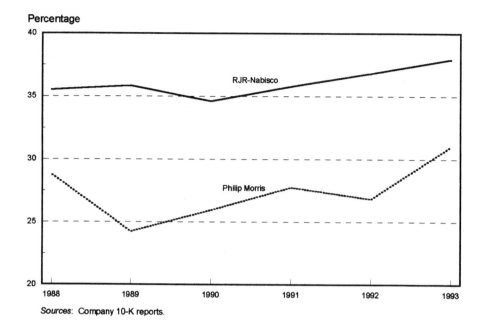

Sources: Company 10-K reports.

Figure 4.10
Overhead expenses in relation to sales at RJR-Nabisco

a product of more than $100 million of research and development, into a running gag: "It tastes like s——." In addition, critics pointed to the $2 billion planned investment in Cookieville, a pair of highly automated bakeries. The investment would have yielded an internal rate of return of less than 5 percent, evidently below the hurdle rate for any investor in RJR. Such an investment would simply waste investors' money on an engineer's dream, involving, for instance, spending $10 million on robots to replace three (human) forklift drivers.[22] On the other side are critics of leveraging who diagnose it as an anorexia that starves firms of needed investment.

However one interprets the fact, one cannot escape the observation that capital spending as a fraction of sales declined markedly for RJR-Nabisco after its LBO (figure 4.11). Note that RJR's capital spending in

Percentage

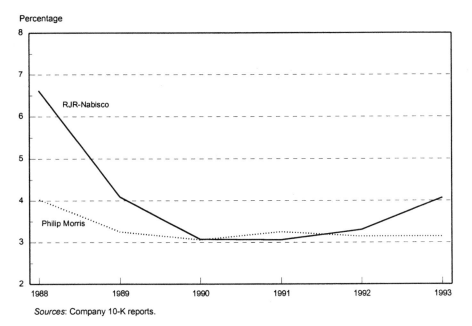

Sources: Company 10-K reports.

Figure 4.11
Capital spending in relation to sales for RJR-Nabisco and Philip Morris

relation to sales declined toward the lower level characteristic of Philip Morris. Defenders of the buyout might argue that these data show that the right firm, not merely the smaller and therefore more affordable firm, was bought.

Employment and Wages

Many critics of buyouts have argued that any financial gains to shareholders (again, these are not obvious over time) come out of workers' backs. One version of this view looks to cost savings from layoffs; another looks to savings from union busting; still another to cost savings arising from breaking implicit contracts of long-term employment and postretirement income security. Here we confine our attention to the

Thousands of dollars

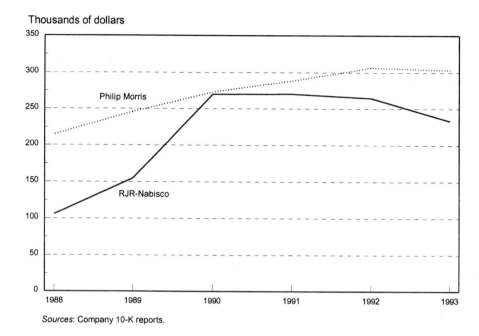

Sources: Company 10-K reports.

Figure 4.12
Sales per employee at RJR-Nabisco and Philip Morris

first question of workforce reductions. Note that any cost savings on the wage bill cannot be readily ascribed to efficiency gains as opposed to redistributions from the affected employees.

One crude measure of labor productivity casts the buyout in a good light. Sales per employee at RJR-Nabisco rose from just over $100,000 in 1988, about half that of Philip Morris, to more than $250,000 by 1990 (figure 4.12).[23] Thereafter, sales per employee ceased rising at RJR-Nabisco, even as they continued to rise at Philip Morris (before Marlboro Friday). By this measure, RJR-Nabisco shows a marked absolute and relative performance. RJR-Nabisco's disposals in the quarters following the buyout render any strong conclusions from these observations hazardous, however. Del Monte Fresh Fruits, for instance, may well have had a disproportionate share of employees.

Because of such problems, those who have examined the effects of takeovers on labor have focused on announced layoffs at firms that have been taken over.[24] Here accounts of the buyout recognize off-setting moves: "The new tobacco chief, Jim Johnston, dismissed 1,525 workers in August 1989, shrinking the domestic tobacco division's payroll by 13 percent"; but "the foregone wonders of the proposed Cook-ieville factories preserved a lot of reasonably well-paying factory jobs that otherwise would have been eliminated by costly automation."[25]

Again a comparative approach rewards the effort. U.S. companies could and did downsize—or "rightsize," cut fat, eliminate unnecessary management layers, or whatever one wants to call it—without the compulsion of debt or hungry new managers.[26] So we consulted the *Wall Street Journal* index for announcements of layoffs at RJR and Philip Morris.[27]

In the first full year after the RJR buyout and Philip Morris's acquisition of Kraft, RJR clearly reduced its workforce more than its competitor (table 4.5). After canceling the hand-held Edsel, namely Premier, the smokeless cigarette, "one of the most stunning new product disasters in recent history,"[28] RJR-Nabisco announced that it was letting go 10 percent of its domestic cigarette factory workers, or 700 employees. Later, in August, the company announced the dismissal of 1,640 workers, or 12 percent of its total domestic tobacco workforce. One source estimated savings of $60 million, or about $36,000 per employee; a study later found that 72 percent of 2,000 employees fired had found work but that they averaged only 47 percent of their RJR wages.[29] By contrast, Philip Morris announced only the elimination of 250 white collar jobs as it consolidated Kraft into its General Foods unit.

Taking a longer view, it remains true that the aftermath of the RJR-Nabisco buyout brought noticeably larger workforce reductions than observed at Philip Morris in the same time period. In the four years, 1989–92, announced layoffs at RJR-Nabisco amounted to 2,440 out of a workforce of 63,000, or 3–4 percent. By contrast, Philip Morris cut only 1,690 jobs out of about 175,000, or about 1 percent. The responses

Table 4.5

Announced layoffs at RJR-Nabisco and Philip Morris, 1989–93

	RJR-Nabisco			Philip Morris		
	Total	Blue collar	White collar	Total	Blue collar	White collar
1989	700	700[1]		250		250[2]
	1,640	815[3]	825[3]			
1990	0			0		
1991	100+	100[4]	10% reduction[5]	1,440	1,440[6]	
1992	0					1,000[7]
1993	200+	200[8]		1,000		
	1,000	1,000[9]			14,000[10]	
	5,000	5,000[11]		14,000		
Total	8,640	7,815	825	16,690	15,440	1,250

[1] James R. Schiffman, "RJR to Cut Cigarette-Factory Staff 90% in First Reduction Since KKR Buy-Out," *Wall Street Journal*, March 22, 1989, p. A5.

[2] Philip Morris Cos.: Kraft to Cut 250 Jobs," *Wall Street Journal*, January 17, 1989, p. A10.

[3] Betsy Morris and Michael J. McCarthy, "RJR, in Long-Awaited Move, to Dismiss About 12% of Workers at Tobacco Unit," *Wall Street Journal*, August 11, 1989, p. A3: "When RJR Nabisco's headquarters was moved to New York from Atlanta [sic] this summer, the headquarters staff shrank to 350 from, 650."

[4] "RJR Nabisco Inc.," *Wall Street Journal*, August 15, 1991, p. B4.

[5] Robin Goldwyn Blumenthal, "RJR Nabisco Plans A Reorganization of Food Business," *Wall Street Journal*, October 9, 1991, p. A7.

[6] "Philip Morris Cos.," *Wall Street Journal*, December 6, 1991, p. B7.

[7] Suein L. Hwang, "Philip Morris's Kraft to Make 1,000 Job Cuts," *Wall Street Journal*, May 6, 1992, p. A4.

[8] "RJR Completes Sale of Cereal Business, Sets Charges for Some Job Cuts and Debt," *Wall Street Journal*, January 5, 1993, p. B4. The 200 jobs were not identified as blue or white collar.

[9] Eden Shapiro, "Tobacco Unit of RJR to Cut 9% of Its Staff," *Wall Street Journal*, September 15, 1993, p. A4.

[10] Eden Shapiro, "Philip Morris to Slash Staff, Shut 40 Plants," *Wall Street Journal*, November 26, 1993, p. A3.

[11] Eden Shapiro, "RJR Nabisco to Cut 9.5% of Work Force, Take 4th-Quarter Charge of $445 Million," *Wall Street Journal*, December 8, 1993, p. A2. The employees were not identified as blue collar or white collar.

of the two competing firms to the decline in revenues in the wake of Marlboro Friday only reinforced the differences over the previous four years. After Philip Morris shocked the pricing in this cozy oligopoly—one might almost say duopoly—RJR-Nabisco announced 6,000 job cuts (almost 10 percent of employment) while Philip Morris announced only 14,000 (about 8.5 percent of employment). Analysts guessed that Kraft General Foods, the profits of which faltered in 1992, would bear the brunt of Philip Morris's layoffs and plant closings.

What might the extraordinary squeeze on employment have done for the RJR-Nabisco buyout? Consider the 1989–92 job cuts under the strong assumption that every job cut reduced costs without reducing revenues. The 2,440 announced job cuts under that assumption might have saved RJR-Nabisco as much as $50,000 per year per job. Total savings might then reach $122 million per year. Capitalized at 10 percent, the shareholders of RJR might net as much as $1.2 billion from RJR-Nabisco's postbuyout downsizing.

This sum is not inconsiderable, but in the perspective of the biggest buyout ever, it is not big money. This sum amounts to only about 10 percent of the premium KKR paid to RJR-Nabisco shareholders. This admittedly falls within the estimation error in our valuation exercise. That the gains from squeezing the workforce work out to an amount within spitting distance of the fees Wall Street collected should be taken as no more than happenstance.

4.4   Conclusion

RJR-Nabisco exemplifies the determined leveraging of the 1980s and serendipitous deleveraging of the 1990s. Marty Whitman, founder of a vulture fund that bears his name, holds that RJR-Nabisco would have gone into bankruptcy if an equity market receptive to new issues had not come along at just the right moment.[30]

A comparison of the market valuation of RJR-Nabisco and Philip Morris shows that RJR leapt ahead of its competitor during the frenzied bidding in late 1988. Later, however, the paths of the market value of the two firms converged to the point that it becomes very difficult to claim that the buyout created any value. Philip Morris plodded along like Aesop's tortoise and ended up neck and neck with the hare, RJR-Nabisco. This finding stands in stark contrast to early readings taken through the first half of 1991. An apologist might contend that RJR's deleveraging spoiled the experiment, but few doubt that RJR-Nabisco ended 1993 with extraordinarily concentrated and interested shareholders. While the jury was hung on the buyout, fees amounting to no less than $1.3 billion had already been paid.

One might argue that the bidding became so extreme and the final buyout price went so high that little wonder should attach to the finding that the buyout did not work out so well. But an excessive price all by itself would merely have favored the sellers of RJR-Nabisco equity (the original shareholders) over the buyers (both the KKR partnerships and the buyers of the public shares issued in April 1991). Indeed, the former did well, whereas the latter have not.

An excessive price could damage all shareholders and creditors, however, if leverage were pushed up so high that management had to spend all its time cutting deals to stay a step ahead of default. On this view, a management that indulged in perks and tolerated fat yielded control to a management that spent too much time dodging the bailiff to run the firm efficiently.[31]

Judging from RJR's results as reported to its shareholders, the firm put in a mixed performance as a leveraged buyout. It slashed investment spending in relation to sales to a ratio close to that of Philip Morris, consistent with the view that the firm was overinvesting before the buyout. It laid off its workers faster than its more well heeled competitor. Despite all the talk of headquarters fat at RJR, overhead costs failed to fall in relation to sales after the buyout. And despite its abandonment of investment plans and firing of workers, RJR-Nabisco's management did not succeed in widening profit margins.

KKR finally threw in the towel on RJR by swapping its equity in the firm for that of a beat-up conglomerate, Borden. In 1999, an Icahn of the 1980s (Carl, who ran TWA after an LBO) threatened to rally RJR's institutional investors to vote in directors keen to split cookies from cigarettes. Management conceded by selling RJR's foreign business to Japan Tobacco and by promising to pay out shares in R.J. Reynolds to shareholders of RJR Nabisco Holdings (to be renamed Nabisco Group Holdings). While the dramatis personae came from the 1980s, the plot was in line with the 1990s. Chapter 9 discusses restructuring without leverage and chapter 10 institutional investors as responsible owners.

Appendix 4.1   Data Sources and Method for RJR-Nabisco–Philip Morris Comparison

This appendix offers the reader greater detail on the sources of data and the method of their combination that underlies the analysis of this chapter. All data were collected for end-September 1988, and end-December 1988, 1989, 1990, 1991, 1992, and 1993, a total of seven observations.

Balance Sheet

Arriving at a market value for each company requires the summing of the value of equity and debt outstanding. The value of equity outstanding is just the product of the market price of the shares and the number of shares outstanding. To this product we add a minimum and maximum value of the outstanding options on shares. We obtained the share price information from Bloomberg and the number of shares outstanding from the 10-Ks and 10-Q (including in this context and below the annual reports of Philip Morris, which are incorporated by reference in the 10-Ks). Information on options outstanding in the 10-Ks was limited to the number outstanding within ranges of strike prices, with no information given on strike prices. Accordingly, the maximum price assumes an exercise price of 0, so that options reduce to shares; the minimum price is taken as the difference between the highest strike price in the range and the shares' current market value.

To value the debt, we add the book value of floating-rate debt—drawn bank loans and commercial paper outstanding—to the value of long-term debt priced at market value. Consistent with market practice, we ignore trade debt and implicitly take it as part of the business rather than part of its financing. For RJR-Nabisco, we obtain market values for each of two score different debt securities listed as outstanding in the 10-Ks and 10-Q over the seven observations. Our sources for price data were Bloomberg, Standard & Poor's, Moody's, and the *Wall Street Journal*. For the relatively low-leverage Philip Morris, which had even more numerous issues of debt, we take a shortcut in the valuation of long-term debt. We read in Philip Morris' *1993 Annual Report,* p. 35, that the market value of long-term debt in 1993 was $18.1 billion, as compared to a book value of $17.0 billion. The market value of debt is further described as not materially different from the reported book value for 1992. We therefore use the reported market value in 1993, accept the book value in 1992 as materially correct, and take the risk that book values fairly represent market values for the earlier dates. Our sources for the value of long-term debt are accordingly the 10-K and 10-Q.

Philip Morris's acquisition of Kraft was effective in the fourth quarter of 1988, but we needed to start the comparison before the bidding for RJR got under way. So we constructed a pro forma market value of the merged firm for September 30, 1988, by summing the value of Philip Morris's equity at September 30, 1988, with Philip Morris's end-1988 debt. From this sum we subtracted the difference between cash on hand at both Philip Morris and Kraft at the end of the third quarter plus net cash flow in the fourth quarter, on the one hand, and Philip Morris's cash holdings at the end of the fourth quarter, on the other hand.

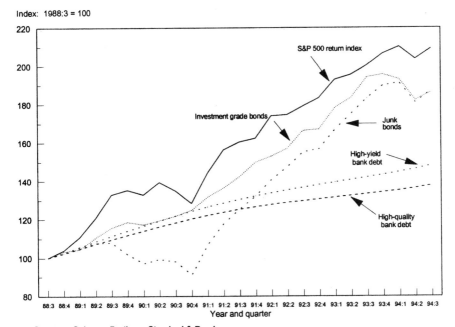

Index: 1988:3 = 100

Figure 4.A.1
Cumulated returns on equity and debt

Cumulated Cash Flows

All information on cash flows was derived from the 10-Ks and 10-Qs. Rates of return on public equity, private equity, investment grade bonds, junk bonds, and high-quality and HLT bank debt (figure 4.A.1) used to cumulate the cash flows were derived from a number of sources. Standard & Poor's was the source for returns on the S&P 500, and we took the cost of LBO equity to be 7 percent per quarter, or 30 percent per annum. Returns on investment grade and junk bonds were taken from Salomon Brothers. Philip Morris's commercial paper and bank debt was taken to cost the A2/P2 rate plus 10 basis points; RJR-Nabisco's bank debt was taken to cost LIBOR plus 200 basis points.

For the tax adjustment of the cumulated cash flows, educated guesses had to serve on a number of fronts. One-quarter of the shareholders were taken to be nontaxed institutions, consistent with the share of corporate and state and local pension funds among the holders of corporate equity.[32] Similarly, one-fifth of the holders of corporate bonds were taken to be nontaxed institutions. Holders of commercial paper and banks were taken to be taxed. Top federal tax rates of 28 percent before 1990, 31 percent after, and 36 percent in 1993 (ignoring the millionaire's surcharge) were used; the capital gains tax employed was 28 percent consistently.

The tax basis for the original shareholders of RJR-Nabisco and for Philip Morris shareholders who have sold shares back to the company in the company's ongoing share repurchase program is hard to estimate. Fortunately some scholars from North Carolina have gotten their hands on the shareholder list for RJR in that state and have determined that the average basis was $21.[33] Recognizing that North Carolina, the home state of Reynolds Tobacco, had more than its share of long-term holders, however, these analysts take the average basis for all RJR shareholders to be $40. The tax status and basis for those who have sold Philip Morris shares back to the company are necessarily a matter of some conjecture. But the North Carolina scholars found that shareholders with the highest basis sold their shares earlier in the takeover battle than did those with a lower basis. This finding, as well as the higher turnover of institutional as against individual investors, suggests that taxable investors have sold perhaps only half of repurchased shares, and that the taxable investors have a basis not far below, say 10 percent below, the repurchase price.

Armed with these assumptions, we find that the shareholders of RJR had to pay almost $3.5 billion in capital gains taxes. This estimate is not much different from that of others.[34]

II   The 1990s

5   The Legacy of Debt and Corporate Refinancing in the 1990s

As the 1980s yielded to the 1990s, default and the threat of default hammered a new notion into managers' and investors' minds: "Debt is out, equity is in." U.S. corporations floated stocks in unprecedented amounts in the 1990s. Private firms going public, public firms growing fast, and mature firms running losses all sold shares on Wall Street. And as long-term interest rates dropped, corporate treasurers flooded underwriters with notes and bonds even though short-term borrowing remained much cheaper.

To some extent, corporate treasurers were no more than doing what came naturally. After the invasion of Kuwait, U.S. share prices rallied. With Wall Street suddenly offering more for equities, corporate treasurers took the opportunity to print more share certificates and to sell their paper to Wall Street underwriters. The story in the bond market through 1993 differed only in detail. As long-term interest rates fell, bond prices rose. Old bonds carrying high interest rates, unlike shares sold when prices were low, can often be called, and some bonds are maturing at any given time. So corporate treasurers could not only seize their opportunity to sell new bonds into a rising bond market, but also retire old bonds and replace them with bonds carrying lower coupons. Millions of home owners similarly cashed in on their opportunity to refinance their mortgages to lower their monthly payments.

The rapid issuance of securities in the 1990s, then, did not show the unfolding of a well-developed plan. Rather corporate treasurers committed "crimes of opportunity" by trading paper for cash at what looked like favorable rates.

Mixed in among the opportunistic sellers of paper who came to market when prices turned in their favor were rather more motivated sellers, however. Here was the RJR-Nabisco treasurer from chapter 4 who used equity to defuse junk bond bombs. Over there were the treasurers of General Motors and Ford, scrambling to avoid the downgrade of their credit standing in the market and the risk of runs against their near-bank financing arms.

We show in this chapter[1] that surprisingly few of the corporations that tapped equity investors in the early 1990s were seeking funds for the purpose of expanding business operations. Instead, much of the record financing served to strengthen corporate balance sheets, to unburden cash flows of the weight of debt service, to forestall costly credit rating downgrades, and to guard against rises in short-term interest rates.

The full-scale return of U.S. firms in 1991–93 to their traditional role as sellers of equity decisively reversed seven extraordinary years of firms' buying their own and one another's equity. As described in chapter 2, only the most conservative corporations refrained from increasing leverage after 1984. Indeed, management often found it in its own interest to pile on debt to discourage corporate raiders from bootstrapping their way into the executive suite with borrowed money.

The about-face of corporate treasurers from retiring to floating equity in 1991–93 caught the attention of policy makers trying to understand the anemia in the U.S. economy from the end of the Gulf War in early 1991 to the pickup in growth at the end of 1993. Observers pointed to the U.S. firms' preoccupation with reducing debt as the chief source of the firms' extraordinary caution in planning fixed investment, in managing inventories, and especially in taking on new employees. Obsessed with the risks of debt, many firms used higher business cash flows resulting from any spending impulse in the economy to pay down debt faster rather than to invest or to hire. For example, the 5 percent rise in consumer spending in the first quarter of 1992 did not generate a self-reinforcing surge in production and employment.

This chapter assesses the motives and progress of corporate refinancing in the 1990s. We find that U.S. corporations returned to the equity market as sellers for reasons that go beyond the attractive pricing of shares in 1991–93. In addition, firms found that the debt they had taken on in the late 1980s proved difficult to manage. As bankruptcies surged and bond investors and banks tightened credit to highly leveraged firms, organizers of leveraged buyouts scrambled to sign up new public equity investors. And unprofitable firms, especially industrial firms that had built up finance company subsidiaries in the 1980s, sold equity to offset weak cash flows and to retain their access to commercial paper funding.

5.1 Motives for Restructuring

Understanding U.S. corporations' financial restructuring requires some perspective on the short- and long-term motives behind the process. U.S. corporations seized the opportunity to sell shares and thereby infuse equity into their capital structure in 1991–93 both for cyclical reasons and for reasons relating to the extraordinary developments in U.S. corporate finance in the 1980s. The 1991–93 period resembles 1982–83, the corresponding phase of the prior business cycle, in two respects: Stock prices rallied to mark the end of a recession, and corporations, including heretofore private firms, issued equity aggressively. But 1991–93 also differs from the earlier period in important features. In the 1980s many U.S. corporations leveraged up, and some firms rapidly expanded into financial services through their finance companies. These developments carried unusual risks that manifested themselves in 1989–90 and spurred treasurers to deleverage their firms' finances aggressively.

Cyclic Influences: The 1982–83 Record

Both demand- and supply-side forces can contribute to the rise in equity issuance when a recession ends. On the demand side, stock market investors, anticipating an upturn in the economy and an associated surge in earnings, bid up prices relative to current earnings. Declining interest rates reinforce the effect of higher anticipated earnings on price-earnings ratios as investors capitalize anticipated earnings at a higher rate. On the supply side, corporate treasurers readily issue shares into a more buoyant market to augment cyclically low cash flows.

After the 1981–82 recession, these forces combined to produce an unusually timed burst of equity issuance (figure 5.1) that reduced the burden of interest payments on U.S. corporations' cash flows. With little equity being withdrawn through debt-financed mergers or share repurchases, U.S. nonfinancial firms' net equity issuance ran at an annual rate of $15 billion in the 18 months between July 1982 and December 1983. Depending on equity financing rather than debt financing saves on interest costs. Given the high interest rates then prevailing, the equity issued in 1982–83 saved the issuers some $3 billion in interest payments by the fourth quarter of 1983 (and sliced 0.5 percent off the ratio of interest to cash flow).

U.S. corporations' resort to equity finance in 1991–93 bears some resemblance to equity issuance in 1982–83. The rates of gross and net equity issuance in the later period ran about double those of the earlier period, but taking account of economic growth and inflation in the intervening years narrows the difference. Owing to the higher interest rates prevailing in 1982–83, the interest saved in relation to corporate cash flows during the earlier cycle was comparable to that saved in the recent period. The 1990s' surge of equity issuance distinguished itself,

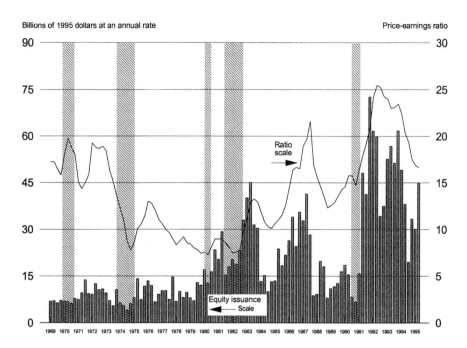

Source: Board of Governors of the Federal Reserve System.
Note: Shaded areas indicate recession periods designated by the National Bureau of Economic Research.

Figure 5.1
Gross public equity issuance and price-earnings ratio of the Standard and Poor's 500 companies

however, by its composition, its longevity, and the high price-earnings ratios underpinning it.

The Hangover of 1980s Leveraging

The outsize accumulation of corporate debt in the 1980s, the greater than anticipated difficulty of servicing it, and the resulting unprecedented pileup of business bankruptcies also spurred treasurers to issue equity in the 1990s.[2] Evidence suggests that in 1990–92, U.S. corporations found managing their debt in a period of weak cash flows more difficult than anticipated. It should have come as no surprise that highly leveraged firms lose market share in an industry downturn as customers switch to less-risky providers of goods and services.

Perhaps practical managers took seriously the argument that highly leveraged firms with weak cash flows could generally reorganize their debt without resorting to bankruptcy—that bankruptcy had been "privatized."[3] The argument held that, in the event of trouble, creditors would grab the controls and pull highly leveraged firms out of a nosedive while considerable value still remained in the firm. That is, because creditors of a very leveraged firm would, by definition, be exposed to loss early on as the value of a firm dropped, they would have more incentive than the creditors of an unleveraged firm to intervene early in a troubled firm. The argument concluded that creditors would avoid the dead-weight losses of bankruptcy by collectively reducing their claims without resort to the courts. The argument understated the difficulty of forging an agreement among different classes of creditors, a problem that the proliferation of creditor classes during the leveraging boom of the 1980s exacerbated. In the event, instead of one creditor's entering the cockpit to seize control from a failing pilot, a host of creditors out in the cabin argued among themselves.[4]

Recent research has confirmed that the strategic interaction of multiple classes of creditors—in plain English, the games played by disappointed investors and newly arrived vultures—has made it harder for firms to manage their debt. A study of distressed firms that had issued junk bonds in the 1970s and 1980s found that the weakness of cash flow had no power to predict Chapter 11 bankruptcy filings. Instead, the more complex the capital structure, as measured by the number of public debt issues outstanding or the number of priority tiers among claimants, the more likely Chapter 11 proved to be.[5]

As we saw in chapter 3, even when companies forged agreements among different classes of creditors in an effort to avoid a bankruptcy filing, they frequently could not achieve the near unanimity required as a practical matter. As a result, they had to seek the protection of

Chapter 11 to force deals on a minority of holdouts. The volume of these "prepackaged" bankruptcies increased in the 1990s as a share of large-company bankruptcies (table 2.3). Although the prepackaged bankruptcy has been called a "variation on the privatization theme,"[6] its development points instead precisely to the element of compulsion that possibly cheaper private arrangements lacked. In the end, the accretion of successive bond issues or layers of priority that typified the junk bond business of the late 1980s multiplied the chances for a holdout problem and thereby made it more difficult for a distressed firm to work out its debt without resort to the courts. The pied pipers of leverage had not sounded any warning about the hazards of fractious creditors.

Firms with Major Finance Companies and Access to Commercial Paper

Another important reason for the extraordinary burst of equity issuance in 1991–92 was the need on the part of a minority of industrial and commercial firms to buttress the balance sheet condition of their finance company affiliates. The balance sheets of finance companies, which are part of what has been termed the parallel banking system, generally grew faster than the economy in the 1980s, and finance companies owned by industrial firms tended to grow faster than their parent firms.[7] At the same time, finance companies' reliance on credit markets for funds increased in the 1980s. In particular, they financed themselves very heavily in the commercial paper market, where investors show limited tolerance for questionable credit. Fast growth and reliance on risk-averse investors combined to heighten the importance of retaining a high credit rating.

Chrysler's experience illustrates the costs of a downgrade in credit rating. When Chrysler Financial's commercial paper was downgraded to the second tier of prime, the firm had to turn to its banks for financing, at an immediate cost of something like 0.5 percentage points on the funds formerly raised from the commercial paper market. And when it came time for Chrysler to renegotiate its bank credit, the cost rose still more. The lesson was not lost on other financially troubled firms with finance company affiliates.

Tighter Supply of Credit for Heavily Leveraged Firms

As described in chapter 2, the junk bond market seized up in late 1989. This seizure not only eliminated a source of leveraged finance but also increased the incentive for equity issuance, owing to the structure of outstanding junk bonds. The largest leveraged buyout, that of RJR-Nabisco, provided a telling example in the last chapter. Part of its debt consisted of so-called reset notes,[8] which promised to trade close to par owing to the periodic resetting of their interest rate. In late 1989, however, with junk bonds selling at a deep discount, the interest rate required at reset to enable them to trade at par threatened to climb so high that it would push the firm into default. The need to refinance these notes spurred RJR-Nabisco's issuance of equity in February and April 1991. In short, engineered into the stock of junk bonds were features that presumed the junk bond market's health; that market's malady forced leveraged companies to resort to unexpected equity issuance.

The tightening of bank credit in 1990 reinforced the crisis in the junk bond market. Banks with substantial claims on troubled real estate projects, as well as undercapitalized or downgraded banks, started to restrict commercial and industrial loans. In one of the earliest studies, Ronald Johnson examined commercial and industrial loan growth at banks grouped according to whether they were carrying a light or heavy burden of troubled real estate loans and whether their regulatory capital was ample or insufficient.[9] He found that commercial loan growth was greatly reduced at banks carrying a heavy burden of troubled real estate and somewhat reduced at banks operating on a particularly narrow margin of capital. Other studies, using different research designs to study the same data and using survey data instead of balance sheet data, reached similar conclusions.[10] For companies seeking loans, this tightening of bank credit meant wider spreads over banks' cost of funds, stiffer collateral requirements, and in some cases sheer difficulty in obtaining funds. Equity finance then became more attractive on grounds of price or availability.

5.2   U.S. Corporations' Return to Net Issuance of Equity

Through mergers and acquisitions, leveraged buyouts, and share re-purchases, U.S. nonfinancial corporations removed more equity from the stock market than they issued into it from 1984 to 1990 (figures 5.2 and 5.3). During that seven-year period, a net $640 billion dollars

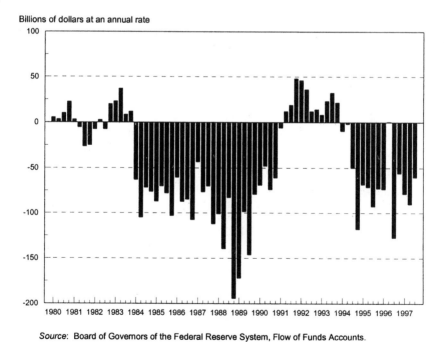

Billions of dollars at an annual rate

Source: Board of Governors of the Federal Reserve System, Flow of Funds Accounts.

Figure 5.2
Net equity issuance by U.S. nonfinancial corporations

Billions of dollars

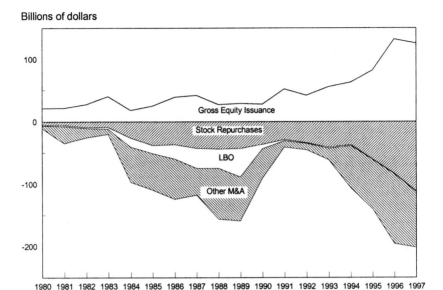

Source : Board of Governors of the Federal Reserve System, Flow of Funds Accounts.
Note: 1997 data are annualized first-half data.

Figure 5.3
Components of net equity issuance

of equity was retired. Net retirements peaked at an annual rate of almost $200 billion, or about 7.5 percent of the total outstanding equity,
in the fourth quarter of 1988.[11]

At the end of the Gulf War, this trend reversed. Positive net issuance
returned in the second quarter of 1991 and totaled $18 billion for the
year. In 1992, U.S. nonfinancial corporations accelerated their net issuance of equity to a $27 billion dollar annual rate. In 1993, with banks
offering depositors yields of 1 or 2 percent, equity investors put a net
of $22 billion into U.S. corporations.

These figures reflect not only a surge in gross new issuance but also
a decline in debt-financed mergers and acquisitions, including a virtual
disappearance of the leveraged buyout and much-reduced repurchasing of shares. We first consider briefly the falloff in equity retirement

through mergers and repurchases, then take a close look at the extent and nature of equity issuance.

U.S. Corporations' Slackened Retirement of Equity

In the early 1990s U.S. corporations chipped away at the overhang of debt built up in the late 1980s, and the pace of decapitalization through mergers and acquisitions slowed to rates observed before the break in behavior in 1984. Although share repurchases also fell back somewhat in the early 1990s, their persistence suggested their endurance as a means of managing leverage and putting cash into shareholders' hands.

Debt-Financed Mergers and Acquisitions

High share prices and tight credit for leveraged deals well into 1993 curbed mergers and acquisitions involving the replacement of equity with debt. Well-capitalized firms accounted for much of the remaining merger activity, and with share prices high, treasurers were more inclined to use share exchanges in mergers.

Leveraged buyouts: Between 1984 and 1990, more than 18,000 U.S. nonfinancial corporations underwent leveraged buyouts, and the total dollar value of these deals exceeded $250 billion (figure 2.5). Of this sum, approximately $165 billion in equity, or about two-thirds of the total, was replaced with debt or otherwise retired.[12] It may seem strange that LBOs did not retire more equity, given the high debt-to-equity ratios described in chapter 2. The key to understanding why LBOs did not retire even more equity, though, is that divisional LBOs need not result in any retirement of equity. That is, the cash paid by the LBO organizers to a corporate seller does not retire equity as does the payment of cash to the public shareholders in the LBO of an entire public firm. (The cash that a company raises by selling a division to an LBO partnership might be returned to shareholders through the cash acquisition of another firm or repurchases of shares, but then the equity retirement would be counted in these categories below.)

After the peak in 1989, LBO activity fell off sharply, the result at first of a collapse in the junk bond market and the tightening of bank credit, and then of high stock prices in relation to cash flow. Transaction volume in 1990 was comparable to that in 1984 and 1985, but the deals could be completed only if they involved less debt, so much less equity was retired in 1990 than in those earlier years. Leveraged buyouts went out of fashion in 1991 and showed only a slight recovery through the mid-1990s. Moreover, the deals still made were less leveraged than they were in the 1980s, probably for the same reasons that explain the fall in activity.[13] LBOs have retired only about $1–2 billion in equity per annum in the 1990s, so little that the Flow of Funds Section at the Federal Reserve Board has stopped keeping separate totals for equity so retired. Looking forward, institutional investors' willingness to commit funds to organizers of buyouts (figure 2.1) points to more LBOs—if stock prices falter.

Other Acquisitions

Leveraged buyouts are not the only means by which mergers and acquisitions can retire equity. When one company buys another whole company with borrowed money or cash, as when Philip Morris bought Kraft, the transaction retires equity as well. In either case, target shareholders receive cash and the acquiring company issues no shares. When a cash payment to shareholders is financed with a debt issue, clearly debt substitutes for equity. When cash is used, the buying firm's *net* debt rises, and with it its net interest obligation, in a manner similar to that in a debt-financed purchase.

In fact, the total dollar volume of non-LBO mergers and acquisitions of U.S. nonfinancial corporations exceeded $1.2 trillion between 1984 and 1990 (figure 5.4). Of this total, about $420 billion of equity, or roughly one-third, was retired.[14] Mergers and acquisitions other than LBOs fell off after 1989, though not as sharply as did LBOs. Like LBOs,

Billions of dollars

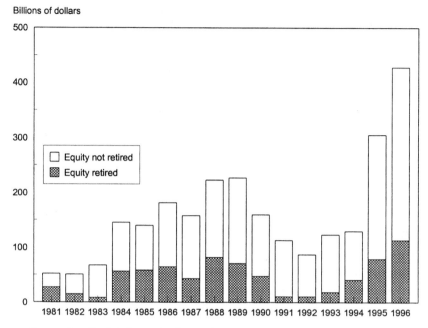

Sources*: Securities Data Corporation; Board of Governors of the Federal Reserve System; Mergers and Acquisitions Magazine.

Figure 5.4
Value of mergers and acquisitions and equity retired

however, other mergers and acquisitions came to rely less on debt for their financing. In 1991–92, equity retirements from non-LBO mergers and acquisitions were estimated at about $10 billion. Mergers and acquisitions activity revived in the mid-1990s and equity retired rose as well.

In 1994, television companies Viacom and QVC engaged in a bidding war for Paramount. As the bids rose, equity gave way to cash as a means of payment. In the event, two-thirds of the $11 billion deal was financed with debt as Viacom cashed out Paramount's shareholders to the tune of $6.6 billion. This deal raised the question, regarding both the law (that is, Delaware case law—see chapter 3) and the merger market, whether the pace and character of mergers and acquisitions might revert to those of the 1980s. In motivation if not in financing, the deal calls the merger wave of the 1960s to mind: The deal intended to achieve synergies between Viacom's strengths in cable and Paramount's in moviemaking. (The apparent absence of synergies between hardware and software in the takeovers by Matsushita and Sony of Hollywood studios has not dulled the enthusiasm in some quarters for uniting various strands of the entertainment business.) In general the pattern of financing of mergers and acquisitions in the 1990s leaves Viacom-Paramount the exception. In contrast to the 1980s, swaps of high-priced shares dominate. Chapter 9 provides an in-depth look at the mergers and acquisition market of the 1990s.

Stock Repurchases

Share repurchases took off in 1984 as a defense against takeovers but have since found a broader, more lasting role in corporate finance. To defend against a takeover, a firm would make a public tender offer to buy back a substantial portion of its equity, often a sixth or a fifth of the shares outstanding, at a premium above the market price. Sometimes defensive repurchases generated controversy because they took the form of so-called greenmail, a targeted repurchase from a troublesome shareholder at an above-market price—excluded shareholders did not take such transactions well. For instance, Goodyear Tire, stalked by Anglo-French financier Goldsmith, repurchased a large bloc of its own shares. In contrast to such one-off tender offers, firms can repurchase a small fraction of their shares through brokers at the market price as part of a preannounced program, often spanning more than one year. These mostly quiet market operations were encouraged by a 1982 SEC ruling that created a "safe harbor" for such programs. As a result, rules against price manipulation did not impede firms' ability to buy in their shares.

Repurchases jumped from less than $10 billion per year in 1983 to $35 billion to $45 billion in 1984–90 (figure 5.5). In the 1990s, however, defensive repurchases have become rare. The staying power of

Billions of dollars

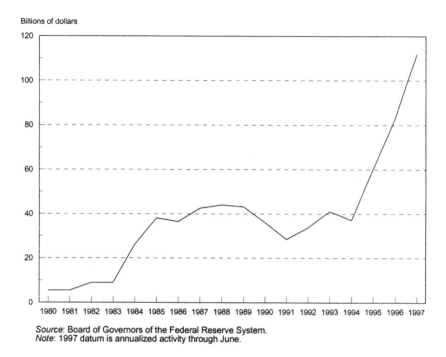

Source: Board of Governors of the Federal Reserve System.
Note: 1997 datum is annualized activity through June.

Figure 5.5
Share repurchases by U.S. nonfinancial corporations

repurchases is evident, though, from the smallish decline they showed in the 1990–91 recession, especially as compared to other sources of equity retirement (figure 5.3).

Repurchases tended to contribute to the rise in leverage in the 1980s. Repurchasing firms were generally larger firms showing asset growth no faster than the economy at large, both in the 1980s and in the 1990s. But in the 1980s, repurchasing companies were often no more profitable than those not repurchasing their shares. What is more, repurchases tended to be associated with rising debt in relation to assets in the 1980s.[15] Even in the 1980s, however, much repurchasing served less to raise leverage than to return cash to shareholders. Thus Exxon regularly spent billions per year repurchasing its shares from the mid-1980s—an alternative, perhaps, to the cash-financed acquisitions in the oil industry in the early 1980s. As noted in the last chapter, Philip Morris spent billions on repurchases, and thereby permitted shareholders to realize capital gains only if they wanted them. IBM did likewise until its mainframe business fell on hard times (although it has resumed repurchases in the 1990s). The Big Three automakers repurchased shares in the late 1980s only to find themselves in uncomfortable financial shape at the end of the decade (see below under "Loss-incurring and De-leveraging Firms as Issuers of Seasoned Public Offerings.").

Repurchases have graduated from their role as a defensive leveraging tool in the 1980s to that of a standard corporate financial choice in the 1990s. When General Electric, a firm enjoying a reputation for good management, decided to start repurchasing its shares in the early 1990s, it signaled that returning cash to shareholders was no sign of failure. In fact, repurchases in the 1990s typically were the policy of particularly profitable firms and were generally associated with falling leverage. Although they possess tax advantages over dividends, they appear to complement, rather than substitute for, the traditional means of returning cash to shareholders. Most firms repurchasing their shares also paid dividends and indeed showed respectable growth in dividend payments. Even critics of the leveraging business recognize repurchases as exerting a useful discipline on managements.[16] Thus, management examining alternative uses of cash, either new capital expenditure or an acquisition, have an alternative use that tends to help boost the share price.

U.S. Corporations' Record Flotation of New Equity

U.S. corporations took advantage of the relatively high valuation of current earnings in the stock market of the 1990s. U.S. nonfinancial corporations issued $45 billion of new equity in the public markets in 1991, $48 billion in 1992, and $59 billion in 1993. The rate of equity issuance appears to respond promptly to the market's valuation of a given stream of earnings (figure 5.1). In particular, surges in gross equity issuance coincided with high or rising price-earnings ratios in 1982–83, 1985–87 and 1991–93. Both seasoned public corporations and firms issuing public stock for the first time (commonly termed initial public offerings or IPOs) tend to time their offerings to receive the most favorable prices for their shares.

While rising valuations supported heavy stock issuance in this, as in previous cycles, forestalling financial distress emerged as a new motive in the early 1990s' stock issuance. Thus firms liable for about half the value of junk bonds outstanding in the early 1990s sold equity.[17] The spate of reverse LBO IPOs (IPOs that partly unwind the high leverage of earlier LBO deals) and the heavy volume of equity issues by loss-running and deleveraging firms set the 1991–93 cycle apart from previous cycles.

Ordinary IPOs

The IPO market sustained itself at white-hot temperatures in the early 1990s. Gross proceeds of initial public offerings reached $16.5 billion in 1991, $24 billion in 1992, and $42 billion in 1993. Ordinary IPOs (as opposed to reverse LBOs) accounted for $9 billion in 1991, $18 billion in 1992, and $34 billion in 1993 (figure 5.6).

IPOs are generally thought to provide growing corporations with new funds for expansion and to offer private investors, such as venture capitalists and top management, a means of liquidating their holdings. An analysis of IPOs, excluding reverse LBOs, by U.S. nonfinancial corporations in 1991 and the first half of 1992 confirms this conventional view (figure 5.7).[18] About 31 percent of gross proceeds were reportedly devoted to "general purposes," which includes new hiring and investment in new plant and equipment. About 28 percent of the offering value was "secondary," meaning that this fraction of the proceeds allowed existing shareholders to cash out and thus was not available to the offering firms. In addition, about 28 percent of the proceeds went toward the retirement of debt (deleveraging).

Billions of dollars

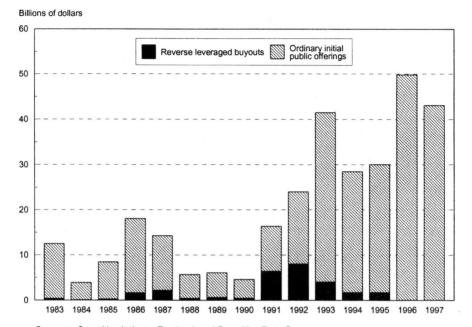

Sources : Securities Industry Factbook and Securities Data Company.
Note: Figures for reverse leveraged buyouts not available for 1996 and 1997.

Figure 5.6
Gross proceeds of initial public offerings and reverse leveraged buyouts

Reverse LBOs

Reverse LBOs are distinguished from ordinary IPOs by more than the issuer's financial history. The proceeds of the $7.5 billion raised in 1991 and the $5 billion raised in the first half of 1992 from reverse LBOs served very different purposes than the funds raised by ordinary IPOs. Only 2 percent of the funds generated by these reverse LBOs went to general purposes, whereas almost three-quarters went to pay down debt. These observations confirm that the primary motivation for IPOs by LBO companies is the retirement of debt taken on in going private.

Those taking companies private via LBOs probably did not initally intend to reverse them under the circumstances in which many such companies found themselves during the early 1990s. Earlier reverse

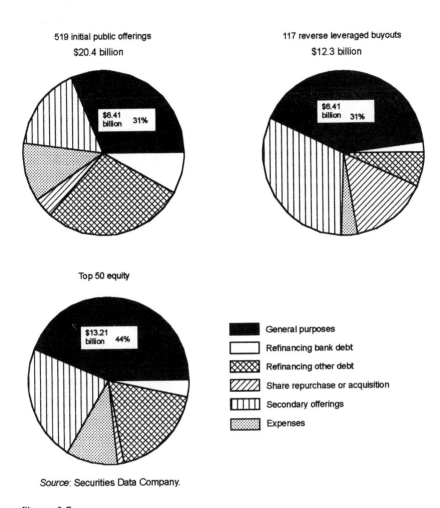

Source: Securities Data Company.

Figure 5.7
Uses of proceeds from public stock offerings, January 1991–June 1992

LBOs—such as that of Gibson Greeting Cards in the early 1980s—
cashed out the existing LBO partners. In the reverse LBOs of the early
1990s, by contrast, little of the proceeds was used to cash out existing
shareholders. In particular, only 16 percent of the proceeds went to
existing shareholders on average—much less than for regular Ipos or
for the more successful LBOs in the past. Difficulties in meeting debt
payments, in refinancing junk bonds, and in selling assets at planned
prices, combined with a window of opportunity in the stock market,
seem to have led to premature public equity issuance by the LBOs of
the early 1990s. We examine their performance in chapter 7.

Loss-Incurring and Deleveraging Firms as Issuers of Seasoned Public Offerings

The composition of seasoned equity issuance in the early 1990s also
had its unusual aspects. New offerings of stock by U.S. nonfinancial
firms that were already public totaled about $47 billion from January
1991 through June 1992.[19] Approximately two-thirds of the transaction value for this period was concentrated among the top fifty deals
(table 5.1). An analysis of those deals shows that approximately 44 percent of the gross proceeds went toward general corporate purposes,
much more than the 31 percent of IPO proceeds directed toward the
same end (figure 5.7). Nevertheless, this finding does not imply that
seasoned companies were investing more in plant and equipment than
did IPO companies.

The largest group of the seasoned firms offering equity in this period
consisted of firms losing money at the time of issuance, epitomized by
the automakers. In these cases, funds devoted to "general corporate
purposes" were probably used to make up for subpar cash flows, not
to finance expansion.

We argued above that firms running losses that have major finance
company subsidiaries faced particularly sharp incentives to sell equity
to protect their prime commercial paper ratings and thereby to maintain their access to commercial paper funding. We observe that no

fewer than five firms with sizable finance company subsidiaries appear on the list of loss-incurring stock issuers (table 5.1). To test the relationship between profitability and equity issuance among firms with major finance companies, we arranged industrial and commercial companies that owned any of the fifty largest finance companies by profitability and stock issuance (table 5.2).[20] No less than five-sixths of the value of equity sales among companies in this group is accounted for by firms suffering losses. By number, firms running losses were as likely as not to issue equity, whereas only one profitable firm among twelve did so.

Deleveraging was another force driving equity issuance. Among the top fifty seasoned issuers of stock, high-leverage companies—those with a debt-to-book equity ratio above 70 percent—represented the second largest group. These firms were undoing all the various modes of leveraging observed in the 1980s. Some swelled their debt by acquisitions (Time Warner), others were following up on well-received reverse LBOs (Safeway and Duracell), and still others were paying down debt incurred in massive and defensive repurchases (Goodyear).

Ordinary motives were represented by secondary issues and by issues for expansion. When stock prices are high in relation to earnings, founding families cash out, as at Reader's Digest. Or a rapidly growing firm such as Kmart comes to market for the wherewithal to open new stores and to hire more people. But stock issues by such firms accounted for less than a third of the top 50 issues.

This look at the top issuers of equity indicates that loss-incurring and quite leveraged firms bulked large on the list. In the next section, we take a look at which of the largest 600 firms issued equity and find that 1991 did introduce a change in the character of equity-issuing firms.

Equity Issuance, Leverage, and Profitability

To test the hypothesis that the boom in equity issuance in the early 1990s was part of a general deleveraging trend, we drew selected operating and balance sheet statistics for the largest U.S. nonfinancial

Table 5.1
Composition of top 50 equity issues by seasoned firms, January 1991 through June 1992

Ranking by size	Firm	Date	Type[1]	Amount (millions)
Losses				
2	General Motors	May 20, 1992		$2,150
3	Ford Motor	November 13, 1991	p	2,128
5	General Motors	February 11, 1992	p	1,350
7	Delta Air Lines	June 24, 1992	p	1,050
9	General Motors	December 5, 1991	p	1,000
11	General Motors	June 26, 1991	p	641
12	Westinghouse Electric[2]	June 3, 1992	p	559
13	Tenneco[2]	December 17, 1991	p	516
20	USX-Marathon Group[3]	January 14, 1992		461
21	Westinghouse Electric	May 9, 1991		451
24	Federated Department Stores	May 20, 1992		437
27	Delta Air Lines	April 8, 1991		416
30	AMR	January 30, 1992		371
33	Chrysler	October 2, 1991		349
38	Texas Instruments	September 11, 1991		306
43	Burlington Northern[2]	November 19, 1991		257
48	Viacom[2]	June 4, 1991		239
49	Texas Utilities	January 31, 1991		218
50	AMR	January 24, 1991		210
Subtotal				13,109

		Date		Amount
Deleveraging				
1	Time Warner	July 5, 1991		2,760
4	RJR-Nabisco	November 1, 1991	p	2,025
6	Sears Roebuck	February 20, 1992	p	1,075
10	Dillard Department Stores[4]	April 3, 1991		789
17	York International Corporation	March 26, 1992		478
18	International Paper	January 16, 1992		466
19	Goodyear Tire & Rubber	November 13, 1991		465
22	Freeport-McMoRan Resource	February 4, 1992		449
29	Black & Decker	April 24, 1992		398
32	IBP[4]	September 5, 1991		360
34	Sears Roebuck	November 1, 1991		325
35	Santa Fe Pacific[4]	June 4, 1992		319
39	Colgate-Palmolive	November 19, 1991	p	300
40	Safeway	April 9, 1991		287
41	Duracell International	October 21, 1991		276
45	The Vons Companies	May 30, 1991		251
Subtotal				11,023
Secondary/ Repurchase				
14	ConAgra	September 26, 1991		507
15	National Health Laboratories	April 30, 1991		501
16	Reader's Digest Association	June 10, 1991	p	499
23	Tandy	February 14, 1992		443

Table 5.1 (continued)

	Ranking by size	Firm	Date	Type[1]	Amount (millions)
	25	ConAgra	May 28, 1992	p	425
	28	Marlon Merrell Dow	May 12, 1992		410
	31	Long Island Lighting	May 21, 1992	p	363
	37	Reebok International	December 10, 1991		310
	42	National Health Laboratories	February 13, 1992		259
	47	Santa Fe Pacific	October 8, 1991		242
Subtotal					3,959
Expansion	8	Kmart	August 16, 1991	p	1,012
	26	Amerada Hess Corp	June 9, 1992		425
	36	Home Depot	April 12, 1991		315
	44	MGM Grand	July 16, 1991		256
	46	Browning-Ferris Industries	June 10, 1992		244
Subtotal					2,252
Total					30,343

Sources: Securities Data Company, Compustat, Reuter's Textline.
[1] Items in this column marked *p* were preferred issues.
[2] Debt retirement is listed as use of funds.
[3] Losses are at consolidated level.
[4] Parent company used funds to retire debt.

Table 5.2
Industrial firms with finance companies: Profitability and equity issuance in 1991–92

	Firms reporting a profit*	Firms reporting a loss*	
Firms not issuing stock	General Electric	IBM	
	ITT	Deere & Co.	
	AT&T	Caterpillar	
	Xerox	Greyhound	
	Philip Morris	Navistar	
	McDonnell Douglas		
	Pitney Bowes		
	J.C. Penney		
	Textron (Avco Financial Services)		
	Whirlpool		
	GATX		
Firms issuing stock (amount issued in parentheses)	Sears Roebuck & Co. ($1.4 billion)	General Motors	($6.9 billion)
		Ford	($2.1 billion)
		Chrysler	($0.3 billion)
		Westinghouse	($0.5 billion)
		Tenneco	($0.5 billion)
		(Total)	($10.3 billion)

* 1991 net income.
Sources: Wall Street Journal, New York Times, Securities Data Corporation.
Note: Computed chi-square statistic is 4.77 with one degree of freedom. A statistic in excess of 3.84 allows the rejection, with a probability of error less than .05, of the null hypothesis that the equity issuance of a firm and its profitability are independent factors. Equity issuance by General Motors includes $0.5 billion in Hughes Aircraft shares.

corporations from the Compustat database. For each year from 1988 through 1991, 600 firms with the largest assets were singled out. They were then broken up into three groups—the 50 with the largest positive net equity issuance, the 50 with the largest negative net equity issuance, and the remaining 500.

For each company and each year, six ratios were constructed. To measure each company's leverage, we calculated the ratios of interest to cash flow and the ratios of interest-bearing debt to the book and market values of equity. To measure each company's profitability, we took the ratios of net income to book and market values of equity. Finally, to measure the magnitude of investment in plant and equipment, we took the ratio of capital expenditures to assets.[21]

Table 5.3 presents the median of each statistic for each group in each year. For the two extreme groups of fifty each, we also present the p-value corresponding to the nonparametric Wilcoxon Rank Sum test of the null hypothesis that the ratio for the group of fifty is the same as the ratio for the middle group of 500 (table 5.3). The p-value is the probability that the medians are the same, given the observations. Consequently, p-values close to 0 indicate significant differences, with almost no probability that the medians are the same.

As the table shows, the largest net equity issuers did not differ consistently from other large firms in their profitability or debt burden from 1988 through 1990. In 1991, however, notable differences emerged: The large equity issuers were significantly less profitable and more highly leveraged by all measures. These observations lend strong support to the claim that equity issuance was concentrated among those companies that needed it most.

In 1991 a behavioral symmetry arose: Large equity issuers and re-purchasers were mirror opposites in profitability and debt burden. For each year from 1988 through 1991, those companies that were the largest net repurchasers of equity showed significantly more profitability as measured by the ratio of income to book equity and a significantly lighter debt burden as measured by the ratio of interest to cash flow.[22] In the latter two years, the large net repurchasers also showed a significantly lighter debt burden as measured by the ratios of debt to equity. Thus the public firms that bought back their own stock in greatest quantities could best afford to do so. Note also that net equity retirements by more-profitable and less-leveraged companies continued through 1991, even as a general deleveraging trend took hold in the rest of the economy.

Finally, large issuers and large repurchasers did not consistently differ from the average in the intensity of their capital expenditures. This finding lends support to the claim that equity financing in the early 1990s supported financial restructuring as opposed to investment.

5.3 Debt Restructuring

U.S. corporate treasurers reinforced the effect of their return to the equity markets in 1991–93 with a massive restructuring of their bond debt. Whereas the resumption of net equity issuance served to reduce the stock of debt and the annual interest charges on it, calling bonds yielding 9 or 10 percent and selling new bonds carrying yields of 6 or 7 percent served to reduce the costs of debt.

Bond calls accelerated as U.S. long-term interest rates dropped to their trough in October 1993 and cumulatively affected a remarkable fraction of the corporate bonds outstanding. Firms exercised their right to repurchase—at 102 or 101 or even at par of 100—high-coupon debt in the amount of $38 billion in 1991, $102 billion in 1992, and $130 billion in 1993 (table 5.4). Altogether the called-in bonds amounted to $270 billion, or more than a fifth of outstanding bonds.

The bond calls offered relief from interest burdens where the relief was most needed: junk bond issuers. Junk bond issuers called about 24 percent of the total in 1991–93, while investment grade issuers

Table 5.3
Leverage, profitability, and investment by magnitude of net equity issuance in the 600 largest U.S. nonfinancial corporations

		1988		1989		1990		1991	
Debt burden measures (ratios)									
Interest/ cash flow	50 largest net issuers	18.06%	(0.100)	20.96%	(0.802)	18.32%	(0.147)	49.89%	(0.000)
	Middle 500	23.44%		24.05%		25.72%		25.82%	
	50 largest net repurchasers	14.00%	(0.004)	14.52%	(0.002)	16.07%	(0.000)	10.26%	(0.000)
Interest-bearing debt/ book value of equity	50 largest net issuers	69.39%	(0.130)	89.80%	(0.448)	96.32%	(0.725)	154.68%	(0.000)
	Middle 500	83.11%		90.93%		93.19%		90.55%	
	50 largest net repurchasers	77.87%	(0.663)	74.54%	(0.090)	59.04%	(0.007)	49.31%	(0.000)
Interest-bearing debt/ market value of equity	50 largest net issuers	38.07%	(0.107)	46.08%	(0.871)	48.19%	(0.081)	86.02%	(0.012)
	Middle 500	59.96%		53.58%		73.96%		58.07%	
	50 largest net repurchasers	43.96%	(0.122)	35.37%	(0.030)	35.61%	(0.000)	19.02%	(0.000)
Profit measures									
Net income/ book value of equity	50 largest net issuers	14.22%	(0.486)	11.28%	(0.075)	12.98%	(0.278)	6.04%	(0.001)
	Middle 500	13.48%		13.10%		11.78%		10.33%	
	50 largest net repurchasers	18.00%	(0.000)	16.87%	(0.000)	15.04%	(0.000)	17.71%	(0.000)
Net income/ market value of equity	50 largest net issuers	7.30%	(0.183)	6.14%	(0.069)	5.94%	(0.029)	3.16%	(0.000)
	Middle 500	8.88%		7.11%		7.67%		5.14%	
	50 largest net repurchasers	9.04%	(0.432)	8.62%	(0.025)	7.47%	(0.880)	4.55%	(0.958)

Investment intensity								
Capital expenditures/ assets	50 largest net issuers	6.90%	(0.977)	7.54%	(0.875)	8.72%	(0.023)	5.78%	(0.162)
	Middle 500	6.29%		7.24%		6.96%		6.50%	
	50 largest net repurchasers	6.92%	(0.975)	7.00%	(0.699)	7.47%	(0.251)	7.02%	(0.451)

Source: Compustat.

Note: The table shows median values. The *p*-value of Wilcoxon Rank Sum tests for difference of medians are shown in parentheses. The *p*-value is the probability of observing a value different from the middle 500's median under the null hypothesis that the medians of the two groups are the same. Consequently, *p*-values close to zero indicate significant differences in median values.

Table 5.4
Bond calls by U.S. nonfinancial corporations, 1991–93

	1991	1992	1993	1991–93
Investment grade	28	78	100	206
Junk	10	24	30	64
Total	38	102	130	270
Total bonds outstanding of nonfinancial corporations	1,087	1,154	1,230	

Sources: Salomon Brothers, Merrill Lynch, First Boston, Board of Governors of the Federal Reserve System.
Note: Figures presented are in billions of dollars.

called less than a fifth of their outstanding bonds. This finding is consistent with the observation that almost all junk bonds were callable, whereas a declining fraction of investment grade bonds were (perhaps because bond buyers started charging issuers for the options once the Black-Scholes option pricing model diffused).[23] Moreover, as we shall demonstrate in the next chapter, the interest savings on junk bonds well exceeded those on investment grade issues. Whereas the collapse of the junk bond market in 1990 kept junk bond issuers from refinancing, when the market reopened in 1991, they made up for lost time.

Readers who attended suburban cocktail parties in early 1993 and who recall that mortgage refinancing terms and savings regularly came up in conversations may find the one-fifth to one-quarter rate of refinancing of corporate bonds unimpressive. Did home owners not refinance their liabilities to a greater extent than supposedly more sophisticated corporate treasurers? Home owners may well have been busier, but remember that just about all U.S. mortgages can be prepaid without (ex post) penalty, whereas only some corporate bonds allow the issuer to call them before maturity. The study remains to be done, but the authors would be willing to bet that few corporations leave outstanding for long bonds that can be refunded at lower cost.

Billions of dollars at an annual rate

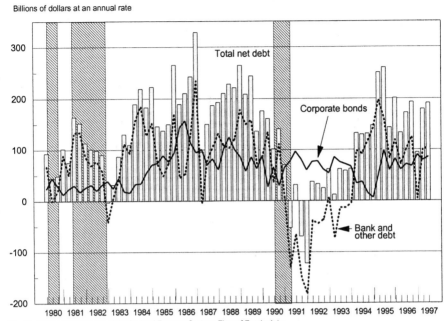

Figure 5.8
Net debt issuance by U.S. nonfinancial corporations

U.S. corporate treasurers accompanied their refinancing of their bonded debt with a restructuring of their overall debt toward bonds. Net bond issuance remained remarkably steady at the roughly $80 billion level characteristic of the late 1980s (figure 5.8). Treasurers maintained their (net) reliance on the bond market, but they reduced their reliance on bank loans and commercial paper sharply. Whereas in the 1980s, borrowing from banks had paced bond issuance, in the early 1990s corporate treasurers paid down their bank and commercial paper debt.[24]

In some ways, corporate treasurers shifted to the bond market in a manner fairly typical of their behavior in the latter part of a recession and the onset of a recovery. Weak investment and inventory

Billions of dollars at an annual rate   Percentage of par value

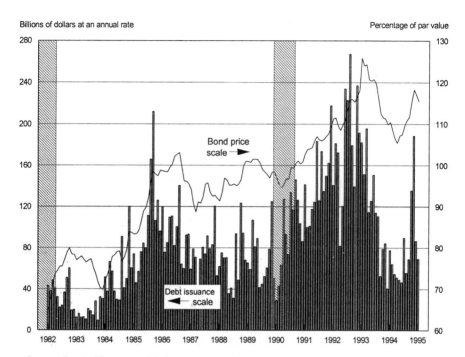

Sources: Board of Governors of the Federal Reserve System; Moody's.
Notes: Bond prices refer to hypothetical 15-year Baa bond with 10 percent coupon. The first data point in the figure is August 1982. Shaded areas indicate recession periods designated by the National Bureau of Economic Research.

Figure 5.9
Gross public debt issuance by U.S. nonfinancial corporations

accumulation reduce the need for outside funds while a rallying bond market affords the opportunity to extend maturities. But this cycle offered the added incentive of the tightening of bank credit standards, which induced treasurers to raise equity as well as to sell bonds to meet the demands of suddenly exigent bankers.

The steady growth of bonds outstanding should not obscure U.S. corporate treasurers' record flotation of bonds in the early 1990s. Just as bond calls accelerated into 1993, so too did gross issuance, exceeding the previous records for issuance set in 1986. The trend of bond prices tells the story (figure 5.9): Just as treasurers sell equity into surging markets (figure 5.1), so too they sell bonds into surging bond markets.

5.4 Market Timing by Corporate Treasurers

Eyeballing figures 5.1 and 5.9 provides prima facie evidence of market timing by corporate treasurers. One might argue that firms sell bonds into rallying markets because they can profitably call their bonds when interest rates are falling. But a recent study finds that for investment grade bond issuers, there is generally not a strong link between calling an old bond and issuing another.[25] Corporate treasurers apparently take their opportunities as they present themselves in the capital markets. Treasurers sell stocks and bonds when their prices are high. Anyone unburdened with any finance courses might respond to these observations with a shrug: What else are corporate treasurers paid to do?

But a more educated response would start with the recognition that there are two sides to any market. If the corporate treasurer is on the sell side, plenty of ring-wise investment managers are on the buy side. If there is market timing, the sell side would be systematically putting one over on the buy side. Besides, the educated response would continue, does market efficiency not preclude corporate treasurers' getting their timing right?

Quick, open a leading corporate finance textbook to its discussion of the stylized fact, ignored in many other texts, that corporate treasurers sell equity when its price is high:

Why should managers act in this way? Do they believe that equity is cheap when stock prices are historically high? As we pointed out in Chapter 13, in an efficient market buying or selling stock is a zero-NPV [net present value] transaction regardless of whether the price is historically high or historically low.

We don't know why managers tend to issue equity rather than debt after a rise in the stock price. It may reflect confused interpretations of price-earnings . . .

ratios. Some financial managers still think that a high P/E indicates a low rate of return demanded by stockholders and a good time to issue equity. . . . These managers defer issues when stock price is low, and their stored-up demand for fresh equity is released after prices rise.[26]

In other words, myth persistently grips corporate treasurers' behavior. So strong has been the grip of theory on students of corporate finance that only recently have they performed tests of whether corporate treasurers' timing is good. Starting with initial public offerings, then proceeding to seasoned equity issues, one line of research has found that investors in equity that is issued when issuance is heavy realize low returns in the years after issue. The following analysis comments on the textbook passage above: "Managers are right. It is not managers who are confused. It is investors who are systematically mispricing securities, and these managers are taking advantage of it."[27]

Some recent studies have attempted to provide explanations for this phenomenon.[28] Lee Crabbe, formerly an economist at the Board of Governors and now at Merrill Lynch, suggested to one of the authors the following interesting possibility: that the "buy side" investors are agents whose portfolios are marked to market and who are judged frequently against a benchmark, whereas the "sell side" issuers are not similarly constrained. Financial economists are hard pressed to provide a convincing account of market timing.

5.5 Conclusion

The timing in the business cycle of the 1991–93 surge in equity issuance had a precedent in 1982–83, but the who's who of firms selling shares in the early 1990s reflected the wave of corporate leveraging of the 1980s. Firms running losses, especially parent firms of major finance companies, assumed unusual prominence among equity issuers. And quite mature businesses that had endured leveraged buyouts showed up in the corporate nursery in the "initial" public offering market.

Corporate treasurers reinforced the strengthening of their balance sheets through equity issuance with a massive recasting of their debt. They called more than a fifth of their outstanding bonds and replaced them with paper substantially cheaper to service. And they reduced their reliance on banks not only in reaction to the availability of bond finance at favorable rates but also in reaction to banks' constriction of credit. In the next chapter we consider the relative contribution of equity issuance and bond refinancing, on the one hand, and lower short-term interest rates, on the other, to the decline in the burden of interest on corporate cash flows.

The timing of corporate treasurers' issuance of both stocks and bonds appears on its face very good. Treasurers flog more paper into investors' hands when the prices are high. This observation flatters the sell side but raises questions about those on the buy side who manage other people's money. In particular, in the early 1990s, the opportunities the strong equity market afforded could hardly have come at a more serendipitous time for firms that had leveraged up in the 1980s. But how did the investors in the reverse LBO initial public offerings fare? Chapter 7 addresses this question.

6   *Relieving the Burden of Interest on Cash Flow*

Critics of the substitution of debt for equity in the finances of U.S. corporations in the 1980s prophesied that a time would come when paying the interest on the new debts would prove very difficult. The legacy of the 1980s, according to these critics, would be sluggish growth that would lead to widespread bankruptcy and layoffs, unless short-term interest rates were allowed to fall to an extent that would risk an acceleration of inflation.[1]

Events appear to have put the lie to this prophecy. Did the success of corporate treasurers and their investment bankers in floating equity in unprecedented amounts, as described in the last chapter, not demonstrate an unappreciated recuperative power?

If this question is answered in the affirmative, the leveraging of the 1980s and deleveraging of the 1990s would show much symmetry. This chapter argues, however, that the equity issuance of the 1990s only reversed as small part of the retirement of equity in the 1980s.

Instead, the critics' prophecy mostly came true. We find that lower short-term rates were necessary to lighten the burden of interest payments on cash flow. As Federal Reserve Chairman Alan Greenspan testified to Congress, "We judged that low interest rates would be necessary for a time to overcome the efforts of a number of factors that were restraining economic expansion, including heavy debt burdens

Ratio

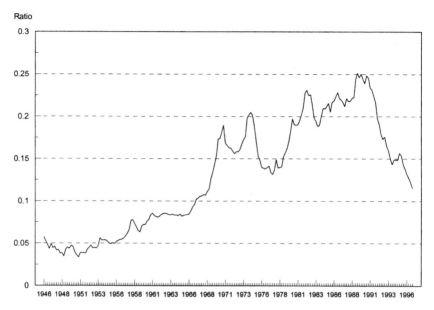

Source: Federal Reserve System, Flow of Funds Accounts.

Figure 6.1
Interest to cash flow ratio

of households and businesses and tighter credit policies of many lenders."[2] Spending a fair amount of time on airplanes, Greenspan termed
these restraining forces "head winds." The critics' prophecy erred,
however, in positing that the policy response to these head winds,
namely, interest rates low enough to make the legacy of debt bearable,
would push inflation upward.

This chapter puts the subject of this book into perspective. We take
the measure of U.S. corporate treasurers' operations in the stock and
bond markets in the early 1990s by examining their effect on the ratio
of interest payments to cash flow for the broad nonfinancial corporate sector. This ratio declined from about 24 percent to 19 percent
from the end of 1990 though the end of 1993 (figure 6.1). Again, the
interest–to–cash flow measure of leverage recommends itself because

of its power to predict corporate distress, on the one hand, and its effect on investment spending, on the other. Unlike measures of the stock of debt in relation to assets or equity, its measurement is fairly straightforward.

Further perspective is gained by juxtaposing the effect of corporate refinancing with that of the other two forces that worked to relieve the burden of interest on cash flow: lower short-term interest rates and cash flow growth. Both these forces did more than corporate refinancing to bring interest payments and cash flows into healthier balance.

This chapter's analysis establishes the fortuitous, almost providential, nature of the relief that U.S. corporations received in the 1990s from the interest burdens they took on in the 1980s. Certainly, corporate treasurers to some extent bailed themselves out of their high interest payments, but forces outside their control also bailed them out.

Leveraged firms and their bankers did not avoid a financial crisis "through sheer luck,"[3] however. The firms and their bankers acted with the kind of prudence that Keynes described, in which one makes the same mistake that everyone else is making. When lots of smart people blow it in the same way, head winds result.

The objection that it is not unusual for interest rates to fall during a recession carries some force. But recall that short-term rates began to fall in 1989, well before the recession set in at the time of the Gulf War. The strains in the junk bond market of September 1989, the collapse of the United Air Lines deal in October of that year, the defaults in the commercial paper market in the year's fourth quarter, the bankruptcy of Allied/Federated Department Stores in January 1990, and the bankruptcy of Drexel the next month all had as comforting backdrops the decline of short-term interest rates.

The first two sections of this chapter discuss, in ascending order of importance, the three forces bearing on the burden of interest payments on cash flows: refinancing, macroeconomic factors, and lower short-term interest rates. Because measuring the effects of refinancing takes a disproportionate fraction of this chapter, the finding of its modest impact is not purchased cut-rate. In recognition that the interest burden continued to fall in the mid- to late 1990s (figure 6.1), the third section of this chapter examines the causes and consequences of this ongoing decline. In the latter 1990s, cash flow growth and the trend to lower bond yields worked together actually to lower net interest payments. Understanding the decline of interest payments provides a key to understanding the growth of corporate earnings that helped propel the surge of stock prices after 1994.

6.1 Interest Savings from Corporate Refinancing

Our starting point is the five-percentage-point decline in the ratio of interest payments to cash flow from the end of 1990 through the end of 1993. Corporate treasurers contributed to this reduction by transacting in both the stock and bond markets. In the stock market, new equity issuance exceeded retirements through mergers, and acquisitions and repurchases and thereby directly reduced reliance on debt. In the bond market, corporate treasurers followed their investment bankers' advice to call outstanding bonds, some carrying double-digit coupons, in order to refinance them with freshly issued IOUs carrying single-digit coupons.

Offsetting the savings from stock issuance and bond calls, however, was the generally unnoted and, in the first instance, at least, costly extension of maturity on corporate debt. In some measure, this shift should be understood as a normal response to falling bond yields. In addition, some corporate treasurers worked to reduce their dependence on banks in the face of banks' tougher lending standards. The substitution of tens of billions of dollars of bond debt for bank and commercial paper debt when long-term interest rates stood at twice short-term interest rates cost firms a significant fraction of their interest savings from equity issuance and bond calls.

Interest Savings from Equity Issues

A company that issues equity reduces its net interest payment no matter how it disposes of the proceeds. If the company adds to its financial assets—say, by investing in U.S. Treasury paper—it stands to receive interest that will lower its *net* interest payments. If it uses the proceeds of an equity issue to pay down debt, its interest payments are reduced. If it uses the equity to finance expansion—buying plant and equipment, for instance—then its use of equity instead of debt holds down its interest costs. Abstracting from the difference between the interest rate received and paid, net interest payments fall (or do not rise) in any case.

U.S. corporations in 1991–93 sold new equity in excess of equity retired in acquisitions and through repurchases in the amount of $67 billion. With average interest rates of 8 percent at the beginning of the period and 7 percent at the end of the period, the interest saved came to about $5 billion per year by the end of 1993 (table 6.1).

These measures of the savings from equity issuance do not attempt to capture the full savings on debt that result from equity issuance. For instance, when an industrial firm that owns a finance company sells equity and succeeds in maintaining its access to the commercial paper market, it saves more interest payments than those associated with the debt directly replaced by equity. This "saving" does not actually show up in observed interest payments, however: Interest payments would have gone up without the equity issue. Our measure of the savings from junk bond calls, described below, does capture some effects of equity issuance, however. For instance, RJR-Nabisco could call its 17 percent bonds and refinance them at 10.5 percent in the spring of 1991 not so much because of generally lower rates but because of the firm's sale of equity.

Table 6.1
Contribution of refinancing and lower short-term rates to U.S. corporate interest savings in 1991–93

	1991	1992	1993	1991–93
Refinancing	*0.7*	*4.1*	*2.3*	*7.1*
Net equity issuance[1]	1.5	2.0	1.5	5.0
Fixed income	−0.8	2.1	0.8	2.1
Bond calls	0.8	1.6	2.0	4.4
Investment grade[2]	0.3	0.9	1.1	2.3
Junk[3]	0.5	0.7	0.9	2.1
Maturity extension[4]	−1.6	−0.5	−1.2	−2.3
Direct effect of lower short-term rates[5]	*13.2*	*12.4*	*3.1*	*28.7*

Sources: For net equity issuance—Board of Governors of the Federal Reserve System, Flow of Funds data for nonfarm nonfinancial corporate business; authors' estimates. For investment grade bond calls—Salomon Brothers Corporate Bond Research, "Notice of Corporate Bonds Called," Industrials' Utilities; Bloomberg data base. For junk bond calls—First Boston High Yield Research. For maturity extension—Board of Governors of the Federal Reserve System, Flow of Funds data. For effect of short-term rates—Board of Governors of the Federal Reserve System, Flow of Funds data and *Federal Reserve Bulletin.*
Note: Numbers represent billions of dollars at an annual rate.
[1] Estimates assume that $18 billion in equity replaced 8 percent debt in 1991, that $27 billion in equity replaced 7.5 percent debt in 1992, and that $21 billion in equity replaced 7 percent debt in 1993.
[2] Estimates are based on $28 billion called in 1991, $78 billion in 1992, and $100 billion in 1993.
[3] Estimates are based on $10 billion called in 1991, $24 billion in 1992, and $30 billion in 1993.
[4] We estimate that $41 billion in net fixed-rate debt replaced floating-rate debt in 1991, $9 billion net floating-rate debt replaced fixed-rate debt in 1992, and $26 billion net fixed-rate debt replaced floating-rate debt in 1993.
[5] Estimates assume that one-fourth of net short-term debt is repriced each quarter.

Savings from Bond Calls

The convergence of two trends encouraged bond calls over the years 1991–93: lower interest rates and less erosion of corporations' credit standing.[4] The latter trend was a consequence of lower interest rates and net equity issuance as well as an underlying recovery of economic activity.

We start with estimates that U.S. corporations called more than $200 billion in investment grade bonds and more than $60 billion in (face value of) junk bonds in 1991–93 (table 5.4). We base our calculation of interest savings on samples of investment grade bonds and junk bonds that were called. We find that the pace at which U.S. nonfinancial corporations called and refinanced their bonds saved $1.6 billion a year in interest payments.

The savings from calls of investment grade bonds stemmed from strong refinancing activity and relatively modest average savings. A sample of 153 issues called between January and May 1992 with an aggregate face value of $10.3 billion[5] showed a weighted average original coupon of 9.3 percent, call price of $102, and a refinancing cost of 8.04 percent. These averages indicate interest savings of $1.10 per $100 of face amount called: the difference between the original coupon (9.3) and new coupon scaled by the call price premium (8.04 times 102 divided by 100). This finding suggests that the annual interest savings on $28 billion of called investment grade bonds in 1991, $78 billion in 1992 and $100 billion in 1993 were $0.3 billion, $0.9 billion and $1.1 billion, respectively. Our calculation is biased on the side of greater savings because it neglects the higher principal repayment of refinancing implied by the call price premium.[6]

The savings from junk bond calls stemmed from more modest refinancing activity and very considerable average savings. Companies like RJR Nabisco, which sold new equity to improve its credit standing so as to refinance its debt at lower interest charges, derived significant benefits from refinancing. Thus, savings on junk bond calls arose from credit upgrades as well as lower interest rates for a borrower of a given credit[7]. A sample of $3.7 billion junk bonds called in 1991[8] showed a weighted average original coupon of 15.1 percent, a call price of $101.8 per $100 of face amount, and a refinancing coupon of 10.1 percent (table 6.2). Taking the difference between the original coupon (15.1) and the new coupon scaled by the call price premium (10.1 times 101.8 divided by 100) yields an interest savings of $4.78 per $100 of face amount called. This finding translates into annual interest savings of $0.5 billion on $10 billion in called junk bonds in 1991. Junk bond calls accelerated in 1992 but proved on average less lucrative. First Boston High Yield Research reports that in the first half of 1992, the average coupon on new issues replacing those that were called or tendered was about 300 basis points lower.[9] We estimate therefore that the $24 billion called in 1992 saved $0.7 billion in annual interest charges. For 1993, we estimate a further saving of 300 basis points on the $30 billion called, for savings of $0.9 billion.

Benjamin Cohen[10] has posed the question of why savings from bond calls are so much larger for junk bond issuers than for well-rated corporations. One way of looking at the question is to recognize that junk bond issuers have less flexibility than investment grade issuers in managing their liabilities. For the latter, a bond can be called when it is profitable to do so, without regard for whether the time is judged right for a new bond issue. A junk bond issuer has more limited access to cash or short-term debt to bridge a bond call and a new issue. Moreover, rating agencies can take a dim view of replacing long-term liabilities with short-term liabilities, and loan contracts with banks may prohibit such risk taking.

Clearly another factor is at work: underwriting costs. We noted in chapter 2 that in 1985 Drexel earned more from underwriting bonds than market leaders Salomon Brothers, First Boston, and Goldman Sachs because Drexel underwrote more lucrative junk bonds while its competitors racked up more dollar volume in less remunerative investment grade bonds. Higher underwriting fees on junk bonds all by themselves would tend to slow junk bond issuers from calling their paper. Well-rated firms pay no more than 0.5 percent of the value of a bond to the underwriters. This fee works out to about 10 basis points per year on a 10-year bond, so the refinancing savings have to exceed 10 basis points just to make the game worth the candle. Junk bond underwriting spreads amount to about 3 percent, by contrast.[11] Thus a new 10-year bond must save an issuer some 60 basis points per year simply to recover the up-front costs of flotation. Moreover, these fees vary positively with maturity.

The (Immediately) Costly Extension of Debt Maturities

A large offset to these interest savings arose from the normal cyclical funding of commercial paper and bank debt with bond debt in the face of an extremely steep yield curve. Of course, if long-term interest rates simply represent the average of short-term rates over the relevant period, the extra interest paid now simply saves higher interest payments down the road. However, the power of long-term rates to predict future short-term rates has proven weak in the past. Corporate treasurers and rating agencies view securing long-term, fixed-rate financing as insurance against swings in short-term interest rates. Such financing, however, introduces the risk that a drop in inflation will leave the firm saddled with a very high real interest rate.

In keeping with our focus on net interest payments, we consider corporate liabilities net of financial assets. At the end of 1990, U.S. nonfinancial corporations had $1,240 billion in fixed-rate debt (net of fixed-rate assets) and $677 billion in net floating-rate debt outstanding.[12] At the end of 1991, these outstandings were about $1,287 billion and $594 billion, respectively. In 1991, corporations reduced the ratio of net floating-rate debt to total debt from 35.3 percent to 31.6 percent, partly by shifting about $47 billion worth of that debt from a floating

Table 6.2
Interest savings on junk bonds called in 1991

Company	Month	Coupon (percent)	Amount (millions of dollars)	Premium over par	New coupon (percent)	Dollar savings (millions of dollars)	Savings (percent)
Century Communications	Oct.	12.750	200	101.00	11.875	1.5	0.76
Ferrellgas Inc.	Dec.	13.375	61	106.69	11.375	0.8	1.24
Ferrellgas Inc.	Dec.	12.750	149	104.78	11.375	1.2	0.83
FMC	Jun.	12.500	150	106.25	7.500	6.8	4.53
Illinois Central	Aug.	15.500	150	100.00	10.210	7.9	5.29
Kelsey Hayes	Nov.	13.250	124	100.00	11.375	2.3	1.88
Maxxam Group	Nov.	13.625	140	100.00	12.750	1.2	0.88
Owens-Corning Fiberglass*	Dec.	15.000	208	100.00	7.400	15.8	7.60
Playtex Apparel	Dec.	14.000	182	110.89	11.625	2.0	1.11
RJR Holdings Group	Jun.	17.000	1,500	100.00	10.500	97.5	6.50
Safeway Stores**	Nov.	14.500	420	102.90	7.930	26.6	6.34
Safeway Stores	Dec.	11.750	250	104.61	9.650	4.1	1.66
Viacom Inc.	Aug.–Oct.	15.500	200	100.00	10.250	10.5	5.25
Total/weighted average		15.081	3,734	101.77	10.127	178.4	4.78

Sources: Reuter's *Textline*; Moody's; First Boston *High Yield Handbook*; Euromoney Loanware; *International Financing Review.*

Note: Amount column indicates the amount of the call that could be attributed to a recent debt issue of bank loan. Percentage savings are calculated as the difference between the old coupon rate and the new coupon rate adjusted upwards by the ratio of the call price to 100. Dollar savings are the percentage savings multiplied by the amount.

* Bond was refinanced with bank loan. New coupon assumed spread of 75 basis points over LIBOR on the loan converted into equivalent fixed rate using the mid-December 1991 five-year interest rate swap spread. Seventy-five basis points was the average spread over LIBOR on syndicated loans for a sample of Baa3-rated borrowers in 1991.

** Bond was refinanced with bank loan, as in the case of Owens-Corning. New coupon assumed a spread of 83 basis points converted into equivalent fixed rate using a seven-year swap spread to match the maturity of the Safeway syndicated loan. Eighty-three basis points was the average spread over LIBOR for a sample of Ba2- and Ba3-rated borrowers in 1991.

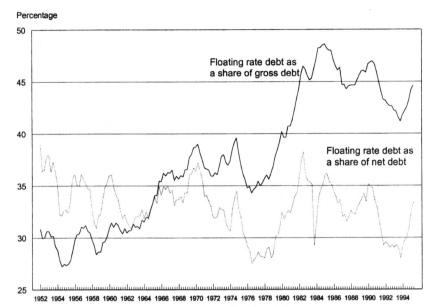

Percentage

Source: Board of Governors of the Federal Reserve System, Flow of Funds data.
Notes: Floating rate debt includes bank loans, finance company loans, and commercial paper. Net floating rate debt is floating rate debt minus all liquid assets except currency, checkable deposits, government securities, and tax-exempt securities. Net debt is gross debt minus all liquid assets except currency and checkable deposits.

Figure 6.2
Ratio of floating debt to total debt for U.S. nonfinancial corporations

rate to a fixed rate and partly by paying off loans with internal cash flows. This behavior is consistent with the historical relationship between maturity shifts and changes in interest rates. During periods of declining interest rates, corporations tend to shift from floating- to fixed-rate debt to lock in favorable interest rates. Such moves occurred in 1970–71, 1975–76, and 1985–87. Conversely, when interest rates rise, as they did in 1973–75, 1979–81, and 1983–84, corporations tend to shift into floating-rate debt to avoid locking in unfavorable interest rates (figure 6.2).

As U.S. nonfinancial corporations shifted unevenly out of floating-rate debt and into fixed-rate debt in 1991–93, they undertook higher interest obligations. Although this shift may have promised the beneficial effect of locking in lower long-term rates, the immediate effect was to increase interest expense. The slope of the corporate yield curve, defined as the difference between the commercial paper rate and the yield on Baa-rated bonds, was about four percentage points. Therefore, the maturity shift that occurred increased annualized interest expense an estimated $1.6 billion in 1991 and $1.2 billion in 1993, whereas a mild shortening of maturities in 1992 produced $0.5 billion in savings.

In summary, corporate treasurers' operations in the debt markets in the early 1990s served not only to pare interest payments through bond calls but also to lock in higher payments through maturity extension. Our calculation of the net cash flow benefits of these operations attempts to capture only immediate, not ultimate, effects. In the event, corporate treasurers who had locked in their debt costs in 1993 patted themselves on the back as short- and long-term interest rates rose sharply in 1994. In 1995, however, short-term rates stabilized and long-term rates resumed their fall. By the late 1990s, with inflation falling to 2 percent and long-term bond yields at generational lows, some of the extension of maturities in the early 1990s looked, with twenty-twenty hindsight, premature.

6.2 Short-Term Interest Rates and the Interest Burden

Financial restructuring contributed to reducing U.S. nonfinancial corporations' interest burden, but the decline in short-term interest rates from 1989 to 1993 unburdened corporate cash flows quite apart from any refinancing. This influence took effect as interest charges on floating-rate debt were reset to prevailing market rates on a monthly, quarterly, semiannual, or annual basis. To compare the effects of refinancing activity and lower short-term interest rates, we need to quantify the relation of lower rates to corporate net interest payments.

Lower Interest Payments on Short-Term and Floating-Rate Debt

If almost all floating-rate assets and liabilities are reset at least once a year, then the savings from lower rates should be roughly equal to the product of the change in interest rates and the dollar amount of net floating-rate debt outstanding. We employ both simple arithmetic and regression analysis to estimate interest savings.

If we assume that one-fourth of net short-term debt is repriced each quarter, the savings owing to lower short-term rates (measured by the change in the three-month commercial paper rate) amounted to $28.7 billion in 1991–93 (table 6.1). Regression analysis provides some ground for the assumption that changes in short-term rates transmit themselves to net interest payments fairly smoothly over four quarters (see box 6.1).

Comparing Lower Short-Term Interest Rates and Corporate Refinancing

Summing the effects of corporate activity in the stock market and in the debt markets shows the net impact of corporate refinancing (table 6.1). In 1991, treasurers extended the maturity on so much debt while facing such a steep yield curve that the effects of the net equity issuance and bond calls were almost nullified. In 1992, with some shortening of maturities, there was no offset to the relief from $27 billion in net equity issuance and $100 billion in bond calls. As a result, refinancing trimmed more than $4 billion off of annual interest payments. In 1993, although bond calls accelerated, the pace of net equity issuance slackened and the costly extension of maturities resumed. The savings from refinancing slipped to $2.3 billion.

Our calculations suggest that in 1991–93 lower short-term interest rates played a preponderant role in lowering corporate interest payments. The immediate relief that lower rates afforded U.S. nonfinancial firms in lightening the interest burden in 1991–93 was four

Box 6.1
Regression Analysis of the Pass-Through of Short-Term Interest Rates to Corporate Interest Payments

Table 6.3 reports the results of our regression analysis. The product of the quarterly change in the three-month commercial paper rate and the lagged quarter-end level of net floating-rate debt predicts fairly accurately the change in seasonally adjusted annualized net interest payments. As the table shows, the estimated relationship is significant both contemporaneously and lagged three quarters.[1] Moreover, the null hypothesis that the four coefficients on quarterly lags add up to 1 can be accepted at any reasonable level. In other words, a change in short-term rates exerts its full impact within a year. Finally, the null hypothesis that the transmission of short-term market interest rates to corporate interest payment occurs smoothly (one-quarter per quarter) can be accepted.

The regression also confirms the linkage of net debt levels and net interest payments. A proxy for the change in net interest payments resulting from increasing levels of debt is computed as the sum of two products: (1) the change in net floating-rate debt outstanding multiplied by the short-term interest rate, plus (2) the change in net fixed-rate debt outstanding multiplied by the long-term interest rate. Absent any changes in interest rates, net interest payments should increase by an amount roughly equal to this sum. Consistent with this simple hypothesis, the expected coefficient value for this variable is 1. As the table shows, the data appear to confirm this hypothesis.[2]

To isolate the effect of changes in interest rates, we repeated the regression, this time holding the value of the coefficient on the leveraging variable at 1 (see table). Because the results were similar to those for the unconstrained regression, the coefficients from this second regression were used to estimate the effects of changes in short-term interest rates on aggregate interest expense.

Notes

1. The product using the first and third lags is significant at the 0.5 percent level (the critical value [c.v.] for the two-sided t-test is 2.70), the product using the third lag is significant at the 2 percent level (c.v. = 2.42), and the contemporaneous product is significant at the 2.5 percent level (c.v. = 2.02).
2. The intercept in the regression was forced to be 0 on the assumption that no factor other than the accumulation of debt and changes in interest rates systematically influences the level of interest payments. The data do not challenge this assumption. The intercept in the unconstrained regression (not reported) is not significantly different from 0.

Table 6.3
Effects of short-term interest rates and debt accumulation on interest payments by U.S. nonfinancial corporations: Results of regression analysis

	Change in commercial paper rate times floating-rate debt				Change in net debt times interest rate	Sum of commercial paper coefficients
	No lag	One-quarter lag	Two-quarter lag	Three-quarter lag		
Coefficient	0.205	0.338	0.27	0.358	0.839	1.175
(*t*-statistic HO: $x = 0$)	(1.88)	(3.17)	(2.65)	(3.63)	(6.86)	—
(*t*-statistic HO: $x = 1$)	—	—	—	—	(1.31)	—
(*t*-statistic HO: $x = .25$)	(0.42)	(0.83)	(0.24)	(1.09)	—	(0.84)
R^2	0.604					
Adjusted R^2	0.564					
Observations	44					
Degrees of freedom	39					
Durbin-Watson	1.98					

Note: Dependent variable: Change in seasonally adjusted annualized net interest payments (billions of dollars at an annual rate). Independent variables: Change in net floating-rate debt times the three-month commercial paper rate plus the change in net fixed-rate debt times the corporate bond yield (billions of dollars); intercept suppressed.

	Change in commercial paper rate times floating-rate debt				Change in net debt times interest rate	Sum of commercial paper coefficients
	No lag	One-quarter lag	Two-quarter lag	Three-quarter lag		
Coefficient	0.219	0.346	0.265	0.365	held at 1	1.194
(t-statistic HO: $x = 0$)	(2.03)	(3.29)	(2.58)	(3.76)	—	—
(t-statistic HO: $x = 1$)	—	—	—	—	—	(0.94)
(t-statistic HO: $x = .25$)	(0.29)	(0.91)	(0.15)	(1.18)	—	—
R^2	0.587					
Adjusted R^2	0.556					
Observations	44					
Degrees of freedom	40					
Durbin-Watson	2.05					

Note: Independent variable: Change in quarterly average three-month commercial paper rate times net floating-rate debt outstanding (billions of dollars).

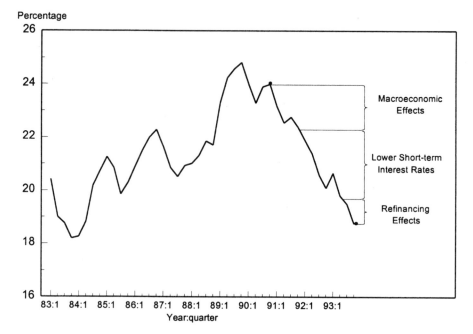

Source: U.S. Department of Commerce, Bureau of Economic Analysis; authors' estimates.

Figure 6.3
Decline in the ratio of interest to cash flow

times the relief that refinancing provided: $28.7 billion as against $7 billion.

Another way to juxtapose the two effects is to draw an equivalence between a (permanent) change in short-term interest rates and the effect of refinancing activity at its 1992 pace. Each year at that pace provided as much relief to corporate cash flows as a permanent cut of 40 basis points in short-term corporate rates.

Decomposing the total change in the aggregate ratio of interest payments to cash flow in the twelve quarters from the end of 1990 through the end of 1993 (figure 6.3 and box 6.2) reveals the relative effectiveness of lower interest rates and corporate refinancing in unburdening corporate cash flow. This ratio ratcheted up to a record vulnerability before the start of the last recession as firms replaced equity with debt. By the end of 1990, the ratio had reached 24.25 percent, a level indicating that in aggregate, cash flow covered interest payments only four times over. The apparently low level of this ratio (or the apparently comfortable interest cover) did not by itself fully reflect corporate finances' fragile state, because it must be understood as an average that includes many firms barely able to cover their interest payments. By the end of 1993, this ratio had fallen 5.25 percentage points to 19 percent.

Three forces worked together to bring down this ratio: macroeconomic factors, lower short-term interest rates, and corporate refinancing (figure 6.3). Macroeconomic factors included the growth of cash flow and the need for outside finance. As economic recovery gained momentum over 1991–93, the cash flow wherewithal to meet interest payments grew and the ratio of interest payments to cash flow declined. At times offsetting the growth of cash flow, however, was the need for outside finance, or the gap between retained earnings and depreciation charges, on the one hand, and investment spending, on the other. Filling this gap with new debt would tend to raise interest payments. Taken together, these macroeconomic factors eased the burden of interest payments on cash flows by about 1.5 percent (figure 6.3).

Lower short-term rates did the heavy lifting. They reduced the fraction of cash flow claimed by interest charges by about 2.5 percentage points through the end of 1993.

The net effects of refinancing activity accounted for a surprisingly small share of the decline shown in figure 6.3. Equity issuance and bond calls alone would have driven the ratio down by about another 1.5 percentage points. But the extension of maturities from short-term debt to higher-cost long-term debt took a sizable bite out of the savings from equity issuance and bond calls. Thus, refinancing pared little more than a percent off of the burden of interest on cash flows.

Box 6.2
The Changing Burden of Interest on Cash Flow

This box defines the ratio of interest to cash flow and decomposes its decline from the end of 1990 through the fourth quarter of 1993. This ratio fell 5.25 percentage points, from 24.25 percent to 19 percent, in the eleven quarters. The exercise is fairly straightforward in concept, although it requires some baseline from which to measure the contribution of equity finance. Our approach here is to take zero net equity finance as the baseline. If, on average, U.S. corporations have had a modest resort to equity finance, over time our baseline may overstate the size of corporate refinancing somewhat.

Defining the Ratio of Interest to Cash Flow

The ratio of interest to cash flow is constructed to indicate the burden of net interest payments on cash flows. This measure has been shown to predict corporate distress and bankruptcy.

The numerator is net interest payments of nonfinancial corporate business as reported in the National Income and Product Accounts. We exclude imputed net interest receipts associated with non-interest-bearing deposits from total interest receipts on the ground that they are noncash, in-kind receipts that cannot be used to avert default.

The denominator, also drawn from National Income and Product Accounts data, is earnings before interest, taxes, and depreciation (EBITD). These earnings are operating cash flows available to pay interest. It is important that net interest payments be included in the denominator so as not to confound the effect of economic growth on cash flows with the effect of lower short-term rates on interest payments. Consider a company with EBITD of 5 and net interest payments of 2 falling to 1. We would measure the ratio of interest to cash flow as 2:5 falling to 1:5. If net interest payments are excluded from cash flow, however, the ratio would be measured as 2:3 falling to 1:4, with cash flows apparently rising by a third.

Decomposing the Change in the Ratio of Interest to Cash Flow

The ratio of interest to cash flow can be decomposed into three partial effects: the effect of lower interest rates (i), the effect of lower debt (D), and the effect of stronger cash flows (CF) (see figure 6.4). The effect of lower interest rates it-

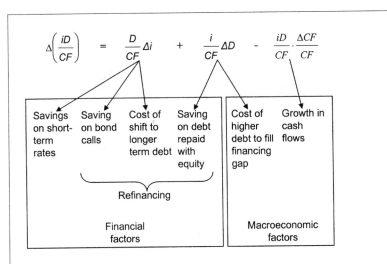

Figure 6.4
The changing burden of interest on cash flow

self is a compound of the effect of lower short-term rates, lower long-term rates on called or maturing bonds, and a shift in the mix of floating- and fixed-rate debt. The effect of lower debt may be thought of as a compound of debt growth (under the assumption that external financing exclusively takes the form of debt) and the separate effect of any net equity issuance.

It is useful to regroup terms into the economic forces bearing on the ratio. The two macroeconomic factors affecting the ratio are economic growth's influence on cash flow and the financing gap's influence on the need for external debt financing. The two financial factors are the direct impact of lower short-term interest rates on net floating-rate debt and the effect of corporate financial restructuring on the stock of net debt, the rates on long-term debt, and the composition of debt.

6.3 The Falling Interest Burden and Profit Growth

The refinancing of corporate debt did not come to an end in 1993, but its character changed markedly. In the second phase of corporate refinancing in the 1990s, which started in 1994, the action centered on the bond market. As we have demonstrated, the Federal Reserve played the dominant role in reducing the burden of debt in 1990–93, but its direct role would be limited—and for a time unhelpful—from the end of 1993. Starting in February 1994, the Federal Reserve raised short-term interest rates, doubling them from 3 percent to 6 percent. Similarly, the net equity issuance that had helped in the early 1990s returned to equity retirement in 1994 as the mergers and acquisitions market heated up again (see chapter 9). If the ready availability of equity finance came to the timely rescue of corporations suffering under the debt piled up by the leveraging business in the early 1990s, in the mid- to late 1990s, the bond market returned the favor to the equity market. As corporate treasurers retired maturing bonds and sold new bonds with lower interest coupons, corporations' overall interest payments fell. The funds that had been paid out to bondholders flowed instead into corporate earnings. Earnings growth thus reflected not only good underlying cash flow growth but also the declining burden of interest payments on corporate cash flows, which made a substantial, and not generally recognized, contribution to the growth of corporate earnings and thus to stock market gains.

A long-term view offers a useful perspective. Essentially, U.S. corporations' reliance on bonds means that today's cost of debt has echoes of bond yields from the last five, ten, and even thirty years. Looking across several business cycles, long-term dollar yields showed a trend rise into the early 1980s and have shown a trend decline ever since. These yields, in turn, embody investors' outlook on inflation. This outlook took a while to catch on to the dangerously loose policy in the 1970s and then gave only grudging and slow recognition to the Federal Reserve's success in lowering inflation in the 1980s and 1990s. Based on these broad swings in inflation and bond yields alone, one would expect a long trend upward in the corporate interest burden into the 1980s and a broad decline since.

Of course, the leveraging business in the 1980s intervened to offset and even for a time reverse the underlying trend toward a lower interest burden. Then as we have seen, the Federal Reserve response to the head winds created by the demise of the leveraging business resulted in an accelerated decline in the interest burden only somewhat related to the decline of bond yields. After these perturbations of the long-term trend, however, the underlying trend decline in the interest burden reasserted itself in the 1990s.

Thus, all through the 1990s, maturing bonds bearing double-digit yields or yields in the high single digits could be replaced with bonds offering lower coupons. This gradual process of shaving interest cost off of the $1.5 trillion stock of bond debt has lowered corporate interest payments. The spate of bond calls in the early 1990s only accelerated and drew attention to an underlying process that continued to work well into the late 1990s.

Understanding this process of quiet debt restructuring is key to understanding the stock market's performance in the 1990s. Above we argued that the ready availability of equity finance prevented a cascade of defaults in the early 1990s. The bond market paid the stock market back in the course of the 1990s. What the coupon-clipping rentier has lost, the residual claimant, the capitalist, has gained. Or to put the same point in more modern terms, the same decline of yields that left bond mutual funds an uninspiring investment has helped power the growth of corporate earnings that have in turn underpinned the performance and growth of equity mutual funds.

Lower interest costs in the 1990s have allowed earnings to grow faster than cash flow. Taking the trough of the recession in 1991 as a base of 100, the net interest payments of the U.S. nonfinancial corporate sector collapsed to 65 by 1997 (figure 6.5). This reduction of the interest burden helped pretax profits soar over the same period from 100 to 235, a spectacular performance that has led to much discussion of a new age of the U.S. economy. The underlying cash flow growth, however, looks more down to earth, with a 1997 reading of about 150.

How important to the equity market performance of the 1990s was the lighter debt service? An answer necessarily depends on a hypothetical baseline, also known as a counterfactual, or in science

Index: 1991:1 = 100

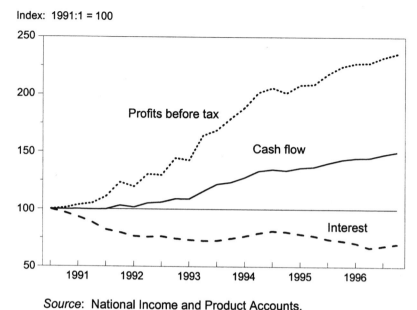

Source: National Income and Product Accounts.

Figure 6.5
Profits before tax, cash flow, and interest payments

fiction, a parallel universe. A straightforward baseline for comparison is a straight line: What would have happened to corporate profits if everything had stayed the same except that net interest payments remained stuck at their 1991 level? Figure 6.6 answers this question. After-tax profits would have grown noticeably less quickly without the boost of falling net interest payments. A slightly more sophisticated approach is to ask what would have happened if the blended average (net) interest rate on corporate debt had not fallen in the 1990s. This assumption implies rising net interest payments once the substitution of equity for debt ceased in 1993 and corporations began once again to retire their equity thereafter. Accordingly, the rise of after-tax profits would have generally been slower under this scenario.[13]

At this stage, most readers may be nodding, "Yes, I knew that lower long-term interest rates are good for the stock market because a given

Index: 1991:1 = 100

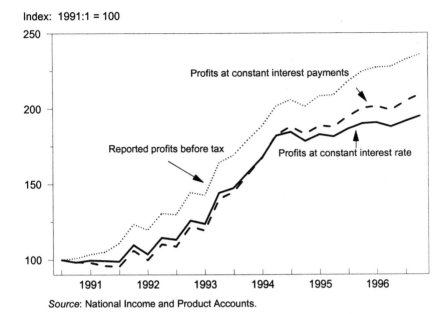

Source: National Income and Product Accounts.

Figure 6.6
Profits at constant interest

stream of earnings is discounted at a higher rate. Now you are telling me that, in addition, lower rates mean higher earnings." So conclude Jason Benderly and John Duca, who want to demonstrate that corporate earnings growth is not derived from some unusual compression of the labor share of income.[14]

The truth of the matter is at once more subtle and less fundamentally supportive of the rise in U.S. equity prices. Much of the decline in interest rates in the 1990s reflects lower nominal interest rates but not lower real interest rates. The key insight is that as lower inflation feeds through to lower interest costs, it flatters the growth of earnings.

To see this, consider a single company with $100 million of debt and $100 million of equity, with cash flow of $16 million. (Let's neglect depreciation and taxes for simplicity.) If inflation is 4 percent, and interest rates are 7 percent, then $7 million of the cash flow is paid out to bondholders and $9 million represents profits. Now let inflation fall to 2 percent and interest rates to 5 percent. Real interest rates remain the same. But interest payments eventually go down to $5 million and profits rise to $11 million. How should one view that $2 million increase in profit? It is unreal. Basically, the real cost of debt did not change—the standard of living that the bond holder can support without reducing the real value of his capital did not change. At 4 percent inflation, $4 million of the $7 million payment to bondholders actually served to reduce the real value of the debt. This reduction of the firm's debt liability is no more a real expense of the firm than it is real income to the bondholder. It is really part of the firm's profit. Looking through the veil of inflation, profits are $13 million at 4 percent inflation and $13 million at 2 percent inflation. The rise in stated profits of from $9 million to $11 million represents a transition from substantially understated profits to only somewhat understated profits, from worse accounting to merely bad accounting.

No originality is claimed for this argument. Modigliani and Cohn argued that the rise of inflation in the 1970s had meant that accounting profits progressively understated economic profits.[15] We are only turning around their argument and saying that falling inflation produces a better accounting for profits but spuriously stronger profits in the transitions. Further, Modigliani and Cohn argued that stock market investors failed to look through the veil of inflation and so undervalued shares. If rising inflation condemned stated profits to look worse and worse, falling inflation in the 1990s has tended to flatter the growth of profits.

The Modigliani-Cohn effect bulks very large in the 1990s. U.S. nonfinancial corporate business carried about $2.7 trillion in net debt in the third quarter of 1997. If inflation fell by 2 percent over the 1990s from roughly 4 percent to 2 percent, then corporate interest payments should eventually fall by $54 billion without falling in real terms. This sum represents more than 10 percent of pretax corporate profits and more than 20 percent of the growth of those profits since 1991. Looking back at figure 6.6, one could interpret most of the difference between observed profits and profits at a constant interest rate as reflecting the Modigliani-Cohn effect.

We shall resist the temptation to calculate where the Standard & Poor's index of 500 stocks or the Dow Jones Industrial Average would be without the spurious boost from lower nominal interest payments. Apart from avoiding the heroic assumption that the observed price-earnings ratio would have held in the presence of lower reported profit growth, we also recognize that there is quite a gap between the national income profits that we have analyzed here and the profits discounted in the stock market.[16] Suffice it to say that a substantial part of the double-digit profit growth of the 1990s spuriously arises from lower inflation.

6.4 Conclusion

Short-term interest rates fell to and remained at 3 percent in the early 1990s with the express purpose of permitting companies and financial institutions to rebuild their balance sheets. Low interest rates worked: Nonfinancial firms bolstered their finances by selling shares and refunding their bond debt, both at unprecedented rates.

This chapter took as its starting point the 5-percent-plus decline in the ratio of interest to cash flow in 1991–93 and asked how it came about. Did refinancing, or the lower short-term rates that spurred it, do more? Alternatively, did the upswing in cash flows that normally accompanies a recovery do most to relieve the burden of debt?

We find that lower interest rates amid accelerating economic growth far surpassed corporate refinancing's modest effect in relieving the burden of interest charges on cash flows in 1991 through 1993. The exertions of corporate treasurers and their investment bankers in the equity and bond markets played an important role in relieving the cost of debt, to be sure. But by taking out an insurance policy against higher rates, that is, by extending the maturity of their debt, corporate treasurers limited their savings from refinancing. Washington and Main Street did more than Wall Street to make debt manageable in the 1990s.

These aggregate results should not obscure the key role the equity market played in undoing the damage of the leveraging business of the 1980s. The next chapter analyzes the performance of reverse LBO public offerings.

This chapter has also established that the ongoing refinancing of corporate debt has made a substantial contribution to corporate profit growth in the 1990s. This finding alone casts doubt on some of the claims that the U.S. economy has entered a new age in the 1990s. James Poterba examines the data on total returns to capital in the 1990s—interest and profit—and concludes that although the overall return to capital is higher than it has been for two decades, it is still too early to conclude that there has been any departure from past experience.[17] We have argued in addition that lower inflation has tended to lower interest payments and to raise reported profit in a spurious fashion.

Stepping back, we glimpse an ironic result. The Federal Reserve is rightly proud of the decline in inflation in the 1990s. Yet this very decline has contributed to a rise of corporate earnings in excess of underlying cash flows that is not altogether real. If equity investors do not distinguish nominal earnings growth from real earnings growth, as Modigliani and Cohn claimed, then some part of the "irrational exuberance" Chairman Greenspan alluded to in 1996 is based on a misapprehension of the lower burden of interest on corporate cash flows. The Federal Reserve's success in lowering inflation may itself have contributed to exuberance. Chapter 10 discusses policy responses to asset inflation.

7 The Equity Infusion—Reverse LBOs

For a host of leveraged firms, enthusiasm for buying shares gripped investors none too soon after the conclusion of the Gulf War. Deep craters in the junk bond market precluded these firms' taking advantage of the lower long-term rates that permitted investment grade companies to refinance their debt. Once-eager bankers to LBOs, in many cases themselves humbled by unknown but vast losses on their real estate portfolios, were seeking only to reduce their now carefully watched sums of highly leveraged loans. For more than a few firms, what Moody's dubbed "coupon events" loomed: A coupon had to be "reset" to bring to par a junk bond trading at a deep discount (in the manner of RJR-Nabisco, as described in chapter 4), or a payment-in-kind bond had all at once to pay cash. Saddam Hussein's invasion of Kuwait, which pushed the U.S. economy into recession, certainly did not help leveraged firms' cash flows. These firms needed above all an infusion of cash, with no strings attached, with which interest could be paid, debt could be paid down, and bondholders and bankers could be persuaded to refinance their claims. Such cash was and is to be had in one place: the stock market.

The buoyant stock market in the early 1990s thus provided a timely life raft for some troubled leveraged firms. Thanks to a favorable stock market, many firms that had been taken private with largely borrowed money were able to survive by issuing public equity in the early 1990s. Such transactions, termed reverse LBOs, probably saved a number of firms from falling into bankruptcy.

These transactions provided timely cash to the issuing firms, but how have they performed for investors? Our review of the data finds that as a whole, reverse LBO IPOs of the early 1990s have not proven spectacular investments.

7.1 Reverse LBOs and the Performance of Initial Public Offerings

Initial public offerings of reverse LBO are a subset of all IPOs. An ordinary IPO occurs when a firm first issues public equity, typically because it needs the capital for expansion. Reverse LBOs differ from traditional IPOs in their age, size, use of funds, and professional direction.

Differences between Reverse LBOs and IPOs

Firms that offer public shares after an LBO have generally been around longer than typical IPO firms. The average age since incorporation of U.S. IPO firms on NASDAQ is reportedly only five years.[1] By contrast, reverse LBO firms like RJR-Nabisco, Dr. Pepper, and Duracell have been around long enough to be household names.

Reverse LBOs are typically much larger than ordinary IPOs. The sample examined later in this chapter includes only reverse LBOs of more than $100 million, and that sample accounted for about 85 percent of the dollar volume of all reverse LBOs in the sample period. IPOs typically range in size from $10 to $20 million. Thus the offerings examined here are roughly ten times the size of the typical IPO.

Stock market investors ought to be able to value these older and larger reverse LBOs more readily than ordinary IPOs. In a reverse LBO, some chunk of a company is typically returning to the stock market.

In the case of a whole-company buyout like RJR-Nabisco, a slew of stock market analysts already has its spreadsheets laid out and ways of looking at the firm well practiced. Even in the case of a divisional LBO, some analysts of the former parent may have built up expertise in analyzing the division that will carry over to the new firm. Even when the Wall Street analysts come to a reverse LBO fresh, its product and market are less likely to be new or unproven than in the case of an ordinary IPO.

As mentioned in chapter 5, the proceeds of recent reverse LBO IPOs have served very different purposes than the funds raised by ordinary "first time" IPOs or earlier reverse LBOs. Ordinary IPOs usually list general corporate purposes as the main intended use of the proceeds of their debut in the stock market. By contrast, only 2 percent of the $7.5 billion raised in 1991 and the $6 billion raised in 1992 by reverse LBOs went to general purposes, whereas almost three-quarters went to pay down debt. Earlier reverse LBOs, such as that of Gibson Greeting Cards in 1983, cashed out the existing LBO partners at substantial profit. The primary motivation of reverse LBOs in the early 1990s, by contrast, was the retirement of debt taken on in going private: Cash outs would have to wait.

The managers of reverse LBOs bring unusual market savvy to the negotiations over price with the Wall Street firms that underwrite new issues. The promoters of LBOs generally started their careers in the securities industry. However much these promoters protest that they leave the operations of LBOed companies to the managers, it begs credulity that the promoters do not have a strong voice in such decisions as when an LBO returns to the public equity market and at what price. Thus those calling the plays at reverse LBOs are extraordinarily wise to the ways of the Street. This is not to say that managers of IPOs are necessarily financial naïfs (perhaps played by Jimmy Stewart) compared to the managers of reverse LBOs (Michael Douglas). Many ordinary IPOs owe their existence to investments by venture capitalists who have jumped through the IPO hoop before.

A question arises whether the market prices of reverse LBO IPOs, as a peculiar subset of all IPOs, perform in a manner similar to those of ordinary IPOs. There has been considerable investigation of the so-called aftermarket performance of initial public offerings, both over the span of days or weeks and over the medium term of three to five years. The prices of IPOs frequently rise substantially from the offering price in the immediate aftermarket, yet on average, IPOs prove a poor investment over the medium term.

IPOs' Initial Price "Pop"

IPOs reportedly achieve sizeable average returns over a very short period of time following the offering. Various studies have reported average initial returns ranging from 6.5 percent to over 20 percent. If IPO stock prices were set fairly and thereafter followed a random walk, one would expect the average initial return of a large sample of IPOs to be close to 0. Several studies have documented positive average short-term returns, leading to much speculation about why this occurs.

Rationales abound for the initial price run-up of IPOs, and the rationales do not necessarily exclude one another. In fact, a number of factors probably contribute to the positive average initial returns of IPOs. Perhaps the most obvious rationale for positive average initial IPO returns—their price "pop"—is that underwriters and issuers have difficulty determining an appropriate share price and are willing to err on the side of underpricing of the initial offerings. All the differences between reverse LBOs and ordinary IPOs just reviewed—the age and market record of the firm involved, the size of the offering and the presence of former investment bankers on the sell side—suggest that as a group reverse LBOs would be priced more accurately than ordinary first-time IPOs.

Many academic theories proposed to explain the high average initial returns of IPOs assume that deliberate, systematic underpricing occurs for any of the following reasons: (1) an informational advantage of underwriters over issuers,[2] (2) an informational advantage of informed investors over uninformed investors,[3] (3) as insurance against shareholder lawsuits,[4] and (4) to signal that the firm is of high quality.[5] Some of these theories bring Kipling's *Just So Stories* to mind. At least Kipling's stories, such as "How the Camel Got Its Hump," end up with an empirical regularity (camels do have humps). Some theorists have spun IPO underpricing stories whose predictions do not even match reality.

The reasoning behind the theory that underwriters' informational advantage could contribute to IPO underpricing is straightforward. Underwriters are selling insurance that an issue will fly. Thus they have an incentive to recommend an offering price that is lower than their best estimate of the market clearing price, because a lowball price reduces the effort necessary to sell the issue and reduces the chance that the underwriters will be left with unsold shares that may be salable only at loss. However, a clever test of this theory examined the IPOs of thirty-eight investment banks that marketed their own IPOs. This group of IPOs would not pit a naive issuer against a street-smart underwriter, because issuer and underwriter are one and the same. According to the theory at hand, such IPOs with no "informational asymmetry" should consequently exhibit little or no underpricing. Contrary to what the theory predicts, however, such offerings did display underpricing comparable to that of other IPOs.[6] Were the investment bankers shortchanging themselves?

The theory that the existence of informed and uninformed investors could give rise to systematic IPO underpricing is based on the rationale that underpricing is necessary to widen the market for IPOs. Without underpricing, informed investors (the smart money) would crowd out the uninformed investors (the dumb money) for allocations of promising issues. Consequently, the IPOs left for uninformed investors to buy would consist of unpromising issues. In this world, even uninformed investors would eventually catch on and take their marbles and go home (or to the race track for better odds). Therefore, to compensate the uninformed investors for this adverse selection and thereby to induce uninformed investors to participate in the IPO market, firms must underprice their IPOs. As an explanation for IPO underpricing this theory suffers from a debilitating handicap: a free-rider problem among issuers. Even if all issuers know that IPOs need to be underpriced in the aggregate to attract uninformed investors, no individual issuer would be willing to underprice. Further, extensive oversubscription of IPOs reported both in studies and in news accounts raises a question whether underpricing is necessary to attract uninformed captial.

The jury is still out on whether IPOs are underpriced to avoid shareholder lawsuits. This rationale is appealing, in that it gives us a plausible reason why issuers would tolerate deliberate underpricing and even a reason why investment bankers would underprice their own IPOs. However, the evidence provided for this theory—a comparison of the initial returns of samples of IPOs before and several decades after the passage of the Securities Act of 1933—is quite indirect and overlooks the effects of many other factors. For example, greater underpricing of IPOs in the latter period can quite possibly be attributed to reduced competition among underwriters, because 1933's Glass-Steagall Act prohibited banks from underwriting stock in the latter period.

Signaling models of IPO underpricing, such as those of Allen and Faulhaber, Grinblatt and Hwang, and Welch[7] suggest that better firms purposely underprice their IPOs to signal that they are high-quality firms. The firms purportedly have an incentive to underprice because they assume that their subsequent equity offerings will be priced higher than they would have been had their IPO not been underpriced. The signaling theory of IPO underpricing predicts that more high-quality firms will undertake IPOs during hot issue markets than during cold issue markets.

Helwege and Liang's (1997)[8] evidence debunks the signaling theory premise for IPO underpricing. They examine IPO firms' operating performance and stock returns for up to five years after the IPO, during which time frame the firms' quality would presumably be revealed. They find the operating performance of hot-market IPO firms indistinguishable from cold-market IPO firms. Furthermore, they find hot-market IPO firms have quite poor returns for several years, whereas cold-market IPO stocks have returns comparable to those of NASDAQ stocks. Thus, the empirical evidence they marshall indicates that if anything, hot-market IPOs come from inferior firms—the opposite of signaling theories' prediction.

A simpler, more compelling explanation for IPOs' positive average initial returns, namely underwriter price support, does not presume that the issues are necessarily underpriced and moreover accounts for a regularity most observers overlook. Underwriters supporting the price of some IPOs could create an appearance of mispricing. In contrast to the view that IPO underpricing is undertaken deliberately, apparent underpricing (that is, high average initial returns) may simply reflect the practice of underwriter price support or stabilization.[9] Underwriters support a price by standing ready with a bid order to buy the newly issued shares at or slightly below the offering price, thus preventing the market price from falling at all or much below the offering's fixed selling price. When underwriters support prices in the aftermarket, they effectively skew the distribution of initial returns by propping up returns that would have been negative, thus raising the average return. One of the authors has documented that the distribution of IPO first-day returns for a sample of 463 IPOs has very few negative returns—far fewer than one would expect if stock price changes followed a random walk. A significant and suspicious fraction (one-fourth) of IPOs trade at their issue price at the end of their first day on the market. Both of these observations, the rarity of losing shares and the superabundance of issues breaking even, point to underwriter price support. Moreover, most IPOs with first-day returns of 0 subsequently dropped in price over the following days and weeks, whereas those with positive first-day returns showed a fairly even mix of subsequent rises and falls. This contrast suggests that underwriters propped up those IPOs that closed the first day with no price change and that as the underwriters withdrew their propping bids, the prices tended to drop.

More recent research has confirmed the importance of underwriter support. On careful inspection of over-the-counter quotes and trading records, underwriters tend to offer the best price for IPOs selling at or below their issue price and appear to repurchase a substantial fraction of the shares of cold IPOs.[10]

Long-Term IPO Performance

IPOs over a period of years turns out on close inspection to perform rather dismally on average. One study of IPOs' long-term performance reported an average cumulative return, relative to non-IPO firms with the same market capitalization, of negative 15.08 percent over the 36 months following the IPO.[11] Another study showed that the strategy of investing a fixed-dollar amount in every IPO (at the first-day closing price) that hit the market between 1970 and 1990 and holding each investment for five years would have produced an average annual return (not market-adjusted) of only 5 percent[12]—less than that of Treasury bills!

The relatively poor medium-term performance of IPOs results from a combination of their coming onto the market when stock valuations are high and from their subsequent underperformance even given the timing of issues. IPOs occur in waves: High volumes are issued when market valuations are high. Such windows of opportunity may open and remain open because investors are overly optimistic about the chances of buying a stock that is going to skyrocket in price. If one assumes that managers of LBO firms are even more astute at market timing (that is, issuing when stock prices are high) than the typical IPO firm management, relatively poor medium-term performance would also be expected for reverse LBO IPOs. The underperformance over time even given the timing of issues may reflect the fact that investors, in looking for the single stock that will make them rich, buy lots of firms that disappear without a trace. As time-tested businesses, firms offering reverse LBOs may have better survival rates than ordinary IPOs.

7.2 $12 Billion of Reverse LBOs and How They Fared

We investigated the record of the stock price returns of U.S. reverse LBOs of more than $100 million occurring between January 1, 1991, and September 30, 1993. We found that on average, reverse LBOs exhibit a smaller initial price run-up than do ordinary IPOs, but that in contrast to ordinary IPOs they maintain their initial lead against the general market over the medium term (three years). A relative few big winners drive the modestly favorable average return.

Another study of reverse LBO performance by Holthausen and Larcker[13] reported findings similar to ours in examining the returns of a sample of reverse LBOs that went public between 1983 and 1988. They also found that reverse LBOs have smaller first-day returns than ordinary IPOs. Over the longer term, the stock market returns of their reverse LBO sample slightly outperformed those of the broad market.

The Sample

We compiled our sample of domestic reverse LBO IPOs of more than $100 million that tapped the market between January 1, 1991, and September 30, 1993, by cross-referencing the lists of reverse LBOs reported by Securities Data Company, *Mergers & Acquisitions,* and *Going Public: The IPO Reporter.* We tried to eliminate reverse LBOs of foreign firms and equity carve outs (offers by a firm for sale to the public of a portion of a wholly owned subsidiary's common stock). Equity carve outs were excluded because the focus of this investigation is standalone leveraged private companies reverting to public ownership. The sample (forty-eight issues totaling about $12 billion, listed in table 7.1)

Table 7.1
Sample of reverse LBOs of more than $100 million occurring between January 1991 and September 30, 1993

Date	Name of firm	Amount (millions)
04/11/91	RJR	$1,129.4
04/24/91	Caldor	108.2
05/01/91	Duracell Int.*	450.0
05/16/91	Ann Taylor Stores	158.6
05/23/91	BWIP Holding*	116.0
06/24/91	International Specialty Products*	269.7
07/11/91	Kaiser Aluminum	101.5
07/19/91	Enquirer/Star Group*	189.0
07/24/91	Interstate Bakeries*	250.0
10/01/91	York International Corp.*	246.1
10/11/91	RP Scherer	180.0
10/11/91	Warnaco Group	120.0
10/17/91	Health Care & Retirement Corp.	263.1
11/08/91	Amphenol	160.0
11/14/91	Horace Mann Educators*	252.0
11/15/91	Joy Technologies	153.0
11/22/91	Stop & Shop	212.5
11/26/91	Agricultural Minerals*	164.2
12/11/91	Owens-Illinois	660.0
12/12/91	Healthtrust Inc.–The Hospital	560.0
12/16/91	Perrigo Co.	128.0
01/29/92	National Re Holdings*	165.6
01/30/92	Infinity Broadcasting	107.2
01/31/92	Scotts	218.5
02/13/92	Living Centers of America	112.8
02/26/92	MusicLand Stores	216.1
02/26/92	HCA Hospital Corp of America	672.5
03/04/92	Foodmaker	180.0
03/19/92	Burlington Industries Equity	469.4
03/25/92	Coltec Industries	462.0

Table 7.1 (continued)

Date	Name of firm	Amount (millions)
03/31/92	Chicago and North Western Holding	170.4
05/05/92	Reliance Electric	286.1
05/07/92	Sybron	107.0
05/13/92	Arkansas Best*	175.8
05/18/92	Kohl's	108.4
06/10/92	General Instrument	264.0
07/22/92	GTECH Holdings	115.0
08/14/92	Computervision Corp.	240.0
10/01/92	Caraustar Industries*	120.0
10/27/92	Life Re Corp.*	186.7
01/26/93	Dr. Pepper/Seven Up	247.8
01/28/93	American Re Corp.	287.7
03/08/93	Payless Cashways Inc.	285.6
03/10/93	Ethan Allen Interiors	105.9
03/25/93	Life Partners Group Inc.*	206.7
07/01/93	Carr-Gottstein Foods	102.0
07/01/93	Levitz Furniture	145.6
08/10/93	Southern Pacific Rail Corp.	330.8
Total		$11,960.9

* Denotes firms that began paying dividends within three years of their reverse LBO.

accounts for about 85 percent of the dollar volume of all reverse LBOs occurring between January 1, 1991, and September 30, 1993 (approximately $14 billion).

Strictly speaking, RJR common stock began trading publicly a couple of months before the company offered shares to the public, when it converted debentures to common stock in February 1991. However, we included its $1.1 billion initial public offering in April 1991 as a reverse LBO. As such, it is the largest reverse LBO in history.

Another debatable inclusion in the sample was the offering of Kaiser Aluminum, because its parent, MAXXAM, was publicly traded at the time of Kaiser's IPO. However, reports indicated that the deal had many characteristics of a reverse LBO and for practical purposes was viewed as a reverse LBO by the market.[14]

The sample excluded some relatively famous reverse LBOs that did not meet the $100 million size cutoff. Some of these firms (as well as several firms in the sample), such as Safeway and Filene's Basement, "double-dipped," so to speak, by issuing additional equity within a year of their initial public offering. In a number of these cases, the purpose of the second offering was to allow insiders to cash out.

None of the reverse LBOs examined was de-listed owing to liquidation, but four of the firms in the sample, Hospital Corporation of America, Agricultural Minerals, Dr. Pepper, and Reliance Electric were acquired by other companies within three years of their reverse LBOs. Their returns were calculated to their final listed price. Subsequent to their exit from the market, their returns were assumed to be those of the S&P 500 Total Return Index. This treatment corresponds to a scenario in which an investor in the reverse LBO IPO offering that was subsequently acquired for cash simply reinvested the money received in the broad stock market as represented by the S&P 500.

Evaluation of Performance

We evaluated the performance of reverse LBOs by examining the resulting returns corresponding to two different investment strategies. The first performance measure captures the results of a strategy of investing a fixed amount, say $100,000, in each reverse LBO over our size threshold. The second performance gauge measures the outcome of a strategy of investing in the same proportion, say one-tenth of a percent, of every reverse LBO. In the latter case, the investor puts $100,000 into a $100 million issue, but $200,000 into a $200 million issue. Both measures take opportunity cost into account by evaluating the reverse LBO returns in relation to the overall market return. The latter strategy, termed a value-weighted approach, probably best measures reverse LBO performance, because it reports the return per dollar invested in all reverse LBOs.

These performance measures accurately tracked the returns of our two stylized investment strategies but nevertheless probably flattered the performance of the reverse LBOs. This flattery arose from our assumption that an investor could in fact pursue these two strategies and in particular lay hands on the assumed amounts of the stocks in most demand. The flattery also arose from our assumption that the returns from holding the 500 largest stocks in the stock market represent the opportunity cost for these rather more risky reverse LBOs. Consider each of these sources of bias in turn.

Our results probably overstated what real investors could have realized because individual investors might not have been able to get allocations of all reverse LBO IPOs. Allocations of "hot" issues are at the underwriter's discretion, and it is widely believed that underwriters effectively shut out the mass of individual investors in allocating plum IPOs. Instead, Wall Street firms choose to reward large institutional investors and favored (perhaps high-turnover) customers with allocations of the best offerings.[15] Thus, in practice the small investor's portfolio of reverse LBOs is likely to contain more than its fair share of the poorer performers. Our measures, by contrast, assumed that the investor obtained a certain dollar amount or certain fraction of each issue.

We also flattered the reverse LBOs by using the returns on the largest 500 shares traded in the U.S. stock market as a benchmark for their performance. As described below, we adjusted the reverse LBO returns for their opportunity cost, that is, what the investor might have earned on an investment with similar risk. To use the returns on the Standard & Poor's 500 to perform this adjustment meant assuming that the reverse LBOs were no more risky than the largest stocks in the market. Because reverse LBOs remain substantially more leveraged than the market as a whole, one would expect their price changes to exaggerate those of the Standard & Poor's 500. In particular, falling interest rates over our sample period were good news for the shareholders of the largest companies on the stock market but even better news for the shareholders of our still leveraged companies. And stronger cash flows from a reviving economy—our earliest reverse LBOs occurred in April 1991, at the end of the recession—were good news for the shareholders of the largest companies but even better for the shareholders of leveraged companies because there would be lots more cash left after debt service.

The market adjustment of subtracting the corresponding return on the S&P 500 Total Return Index, by contrast, implies that the firms in the sample were all expected to move exactly as the market moves. Beta is a measure that relates the volatility of a single stock to the volatility of the market as a whole. If a stock moved exactly as the market moved, it would have a beta of 1. Stocks with betas greater than 1 are more volatile than the market. A stock with a beta of 1.5, for example, tends to increase 50 percent more than the total market when the market is going up and drop 50 percent more than the market when it is going down. In general, the higher the beta (the greater the risk one undertakes), the higher the expected return required.

Most of the reverse LBOs in this sample probably had betas greater than 1, owing to their leverage alone. Indeed, evidence from firms with debt-to-equity ratios similar to those of firms offering reverse LBOs suggests betas well in excess of 1. An investigation of 12 firms that undertook less radical leveraging transactions than LBOs (through large special dividends or buybacks of shares) reported that the shares subsequently traded with betas of 1.3 to 1.5.[16] The average debt-to-total capital ratio for this sample of so-called leveraged recapitalizations, at 81.3 percent,[17] resembled RJR's debt-to-equity ratio of about 75 percent after its April 1991 reverse LBO. Thus, if it is plausible that the betas of the firms in our sample of reverse LBOs range between 1.3 to 1.5, then our performance benchmark assuming a beta of 1 sets a minimal hurdle. Subtracting only 1 times the market return (rather than say, 1.5 times the market return) biases the adjusted returns upward.

Return Calculations

Aftermarket prices were collected for the first day and for the one-week, four-week, six-month, and one-year intervals after the reverse LBO. In cases where the price history was long enough, two- and three-year returns were also calculated. Raw returns were calculated over each interval, taking dividend payments and stock splits into account along with price appreciation. Five firms in the sample had one or more stock splits (Infinity Broadcasting, one of the top performers in the sample, had two three-for-two stock splits within two years of its reverse LBO), and thirteen firms paid dividends within three years of reverting to public ownership.

One might have expected that the group of dividend-paying firms would exhibit higher average total returns than the overall sample, but this was not the case. In almost every case, these firms declared token dividends of five cents or less per quarter that left stock price changes the overwhelming determinant of the firms' total return. With the exception of Duracell and International Specialty Products, all the dividend-paying firms initiated dividend payments within six months of their reverse LBOs. Dividend-paying firms are identified by asterisks in table 7.1.

The performance measure that matters most to an investor is the market-adjusted return. For example, the record of a stock that posted a 7 percent return would be evaluated quite differently depending on whether the overall market dropped 10 percent over the same period or increased 30 percent over the same period. The raw returns were therefore adjusted by subtracting the corresponding change in the S&P 500 Total Return Index over the same interval, thereby giving an indication of how the firms performed relative to the market in general. The Total Return Index was used rather than the more widely available S&P 500 index to include the dividends received in the returns, as we have done for the thirteen dividend-paying reverse LBOs.

Initial Price Performance

Reverse IPOs hit the market with a splash, but with a somewhat smaller splash than ordinary IPOs. We measured the initial price performance and the very short-term performance of IPOs with raw returns, not market-adjusted returns, because over the short term (a day or a week) the market's movement is usually insignificant relative to the movement of an individual new share price. The average return from the offering price to the first-day close—not an annualized return, but the return on the first day—was 6.54 percent. This is a lower first-day average return than has typically been reported for ordinary IPOs,[18] and also lower, though only slightly, than the first-day average return reported by Ruud.[19] Thus it appears that the first-day price pop of reverse LBOs is at the low end of the spectrum observed for IPOs in general. The average first-day return when each return was weighted by the issue's dollar amount was 6.6 percent. The fact that the weighted average is nearly identical to the simple average indicates issue size had no strong relation to first-day return.

This lower price pop for reverse LBOs is consistent with the "information asymmetry" explanation for IPO underpricing. There is, for a number of reasons, less uncertainty about the value of firms offering reverse LBOs. First, because the firms have been public before, stock market analysts are familiar with them. Second, these firms' products and markets are likely to be well-established, rather than new and unproven. Furthermore, the executives calling the shots at these reverse LBO firms are probably more savvy to the ways of Wall Street than those executives at the typical ordinary IPO firm. For all these reasons, underwriters have less of an informational advantage and consequently are less able to lowball the offering price.

Table 7.2
Descriptive statistics of raw returns of reverse LBOs

Time period	Mean	Median	Minimum	Maximum
1-day ($n = 48$)	6.54%	2.54%	−4.55%	45.31%
1-week ($n = 48$)	7.11	3.26	−15.18	50
4-week ($n = 48$)	11.40	7.95	−18.38	84.38
6-month ($n = 48$)	14.70	11.83	−61.46	155.88
1-year ($n = 48$)	24.43	10.87	−75.00	178.57
2-year ($n = 48$)	46.62	30.45	−75.00	317.86
3-year ($n = 48$)	54.39	28.79	−73.33	335.00

Note: The sample consisted of reverse LBOs of more than $100 million occurring between January 1, 1991, and September 30, 1993 ($n = 48$). All stock prices were adjusted for stock splits and dividends. Returns have not been annualized but are the return over the period indicated.

The raw average returns in the second column of table 7.2 over periods of one day through one year might lead one to conclude that reverse LBOs are winning investments. The descriptive statistics of the distributions in the following columns temper that view, however. The minimum and maximum columns show a wide range of returns over each period, both positive and negative. The two firms with the biggest first-day price run-up were Perrigo, with a 45 percent increase, and Duracell, with a 38 percent increase. A useful summary measure of the distribution is the median, the middle value of the distribution. Thus, a median 2.5 percent return for the first day means that half of the firms had one-day returns of less than 2.5 percent. The medians of all the return periods are less than the means, indicating that a few positive outliers drive the mean (or average).

Don't Buy If the First Day Return Is Zero

A suspiciously large fraction of firms exhibiting one-day returns of 0 provides some indication of the frequency of underwriter price support. Twenty-nine percent of the reverse LBOs in the sample had first-day returns of 0. This exceeds even the 25 percent found to have no first-day price movement in a sample of 463 ordinary IPOs encompassing a previous hot IPO market in 1983.[20] Twenty-five percent or more is a large fraction of firms having no price movement, particularly considering the high volume of trading on the day of issuance. If an eerie silence pervaded the busy traffic in reverse LBOs that remained at issue price at the end of the first day of trading, it was the sound of losses soon to be realized.

Examination of the issues that showed no price action (neither a rise nor a fall) on the first day revealed that they were hazardous to the investors' wealth. Stocks with one-day returns of 0 tended subsequently to fall in price in a manner consistent with underwriters' gradually withdrawing their price support. Among the 14 firms (29 percent of the sample) that had initial one-day returns of 0, nearly three-fourths (ten out of fourteen) had negative four-week returns (figure 7.1). In contrast, firms with first-day price run-ups divided evenly between increasing and decreasing price movements in the week after the offering. Stocks with initial price run-ups presumably were not being supported and consequently would be expected to have equal probability of increasing or decreasing subsequent returns. In fact, only 41 percent of the thirty-two firms with positive one-day returns (thirteen out of thirty-two) decreased in price over the subsequent four weeks.

The bulk of ordinary IPOs with no first-day price change also subsequently sank in price, indicating initial price support and subsequent withdrawal of that support. For the sample of ordinary IPOs with initial returns of 0, 69 percent experienced subsequent 0 or negative one-week returns. Of those firms with no price change on the first day, 60 percent remained the same or declined in price over the subsequent four weeks (figure 7.1).

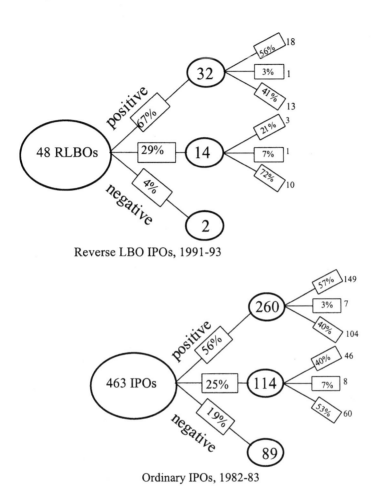

Reverse LBO IPOs, 1991-93

Ordinary IPOs, 1982-83

Figure 7.1
First-day and four-week price changes for IPOs

Table 7.3
Descriptive statistics of market-adjusted returns of reverse LBOs

Time period	Mean	Median	Minimum	Maximum
1-week ($n = 48$)	6.84%	4.16%	−15.71%	45.59%
4-week ($n = 48$)	10.02	7.29	−19.12	79.03
6-month ($n = 48$)	9.07	5.69	−66.33	148.17
1-year ($n = 48$)	13.39	−0.04	−85.88	168.74
2-year ($n = 48$)	24.32	6.55	−91.25	293.89
3-year ($n = 48$)	17.70	−9.54	−133.60	293.15

Note: The sample consisted of reverse LBOs of more than $100 million occurring between January 1, 1991, and September 30, 1993. All stock prices were adjusted for stock splits and dividends. Market adjustment was made by substracting the return on the S&P 500 Total Return Index for the relevant period. Returns have not been annualized but are the return over the period indicated.

There are exceptions to any rule, and some firms that may have been supported initially did go on to perform well. General Instrument and Amphenol are examples of reverse LBOs that had no first-day price increase and negative one-week returns but have since more than doubled in price.

Results for Simple Market-Adjusted Average Returns

The returns of reverse LBOs, if an investor followed the strategy of investing a fixed amount in each offering, look better than those available elsewhere in the stock market. The second column in Table 7.3 shows that returns on these firms outperformed the market by 13.39 percent on average over one year and by 24.32 percent over two years. By three years (following the initial public offerings), however, an investor employing this strategy would have been only a bit better off than he was at the end of one year. Again, remember that we have stacked the deck in favor of the reverse LBOs by assuming that the firms had a beta of 1, even though a number of them likely had betas greater than 1.

The best explanation for why investors continue to invest in IPOs, despite documented mediocre average performance over the medium term, is that investors hope to get in on the ground floor of the next Microsoft. That is, the existence of extreme (positive) outliers lures investors, much as a lottery does, into an unfair bet. Among the reverse LBOs in our sample were some big winners—but also some big losers. The firms with the best one-year performance relative to the market were Kohl's, Perrigo, and General Instrument with 169 percent, 151 percent, and 147 percent increases, respectively. The firms with the worst one-year market-adjusted returns were Computervision Corp. with a −86 percent return and Carr-Gottstein Foods with a −61 percent return. RJR-Nabisco's one-year market-adjusted return was −26 percent. The sample divided exactly in half in terms of the number with positive and negative one-year market adjusted returns, and the median was −0.04 percent.

By the end of the second year, most of the previous winners continue to soar, while the losers plumbed new depths. The three best two-year market-adjusted performers were Infinity Broadcasting (+294 percent), Perrigo (+278 percent), and General Instrument (+267 percent). The three firms with the worst two-year returns were Computervision Corp. (−91 percent), International Specialty Products (−81 percent), and RJR-Nabisco (−73 percent). Twenty-nine firms had positive two-year market-adjusted returns, and nineteen had negative two-year market-adjusted returns. The median two-year market-adjusted return was 6.55 percent.

Results for Size-Weighted Market-Adjusted Average Returns

The results we obtained for investing proportionally in reverse LBO IPOs (table 7.4) did not paint as rosy a picture as the previously reported measures corresponding to fixed-amount investing. The

Table 7.4
Descriptive statistics of market-adjusted reverse LBO returns weighted by offering size

Time period	Mean	Median
1-day ($n = 48$)	6.60%	2.22%
1-week ($n = 48$)	6.88	3.77
4-week ($n = 48$)	10.24	5.02
6-month ($n = 48$)	5.90	−5.36
1-year ($n = 48$)	6.18	−3.85
2-year ($n = 48$)	15.04	1.37
3-year ($n = 48$)	12.22	−16.21

Note: The sample consisted of reverse LBOs of more than $100 million occurring between January 1, 1991, and September 30, 1993. All stock prices were adjusted for stock splits and dividends. Returns shown are the market-adjusted returns weighted by the size of the offering. Returns have not been annualized but are the return over the period indicated.

weighted average returns for one day, one week, and four weeks do not differ substantially from the unweighted averages, indicating the initial performance was not particularly correlated with the size of the issue. However, the six-month, one-year, two-year and three-year return per dollar invested in reverse LBOs in the early 1990s, at 5.90 percent, 6.18 percent, 15.04 percent, and 12.22 percent, respectively, are considerably lower than the simple market-adjusted average returns (table 7.4).

Furthermore, the generally negative size-weighted median returns indicate that half the money invested in these reverse LBOs was substantially underperforming the market by six months after issue. This reflects the relatively poor performance of some large issuers, such as RJR-Nabisco and Owens-Illinois.

How should the investors in reverse LBO IPOs evaluate a 12.22 percent market-adjusted return over three years? First, note that this figure is not annualized; the corresponding annualized return is about 4 percent. Second, qualitatively, it represents performance above a broad market index, while ordinary IPOs tend to underperform the market on average over the medium-term.[21] Given the sample size and, more importantly, the timing of our sampling at the beginning of a long economic upswing, perhaps too much should not be made of this difference.

Two further considerations bear on the interpretation of this finding. One is the weighting of technology and media firms in the sample as compared to the Standard & Poor's index. It may be unfair to compare a sample of firms selected by their debt-carrying capacity in the 1980s to a broad index showing by the mid-1990s the effect of investors' enthusiasm for technology stocks. But it would be a mistake to consider such shares as absent from our sample (such as General Instrument and Infinity Broadcasting), and easy to overstate their representation in the Standard & Poor's 500. Another aspect of this point is that the share of RJR Nabisco in our size-weighted reverse LBO sample is larger than the share of Philip Morris in the Standard & Poor's 500. The second consideration probably carries more weight than such compositional questions: leverage. Substantially leveraged firms should be expected to outperform the general market in an environment of macroeconomic growth and generally well-behaved interest rates. Almost any allowance for the greater risk from higher leverage would leave investors in reverse LBOs feeling a little short-changed.

7.3 Conclusions

These findings indicate that, from an investor's point of view, reverse LBOs that were launched primarily to deleverage have proven to be acceptable, although in view of their risk, unspectacular investments

over the medium term. Nevertheless, evidence indicates these large reverse LBO IPOs have performed better over the medium term than ordinary IPOs—reverse LBOs' initial average price run-up may be smaller,
but their performance over three years looks better.

This investigation of the initial returns of reverse LBOs sheds some
new light on postulated theories for IPO initial price run-ups. The initial price pop of reverse LBOs is the same as or smaller than that of
ordinary IPOs, depending upon which IPO study you use for comparison. A smaller price pop for reverse LBOs would be consistent with the
asymmetric-information theory for IPO price run-ups. The finding of
no correlation between issue size and size of initial return offers some
evidence against the interpretation that IPO prices shoot up because
there is not enough paper to go around. The large fraction of reverse
LBOs showing no price change on the first trading day and the subsequent four-week price decline among the issues show the hand of
underwriter price support. However, enough firms' prices rise sufficiently in the weeks following their offerings that the average return
still goes up.

From the reverse LBO issuers' standpoint, these transactions have
been favorable, if not lifesaving in many cases. The reverse LBO IPOs
do not appear to have been systematically underpriced, as ordinary
IPOs are so often characterized, and the window of opportunity for
equity issuance has been long enough to allow many firms to make
second offerings. The first offering has typically provided funds to reduce debt to a manageable level, and the second offering allowed insid-
ers to cash out.

The equity raised by reverse LBOs in the early 1990s eased the aggregate corporate debt burden considerably. Assuming all the equity
raised was used to pay down debt, the equity raised retired approximately $12 billion in debt, and the quality of $36 to $120 billion more
debt was improved by the reduction in leverage. The potential financial
distress averted by the coincidence of voracious investor appetite for

the equity of these highly leveraged companies and the hour of need is perhaps not fully appreciated.

As argued above, a reverse LBO IPO is a peculiar IPO by virtue of the long history of the firm involved, the firm's size, the relatively abundant information regarding the firm's performance, the use of the proceeds, and the sophistication of the directors of the firm. In the next chapter we discuss the more usual IPOs and emphasize the issuers' good timing and buyers' elastic demands for a track record. Viewed from an international perspective, the IPO market, for all its games and fads, appears to be a remarkable mechanism for financing innovation.

8   *Cheap Equity Capital for Young Firms*

To a rocket scientist, "burn" refers to the rate at which a rocket uses fuel. To an investment banker, "burn" refers to the rate at which a new company uses up cash. For a start-up firm with no product yet, and therefore no revenues, the burn rate is simply monthly expenses, consisting largely of the salaries of the firm's officers and employees.

Investors in the stock market of the 1990s have warmed to some surprisingly high burn rates. Technology firms with fairly amorphous products and no revenues have recently been very successful selling their shares to the public in IPOs. This chapter argues that a hot market for IPOs provides cheap financing for young firms in the United States. High-technology firms, among others, can access finance with quite long "horizons," measured by any reasonable expectation of the first dollar in profit. Many individual and institutional investors risk large sums of money capitalizing companies with more ideas than experience.

Hot IPO markets come and go in the United States, but they do not appear to be a random phenomenon. Instead, they seem to be associated with declines in the cost of equity finance, when the stock market puts a higher price on a given stream of current and expected earnings.

When price-earnings multiples rise in the stock market, stock issues surge in general and Ipos in particular find a ready market.

In this chapter, we first examine the cases of four young firms: Orbital Sciences, 3DO, Shaman Pharmaceuticals, and Netscape Communications. We then place their experiences in going public into the larger perspective of hot IPO markets and the timing of IPO issues in the general context of the timing of U.S. equity issues. Here we pick up the theme of market timing sounded in chapter 5.

Later, we offer evidence for the alternation of foreign buy-ins and Ipos over the last ten years. Between the hot IPO markets of 1986–87 and 1991–97, many foreign firms bought into young U.S. technology firms, often exchanging cash for 10 to 50 percent shares. These foreign purchases generated much controversy in the late 1980s. For instance, President Bush's science advisor warned that "[o]ur technology base can be nibbled from under us through a coherent plan of purchasing entrepreneurial companies."[1] The controversy waned in the 1990s as foreign buy-ins fell off.

We argue that the influence of stock market pricing on the nationality of equity financing of young U.S. firms is just a part of a larger picture in which stock market valuations influence global flows of direct investment. As the cost of equity offered by the New York Stock Exchange (NYSE) and the National Association of Securities Dealers Automated Quotations (NASDAQ) has fallen relative to the cost of equity abroad, direct investment has shifted from flowing into the United States to flowing out. The bull stock market of the 1990s has tended to maintain domestic ownership of U.S. firms.

The hot IPO market, by showering cheap equity on new firms, has thus muted discussion of U.S. policy toward industrial innovation and its financing. Those who were concerned that "foreign interests are picking off our technology jewels one by one"[2] could relax, given that a hot market multiplies the price of those jewels. Moreover, the sums mobilized by the hot IPO market of the 1990s have made the market a uniquely American phenomenon: No foreign stock market, no matter how vibrant, matches the U.S. market in providing capital to new firms. It would be easy to overstate the role of IPOs in financing industrial innovation in the United States in view of the importance of research spending in large successful firms out of cash flow. Still, discussions of industrial policy that contrast different governments' support for industrial innovation should not lose sight of how the U.S. equity market can, at the margin at least, finance industrial innovation.

8.1 IPO Tales

Here we review four IPOs, the first in a lukewarm market, the last three in a hot market. The marketplace demanded a track record of successful performance in the first case much more than in the latter cases. We do not claim, in our selection of these four cases, to be scientific, but the ultimately poor performance of the middle two IPOs was not a selection criterion. Instead, one of the present authors had described these cases shortly after their successful launches as firms with more dreams than track record.[3] The choice of Netscape was guided by its youth at the time of the IPO and by its white-hot reception in the market.

One study that compares the operating results of firms that went public in a hot market with the results of firms that went public in a cool market supports more systematically our view that hot markets welcome firms at a very early stage of their development. Helwege and Liang found that firms that went public during the hot IPO market of 1983 were less profitable and somewhat smaller than firms that went public during the relatively cold IPO market of 1988.[4] Furthermore, the stock returns of the hot-issue-market firms were significantly poorer over the five years following the IPO than the five-year returns for cold-market IPOs.

Orbital Sciences

Orbital Sciences' initial public offering in the relatively cool stock market of 1990 offers a striking contrast to the financial debuts of 3DO and Shaman Pharmaceuticals, which took place in hot markets a few years later. The firm, founded in 1982 by three Harvard Business School graduates, seeks to compete with NASA and its counterparts abroad by launching payloads into orbit around the planet. Orbital Sciences' first product, the Transfer Orbit Stage (TOS), was a satellite launcher for use with the space shuttle or Titan rocket. Its second product, developed with Hercules, was a so-called Pegasus booster to launch satellites from an airplane; in February 1993, for instance, Orbital launched Brazil's first satellite into orbit from the wing of a B-52.[5] In its prospectus, Orbital Sciences touted its expectation that "lower-cost space launch vehicles and less expensive satellite systems should expand the use of space products and services by private corporations, educational and research institutions."[6]

Orbital Sciences was burning cash at the rate of $600,000 per month in the nine months prior to September 1989, but in retrospect it looks quite bankable compared with 3DO or Shaman. It had an order backlog of $151 million, including contracts with NASA and the Defense Advanced Research Projects Agency. But a *Barron's* article that appeared shortly before Orbital's scheduled IPO pointed out that "TOS and Pegasus have not yet been launched, though Pegasus is scheduled for an attempt this spring."[7] *Barron's* also cited as "Worth Noting: [Orbital] has never demonstrated profits from operations."[8]

After this report, Orbital scrubbed its IPO.[9] Only after Orbital launched the Pegasus, the first U.S.-made launcher since the space shuttle, did it finally undertake an IPO. In April 1990, Orbital sold 2.4 million shares at $14 each. Thus in the fairly sluggish stock market of 1990, Orbital could not get its IPO off of the ground until it could launch a rocket. Moreover, Orbital's subsequent success demonstrates that profits were not far off. Notwithstanding some "aborted launches, [and] blown-up and misguided rockets," from 1990 to April 1993 the firm "logged 31 successful space missions out of a total of 36."[10] In 1993, Orbital agreed with a Canadian firm to construct and launch a network of small, low-orbiting satellites that would inexpensively relay messages from hand-held communications.[11] The firm reported turning a profit of $2.8 million in 1991 and $3.8 million in 1992, its first years as a public company.[12] At the end of 1997, Orbital's stock closed at $29.75 per share.

3DO

3DO is in the business of making "interactive multiplayers," that is, home entertainment units that combine cable TV, stereo, and personal computers. The multiplayers should allow viewers to turn home movies into cartoons.

At its market launch in May 1993, 3DO was a hot issue. The company had originally sought to sell 2.1 million shares at $10–12 per share, but market soundings led the underwriters to offer 2.9 million shares at $15 per share. In spite of this increase, 3DO's price shot up to $20.25 in the first day's trading.

For our purposes, what is striking is what was said at the time of the IPO: "3DO is 'vaporware' right now—they have no real products, no revenues, no profits—but people who missed out on Microsoft the first time around think that with all the risks, this might be another Microsoft in the making."[13] The firm's founders stayed up all night to assemble a mock-up of its machine for the winter 1992 Las Vegas consumer electronics fair and offered further details at the June 1993 consumer electronics show in Chicago. They shipped their first $700 video game in October 1993.[14]

Investors who could not get their broker to sell them any 3DO shares at the initial offering and who resisted the temptation to buy them at more than $20 per share can claim a reward for their patience. On December 31, 1997, the shares closed at $2^3/_{16}$.

Shaman Pharmaceuticals

In early 1993, Shaman Pharmaceuticals sold three million shares at $15 per share. If Orbital Sciences appealed to Star Trek fans, Shaman conjured up images of Indiana Jones turned Jonas Salk. The firm's concept was to send ethnobiologists to tramp through tropical rain forests gathering plants used by traditional medical providers, then use these plants to develop proprietary drugs. Such searches may sound far-fetched, but large, wealthy firms like Glaxo and Merck already conduct them. Shaman appealed quite broadly to investors seeking a firm narrowly focused on this mode of drug discovery (that is, a "pure play"). One portfolio manager even described the issuer as a Ben and Jerry's of the drug market.[15]

Despite Shaman's appeal, its prospects for profits remained distant at best. The firm, founded in 1989, burned cash at a rate of a half million dollars per month in 1992 on its way to a $6 million loss. Though the firm boasted an investment from major drug firm Eli Lilly to find treatments for fungal infections and a contract with Merck to screen treatments for diabetes and pain, investors could only hope that Shaman's drugs for herpes and viral infections of the respiratory tract reach market by the turn of the century.

Like many initial public offerings, Shaman Pharmaceuticals has not done wonders for its investors. On December 31, 1997, the stock closed at $4^{15}/_{16}$ per share. Investors who paid the offering price of $15 per share had lost two-thirds of their money.

Netscape Communications

Netscape was founded in April 1994 by James H. Clark, founder of Silicon Graphics, and twenty-three-year-old Marc Andreessen, creator of

Internet browser software called Mosaic. Netscape's Internet browser, Netscape Navigator, made its debut in December 1994. To spur the market, Netscape initially gave the browser away and made money by charging for World Wide Web server software, software that enables companies to create interactive "home pages" that may be accessed on the Internet. Within seven months of Navigator's introduction, two-thirds of the browsers used on the World Wide Web were Navigators.[16] Later Netscape began charging for the browser.

Netscape went public at $28 per share on August 9, 1995, rocketing as high as $78 that day and closing at $58¼. By December 1995 its price had soared to more than $170. It would appear that Netscape was the IPO investor's dream, the "next Microsoft." Then the real Microsoft entered the Internet browser market with the introduction of Internet Explorer, bundled at no additional cost with the Windows operating system. By the last quarter of 1997, revenues from sales of Netscape's Navigator had plummeted, and the stock price dove with it. On December 31, 1997, Netscape shares, having split two for one in the interim, closed at 24⅜. Thus a share purchased on the IPO was worth $48.75, well ahead of the IPO price of $28 per share, but noticeably short of the first-day closing price of $58¼ per share.

8.2 Equity Issuance and the Cost of Equity

The years 1992, 1993, and 1996 set records for IPO issuance (see figure 5.6). This statement holds even if one considers only ordinary IPOs and ignores reverse leveraged buyouts. The latter have involved mostly mature companies, such as RJR-Nabisco, that partnerships, employing enormous fractions of debt in the form of junk bonds and bank loans, bought from public shareholders. Such companies stand out like oldsters in the nursery of the IPO market. They offered shares to the public as the difficulty of carrying high debt loads in the 1990s became evident (see chapter 5).

The use of IPO proceeds shows where the deals came in the firms' financial life cycle. Although much of the money generated is available for expansion, or "general corporate purposes," a fair fraction cashes out shareholders (see figure 5.7, "secondary offerings"). These shareholders include venture capitalists who take the opportunity to harvest some or all of their investment. General corporate purposes includes spending for research and development, which, in a sample of 346 firms that went public in 1991–93, averaged more than three-quarters of sales receipts.[17]

The stock market offered a favorable background for the strong IPO issuance of 1992–97. In general, equity issuance jumps when the stock market puts a higher multiple on corporate earnings (see figure 5.1). Hot IPO markets tend to occur during general surges in equity issues—1983, 1986–87, and 1991–97.[18] Founders of new firms as well as managers of older companies look to sell equity when the market price of a given stream of earnings is high or, equivalently, when the cost of equity is perceived to be low.

If new firms benefit from going public, a question arises as to how investors in IPOs fare. A recent study of almost 5,000 firms that went public in the years 1968–87 found that investors in these IPOs did poorly, both because of the timing of the offerings and their price performance relative to already listed firms.[19] Investors did best buying IPOs that were floated in years when price-earnings ratios were low and few firms were going public, and worst buying IPO shares in hot markets such as that of 1991–93. Moreover, investors in IPOs in any given year tended to harvest five-year returns well below those available on already listed firms. Indeed, investors would have been better off buying Treasury bills.

These findings suggest that hot IPO markets offer cheap equity to new U.S. firms, at least cheap in relation to average U.S. equity costs. Looking at the matter from the other side, investors in IPOs have reaped only poor returns on average in pursuit of the next Microsoft. One could argue that investors knowingly and willingly give up expected return in favor of a fat tail of the distribution of returns that offers spectacular returns.

8.3 Direct Foreign Investment in U.S. High Technology

In the early 1990s, IPOs by high-technology U.S. firms largely supplanted foreign buy-ins. Direct evidence for this claim has tended to focus on buy-ins by Japanese firms, but there is reason to believe that firms from countries other than Japan also made fewer foreign purchases of U.S. high-technology firms.

Japanese firms in the late 1980s enjoyed cheap equity and raised the equivalent of hundreds of billions of dollars through various means.[20] Investors in the Tokyo Stock Exchange assigned a value in the neighborhood of 30 to a unit of earnings. By contrast, the NYSE in the late 1980s assigned a value closer to 10 to a unit of earnings. Turning these adjusted price-earnings ratios upside down, investors in Japanese firms seemed content with a return of 3 percent, whereas investors in U.S. firms required a return of ten percent or more (see figure 8.1).

Such differences in the cost of equity determine how patient capital can afford to be. Consider a start-up firm that requires a $100 million investment up front in year t and that returns $25 million in perpetuity starting in year $t + n$. At a 3 percent cost of capital, the investment makes sense even if it bears no fruit for forty-five years. By contrast, at a 10 percent cost of equity, the investment must produce in six years to make sense.

Thus, Japanese firms found themselves well placed to buy into U.S. high-technology firms in the late 1980s, whether one conceives the advantage in terms of how high a price they could offer for a given stream of earnings or how long a stretch they could endure before they realized profits. It is not surprising, then, that as the Tokyo Stock Exchange rose precipitously in the late 1980s, Japanese firms bought more high technology than U.S. firms. Data from Ulmer Brothers show

Percentage

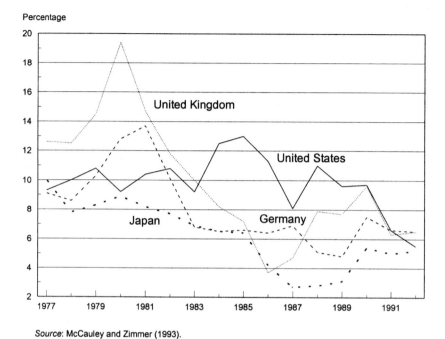

Source: McCauley and Zimmer (1993).

Figure 8.1
Cost of equity

that the Japanese invested increasing sums in buying more and larger U.S. firms in the late 1980s (tables 8.1 and 8.2).

But with the decline of the Nikkei index from 1990 onward and the rise of the U.S. stock market, the cost-of-equity gap between New York and Tokyo narrowed (see Figure 8.2). Paralleling these prices changes, equity issuance dropped to near 0 in Japan as it rose in the United States, as demonstrated above.

At the same time, U.S. high-technology firms found buy-in offers from Japanese firms less compelling after 1990 and pricing talk from domestic investment bankers much more interesting. Thus, while U.S. IPOs boomed in the early 1990s, Japanese firms' investment in U.S. computer firms sank by all measures (tables 8.1 and 8.2).

Table 8.1
Japanese acquisitions in the U.S. computer industry

Year	Number of deals	Number of deals with disclosed value	Amount ($ millions)
1987	24	13	641.25
1988	17	13	1,284.63
1989	44	30	2,113.57
1990	51	39	992.45
1991	48	34	517.70
1992	22	15	158.20

Source: Ulmer Brothers, Inc., *Japanese Acquisitions in the U.S. Computer Industry*, April 1993, p. 2.

Table 8.2
Japanese acquisitions in the U.S. computer industry: Size comparison of deals with disclosed amounts

Year	$10 million	$10–20 million	$20–50 million	$50–100 million	$100–500 million	More than $500 million
1987	7	3	2	—	—	1
1988	7	1	3	1	—	1
1989	12	6	3	3	5	1
1990	22	7	4	3	3	1
1991	20	7	4	3	—	—
1992	12	1	1	1	—	—

Source: Ulmer Brothers, Inc., *Japanese Acquisitions in the U.S. Computer Industry*, April 1993.

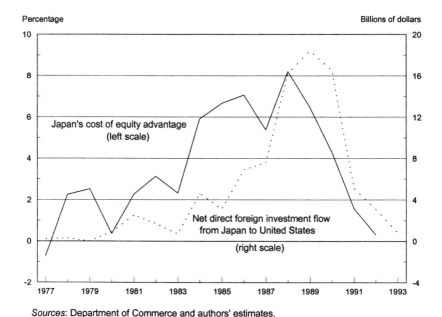

Sources: Department of Commerce and authors' estimates.

Figure 8.2
Cost of equity and direct foreign investment flows

In summary, we offer a straightforward interpretation of the alternation of hot IPO markets and foreign buy-ins that is grounded in
changes in stock market valuations. Just as the IPO market heats up
when the U.S. cost of equity falls, so too can foreign firms afford to
outbid U.S. investors when the cost of equity abroad falls below its
level in the United States.[21] As the U.S. cost of equity has declined in
relation to that abroad, U.S. firms have found it more lucrative to go
public and less necessary to find a foreign partner. In the case of 3DO,
the first licensee, Matsushita, had an equity stake, but U.S. institutions
and individuals among 3DO shareholders held a majority stake as a
result of the IPO.

These developments in new technologies paralleled larger developments in the flows of direct investment between the United States and
Japan. As the equity market in the United States put a higher value on

U.S. earnings and as the crash of the Tokyo market cut off access to cheap equity there, the flood of money out of Japan and into U.S. manufacturing companies, movie studios, real estate, and high-technology firms slowed to a trickle (see figure 8.2).[22] Taking a global view, it is remarkable that the 1990s have seen consistent and substantial net outflows of direct investment from the United States, reversing the large net inflows in the 1980s.[23]

In our view, then, Japanese and some other foreign firms drew on a cost-of-equity advantage in buying U.S. firms in the late 1980s, and that advantage has reversed with the strong performance of the U.S. equity market in the 1990s. In the early 1990s, some analysts sought structural causes for the difficulties of U.S. companies that found expression in the flows of international investment. For instance, in 1992 Michael Porter concluded from a massive research effort, cosponsored by the Council on Competitiveness and the Harvard Business School, that the structure of U.S. capital allocation—principally fractured, passive equity investors as compared to relational investors abroad—had unnaturally shortened the time horizons of American managers.[24] Whatever the virtue of the proposed changes in the U.S. capital allocation process, events have been kinder to the relative-cost-of-equity argument than to the structural argument.

Another strand of the policy debate in the late 1980s was less concerned with the causes of foreign firms' buying up U.S. firms and more with when and how to stop them. We briefly sketch this argument and again suggest that the strong equity market of the 1990s and the strong issuance of IPOs in particular have quieted this discussion.

8.4 Policy Implications

A decade ago, a policy debate over foreign acquisitions of U.S. technology firms focused on whether such deals should be blocked on the grounds of national or economic security. Unease over Japanese purchases of U.S. technology firms has traveled from academic studies to popular novels and movies.[25] Senator J. James Exon (D-Neb.) became concerned with the issue when the Anglo-French financier Sir James Goldsmith tried to acquire Goodyear, along with its plants in Nebraska. After Senate and House hearings on the issue in 1987, Congress adopted an amendment offered jointly by Senator Exon and then-Congressman James J. Florio (D-N.J.) as part of the 1988 Trade Act, which gave the president the right to restrict or to prohibit a proposed merger or acquisition on grounds of national security.[26]

The Bush administration did not exercise its power in this area very often. Between 1988 and mid-1992, the administration received notice of more than 700 deals but extensively reviewed only thirteen and blocked just one: a Chinese company's proposed acquisition of a U.S. aerospace company shortly after the Tiananmen Square massacre.[27] Senator Donald W. Riegle (D-Mich.) argued at the first hearing on the legislation's impact:

Congress's passage of Exon-Florio was a policy directive to the Administration that not all U.S. companies should be open for purchase by foreigners.

There are concerns that the Administration, blinded by its free trade and open investment ideology, has taken a much too narrow view of the authority Exon-Florio gives to it. It has failed to take a broad look at the financial and trade strategies of our industrial competitors and the effect such strategies are having on our technology and financial base. The Administration examines takeovers on an isolated case by case basis and is missing the cumulative impact such takeovers are having on our technology base.[28]

Other commentators cautiously urged blocking deals on grounds of economic security. Laura D'Andrea Tyson, then a professor of economics and business administration at the University of California at Berkeley and subsequently chair of the President's Council of Economic Advisors, suggested possibly blocking deals that concentrate key technologies in a few hands or allow foreign governments to control such technologies:

[F]oreign investment is beneficial. However, when foreign governments are involved or the acquisition results in increasing concentration of the industry—

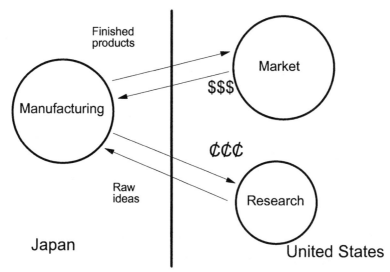

Source: National Research Council, *U.S.-Japan Strategic Alliances in the Semiconductor Industry* (1992), p. 72.

Figure 8.3
"The high-tech banana republic"

thereby jeopardizing either national or economic security—we should look very carefully at the investments. I believe that . . . the McDonnell Douglas acquisition by partly government owned Taiwan Aerospace would jeopardize American economic interests, not just national security interests, and CFIUS [the interagency review Committee on Foreign Investment in the United States] is simply powerless to address that question.[29]

At the heart of the policy debate was the concern that foreign acquisitions could mean lost money and jobs in the United States. One view was that "[o]utside acquisitions of high-technology startups in biotechnology and microelectronics deny this country the large economic 'rents' from emerging technologies. And when the fruits of research are thus appropriated, subsequent development and manufacturing may well be done outside the United States."[30] This concern was portrayed in a diagram, "The high-tech banana republic," found in a National Research Council study of U.S.-Japanese strategic alliances in the semiconductor industry (figure 8.3).

Some observers also worried that foreign acquisitions would result in research and development moving offshore. One commentator, Gregory Tassey, held that "major portions of the first stage in the production chain (research and development) is [sic] reserved for the home country" and "technology is basically appropriated by a foreign production chain with reduced follow-on investment."[31] Tassey demonstrated that, at least in manufacturing, foreign firms in the United States do less research and development in relation to sales than do U.S. firms.[32]

Whatever the validity of these concerns, we contend that the U.S. stock market has made them less salient. In the 1990s, foreign firms wanting to buy into small U.S. firms had to compete with U.S. individuals and institutions eager to invest in IPOs.

In providing generous, if variable, financing for new firms, the U.S. stock market stands out. The number of U.S. IPOs in either of the peak years 1993 or 1996 greatly exceeded the number of Japanese IPOs in the Tokyo market's peak year of 1990 (see figure 8.4). What is more, the peak-to-peak comparison is especially telling if the Tokyo stock market valuation of the late 1980s is taken to be a once-in-a-lifetime (or once-in-three-lifetimes) event. The U.S. stock market has an unmatched capacity to put cash into the hands of dreamers and inventors.

The role of IPOs in financing industrial innovation should not be overstated. Most research and development is financed by large, successful firms out of internal funds. Bronwyn Hall found that the leveraging business in the 1980s put pressure on mature firms to redeploy their internal funds away from research and development and toward debt service. Thus the U.S. corporate sector's general return to equity in the 1990s may have done more for research and development spending than the hot IPO market. In addition, IPOs have limits as channels of finance for industrial innovation. If hot IPO markets depend on stock market valuations, and those valuations vary over time, it follows that hot IPO markets offer only intermittent support for industrial innovation. The tendency of venture capitalists to nurture new

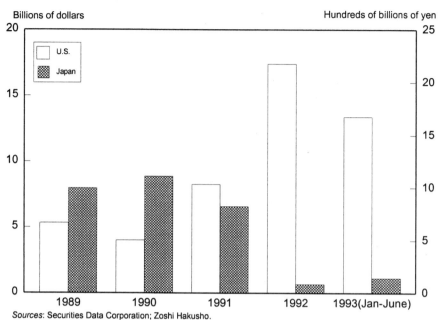

Sources: Securities Data Corporation; Zoshi Hakusho.
Notes: For the sake of comparability, closed-end funds and reverse LBO's are not included in U.S. IPO figures. Scale equates one dollar to 125 yen.

Figure 8.4
Funds raised in initial public offerings: United States and Japan

firms in anticipation of the next hot IPO market somewhat mitigates hot IPO markets' episodic nature.[33]

Moreover, some technologies may not lend themselves to the venture capital–IPO cycle. The venture capitalists who finance start-ups before they go public look to cash out in five to eight years. As a result, any technology with a longer development cycle has a difficult time making it through the pipeline of venture capital and public offering. Some commentators, for example, have argued that new technology for producing semiconductors has drawn inadequate investment because of its long development cycle.[34] Also, IPO investors can develop as much of a taste for fast food chains and steak houses as high-technology firms.

8.5 Conclusion

Hot IPO markets like the very long one of the 1990s offer cheap equity for young firms. The hot market of the 1990s, like earlier hot markets, seems to be part of a more general spate of equity issuance in response to high share prices. The ready availability of cheap equity capital in the 1990s has helped keep foreign companies from buying U.S. high-technology firms. More than its foreign counterparts, the U.S. stock market can help at the margin to finance industrial innovation.

9   *Mergers and Acquisitions in the 1990s*

Chapters 2 and 3 left off at the collapse of the leveraging business and with it the decline of mergers and acquisitions. In the recession of 1990–91, not only did mergers and acquisitions slow for the normal cyclic reason of lower cash flows but also leveraged acquisitions dried up altogether as U.S. corporations struggled to manage the debts they accumulated in the 1980s, as exemplified by RJR-Nabisco in chapter 4. Intervening chapters have concentrated on Wall Street's remarkable run of business in new issues of stocks and, more unevenly, bonds in this decade. Chapter 5 showed how U.S. corporations sought to bolster their finances by selling equity, paying down debt, and refinancing their outstanding bonds. Chapter 6 took the measure of the issuance activity and demonstrated that low short-term rates through 1993 not only made financial markets receptive to the massive equity-for-debt swap but also did the most work in relieving the burden of debt on corporate cash flows. Chapter 7 examined the performance of those equity issues that most immediately reversed the leveraging of the 1980s and found their performance to be no better than par. Chapter 8 focused on history's longest-running hot market for initial public offerings, in which investors will likely reap puny average returns in pursuit of the winning lottery ticket while innovative companies, along with mundane, will have financed themselves on the cheap.

This chapter returns to the mergers and acquisitions business treated in chapters 2 to 4. The pace of mergers and acquisitions continued to accelerate all through the 1990s.[1] As in the 1980s, mergers and acquisitions continue to rise in the 1990s with economic activity in general. But the resemblance does not extend to the effect on corporate capital structures. Although some acquisitions in the 1990s are serving to leverage up the firms involved, overall developments in the merger market echo the theme of the return to equity sounded in the last four chapters.

In the 1990s merger market, executives have had in hand the press to print the currency needed to make deals. Instead of having to persuade creditors to finance debt-heavy deals, executives could issue their own shares in exchange for those of their merger partners or targets. Why go out and ask to borrow when the share-printing press at headquarters could buy so much? While observers argued whether share prices in the mid-to-late-1990s were too high, a massive reallocation of household portfolios into equity mutual funds meant that the market readily accepted freshly minted shares. High prices had an opposite effect on LBO organizers: The quite substantial sums available to LBO partnerships had a hard time finding promising buyout targets.[2] Thus, mergers and acquisitions in the 1990s typically saw one firm exchange (or swap) its shares for those of another firm. Consistent with our image of corporate treasurers as canny timers, the switch from merger debt in the 1980s to merger equity in the 1990s responded to the high share prices prevailing in the 1990s.

The contrast in the financing of mergers and acquisitions in the 1990s and in the 1980s is the most salient of a series of contrasts developed in this chapter. We begin by juxtaposing the character of two particular deals: RJR-Nabisco's leveraged buyout and WorldCom's merger with MCI. The differences between these deals highlight important differences between the aggregate effect of mergers on corporate capital structures in the two eras. Next we examine the role of spinoffs and divestitures in the ongoing return to corporate specialization.

Then we turn to the crosscurrents of the 1990s' acquisition business in the pharmaceuticals and defense industries, where debt played an unusually large part. The picture that emerges is one of a merger market very possibly caught up in its own enthusiasms, which may or may not pan out, but still discriminating enough to continue to refashion companies into more coherent businesses and to drain equity capital out of sectors without debilitating increases of debt.

9.1 WorldCom-MCI and RJR-Nabisco

Chapter 4's review of the archetypal deal of the 1980s, the leveraged buyout of RJR-Nabisco, highlighted the deal's fevered bidding and consequently high leverage. If RJR-Nabisco epitomized the mergers and acquisitions of the 1980s, perhaps WorldCom's merger with MCI in 1997 epitomizes the 1990s wave of mergers and acquisitions. The deal unites businesses only recently created in response to deregulation and brings together under one roof heretofore separate technologies, the so-called convergence theme. Shares valued at $35 billion closed the deal which made it noticeably larger than the RJR-Nabisco buyout. The contrasts between the two deals, far more striking than their similarities, make it clear why the once again very active mergers and acquisitions of the 1990s do not represent a return to the 1980s in respect to their effect on corporate capital structures.

The choice of which merger in the 1990s to compare to RJR-Nabisco is ultimately not very important to the comparison. Any one of several megadeals of the 1990s might have been selected—the $19 billion acquisition of McCaw by AT&T, the $17 billion purchase of Pacific Telesis by SBC Communications (the former Southwestern Bell), or the $13 billion hookup of Bell Atlantic and NYNEX. The choice is not critical insofar as what is said below regarding WorldCom-MCI applies equally to the other cases. Indeed, we shall refer occasionally to AT&T's acquisition of McCaw for the sake of concreteness below.

RJR-Nabisco and the big recent mergers occurred well along their respective cyclic upswings. RJR-Nabisco was the talk of the market seven years into the long upswing of the 1980s; the WorldCom-MCI merger likewise closed seven years after the shallow trough of 1991. Well into 1999, at least, the pace of mergers and acquisitions continued to build, with the proposed merger of Exxon and Mobil perhaps the biggest deal of the cycle.

While the deals are similar in their size and timing, WorldCom-MCI (or AT&T-McCaw) differs from RJR-Nabisco in several important respects. The character of the buyer differed; the process and attitude of the deal differed; the means of payment differed; the horizon of the deal differed; and the fees collected and the effect on the bond market differed.

On the first dimension, the *character of the buyer* involved in the two deals differed starkly, not so much in size as in organization. Whereas RJR-Nabisco's buyer, KKR, was a "financial" buyer, with no business to which RJR-Nabisco was to be attached, WorldCom (AT&T) was an "industry" buyer. True, KKR held a portfolio of companies, but RJR-Nabisco was not to be combined in any operational way with, say, KKR's publishing firm.[3] By contrast, WorldCom merged with MCI (and AT&T bought McCaw) with the express purpose of building up its business long-distance and Internet services (and for AT&T, hooking up its long-distance lines to McCaw's cellular network). WorldCom itself is in some ways an archetypal firm of the 1990s, a virtual merger machine that grew from recent and small roots in Alabama by swapping its shares for telecommunications firms and then rationalizing and reducing their costs.

More generally, public corporations have eclipsed LBO partnerships as buyers in the 1990s. Of course, LBO partnerships never dominated among buyers in the late 1980s. Still, in 1986–89, LBOs put tens of billions of dollars of cash into shareholders' hands each year, mostly thanks to deals of more than a billion dollars. In the four years 1994–97, by contrast, the likes of KKR, Forstmann Little, and Goldman Sachs

Table 9.1
Tender offers, 1989–95

Year	Number	Amount ($ billions)	As a percentage of M&A
1989	208	156	50
1990	74	30	15
1991	55	11	8
1992	44	5	4
1993	127	31	18
1994	115	59	21
1995	155	74	20
1996	154	75	14

Sources: "Robust Revival for Tender Offers," *Mergers and Acquisitions*, March/April 1996, pp. 20, 37, and "A Good Way to Win a Prize Target," *Mergers and Acquisitions*, March/April 1997, p. 20.

Capital Partners II closed only a handful of big deals—those of more than $1 billion—and these put no more than $6.6 billion into shareholders' hands.[4] The biggest deal involving an LBO partnership (described in chapter 4) was KKR's exit from RJR-Nabisco into Borden, and this deal was itself an equity swap.

Similarly, the *process and attitude of the deal making* involved in the two deals could hardly have differed more (table 9.1). Whereas the contest for RJR-Nabisco made good cinema, no screenwriters will bring the sedate discussions among executives and board members of AT&T and McCaw to the screen. The essential question of how many AT&T shares were to be exchanged for each McCaw share was worked out quietly and amicably behind closed doors, albeit subject to the constraint represented by what the market would find acceptable. When British Telecom offered an opportunity by lowering its cash bid for MCI's shares in response to some poor results at MCI, WorldCom wanted to put a bid on the table with a fairly certain cash value. So WorldCom offered MCI shareholders a price nearly fixed in dollar terms: a number of its own shares for each MCI share, that number varying negatively with WorldCom's own share prices. Within limits, MCI shareholders would end up owning more of the merged company if WorldCom shares weakened.[5]

The biggest hurdle for many mergers of the 1990s has not been paying the price but obtaining regulatory approval. The WorldCom-MCI deal remained pending for almost a year as it was vetted by antitrust officials. Moreover, after the precedent of European authorities' imposing conditions on the Boeing–McDonnell Douglas merger, the antitrust vetting now includes European Union officials in Brussels as well as Justice Department officials in Washington.

The contrast between the public, prolonged, and pitched battle among several bidders to set a mostly cash price on the shares of RJR-Nabisco and the technocratic fixing of an exchange rate between two pieces of paper brings the two deals contrasting *means of payment* into focus. As a result of the use of debt in one and equity in another, the deals carried very different implications for the riskiness of corporations' capital structures. KKR's deal stripped capital out of corporate America, whereas WorldCom's (or AT&T's) deal just changed the name on some share certificates. The closing of the RJR-Nabisco deal retired equity, stripping equity out of the firm and putting billions of dollars into the hands of shareholders, including Tar Heels who had received shares in Reynolds Tobacco from their grandfathers and who found themselves suddenly flush. By contrast, MCI (McCaw) shareholders received common shares in WorldCom (AT&T) in exchange for their common shares.

The aggregate means of payment for mergers and acquisitions in the 1990s contrast sharply with that in the 1980s. Figure 9.1 shows that cash was king in the 1980s, whereas shares reign in the 1990s. The strategic mergers of the 1990s leave the equity in the firm and thereby give the merged firm the financial strength, flexibility, and low debt costs needed for further expansion.

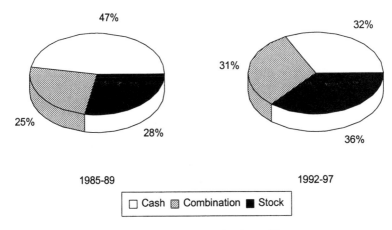

Source: Houlihan, Lokey, Howard and Zinn, *1998 Mergerstat Review*, p. 14.
Note: Percentages are based on number rather than value of deals. For deals over $1 billion, stock swaps represented 46% of all deals by number in 1993-97.

Figure 9.1
Means of payment in U.S. mergers and acquisitions

The buyers in the two deals were casting their eyes on very different *horizons*. KKR told its equity investors that they should not expect to see their money before ten years, and LBO firms generally look to exit from their deals in five years. In the event, KKR exited in half that time from RJR-Nabisco into Borden, but the buyout firm hoped to improve the returns to investors in its 1987 fund, which had been poor, before handing them back their money. By contrast, analysts in the year 2000 would treat any WorldCom divestiture of MCI as prima facie evidence of the failure of their merger.

The difference in *fees* in the 1980s and 1990s accounts for the lower profile of Wall Street deal makers in the present decade. Press accounts often make it out to be a matter of personalities, contrasting the swaggering, macho image of the deal makers of the 1980s with the quiet, bespectacled, backroom industry specialist of the 1990s. But the telling difference is that the friendly deals of the 1990s, with CEOs rather than former investment bankers in control, drop no more than a gentle rain on Wall Street. WorldCom-MCI and AT&T-McCaw paid less than

Table 9.2
Total merger and acquisition advisory fees, 1988–98

Year	Acquiror fees ($ millions)	Target fees ($ millions)	Total fees ($ millions)	Number of deals with disclosed fees
1988	617.6	661.3	1,278.9	312
1989	640.8	598.5	1,239.3	276
1990	234.4	327.8	562.2	218
1991	118.6	197.1	315.7	167
1992	70.8	158.1	228.9	185
1993	118.1	280.8	398.9	227
1994	243.1	451.5	694.6	266
1995	416.0	571.3	987.3	341
1996	294.5	682.4	976.9	369
1997	675.5	1,370.1	2,045.6	391
1998	871.6	1,820.8	2,692.4	498

Source: Mergers and Acquisitions, March/April 1997, p. 58 and March/April 1999, p. 61.

1 percent of the deal value to their investment bankers. In part, the smaller fees paid reflect the investment that big acquisitive firms, particularly in high-tech fields, have made in their own internal acquisition departments. By contrast, LBO firms in effect buy sales "pitches" from investment bankers for possible deals (see chapter 4).

Dollar for merger dollar, the good times did not roll for Wall Street's merger and acquisition departments in the 1990s as they had in the 1980s (table 9.2).[6] Although the deal count and value in 1995 exceeded those in 1988, total fees remained more than a third lower. It is interesting that the leveraging business in the 1980s resulted in a rough balance between acquirers' fees and targets' fees, whereas targets spend more in the 1990s. This imbalance may reflect acquisitive companies' investment in their own merger departments.

A final difference concerns the *effect on the bond market* of the deals in the two decades. Bondholders of MCI, which Drexel often cited as a growth firm funded by junk bonds, could not have been disappointed at an acquisition by a practically debt-free company. (Similarly, the holders of McCaw's bonds could only have been happy to blink at the screen and see that they would have a strong credit behind them.) There was nothing to compare to the sense of betrayal felt by the insurance companies who, having just bought RJR-Nabisco bonds, learned that the shareholders were about to receive the accumulated funds that had justified narrow spreads over riskless Treasury bonds.

More generally, an analysis of big mergers in mid-1994 through early 1997 suggests that mergers can be good for bondholders. Mergers of more than $1 billion resulted in more upgrades of rated debt than downgrades—forty-six compared to thirty-six.[7] By contrast, in 1984–89, downgrades outnumbered upgrades two to one (forty-one against nineteen). Thus, the character of mergers and acquisitions in the 1990s, featuring well-heeled companies buying with their own shares or even with cash, is easy on bond holders.

Our succession of contrasts leaves an important question. What is behind the big deals of the 1990s? An easy answer for telecommunications is the uneasy relationship between the schoolyard organization of the telephone industry—the local monopoly telephone firms in their corners of the playground and AT&T in its—and the technological change that multiplies connections between households or businesses. The 1996 Telecommunications Act abandoned this schoolyard setup in favor of competition and let AT&T purchase Teleport Communications, which supplies businesses with local phone service in several large cities. Deals that subverted the schoolyard organization from the other side of the playground were the mergers first of SBC Communications (née Southwestern Bell) and Pacific Telesis (née Bell), which works to internalize most of the domestic long-distance calls from Texas through California and to capture much of the trans-Pacific phone traffic originating in the United States, and then of Bell Atlantic and NYNEX. Deregulation has also figured importantly in active mergers in banking, where interstate banking is now allowed, in finance more generally (Citigroup), and in electric utilities, which are being required to carry power generated by competitors. A more relaxed view of competition has doubtless been critical in permitting mergers in railroads, which have served to create coast-to-coast and Chicago-to-Mexico networks under single management at Burlington Northern–Santa Fe Pacific, Union Pacific–Chicago & Northwestern, and Union Pacific–Southern Pacific.

Beyond the deals in telecommunications proper, many deals have assembled "software" producers, hardware producers, and electronic delivery systems. In this class of deals were Viacom-Paramount (cable-movies), Viacom-Blockbuster (cable–video rental), Comcast–TCI-QVC, AT&T–Lin Broadcasting, Time-Warner–Cable Vision, Walt Disney–Capital Cities/ABC, and Time-Warner–Turner Broadcasting. These so-called convergence mergers of the 1990s may strike the cynic as no more than a revival of the conglomerate mergers of the 1990s with a high-tech gloss whose demerging will provide jobs for investment bankers of another generation. From this point of view, the current combinations of programming, transmissions, and sound and picture reproduction reflect less the synergies imminent in the technology than the conceits of the executives involved— encouraged by investors' enthusiasm. Sony and Matsushita bought entertainment software to go with their hardware, and Matsushita has already retreated from Hollywood. But at least synergistic arguments are being made, whereas in the 1960s at firms like ITT there was no pretense of any coherence among the businesses gathered under one corporate roof. The next section treats the ongoing breakup of the conglomerates that survived the 1980s.

9.2 Spin-offs and Divestitures

One ground for a less cynical view of convergence mergers is that an enthusiasm for breaking up conglomerates continues elsewhere in the equity market. In the 1980s, high debt often seemed the necessary if not altogether welcome means for breaking up conglomerates. Today, option-holding managers pressured to raise stock prices by the more vocal institutional investors choose corporate breakups.

A prominent early case was USX, formed as a merger of US Steel and an oil company. Institutional holders of USX's stock convinced managers that they wanted to be able to trade the oil and steel companies separately. In addition, perhaps few analysts could figure out the value of the merged entity and the demerged pair of stocks would therefore be worth more than USX.[8]

The mechanisms for divestments vary, but in the easiest case shareholders of the parent firm get shares in a subsidiary as a sort of in-kind dividend. The possibility that no tax may be levied on this stock dividend makes for a more tax-efficient breakup than that achieved by a buyout of a whole firm. Whereas the frequently long-standing individual shareholders of RJR-Nabisco had to pay taxes on their suddenly realized gains, long-time holders of self-divorcing conglomerates like ITT can pick and choose whether and which of the spun-off shares to sell.

ITT offers a particularly ripe example of a conglomerate breaking itself apart through spin-offs. Starting the postwar period as a sleepy operator of overseas telephone companies, the firm diversified under the legendary Harold Geneen by acquisitions of hotels, insurance, car parts, car leasing, and other businesses.[9] Its acquisition of Hartford Fire in 1970 stood as the record postwar acquisition for five years. The conglomerate stood firm against the bust-up acquisitions of the 1980s, and CEO Rand Araskog found himself for some years vilified for earning tens of millions of dollars per year even as ITT's share price underperformed the market. He decided in 1996 to break the firm up into three parts by giving shareholders shares in two new groupings of businesses. Headquarters freed Hartford Fire to return to the New York Stock Exchange as a white-collar ITT Hartford Group Inc. and freed the unsexy automotive and electronic products to return the New York Stock Exchange as the blue-collar ITT Industries. The rump of Sheraton hotels and the newly acquired Caesar's World casinos and Madison Square Garden thus remained on the Big Board as a newly distinguishable leisure-suit ITT Corporation.

The irony is that the trimmed-down ITT quickly attracted the acquisitive interest of Hilton Hotels. A long fight ensued, with ITT using the target-friendly corporate law of Nevada to fend off Hilton. In the end, ITT found a white knight in the form of a hotel company operating in the tax-friendly form of a real estate investment trust.

Westinghouse is another conglomerate looking to divest, acquire and spin off its way to a new coherence. Westinghouse sold its loss-making finance company;[10] bought CBS for $5.4 billion in 1995 to complement the Westinghouse TV and radio networks; bought Infinity Broadcasting for $3.7 billion to add still more radio stations (thanks to the Telecommunications Act); and bought American Radio Systems for $1.4 billion. The firm is looking to spin off its prosaic industrial pieces, including elevators.

Another approach, taken by AT&T with its equipment manufacturing subsidiary, is to offer shares to the public. In this case, shareholders of the parent firm choose whether to acquire a stake in the new company or to decline to buy the new shares, whereas other investors who did not want to own the conglomerate may want to buy shares in the newly separated company. A stock market investor who is offered a so-called equity carve out, however, must ask himself whether the selling company is bringing its subsidiary to market at a time of favorable prices—favorable for the seller, that is, and therefore unfavorable for the buyer.[11] A clear example of such market timing was the sale by U.S. and U.K. companies of their Japanese subsidiaries during the Tokyo stock market boom of the 1980s.[12] AT&T's Lucent proved the counter case, as its stock outperformed that of its former owner after AT&T's potential rivals among the local telephone companies stopped strategically shifting their equipment orders away from Lucent.

Spin-offs and equity carve outs differ in that the former create a new stand-alone firm, whereas often the latter are only partial, with the selling firm retaining a majority stake in the newly listed firm. Moreover, the spin-off just reshuffles corporate assets, whereas the carve out brings fresh equity capital into the corporate sector. The common elements are that Wall Street gets more shares to trade and the stock market tends to push up the price of a parent firm announcing either a spin-off or a carve out.

Although it is clear that investors are high on deconglomeration, it is less clear that today's conglomerates are losers. A careful recent study argued that the stock market valuation of conglomerates is 15–20 percent lower than one would expect from the price-earnings ratios the market assigns to the "pure plays," or monoline firms making up the conglomerates: The whole is less than the sum of the parts.[13] Such a value difference certainly can account for the observed trend toward corporate specialization. But when investors were high on conglomerates, the whole was more than the sum of the parts and conglomerate mergers, in the parlance of modern financial economics, "created shareholder value." So the stock market offers a yardstick of embarrassingly elastic dimensions.

From a business standpoint one can ask, Are conglomerates more or less profitable than one would expect given their business composition? The same study just cited found a very small median shortfall in the ratio of (reported) earnings to sales in relation to what one would expect given industry medians for the underlying constituent businesses. Given the study's exclusion of conglomerates with financial services subsidiaries—which presumably knocked out ITT, AT&T, General Motors, and General Electric[14]—the case that conglomerates perform worse than one would expect on the basis of the composition of the underlying businesses must be considered still open to debate.

Whether a matter of fashion or the market's return to good sense, the trend toward corporate specialization seen in the 1980s continues with spin-offs, carve outs and asset sales in the 1990s.[15] The upshot is that the reshuffling of corporate assets into more coherent piles continues without leveraged buyouts getting the deal.

Taken together, then, mergers in industries undergoing rapid technological change and spin-offs and carve outs of conglomerates suggest
a mergers-and-acquisitions market simultaneously assembling new
businesses and disassembling old businesses. On the face of it, the organizations resulting from such nuanced activity may stand a better
chance of surviving the test of time. In the meantime their general
reliance on equity does not leave them vulnerable, as the late 1980s
deals did, to slightly worse conditions than those foreseen by sanguine
and interested deal makers. Let us consider the counterpoints to the
general use of equity in mergers and acquisitions in the 1990s represented by deals in pharmaceuticals and defense.

9.3   Health Care/Pharmaceuticals and Defense Mergers and Acquisitions

Two industries have returned equity capital to their investors in the
1990s to an extraordinary extent. In health care and pharmaceuticals
new strategies of business and government alike, including the shift
to managed care, prescription guidelines, and tighter fee schedules, reversed a long run of strong pricing power. Defense contractors, for their
part, faced a sharp drop-off in demand at the end of the Cold War.
The response in both industries to the drop-off in expected revenues
has been consolidation to cut costs. Their involvement in the merger
wave does not distinguish firms in these two industries, but their selective decapitalization does.

Pharmaceuticals: Swallowing the Bitter Pill of Price Cuts

The simultaneous challenge the pharmaceutical industry has faced in
major industrial-country markets arises from attempts to control the
costs of health care. Whether pushed by governments trying to rein

Percentage

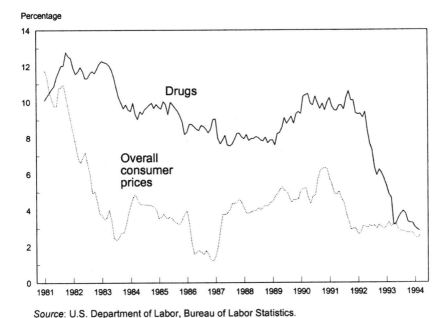

Source: U.S. Department of Labor, Bureau of Labor Statistics.

Figure 9.2
Inflation rate for prescription drugs

in public spending, as in Japan, Germany, France, and Italy, or by corporations belatedly trying to bring employee health costs under control, as in the United States, the worldwide drug industry has faced a sudden loss of pricing power. Figure 9.2 shows that from 1982 through 1992, drug companies managed U.S. price increases almost double the rate of general consumer price inflation. More recently, drug prices have risen only with the general level of consumer inflation. Prices of health care more generally have also decelerated sharply, and consolidation has swept health care corporations as well. We focus on mergers in drugs, however.

Mergers look like a response at both ends of the business to the drug companies' loss of pricing power. At the development end of the business, the hope is to combine research forces, producing wider ranges of drugs and reducing scientific staffs. For instance, the merger of Ciba-Geigy and Sandoz shocked their headquarters city of Basel, Switzerland, where lab coat layoffs could be expected to idle thousands. At the marketing end, the hope was to achieve economies in the sales forces that peddle pills to pharmacists and doctors.

Changes in the marketing of drugs, however, have led U.S. drug companies to make a certain class of acquisitions that are most obviously linked to their loss of pricing power. The telling targets are prescription management firms. Employer health plans and insurance companies, anxious to hold down the growth of drug spending, have signed up these firms to draw up lists of the drugs that are most cost-effective, from which doctors participating in the plans are to choose their prescriptions. Not only are generic drugs favored, but also high-margin but only marginally effective patented drugs are disfavored. In the old days drug marketing went one on one against doctors, with ads in journals, free samples, and personal visits. Faced with professional and cost-conscious corporate buyers, the drug companies have bought them. Thus in 1994 Eli Lilly paid $4 billion for PCS Health System, with revenues of only half that sum but 1,300 health plan sponsors and 50 million members. The year before, Merck paid $6.6 billion for Medco Containment Services.[16]

These drug industry deals have tended to put cash in the hands of shareholders, that is, to retire equity, and it is easy to see why. Given the pricing pressure, the drug industry fell out of favor with stock market investors. Thus drug company executives were less inclined to pay for acquisitions with what they regarded as underappreciated and thus undervalued shares. The Lilly and Merck acquisitions thus between them flushed $10 billion of equity out of the U.S. drug industry. These funds were no longer available to finance new drugs, it is true, and to some extent the drug company executives are right when they argue that lower prices and profits will mean fewer new drugs. But the judgments being made by prescription management firms in effect imply that many new drugs are not producing an increment of good health commensurate with their costs of development. If these judgments are correct, then the selective decapitalization of the drug industry, or perhaps better said, the migration of risk capital from drugs to other industries, makes sense. It is perhaps safer to say that equity retirement from drugs in the 1990s makes more sense than equity retirement from airlines in the 1980s. From pharmaceuticals, we turn to an industry where only those immediately involved can regret its downsizing.

Defense: Returning the Owners' Money

It is easy to argue the logic of defense mergers and acquisitions' departure from the general 1990s pattern of equity-financed deals. The fall of the Berlin Wall, though good news for mankind, was bad news for defense contractors. Figure 9.3 tracks the drop-off in real defense spending from more than 6 percent of national output in the second Reagan administration to about half of that in the second Clinton administration. Supermarkets and department stores, objects of more than their share of LBO activity in the late 1980s, experienced no such drop-off in demand.

Given Uncle Sam's tightening of defense spending in the 1990s, engineers and factory workers would have to find new work. Likewise the capital that was financing the development, production, and marketing of planes, tanks, and ships would have to be put to new use. Would the engineers and capital be redeployed in new businesses into which the defense contractors might diversify? Or would the defense contractors find themselves looking for new jobs even as the capital made its way back to its ultimate owners for reinvestment elsewhere?

Though the first option might seem more humane from the workers' standpoint, the record of such transitions is thick with failure. One thinks of the attempted diversification by Japanese steelmakers into microchip production in the 1980s. Prospects may even be below a low average for defense contractors in particular, because defense procurement's frequent cost overruns and cost-plus pricing hardly bred

Percentage

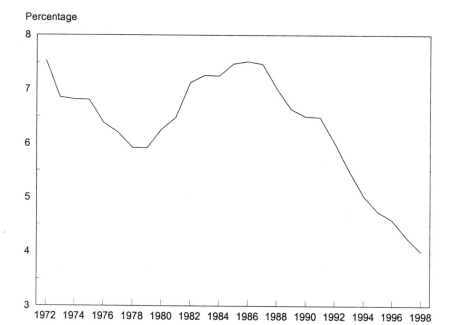

Source: U.S. Department of Commerce, Bureau of Economic Analysis.

Figure 9.3
Real defense spending as a percent of GDP

tight-fisted managers or lean organizations. A hardheaded view suggests returning workers and capital to their respective markets as the least wasteful approach.

It turns out that mergers and acquisitions in defense have been returning capital to the owners. Three examples serve to illustrate this selective decapitalization.

Consider first Northrup's $2.1 billion takeover of Grumann. After heated bidding against Martin Marietta, Northrup paid out cash to Grumann's shareholders and arranged a large syndicated bank loan to finance the payment. The deal thus had the result of substituting debt for equity in the defense industry's capital structure. But in view of the reduced need for capital spending in this shrinking line of business, servicing the debt taken on to finance the merger should not prove too great a challenge. Moreover, the merged firm hopes to eliminate overlap and consolidate production, allowing it to pay down its debt.

General Dynamics offers a striking example of a firm divesting its operations and returning capital to its shareholders. The company sold off various divisions in 1992–94, including Cessna Aircraft to Textron; Missile Systems to General Motors (Hughes); Tactical Military Aircraft, maker of the F-16, to Lockheed; and Space Launch Systems to Martin Marietta. Flush with cash, the firm declared a special dividend and then proceeded to repurchase its shares in quantity. As a result, the firm's payments to its shareholders rose from the roughly $100 million per year paid out in dividends in 1988–91 to $1 billion in 1992 and to more than $1.5 billion in 1993.

The striking feature of the General Dynamics story is that it did not involve debt. The 1980s' argument was that without the discipline of high debt, threatening bankruptcy and loss of job if scheduled payments were not made, managers would invariably prefer the perquisites of running a big company over managing in the shareholders' interests. But General Dynamics actually paid off its debt as well as paying out billions to its shareholders with the funds raised by selling off divisions.[17] The motive force of General Dynamics' shrinkage was not fear but greed, not bonded debt but options: The new CEO who took control in 1991 did not so much fear for his job if he could not make his debt payments as look to win the lottery if he got the share price up. In the event, the CEO pocketed a cool $54 million[18] for four years of selling divisions, laying off workers and returning funds to the shareholders. Even if one imagines that the same job could have been done for, say, $27 million, one must concede that flushing $2.5 billion out of General Dynamics for about $50 million is more cost-effective than flushing $20 plus billion out of RJR-Nabisco at the cost of about $1 billion—2 percent for General Dynamics versus 5 percent for RJR-Nabisco.

Table 9.3
Means of payment in jumbo deals by industry, 1994–November 1997

	Defense/health care and pharmaceutical	Other industries	Total
Equity	38.2	228.2	266.3
Cash/debt	64.0	123.3	187.3
Total	102.2	351.4	453.6

Source: Authors' calculations based on data from Capital Markets Section, Board of Governors of the Federal Reserve System.
Note: Figures quoted are in billions of dollars.

Not all defense deals have returned cash to shareholders, as our third example shows, and it is possible to exaggerate the cash payments to shareholders in the defense sector. Martin Marietta, the frustrated suitor of Grumann, in 1994 tied the knot with Lockheed, paying for its bride in the currency of its own shares, some $5 billion worth. Claims that $10 billion in cash has been returned to shareholders by defense companies by 1995 seem overstated.[19] Lockheed Martin's $7 billion cash purchase of Loral Corporation in 1996 did take equity retirement in the sector to considerably more than $10 billion.

Looking just at deals with a value of more than $1 billion (including assumed debt), it is evident that health care/pharmaceuticals and defense have atypically put cash into the hands of shareholders. Equity retired has amounted to two-thirds of transaction value in the former and more than one-half in the latter. By contrast, all the other nonfinancial industries have shown an equity retirement rate of about a third (table 9.3).

9.4   Implications of the 1990s Pattern of Merger Financing

A happy implication immediately follows from leverage's much reduced role in mergers and acquisitions in the 1990s. In the 1980s some tried to write excuses for leverage as the necessary means to achieve corporate restructuring. But mergers and acquisitions of the 1990s demonstrate that a great deal of restructuring can occur without much leveraging. To be sure, many of the mergers in the 1990s are putting together firms on the premise of technological convergence (with deregulation often serving as a permissive force), and this premise may not prove as valid as now thought. Still, the work done by the 1980s leveraged deals—reshuffling corporate divisions and dealing them into more coherent, specialized firms—clearly continues.

Even the exceptions to the use of equity to finance deals suggest a more discriminating market, at least as compared to the wild and woolly 1980s. Mergers and acquisitions in the 1990s have served to flush equity capital out of an industry suddenly subject to slower revenue growth (health care and drugs) and out of an industry that must shrink (defense). This selective decapitalization makes much more sense than the kind of indiscriminate leveraging that decapitalized supermarkets, department stores, food companies, and airlines in the 1980s.

9.5 Conclusions

The 1990s wave of mergers and acquisitions raises little in the way of financial stability or monetary policy concerns. It is not systematically impoverishing U.S. corporations, making their normal operations vulnerable to any slowdown in growth. Instead, the strategic mergers and acquisitions of the 1990s are in general leaving the resulting firms with the financial strength, flexibility, and low debt costs needed for expansion. On the present evidence, the Federal Reserve will not have to give the economy extra fuel in the next recession to power through the headwinds of corporations suddenly intent on paying down their debt. Redrawing the boundaries between corporations by combining and spinning off equity can be a socially benign activity among consenting adults.

Whether the high equity prices that have made equity the preferred means of payment should raise concern is another matter, one well outside of the scope of this book. In 1998, worrying signs emerged of corporations borrowing to buy their shares. In addition, there may be leverage of a sort on the buy side. Among institutional investors, hedge funds are natural suspects. But perhaps the household sector is an important current locus of leverage. The strong flows into equity mutual funds have exceeded the flow of savings and have represented a draw-down of bank deposits and a deliberate maintenance of mortgage debt. This is leverage of a sort that may put a drag on consumption in the event of a downturn in the equity market.

However the mergers and acquisition wave of the 1990s ends, the leveraging wave of the 1980s raised serious policy issues. Chapter 10 considers how policy should respond when an inflation of asset prices threatens to wreak havoc on the structure of credit. The more benign nature of mergers and acquisitions in the 1990s should not prevent our learning lessons from the mergers and acquisitions of the 1980s.

III   *Lessons*

10   *Policy and Asset Inflation*

Faced with rapid credit growth and asset price inflation, which policy makers should pursue which policies? This question collapses in most treatments into how monetary policy should respond to asset price inflation. After reviewing the debate over whether monetary policy should respond to asset price inflation and deflation, this chapter argues that central banks need more tools than interest rate policy to respond effectively to pronounced swings in asset prices. Central banks must stand prepared with credit policies, including bank regulation, to lean against asset price inflation or at least to prevent the subsequent deflation from wreaking havoc on the credit mechanism. In addition, central banks need help from other policy makers. In response to the 1980s enthusiasm for leveraging corporate assets at high prices in particular, the Federal Reserve needed reinforcements: reforms of tax policy and corporate governance.

10.1   Restrain Asset Price Inflation and Deflation with Monetary Policy?

As a policy precept commands broader and broader assent, the definition of its key terms is more and more debated. So it appears in the case of the proposition that monetary policy should take as its goal maintaining price stability, which goal an increasing number of central banks—not, it must be said, those with the best inflation records—formalize into low target inflation rates. Inflation of company and land prices in the 1980s, not only in the United States, but also in Australia, Britain, and especially Japan and Scandinavia, reopened an old debate on the meaning of price stability. Does price stability mean no inflation in the prices of food, cars, rents, and haircuts—so-called current output prices? Or does price stability require in addition stable prices for companies, land, and even government IOUs and commodities?

Those who have thought about this question have offered three answers:[1] Ignore asset prices, target asset prices, or sometimes target asset prices somewhat. Let us consider each in turn.

Ignore Asset Prices

Milton Friedman and Anna Schwartz suggest ignoring asset prices in their epic *Monetary History of the United States.* As Kindleberger has recently recounted, this advice must be considered the conventional policy wisdom of this century, because it generally enjoyed the support of John Maynard Keynes and of Benjamin Strong, first chief executive officer of the Federal Reserve Bank of New York.

Keynes in the *Treatise on Money* took a clear position that a central bank's job is to maintain stable prices of current output.[2] Friedman and Schwartz fault the Federal Reserve in 1928 and 1929 for paying attention to stock market speculation rather than the general level of prices.[3] Until late 1996, Federal Reserve policy seemed not to concern itself with asset prices, at least on the upswing. Chairman Alan Greenspan's formulation of the Federal Reserve's goal—prices so stable that their change does not enter into business or household decision making—is no more specific on its face than the language of the Federal Reserve Act. But Greenspan's lack of concern in the late 1980s for leveraged takeovers motivated by the prospect of selling off corporate divisions at a profit suggests an implicit qualifier of (output) price stability. Although former Vice Chairman Manuel Johnson often spoke of gold and the exchange rate as price guides and former Vice Chairman David Mullins spoke once in mid-1993 of high bond and stock prices, such views never seemed to affect policy.[4] The price measures employed by such central banks as those of New Zealand, Canada, Australia, England, and Sweden are all variations on the theme of cars, rents, and haircuts, with adjustments for energy, food, taxes, and interest costs.[5] Moreover, attempts to quantify the interest rate policy of central banks, for instance that of Germany, portray them as tightening as consumer prices rise by more than 2 percent and loosening as consumer prices rise by less than 2 percent.[6] Only in policy circles in Japan, still suffering the hangover of the 1980s, is the question a live one. Any proposal to assign monetary policy the job of preventing extreme swings in asset prices faces the weight of received wisdom and current practice.

Target Asset Prices

As Kindleberger has recently emphasized, Benjamin Strong of the Federal Reserve Bank of New York aimed monetary policy at stock market speculation in the 1920s only with evident reluctance and distaste.[7] Despite the Friedman and Schwartz condemnation of Strong, a major central bank has recently taken asset prices as a major goal of monetary policy. The Bank of Japan took a very public bead on asset prices when one of its own, Yasushi Mieno, took over from his predecessor at the end of 1989. Practically from his first day in office, he set out to prick the bubble to restore justice to an economy in which young people without landowning parents or in-laws seemed condemned to residential penury.[8] A former Bank of England official has also embraced this position.[9]

Perhaps as a corollary to the Bank of Japan's success in engineering a collapse of Japanese stock and land prices comes the claim that the

Bank of Japan failed in not preventing the bubble.[10] A common view holds that the Bank of Japan's lowering of the discount rate to 2.5 percent in 1987 to check the rise of the yen against the dollar permitted the bubble in asset prices.[11]

This is the view taken by analysts at the International Monetary Fund, who have taken the position in successive postmortems that monetary policy should have prevented the Tokyo bubble. The second review posed the problem as follows: "Conventional measures of inflation in Japan were below 2 percent throughout the 1980s, yet money and credit growth were excessive and asset prices soared."[12]

There is a danger here of begging the question by concluding that money growth was excessive because asset prices soared. Masaru Yoshitomi, former head of Japan's Economic Planning Agency, argued at a discussion at the Federal Reserve Bank of New York in winter 1994 that the Bank of Japan's main monetary gauge showed no more than marginally excessive growth in the 1980s, certainly nothing in proportion to the asset price surge. Consider interest rates as a measure of monetary policy. If one measures short-term rates against the GNP deflator, Japan does not stand out among industrialized countries with particularly low real rates in the late 1980s.[13] During Japan's bubble years, money was not cheap, but credit was very loose. By the usual measures of monetary aggregates or real short-term rates, it is hard to argue that a large mistake in monetary policy caused the Tokyo bubble.

Armen Alchian and Benjamin Klein set out the general argument for targeting asset prices with monetary policy.[14] In their intriguing argument, most consumption happens in the future, and the price of that consumption is the price of the capital assets that one buys today to finance consumption tomorrow. A rise in the price of capital assets means that today's price of tomorrow's cars, housing, and haircuts has gone up, even if today's *and, in the event, tomorrow's* dollar price of cars, housing, and haircuts remains the same. Higher asset prices can be thought of as raising the cost of retirement. To stabilize the price of tomorrow's consumption as well as today's, the monetary authority must stabilize a mix of today's output prices and asset prices.

In application to corporate leveraging in the 1980s this argument would hold that the LBO firms, the banks, and the junk bond buyers were raising the price of retirement by pushing up publicly and privately traded equity prices. The Fed should have pushed back by raising rates.[15] Conversely, when asset prices dropped after Campeau defaulted, the United Air Lines buyout collapsed, and Drexel went bankrupt in late 1989 and early 1990, the Fed should have eased off.

By this view, of course, the Fed should have responded to the full spectrum of asset price developments in the late 1980s.[16] The assets targeted would have included not only whole companies and publicly traded shares of companies but also residential and commercial real estate. Home prices showed sharply different developments in different regions, although a general uptrend in the late 1980s was evident. Commercial real estate prices also varied by region but, by some measures at least, showed price declines from the middle of the decade onward.[17] If monetary policy is assigned the job of stabilizing asset prices, then declining commercial real estate prices in the late 1980s argued for *lower* interest rates.

The curious case of commercial real estate in the 1980s highlights the difference between treating asset price inflation as a monetary phenomenon and treating it, as below, as a credit phenomenon. Even without a bubble in commercial real estate prices, bank lending to commercial real estate developers expanded very rapidly in the late 1980s.[18] This is an important case to consider, because in 1990–91 soured real estate loans posed a much larger threat to the survival of big banks and to the availability of credit to businesses than did the loans to leveraged corporations.[19] Commercial real estate prices would not clearly have argued for higher interest rates from a central bank prepared to react to asset prices. But the rapid growth of credit that financed innumerable cranes raising "see-through" buildings signaled a dangerous excess in credit to a central bank prepared to act against it.

Stepping back, those who want to include asset prices in the index of prices that the central bank is supposed to stabilize must be willing to sacrifice stable output prices at times. In essence they advise Japan that it should have suffered serious deflation of output prices in the 1980s. A similar view in opposite circumstances was expressed by Alchian and Klein in the early 1970s, when they argued that the Federal Reserve had tightened more than it recognized, given the decline in bond and stock prices. In retrospect, however, the poor performance of the bond and stock markets in the 1970s (which preceded and for a time outweighed the rise of house prices) looks to have been a symptom of rising inflation, not a sign that the Fed was too tight. The more eclectic approach next considered looks to the cause and consequence of an asset price movement before making it a consideration in monetary policy.

Sometimes Target Asset Prices Somewhat

The advice that can be found in Keynes and in broader form in Kindleberger might be phrased as "sometimes targeting asset prices somewhat." Keynes argued for a discretionary policy of responding to an asset price inflation only insofar as it overstimulates investment demand: "[A] Currency Authority has no *direct* [his emphasis] concern with the level of the value of existing securities, as determined by opinion, but . . . it has an important indirect concern if the level of value of existing securities is calculated to stimulate new investment."[20] This advice looks to the effect of an asset bubble on *current* spending in the economy.

Kindleberger, also rejecting a general assignment of monetary policy to the prevention of asset price inflation, looks beyond the bubble's current effect to the implication of the inevitable future collapse of asset prices:

When asset and output prices are stable or move in the same direction, . . . which happen[s] most of the time, such rules [monetary targeting or inflation targeting] are supportable. When speculation threatens substantial rises in asset prices, with a possible collapse in asset markets later, and harm to the financial system, . . . monetary authorities confront a dilemma calling for judgement, not cookbook rules of the game.[21]

At first hearing it may seem that Keynes set out a macroeconomic criterion whereas Kindleberger establishes a financial criterion. We understand Kindleberger's criterion as a broader one, including not only an asset inflation's potential for boosting spending in the upswing but also the subsequent deflation's potential for so damaging financial intermediaries as to crunch spending in the downturn, even in the absence of an earlier boost to spending.

The Federal Reserve appreciates Kindleberger's point, though basically following Keynes in focusing on high stock prices' possible stimulus to spending. Greenspan rocked the world equity markets in December 1996 when he mused aloud on these themes. He echoed Alchian and Klein (noted as A&K) and Kindleberger (CPK):

Certainly prices of goods and services now being produced—our basic measure of inflation—matter. But what about futures prices or more importantly prices of claims on future goods and services, like equities, real estate or other earning assets [A&K]? Are stability of these prices essential to the stability of the economy?

Clearly, sustained low inflation implies less uncertainty about the future, and lower risk premiums imply higher prices of stocks and other earning assets. We can see that in the inverse relationship exhibited by price/earnings ratios and the rate of inflation in the past. But how do we know when irrational exuberance has unduly escalated asset values, which then become subject to unexpected and prolonged contractions as they have in Japan over the past decade? And how do we factor that assessment into monetary policy? We as central bankers need not be concerned if a collapsing financial asset bubble does not threaten to impair the real economy, its production, jobs, and price stability [CPK]. Indeed, the sharp stock market break of 1987 had few negative consequences for the economy. But we should not underestimate or become complacent about the complexity of the interactions of asset markets and the economy. Thus, evaluating shifts in balance sheets generally, and in asset prices particularly, must be an integral part of the development of monetary policy.[22]

The missing element is Keynes's concern that a run-up in asset prices may spill into excessive current spending. As of 1997, this appears to be the Federal Reserve's main point of concern about the stock market:

> . . . unless they are moving together, prices of assets and of goods and services cannot both be an objective of a particular monetary policy, which, after all, has one effective instrument—the short-term interest rate. We have chosen product prices as our primary focus on the grounds that stability in the average level of these prices is likely to be consistent with financial stability as well as maximum sustainable growth. History, however, is somewhat ambiguous on the issue of whether central banks can safely ignore asset markets, except as they affect product prices.[23]

In mid-1997, the Federal Reserve's examination of the effect of stock market wealth on consumption could detect little spillover to spending and therefore potentially to prices, a year later, spillover was evident.[24]

Going back to the policy response to corporate leveraging in the 1980s, consider the difference between Keynes and Kindleberger. Recall from chapter 2 that corporate leveraging departed from the Minsky-Kindleberger pattern in not inducing a boom in real spending; recall in particular from chapter 4 that RJR-Nabisco spent less on capital investments in relation to sales after its leveraged buyout than before. Keynes would therefore view the corporate leveraging of the 1980s as a fairly harmless market development. By contrast, Kindleberger would look past the upswing to the possible harm to the financial system: what losses on leveraged loans and junk bonds might do, respectively, to bank lending and to insurers' purchases of private placements. The risk of financial damage would suffice to motivate a policy response.

This approach, which might argue for higher interest rates even in the absence of overstimulated activity with its risk of inflation, involves a dilemma when output and asset prices are pointing in opposite directions. We look for a way out of the dilemma and submit that central banks should stand ready with credit policies to respond to asset inflation so that one instrument, the short-term interest rate, is not assigned two targets—the stabilization of output and asset prices. But before we get to our prescriptions, we need to consider the somewhat neglected flip side question of how monetary policy should respond to asset deflation.

Monetary Policy and "Headwinds"

The discussion of monetary policy and asset inflation usually concerns policy in the upswing. But a monetary authority may be swept away by the popular stories justifying the asset inflation[25] or otherwise fail to recognize it. Or the central bank may recognize it but judge it, in the manner of Keynes, as carrying little implication for current spending. Or the central bank may lean against an asset inflation with only partial success. In these cases, the central bank faces the question of how to respond when asset price inflation turns to deflation.

"Headwinds": A Bias toward Inflation?

Economist Benjamin Friedman predicted that the Federal Reserve would face a policy dilemma when a recession came along and shook the fragile corporate capital structures created in the 1980s. Overborrowed companies without the cash flow to service their debt, Friedman suggested, would lay off workers and leave their creditor banks and insurance companies with impaired loans and suddenly lower capital. These financial intermediaries would then not be in shape to take the risk of lending to otherwise worthy companies. Faced with a choice between widespread corporate distress with such knock-on effects, and taking risks with inflation, Friedman argued, the Federal Reserve might find itself choosing the latter. Thus he predicted that the leveraging of U.S. corporations would impart an inflationary bias to U.S. monetary policy.[26] At the margin, he held, preventing financial instability would distract policy makers from keeping inflation in check.

In the years between the publication of Friedman's argument and the writing of this book, the underlying rate of inflation in the U.S.

economy has been, and remains, lower than it was then. Where did the argument go wrong?

In an important respect the argument has been proven correct and even prescient. As noted at the outset of chapter 6, Greenspan ascribed the policy of sustained low interest rates of the early 1990s to the need to overcome the effects of heavy debt burdens of businesses and households, dubbed the "headwinds" into which the economy was flying. Balance sheet restructuring and its effect on the economy entered public presentations as early as Greenspan's testimony before Congress in July 1990 and appeared consistently through 1993.[27] Thus corporate leveraging certainly did become a consideration in the making of monetary policy. The Federal Reserve, in the manner prescribed by Keynes above, concerned itself with the decline in asset prices insofar as these were restraining current spending, threatening deep recession.

The question remains why a buildup of debt that tended to constrain monetary policy nevertheless was followed by a decline in inflation. Two answers suggest themselves. First, the constraint disappeared quickly because low interest rates coincided with high equity prices that allowed corporations to issue equity and to retire debt, as described in chapters 5 and 6. On this interpretation, Friedman's criticism of the leveraging mania simply underestimated the financial market's ability to turn on a dime. As Henry Kravis said in 1991, "debt was out; equity was in."[28] The very speed of the restructuring of corporate capital structures in 1991–93 permitted the Federal Reserve to raise rates in early 1994 before the buildup of liquidity had done any more damage than permitting Wall Street to establish large speculative positions in bonds.[29]

Another answer might be that the argument that linked the leveraging mania to an inflationary bias in monetary policy underestimated the macroeconomic drag from the leveraging and subsequent deleveraging. Economists' understanding of how leverage can dampen investment and hiring by individual firms grew in the 1990s.[30] Indirect evidence suggests that the overhang of leverage slowed the macroeco-

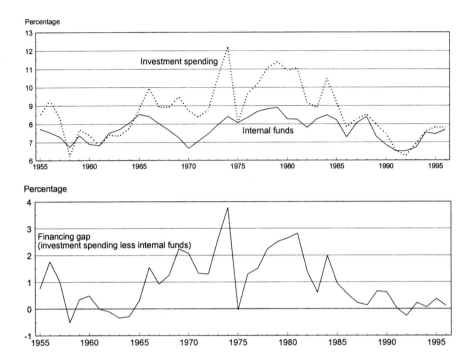

Source: Board of Governors of the Federal Reserve System, Flow of Funds accounts.
Note: Internal funds are retained earnings plus depreciation.

Figure 10.1
U.S. nonfinancial corporations investment spending and internal funds in percent
of GDP

nomy in the early 1990s.[31] But even though much research suggests
that the heavy burden of interest at highly leveraged firms depressed
investment, the 1990–91 recession showed if anything a fairly shallow
decline of investment.

A prima facie case that corporate debt burdens restrained investment
in the early 1990s can be made, however, in relative terms. The decline
of investment in the early 1990s was more substantial when measured
against corporate cash flow (figures 10.1 and 10.2). Investment actually
dipped below cash flow in 1990–91, in a pattern that is very unusual
in the postwar period.[32] We interpret these data to suggest that at the

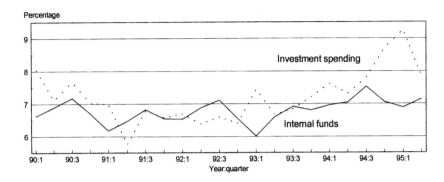

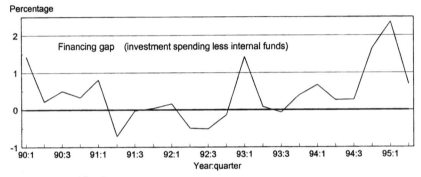

Source: Flow of Funds accounts.
Note: Internal funds are earnings before taxes, depreciation and amortization less taxes, net interest, and dividends.

Figure 10.2
U.S. nonfinancial corporations investment spending and internal funds

macroeconomic level, corporate treasurers' preoccupation with restoring the health of their balance sheets took precedence over undertaking some investment projects.

At present, the conditions that made for a happier outcome for the Federal Reserve than Friedman predicted do not carry altogether happy implications for the U.S. economy. If the need to divert cash flow to serving and reducing debt slowed investment in the early 1990s, then the growth of the U.S. economy in the 1990s may more rapidly run up against capacity limits than it would have in the absence of the need to work off the overhang of debt earlier in the decade. The U.S.

economy today therefore still shows the unfortunate legacy of excessive debt in the 1980s.

Averting the Leveraging Crash: Storing Up Trouble?

If the ex ante critique of the Fed's response to the strains produced by the corporate leveraging of the 1980s overstated the risks of inflation, one ex post critique has faulted the Fed for forestalling a crisis for quite a different reason. Kevin Phillips' point of departure is the finding of chapter 6 to which we just alluded: Lower short-term rates played the predominant role in easing the burden of interest payments on U.S. corporations' cash flow in the early 1990s. Phillips has drawn a parallel between the overt "bailout" of the thrift industry and the "less overt" effect of low interest rates:

> The Fed's action in driving down interest rates was a particular gift for two sectors: overleveraged corporations, especially those in hock from unwise leveraged buyouts, were able to refinance their debts, while shaky banks reveled in huge gains on the spread between high long-term interest rates and low short-term borrowing costs. This indirect assistance was almost as important as the institutional bailouts. By the mid-1990s, banks and investment firms were not only liquid again, but had enjoyed several years of high profitability.

Phillips concedes the danger that maintaining higher interest rates would have run, but draws attention to the distributional consequences of the policy of low interest rates, and decries a perceived coalition:

> There can be no doubt: serious damage *would* have occurred had a willing Washington not joined with a worried Wall Street in history's biggest financial rescue mission. Large banks and corporations guilty of overspeculating and overleveraging would have gone under, as the capitalist process of destruction and renewal suggests they should have. The stock market would have plummeted; so would Wall Street's ascendancy. Instead, overleveraged firms that headed everyone's list of the living dead—from Citicorp, America's largest bank, to RJR Nabisco, the leveraged buyout made infamous in the late 1980s—survived after a year or two of grave-watching. Wall Street had a decent year in 1991 following a bad one in 1990. Then profitability mushroomed. The linchpin was unprecedented Washington–Wall Street collaboration.[33]

Ultimately, the argument comes down to what Phillips calls "federal favoritism" and to moral hazard. On the first point, a lender of last resort in advancing funds to particular institutions is often suspected of playing favorites.[34] But what Phillips calls federal favoritism in the form of "indirect assistance" was simply lower short-term rates in general, which provided relief to all borrowers with interest payments tied to short-term rates. Were lower short-term interest rates as inappropriate for the U.S. economy at large in 1990–93 as they were serendipitous for leveraged firms? The economy's decelerating inflation and sluggish growth well into 1993 suggest that lower rates were both appropriate and serendipitous. It is very hard to maintain that Wall Street demanded one monetary policy and Main Street deserved another (the dilemma faced by Benjamin Strong in the stock market speculation of the 1920s or perhaps by the Bank of Japan in the late 1980s). A policy that permitted an open-ended "capitalist process of destruction and renewal," no matter how deserving its first victims would have been, would not have served the broad goals of stable prices and prosperity.

On the second point, that of moral hazard, because "abuses were protected," according to Phillips, the concern arises that the "bailout itself was part of a new debacle in the making—a bigger speculative bubble blown up around the earlier one that came close to imploding." In view of the "scarcity of insistence on the kind of financial reform typical of a post-speculative era—the regulatory accomplishment of both the Progressive and the New Deal eras," Phillips concludes that the "excesses of the 1980s had only been camouflaged, not pruned." Although it is easy to dismiss Phillips's criticism as a bizarre amalgam of Andrew Mellon–style liquidation and a populist desire to humble Wall Street, it is by no means utterly idiosyncratic.[35]

Phillips's criticism overstates the extent to which "destruction and renewal" were averted. Drexel Burnham Lambert disappeared, though many of its principals escaped with their fortunes. First Boston was so saddled with bridge loans that it had to cede substantial control to its Swiss partners. And after executives at American Express bailed out

Shearson from its bridge loans, they decided that they could leave home without it and proceeded to disassemble the securities firm and to sell it off.

The argument also understates the extent of financial reform. Some of Phillips's outrage may have moved Congress to pass banking legislation in 1991 (the Federal Deposit Insurance Corporation Improvement Act) calling for "prompt, corrective action" to limit regulatory discretion in leaving troubled banks to pull themselves out of their difficulties. In effect, Congress instructed regulators to shut down distressed banks rather than wait for low interest rates to heal them.

Still, there are grounds for concern that the avoidance of a crash in 1990 may have encouraged new excesses. As we have seen, by 1993 the junk bond market had more than fully recovered, digesting more paper and cumulating to greater size than ever before. Big junk issues by leveraging firms did not dominate the junk market in the 1990s as they did in the late 1980s, but the potential is there. Moreover, by 1993, signs were clear that banks were willing to lend to leveraged deals on easier terms. Whether one looked at spreads over interbank rates, at the acceptable coverage of interest payments by cash flow, or at covenants and security, all indications suggested that bank credit, though not quite as loose as in the late 1980s, had still become much less tight than in 1990–91.[36] Also by 1993, some, though not all, foreign banks were planning substantial increases in their U.S. lending.

In late 1993, William McDonough, President of the Federal Reserve Bank of New York, sounded a warning to banks to reexamine the terms to which renewed competitive forces had driven them. Some months later, Greenspan joined in the caution. It is not clear that such warnings have prevented banks from lowering their standards in the mid- to late 1990s.

Easy credit availability to leveraged investment funds in the 1990s could also be cited in support of Phillips's argument that excesses had been camouflaged rather than pruned. The leveraged operators that came to prominence in the 1990s were less specialized than LBO funds insofar as they were prepared to buy (or sell) not only shares but also currencies (notably the deutsche mark in 1992 but also the dollar against yen in 1995–98[37] and against Asian and Pacific currencies in 1997–98), bonds (1992–93, 1995–98[38]) or commodities (gold in winter 1996, copper in spring and summer 1996). But the supercharged returns of the "hedge funds" had a common source with those of the more straightforwardly named LBO funds: borrowed money. The successful stabilization of the previous generation of leveraged credit at the beginning of the decade could only have increased the willingness of banks and other creditors to fund leveraged operators in the 1990s.

Critiques of the "Headwind" Policy Compared

Stepping back, we conclude that both Friedman's ex ante critique and Phillips's ex post critique of U.S. monetary policy's response to the collapse of the leveraging business went wrong in an interesting manner. Friedman prophesied that the Federal Reserve would not be able to respond to the distress of the leveraging business without taking risks with inflation. Phillips holds that the Fed should not have responded and thereby allowed the "guilty" to suffer the consequences of their own imprudence. In effect, economist Friedman argued that the eventual collapse of leveraging would mean that the Fed *could* not do its job, whereas political analyst Phillips argued that its collapse meant that the Fed *should* not have done its job. Events proved correct Friedman's prediction that the Federal Reserve would respond to leveraged firms' difficulties in servicing their debt in an environment of weak activity, but events were less kind to his warning that the Federal Reserve would face a policy dilemma. Low interest rates nurtured a stock market boom that favored deleveraging; meanwhile, imprudent leverage was sufficiently widespread that limiting financial distress did not come in conflict with keeping a lid on inflation. Instead, banks' calling in loans and corporations' diverting their cash flow to pay down bank loans put enough drag on the economy to make low short-term rates less risky. This may be regarded as an instance in favor of Charles

Goodhart's claim that "there should rarely be a serious macroeconomic problem about the provision of support for a banking system in which serious, potentially system bank failures are occurring."[39] Or threatening to occur, we might add. And if the Federal Reserve could both limit financial instability and maintain stable prices, how many citizens would opt for Phillips's "capitalist process of destruction and renewal" at the cost of a deeper recession and more layoffs?

But Friedman was right to warn us of leveraging's challenge to the macroeconomy, and a lucky combination of events does not justify complacency. And Phillips's philippic (after the speeches by Demosthenes condemning the king of Macedonia) reminds us that successful central bank stabilization of the real economy in the aftermath of a substantial financial excess tends to blunt the lesson of probity that collapse, bankruptcy, shame, and even prison teach. The more successful the cleanup operation, the more watchful will policymakers need to be for signs of excess. And the more successful the cleanup, the better equipped they need to be with policies other than short-term interest rates to dampen the excesses or at least to limit their damage to the credit mechanism. The next section suggests credit policies that can be used against financial excess when the real economy cannot bear higher interest rates.

10.2 Adopt Credit and Prudential Policies in Response to Financial Excess

A fundamental insight of the Minsky-Kindleberger model of financial manias, as discussed in chapter 2, is that they involve credit. We contend that authorities faced with an asset inflation can adjust credit policy to slow down the process and to limit the damage from the eventual asset deflation. Credit policy includes prudential policy, such as bank regulation,[40] but can extend beyond it. Authorities can adopt credit policy along one or more of the following four lines: publicize concentrations of credit; regulate the terms of credit; increase capital required to support credit or tax credit.[41] We illustrate each of these policies in subsequent sections with actual measures adopted by central banks. Even though these prescriptions may strike some as unorthodox, they are hardly beyond the realm of recent policy experience.

Publicize Concentrations of Credit Exposed to Inflated Assets

"Sunshine is the best disinfectant" is the motto of this policy. A novel policy toward excessive credit emerged out of the combination of the U.S. bank regulators' defining highly leveraged transactions and the Securities and Exchange Commission's requiring bank holding companies to disclose loans so classified. As related in chapter 3, in late 1988 and 1989 stock market analysts sought to assess the various banks' vulnerability to either a slowdown in the flow of fees associated with highly leveraged transactions or, worse, bad loans cropping up among the stock of leveraged loans retained on banks' own books. As we saw, a consistent regulatory definition of leveraged loans and the SEC's disclosure requirements enabled stock market investors to evaluate the quality of banks' earnings and assets in relation to the investors' own views of the leveraging business. As investors switched from the shares of more-exposed institutions to those of less-exposed institutions, they brought pressure on managers responsive to share price developments to change their behavior by selling off more loans and by making fewer deals. In this manner, disclosure allowed equity investors to assess risks better and in doing so to induce a change in behavior.

Definition and disclosure serve as a paradigm for a very unobtrusive credit policy.[42] Any skepticism in the equity market regarding an asset inflation cannot bear down on managers of credit-granting institutions if information remains so scarce that investors cannot draw distinctions. The definition may have to be creative, as with the highly leveraged loan, which cut across the industry concentrations bank regulators usually considered.

But even creative definition and prompt disclosure may not check credit excesses. Of course, banks' and other intermediaries' equity investors typically believe as enthusiastically in whatever popular models "justify" rising asset prices as anyone else in the economy. In that case, sunshine will not do the job alone, and sober minds may find themselves turning reluctantly to more intrusive credit policies. In doing so they should console themselves with the distaste that Benjamin Strong felt in raising interest rates to rein in Wall Street even as much of the rest of the country was struggling with falling commodity prices.

Regulate the Terms of Credit

Authorities can regulate the terms of credit to hold down the leverage of those buying assets with borrowed money. Examples of policies that regulate the terms of credit include minimum margin for purchases of equities (or in the case of bonds, "haircuts"), minimum loan-to-value ratios in real estate lending, and down payment or maturity restrictions for purchases of consumer durables (known as "hire-purchase" regulation in British English). These are all "stock" measures, and one can imagine a parallel set of flow measures, such as limits on the ratio of interest payments to the dividend yield of stocks bought on margin, limits on interest payments on a commercial mortgage in relation to the cash flow from rent, or limits on the ratio of consumer interest payments to household income.

In application to corporate leveraging, bank regulators could have restrained banks from lending to corporations with debt in excess of a certain fraction of assets, or to corporations with interest payments that bulked large against cash flow. Both the definition of highly leveraged transaction and the Federal Reserve Board's ill fated proposal to subject certain shell acquisition companies to margin requirements, as described in chapter 3, were instances of (stock) leverage tests. Albert Wojnilower recommended limits on nonfinancial corporate leverage—calibrated to respect long-standing differences in leverage across industries—along these lines in 1989.[43]

Recent research has confirmed the dominant role of high loan-to-value ratio in predicting eventual defaults on commercial mortgages.[44] (An interesting research question is whether the consistent 60 percent loan-to-value limit in German banking should get credit for the seemingly lower amplitude of real estate price swings in Germany.) To turn the ratio around, a high fraction of owner's equity permits debt service to remain on schedule even if real estate prices fall, whether because of a decline in rental rates, higher vacancy rates, higher taxes, or higher interest rates. Clearly, the most dangerous combination is a slippage in underwriting standards permitting higher loan-to-value ratios at a time of temporarily high prices.

Minsky and Kindleberger point to the tendency of a market in the grip of a mania to increase leverage as prices rise. That is, effective lending standards such as loan-to-value ratios move with the cycle in prices. Thus competition for real estate loans in Japan in the late 1980s got to the point that one could often borrow more than the market value of a house or building.[45] We saw in chapter 2 that the increasingly fevered mergers and acquisition market burdened newly leveraged firms with greater debt in relation to assets as the 1980s wore on, eventually committing more than the available cash flow to interest payments. If the authorities do no more than hold the line on conventional standards of leverage, so that lending standards do not ease as asset prices rise, they will have succeeded in making the financial system more resilient in the face of any subsequent slump in asset prices.

One objection to such policies is that they prove ineffective because unregulated entities will step in and provide credit. There are two answers to this objection. First, "quacks like a duck" regulations can apply to whatever entity performs a given function. Thus, for instance, U.S. margin requirements apply not just to margin loans by banks but also to margin loans by securities firms.

Another answer is that the goal of such bank regulation may be more modest than limiting the global extension of credit and slowing the asset inflation. One can take a fatalistic view of the mania at hand and seek only to limit the fallout from asset deflation. In particular, one may wish to ensure that banks' ability to extend general business credit does not crumble along with their asset quality when asset prices fall, and so be quite content to limit bank exposure to the asset inflation, even if nonbank lenders make the loans forbidden to the banks under the regulations. Such a strategy puts stress on the boundary of the banking system, and regulators must be on guard against bank-sponsored intermediaries whose mistakes might drown the bank.

The Hong Kong authorities' response to the surge of stock and land prices in the early 1990s illustrates the use of credit policy. As the shock of Tiananmen Square wore off and trade with and investment in China roared, the local stock market and Hong Kong real estate boomed. The local stock market gauge, the Hang Seng Index, roughly quadrupled between the end of 1990 and a peak in early 1994, when rising U.S. rates sent the Hong Kong stock market lower. With real estate loans representing something like 40 percent of all bank loans in the territory, the Hong Kong authorities recognized the danger to the banks were real estate prices first to triple, with banks lending three-quarters or more of appraised value, and then to fall by one-half. Under these circumstances the banks could come to own a significant fraction of Hong Kong's real estate at purchase prices well above market values: a scenario for a banking crisis. As Andrew Sheng, then Deputy Chief Executive of the Hong Kong Monetary Authority, put it: *"[A]sset price inflation is dangerous when it is financed by imprudent bank lending."*[46]

The Hong Kong authorities urged banks to tighten their lending standards in the face of surging real estate prices. In particular, as apartment prices rose in the early 1990s, the authorities saw to it that banks ratcheted down in steps the maximum fraction of a residence's worth that they would lend on mortgage. First, a loan-to-value standard arose

in 1991 as a self-regulatory response by leading banks, perhaps faced
with the possibility of binding rules:

The Commissioner [of Banking] wrote to institutions in May reminding them
of the need for prudence when lending in a buoyant residential property market. A follow-up survey completed in September showed that most institutions
had tightened their lending policies, mainly by reducing the loan to valuation
ratios and the debt to income ratios used in their evaluation of loan applica-
tions. Despite this general tightening, the momentum in the growth of mortgage loans continued. At the end of September, the level of mortgage loans
outstanding stood 41% higher than at the same time in the previous year. In
view of this, the Commissioner wrote again to authorized institutions in November to encourage them to tighten further their lending criteria. . . . A number of major banks took the lead in November by reducing their loan to
valuation ratios [from 80–90%] to 70%. This arrangement spread quickly to
other institutions active in the residential property market. As a consequence,
demand for residential housing loans slowed in the last quarter, the annual
increase dropping to 35%.[47]

Second, in mid-1993, the maximum loan-to-value ratio for luxury
properties was lowered to 60 percent. In February 1994, the head of
banking supervision at the newly formed Hong Kong Monetary Authority recommended that mortgages on residences grow by no more
than 15 percent per annum, in line with nominal GDP growth.[48]

Whether the policy slowed the rapid ascent of Hong Kong real estate
prices through 1993 can be debated, but the policy seems to have protected banks against losses. Apartment prices did not spike with the
Hang Seng Index in 1993 (figure 10.3). Recall the distinction between
slowing the asset inflation and limiting the banks' exposure to it and
consider the evidence on the response of loan growth to the regulation
of the terms of credit. The restrictions on the generosity of credit appear to have slowed, at least for a time, the pace of loan growth (figure
10.4). Thus, a test of the policy came after the Federal Reserve tightening of February 1994. U.S. interest rates exerted an immediate effect
on Hong Kong, given the peg of the Hong Kong dollar to the U.S. dollar
and the generality of floating-rate debt. By late 1994 the Hang Seng
stood about a quarter below peak; by the end of 1995 property prices

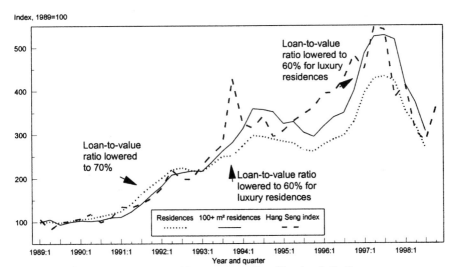

Index, 1989=100

Sources: *Hong Kong Monthly Digest of Statistics*, Hong Kong Monetary Authority
Note: Luxury properties are defined as those costing over HK$ 5million (US$0.6 million) in 1993 and over HK$12 million (US$1.5 million) in 1997. Banks appear to have loosened their lending standards between 1994 and 1997.

Figure 10.3
Hong Kong property and share prices

had fallen by almost the same amount from their later peak fraction.[49] The Hong Kong authorities could congratulate themselves as well as the banks that the loss rate on mortgages remained below 0.5 percent and that bank profits rose in 1995, despite the asset price decline:[50]

The Hong Kong banking community should be congratulated on their remarkable restraint and prudence in lending to property. By progressively reducing their maximum loan-to-valuation ratios from over 88.3% in 1989 to 69.5% in 1994 for small to medium flats, and from 86.8% to 54.8% for luxury flats, the banks have cushioned themselves quite well against sharp declines in property prices. Indeed, our recent residential mortgage survey suggests that the leverage outstanding loan-to-value ratio for residential mortgages in Hong Kong was 53.3% at the end of September 1994.[51]

One of the remarkable features of the Hong Kong economy is the frequency of its asset price cycles. Thus after their sharp setback in

Percentage change over previous four quarters

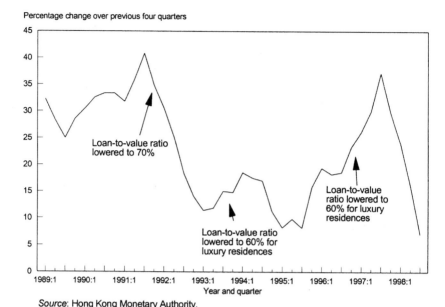

Source: Hong Kong Monetary Authority.
Note: Mortgage loans defined as loans to individuals to purchase private residences.

Figure 10.4
Growth of mortgage and real estate credit in Hong Kong

1994–95, the stock and property markets took off again in 1996 amid easier credit. And the regulators were prepared. In January 1997, the year that Hong Kong became a Special Administrative Region of China, the head of banking supervision at the Hong Kong Monetary Authority wrote as follows to all deposit-taking institutions:

property lending rose by almost 16% in the first three quarters of 1996 (over 20% at an annual rate) . . . property lending as a percentage of other loans for use in Hong Kong rose from 39% at end-September 1995 to 40.7% at end-September 1996. This growth in lending has been accompanied in recent months by a sharp rise in residential property prices, particularly at the upper end of the market, and renewed signs of speculative activity. At the same time, competition among the banks has forced down the margin on residential mortgages to levels which are barely above [the] best lending rate. Thus, the return has fallen while the risks have increased. . . .

We are aware that some banks have already tightened their criteria on more expensive properties. It would be prudent for this to be adopted generally. We therefore recommend that a maximum loan to value of 60% should be adopted for "luxury" property with a value of more than HK$12 million [about US$1.5 million].[52]

From the perspective of more than a full cycle, the Hong Kong authorities may not have slowed the ascent of property prices in Hong Kong, which have quadrupled or quintupled in seven years much like those in the stock market. But they have managed to keep the mortgage credit from growing much faster than nominal gross domestic product in recent years. Most tellingly, the decline of asset prices in Hong Kong by 50% in 1997–98 did not wipe out the banks.

Increase Capital Requirements

Fred Schadrack, then head of banking supervision at the Federal Reserve Bank of New York, used to ask why a higher capital weight might not be applied to highly leveraged loans than to ordinary corporate loans. The Basle Accord, which sets only minimum standards for internationally active banks, throws up no impediment to such a policy. For instance, highly leveraged transactions could have attracted a double weight. Certainly Citicorp's experience with highly leveraged transactions, as reviewed in chapter 2, suggested a loss rate well above what one would expect from a normal commercial and industrial loan book—even given the favorable trends of interest rates and equity raising—and thus provides prima facie support for Schadrack's idea. Moreover, the Basle Committee on Banking Supervision has drawn a distinction in its market risk proposal between junk bonds and investment grade bonds, which is in the spirit of the Schadrack idea.[53] This approach has an advantage over loan-to-value ratios in that banks could still make loans that did not meet loan-to-value criteria as long as they could justify the return in relation to the (constrained) evaluation of the risk.[54] If the regulators were wrong, and bank managers could so persuade their board of directors and shareholders, then the credit would still flow. A disadvantage of such an approach is that it makes the capital regulations more complex and involves regulators' drawing bright lines.

A variant would be to eschew singling out some asset class or classes for higher capital charges and rather to raise levels of required capital across the board during a time of financial excess. Capital requirements have been faulted for operating in a procyclic fashion, because profits appear fat and robust in an asset inflation, but only bite when asset prices crash and with them profits and capital.[55] Moreover, the option of lowering capital requirements below internationally agreed minima during the asset deflation has been rejected because it "would weaken the credibility of the existing ratio requirements, and leave the Central Banks open to political pressures to use, or misuse," this option.[56] No such objections could be voiced against raising capital requirements in a boom. Indeed, the Bank of England has required higher capital levels for smaller and less-diversified banks, and the same rationale of diversification could be used as a reason why requirements had to be stiffened in a boom: Banks are taking on more of the same risk in lending to, for instance, leveraged firms, or to real estate developers.

One could argue that the policy of raising capital requirements in a boom was found to be a failure in stopping the asset inflation in a natural experiment conducted on the Japanese banking system in the late 1980s. There the boom in land and stock prices provided the backdrop for the negotiation of the Basle Accord, which called for an across-the-board rise in the Japanese banks' ratio of capital to (risk-adjusted) capital. Japanese banks started adjusting to the new rules well before their official and phased-in inception, at least as early as 1988. Yet bank credit to real estate and equity and real estate prices boomed through the end of 1989. On the face, higher capital requirements seem to have proven incapable of restraining the asset inflation.

Special circumstances restrict the generality of these experimental results, however. Japanese banks' holdings of the assets subject to the asset inflation meant that there was a strong positive feedback from rising stock prices to banks' wealth. And although observers have criticized the Basle Accord for permitting unrealized gains on equities to be counted as (tier 2, or secondary) capital, the fact is that the Japanese banks engaged in massive matched sales and repurchases of equities to realize the gains. In other words, the Japanese banks proved willing to turn latent wealth into balance sheet wealth to build up their equity, even at the expense of income taxes on the realized gains at a stinging rate of more than 50 percent.[57] So the economic fact of the Japanese banks' ownership of an asset swept up in the asset inflation, rather than any regulatory accounting standard, reduced the experiment's power.

Under either variant of the policy of capital regulation, the question of competition recurs. If foreign banks faced a smaller capital charge against highly leveraged transactions, might not this lucrative business migrate to their balance sheets? The answer to this question, admittedly difficult in the boom phase when seemingly extraordinary profits beckon, is that chances are good that the seeming competitive disability in the boom will serve the affected institution's shareholders well in the bust.

Tax Credit Growth

When the growth of credit appears much too fast but sectoral interventions like loan-to-value ratios or Basle superweights are too distasteful, politically infeasible, or otherwise unavailable, authorities might consider placing reserve requirements against credit growth. These can be crafted to require reserves at the central bank to be held against loan growth in excess of a certain rate. The rationale would be the tendency of the bank with the fastest loan growth in a mania ultimately to show the highest level of dud loans. If the central bank does not pay interest on the loans, then the required reserve amounts to a tax. Note that the tax need not be set at a prohibitive level, which would amount to a dirigiste credit limit ("encadrement" in French usage, or "corset" in

English usage). Instead, the government can permit bank managers to exercise their own judgment but to pay a tax in some instances for doing so. The revenue might even be added to deposit insurance funds against the possibility that government money needed to be used to prop up banks that suffer large loan losses.

Again, recent central bank practice provides an example. Finnish authorities adopted reserve requirements in 1989 to slow wild credit growth. This important instance is in danger of being lost to memory. For instance, one of the studies that the Bank of Finland commissioned to sort through its unfortunate experience of real estate and credit boom and bust at the end of the 1980s reports that Finnish authorities did basically nothing to respond to surging lending and asset prices until hit by the collapse of Soviet trade.[58] In fact, the Finns took a practical step against the boom, one that has no parallel in Sweden.

Faced with banks' merrily increasing their loans at a rate in excess of 30 percent in 1988, the Finnish authorities came to doubt the prevailing story that the growth of credit reflected a "stock adjustment" to the deregulation of their system of credit rationing against a background of ongoing tax relief for interest payments.[59] The governor of the central bank stood up in public and held that such rapid credit growth was dangerous and could not continue, somewhat in the manner of the hero of Ibsen's *The Enemy of the People*, a doctor who reveals that the water on which a spa town's livelihood depends is poisoned. If matters had been left there, we might have just another instance of the inefficacy of moral suasion.

The Bank of Finland, however, gave teeth to the warning. In February 1989, it agreed on an "arrangement . . . which aims at sharply curbing bank lending." It worked by empowering the "Bank of Finland to raise the cash reserve requirement to a maximum of 12 per cent if a bank's or a group of banks' personal lending or a consolidated banking group's total lending increases by more than 20 per cent between February 1989 and December 1989. If, on the other hand, personal lending increases by less than 9 per cent or total lending by less than 11 per cent, the additional requirement will not be applied."[60]

The reserve requirement seems to have been effective. According to one of the authors' discussions at the Bank of Finland in December 1993, one bank actually exceeded the 20 percent limit and paid the reserve, but the other banks restrained their lending. The increase in Finnish banks' real lending had tracked that of their counterparts over the border in Sweden in the boom years of 1986–88. But in 1989, the real increase in Finnish loans fell below 10 percent, while that of the Swedish banks remained about 20 percent.[61] The Finns did not adopt the measure lightly, because it seemed like a step backward to the credit rationing policies that they had operated before, and to this day they do not brag about the measure. But in our judgment, the Finnish authorities saved their banks losses and taxpayers bailout money, and perhaps their fellow citizens some unemployment in the 1990s.

One can argue that such a policy discriminates against companies without overseas operations or without access to offshore bank credit or securities markets. Multinationals or well-known big firms can simply rechannel their demand for credit and avoid paying the tax. On closer examination, however, this objection carries less weight than it might seem at first to carry. For one thing, the reach of a reserve on credit certainly can extend to domestic banks' loans to domestic residents booked offshore.[62] For another, if the policy discriminates against real estate developers in favor of multinational firms and firms in the traded goods sector, it may not be altogether unwelcome insofar as real estate seems so prone to periodic overbuilding. And if foreign banks cannot be stopped from extending credit to domestic borrowers offshore, then at least the authorities can console themselves that any loan losses will be some other central bank's problem.[63]

If the proposal to put reserve requirements against credit growth sounds odd, it is because of the trend in monetary policy toward reliance on prices—the policy interest rate—and a near abandonment of quantitative targets. One does not need to be a monetarist to recognize that the difference between rapid credit growth and the nominal growth of an economy often turns out to be bad loans. A pile of bad loans can leave banks in distress, leading to a drag on the macroeconomy ("headwinds") if not a bill to the taxpayers for a government rescue of troubled banks. Therefore, some policy response to surging credit amid asset inflation is strongly advised. Authorities can publicize loan concentrations (trusting to the capital markets), regulate the terms of credit, increase capital requirements, or tax credit growth. Unthinking adherence to financial laissez faire in the face of a mania can easily lead to the unintended consequence of the government's owning the banks in a form of "lemon socialism."

We have argued that policy makers should stand ready with a variety of credit policies to respond effectively to credit excesses. This is general advice, but a credit excess typically exposes shortcomings in other policies. In the cases of both Japan's and Hong Kong's property booms, government land policies have been criticized as restrictions on supply. In the case of corporate leveraging in the 1980s, however, credit policy needed reinforcement from tax reform and reforms to corporate governance. The next section briefly sketches various policy options for making tax policy neutral in the choice between debt and equity, and the subsequent section discusses policies to persuade the owners of U.S. corporations to act like owners.

10.3 Make Tax Policy Neutral toward Corporate Leveraging

The wave of U.S. leveraging in the 1980s surely exploited the tax code's favorable treatment of debt. To go further and argue that the tax code caused the leveraging wave is to attempt to explain a change—the massive and unprecedented replacement of equity with debt—with a relatively unchanging force.[64] Moreover, we noted above in chapter 4 that (taxed) shareholders had to pay otherwise indefinitely deferred capital gains taxes when, say, their RJR-Nabisco shares were bought out by KKR. Although fairly consistent tax incentives to rely on debt could hardly have suddenly propelled corporate leveraging, a less biased tax code might well form part of the policy response.

The case against the current tax treatment of debt can be stated simply: The current tax deductibility of debt in effect subsidizes bankruptcy. If bankruptcy entails losses that are no one else's gains, then this subsidy can be regarded only as perverse tax policy. The social losses of bankruptcy include the obvious costs of the lawyers' and judges' time. In addition, the disruption of client and employee relations add to these direct costs. The bankruptcy of Texaco offered very striking evidence of the market's evaluation of the cost of corporate distress: The joint value of Pennzoil (the winner in a massive lawsuit) and Texaco (the loser) dropped some $3 billion.[65]

Congressional hearings in early 1989 after the RJR-Nabisco soap opera[66] heard various tax proposals. We saw in chapter 3 that Congress ultimately adopted a proposal to tax "excessive" interest. We also saw that the proposal would have had only a minor impact on the RJR Nabisco buyout.[67] Congress could revisit this terrain, but here we review more-fundamental approaches to lessening the tax code's encouragement of debt.

Investors tap into corporate income through three means: interest payments, dividends, and capital gains, which over long periods of time reflect accumulated retained earnings. The first is taxed, if at all, at the level of the investor; the latter two attract taxes once at the corporate level and again at the investor level. It follows that lowering taxes on dividends or capital gains would reduce corporations' incentives to rely on debt financing. Whereas the tax systems of most industrialized countries give some relief from the double taxation of dividends,[68] the U.S. fiscal position could not easily bear the strain of tax relief for dividends, or over time, for capital gains. Thus we consider two proposals that would leave revenues much the same while removing the tax code's tilt toward leverage.

The Hybrid Approach

One approach, considered in 1989 at the Treasury, is simultaneously to limit the deductibility of interest and to give tax relief to dividends paid. For instance, 20 percent of interest payments might be made not deductible against income for tax purposes, while 80 percent of dividends might be made deductible. The result would be to tax interest and dividends at the same rate: Each would be 80 percent deductible. Something like this fraction would be revenue-neutral, with additional taxes on interest just paying for the tax relief on dividends. Treasury Secretary Nicholas Brady expressed interest in such an approach under questioning before the Senate Finance Committee in early 1989.[69]

The Cash Flow Tax

A more thoroughgoing measure than the hybrid approach would be to adopt a cash flow tax. Like the hybrid approach, such a tax would treat interest payments and dividends the same. In the case of a cash flow tax, the total elimination of the tax deductibility of interest payments (as opposed to the reduction of deductability suggested above) puts interest and dividends on the same footing. The cash flow tax combines this elimination with the immediate expensing of investment expenditures. What corporations would lose from deductibility of interest they would get back from writing off new investment right away rather than over the life of the machinery or building, so that corporate income taxes would remain roughly the same.[70] Essentially a firm would pay tax on the difference between its revenue and the sum of the cost of goods or services and the cost of new investment.[71]

Proponents of the cash flow tax point to its advantage in treating different kinds of corporate investments the same way. As things stand, a firm "investing" in market share via advertising can deduct the cost of a new campaign immediately, whereas the same firm investing in a machine can deduct the cost only over the machine's life.[72] Consider that "investment" in advertising is mostly a zero-sum game in which one firm's gain is another firm's loss. Thus, a cash flow tax would lift a thumb that has weighed against investment in plant and equipment that can raise productivity and living standards.

Our summary treatment of these proposals does not do them justice. One could, for instance, eliminate the deductibility of interest and lower the corporate tax rate to achieve revenue neutrality.[73] Yet it should be evident that any of these approaches makes the tax bite on a dollar of interest payments or a dollar of dividend payment the same. In such a world, corporations would weigh the disadvantage of debt in raising the ex ante costs of possible corporate distress and bankruptcy (as reflected in ratings and risk spreads) against any advantage from debt's binding management to pay out cash flow. The tax system would no longer weigh like a thumb on the scale in favor of debt.

10.4 Reform Corporate Governance Policies

Two-thirds of a century ago, Adolph Berle and Gardiner Means argued that managers ran U.S. corporations without much accountability to shareholders.[74] For better or worse, corporate leveraging propelled raiders into this vacuum of responsible ownership in the modern American corporation. Thus, most highly leveraged transactions were double or joint events. They simultaneously loaded a firm with debt and brought in new managers (or at least aligned the interest of the old managers with the new owners). Proponents of leverage emphasized the new blood and conceived of the debt as the new blood's binding promise not to dissipate corporate resources on projects that did more for its own pay and ego than for the shareholders' bottom line.

Leveraged takeovers, viewed as a means of disciplining managers to act as good stewards for shareholders, depended on large institutional shareholders' exercising their exit option, that is, selling their shares to the leveraged buyout firm. Recall from chapter 2, however, that much the same institutional shareholders subscribed to the leveraged buyout firms' private equity funds, bought the junk bonds, and held the shares of the banks that took the risks of the senior debt. In aggregate, then, the big shareholders did not so much exit from the leveraged firms as pay a new group of agents to keep tabs on other agents. The leveraging business represented a bet that making the LBO organizers rich would pay off by their picking and monitoring good stewards and by their binding their chosen stewards with debt service. What at first blush looks like an exercise of the exit option appears on closer inspection to be something quite different: a Rube Goldberg device for institutions to exercise their voice option and have some say, albeit at some remove and after the payment of fees and more fees, in the firms that they already collectively owned.

As the costs of corporate leveraging became apparent in the early 1990s, simpler and more direct exercise of voice by institutional shareholders gained appeal. As giant corporations like General Motors, IBM, and American Express stumbled, they found themselves under pressure from institutional investors who did not wait around for a corporate raider. To some observers, the trend in state anti-takeover laws and the willingness of the Delaware courts to apply the business judgment rule to takeover situations, as reviewed in chapter 3, put a premium on finding new means to make managers accountable.[75] Institutional investors or their representative would not have to understand the businesses they own better than managers to play a useful role occasionally. It would be enough if they could resist management's proposals to expand by acquiring unrelated businesses, if they could overrule managers' resistance to sensible takeovers, if they could overcome managers' reluctance to return cash through dividends and repurchases, and if they could recognize when corporate decline demands new blood.[76] We therefore consider proposed public policies to give institutional investors, especially pension managers, more voice in governing U.S. corporations.

Consideration of such policies may seen to carry our discussion away from policies concerning corporate leveraging. But those who recognize the destructive potential of corporations hamstrung by their debt would do well to consider how else to make managers accountable. Replace "British" with "U.S." in the following:

> Mergers and acquisitions can play a significant role in the working of the market mechanism, but the question nags insistently whether we have not become too dependent on them as means of securing improvement in underperforming companies. . . . Welcome as the relatively low gearing of British companies is in other respects, it does place on shareholders a bigger responsibility for oversight and influence than in situations where debt plays a larger role and bankers are thus more closely involved. . . . the answer lies in building up critical mass in terms of a wider understanding and expectation in both industry and investing institutions that it is responsible behavior for institutional shareholders to take a closer interest in the boards of their companies than has generally been the case in the past.[77]

The exercise of institutional shareholders' voice can be encouraged in ways that a loose confederation of more-active investors—mostly state and local pension funds—and interested scholars have outlined. Proposals along the lines sketched below were also put forward several years ago by a group of business leaders, academics, and analysts who examined how corporate governance could contribute to long-term investment and growth.[78]

Facilitate Shareholder Communication and Democracy

Given the fragmented nature of ownership of U.S. corporations, the rules governing coordination among these shareholders are key. Rules intended to protect the market place against stock manipulation by a ring of investors, however, seemed to impede legitimate discussions among institutional investors. There has been some recent progress toward better communication among shareholders. In 1989 one of the largest pension funds in the country, that for California's public employees, addressed a letter to the SEC asking for a "roll-back of regulations to allow, inter alia, stockholders to talk with one another more freely."[79] The SEC's proposals along these lines in 1992 drew heavy fire from the Business Roundtable, but the SEC persisted. As a consequence, institutional shareholders have been able to huddle on the future of laggard firms with less fear of lawsuits.

Further progress in giving voice to shareholders might come from shareholder access to more resources for campaigning within the little democracy of the firm.[80] At present, "Managers control the proxy process."[81] Managers have a fix on the identity of shareholders that they could be forced to share with the shareholders.[82] The firm finances all proxy solicitations sponsored by managers, whether successful or unsuccessful; it could be made to finance successful solicitations initiated by shareholders or to include large shareholders' initiatives among those of managers.[83] Management enjoys access to proxies arriving early and can bring pressure to bear on managers of the corporation's own pension funds with the implicit threat to take business elsewhere.[84] Thus confidential voting until the tally, independent tabulation, and full disclosure of how money managers voted (to ensure accountability to beneficiaries) could be required.

A more credible corporate polling system could be put to work to widen shareholder involvement in crucial corporate decisions. In Britain, the 1985 Companies Act authorized share repurchases, but only subject to shareholder approval as to amount and price. There is reason to extend such compulsory votes to acquisitions. As things stand, target shareholders have much more say over acquisitions than acquiring shareholders. For instance, NCR's shareholders got to vote on AT&T's hostile bid, whereas AT&T's shareholders were not consulted. Yet acquiring shareholders face not only a greater risk of an immediate decline in their share price (especially if the target firm is large and its business unrelated) but also the serious chance of long-term drag from an awkward fit and often losses on divestment.[85] Shareholder approval could be required for major acquisitions.[86]

Reserve Board Seats for Direct Nominees of Shareholders

Pension funds could gain voice through legislation granting an exclusive right to shareholders to nominate additional directors making up a significant minority of the board of directors, perhaps 20–25 percent of the board.[87] Shareholders would vote not only on the usual slate nominated by the incumbent board of directors, but also for candidates on a short, separate list who received most nominating votes directly from shareholders. This proposal extends the current New York Stock Exchange requirement for independent directors but structures the selection to produce still greater independence.[88]

This proposal would produce an outcome much like the process that put John Brademas, former congressman and head of New York University, on the board of Texaco. Under attack from Carl Icahn, management received support from CalPERS and other institutional shareholders at the cost of an agreement to choose a board member from a list the institutions provided.

End the Conflict of Interest among Managers of Corporate Pensions

The activity of state and local public pension funds and the relative quiescence of private pensions has encouraged the suspicion that managers of the latter suffer from a conflict of interest (alluded to above). In one view, the earlier policies outlined might helpfully go in the right direction, but as long as managers control corporate pension moneys as trustees, not much can be expected of pensions as responsible owners.[89] There is precedent for depriving management of its command over pensions: The Taft-Hartley Act of 1947 banned exclusive union control of pensions. But such a proposal could not fail to attract managers' opposition.

10.5   Conclusions

Policy lessons from the leveraging and deleveraging of U.S. corporations are four:

Do not task monetary policy, in the usual sense of short-term interest rate policy, with preventing a financial mania. This is especially true for an excess of the credit system like the corporate leveraging of the 1980s that gives little impetus to private spending.

Tighten credit policy in the face of a financial mania. Require disclosure by financial intermediaries of their loan exposures to the affected assets; ratchet down permissible loan-to-value or loan–to–cash flow ratios; attach superweights to highly leveraged transactions in the regulation of banks and other financial intermediaries, or raise capital requirements across the board; and as a last resort subject particularly fast credit growth to reserve requirements.

Eliminate the special favors for debt in the tax code. Either combine taxation of interest payments with lower taxes on dividends or overhaul corporate taxation by adopting a cash flow tax. One way or another, eliminate the tax subsidy to corporate distress and bankruptcy.

Reform corporate governance to further institutional investors' exercise of voice rather than exit in relation to underperforming companies' shares. Let institutional investors act like owners rather than blindly pooling funds to let LBO organizers choose new managers.

11   Conclusion

After collecting the themes from the last ten chapters, this concluding chapter considers the question of the future of corporate leveraging. We end with a warning.

11.1   The End of the 1980s

The Minsky-Kindleberger model offers a telling account of the end of three leveraging manias of the 1980s. A head turner of a deal drew new players into making leveraged deals. The signs of euphoria the model predicts were present in the years following the Gibson deal: expansion of credit, increasing leverage, speculative trading, a manifold of domestic and international market interactions, and—in due time—revelation of swindles and scandals. In one respect only did the leveraging mania depart from the archetype: Whereas most financial manias promote a bricks-and-mortar boom, the burdening of corporate cash flows with debt service tended to depress investment in plant and machinery.

Following half a decade's euphoria, distress emerged in mid- to late 1989 as retail investors took flight from junk bond mutual funds and foreign banks wavered in their willingness to be stuffed with loans from leveraged buyouts. Panic gripped the market almost from first day of 1990 as defaults soared, the leading junk underwriter entered bankruptcy, and the junk bond market seized up. The Minsky-Kindleberger model succeeds in drawing our attention to the features that the late 1980s leveraging movement shared with other financial manias.

One can read entire textbooks on corporate finance without coming upon a single mention of the florid phenomena of manias and panics. This omission is all the more striking when one considers that these textbooks prepare students to deal in a marketplace where vast fortunes are made and lost in just the kind of manias and panics these textbooks ignore.

There are of course a few models of financial bubbles. Such formalisms describe worlds in which single asset prices float away from fundamentals of pricing, for no particular reason, and with everyone involved knowing what the game is ("Of course this market makes no sense, but my expected returns are so high that I'll run the risk of not getting out before the crash"). The evidence of the 1980s leveraging resists being shoehorned into such all too rational views of financial bubbles. Whereas a rational bubble requires investors to demand and to get higher and higher returns to offset the rising risk of a crash, in chapter 2 we saw that investors in private equity did worse and worse over time in the 1980s as more and more players joined the leveraging game.[1]

Observers representing a wide spectrum of perspectives have shown surprising willingness to recognize that corporate leveraging in the 1980s spun out of control. The titles of two papers written by academics and a practitioner whose careers have been closely linked to corporate leveraging offer some flavor of this willingness: "The Evolution of Buyout and Financial Structure (Or, What Went Wrong) in the 1980s"; "What Went Wrong with the Highly Leveraged Deals? (Or, All Variety of Agency Costs)."[2] These papers have savored the irony that, after justifying itself as the solution to the "agency" problem of corporate managers' working for themselves rather than for long-suffering shareholders, the leveraging business ended up beset by its own agency problems. Deal makers took their cut up front without any reference to the deal's success. New managers brought little of their own funds into the leveraged businesses they were hired to run. Bank managers demanded and got higher front-end fees out of which current year bonuses could be paid, leaving the banks' shareholders the risk from the retained exposure to the deals. When junk bond buyers ceased to receive equity kickers, the interests of equity holders and junk holders came into sharper conflict.

Even leveraging's most consistent proponent has conceded that something odd happened. Michael Jensen, who acknowledged support from Drexel Burnham Lambert when he testified before Congress and whose connection to KKR was at least as public as his address to the annual gathering of KKR's investors, has allowed as how the market for leveraged deals "experienced a 'contracting failure'—one that gives rise to boom-and-bust cycles common in venture markets such as real estate development, oil and gas drilling, and the venture capital market." To be sure, Jensen's concession confines itself to the riskiest fringes of the capital market. And the rhetoric "contracting failure" confines itself to the conflicts between principals and agents: "a misalignment of incentives between dealmakers and creditors and investors they bring together." Most importantly the concession offers no threat to laissez-faire: "It can be corrected (without government intervention) by the private parties entering into the transactions." But "I call it *failure* because corrections seem to take too long to appear and the mistakes repeat themselves too often to be consistent with our theory of rational investors."[3] There are more things in heaven and earth than are dreamt of in your philosophy, Horatio.

The most interesting alternative to the mania interpretation of the end of corporate leveraging in the 1980s is the stab-in-the-back theory. As described in chapter 3, this theory envisions the behavior of judges, regulators, and politicians coalescing into a broad political reaction. According to this interpretation, the reaction succeeded in shutting down a debt-driven acquisition market that, although perhaps excessive in some of its aspects, was doing the useful work of disciplining corporate managements.

We took this account of the end of corporate leveraging in the 1980s more seriously than its proponents. We laid out in chapter 3 the legal developments, described their asserted effects, and tried to bring evidence to bear on these assertions.

There is little doubt that court decisions, regulations, and laws began to make the leveraging business more difficult toward the end of the decade. The proponents of the stab-in-the-back theory are generally correct both in their history of legal and regulatory developments and in their assertions about the direction of effects of these developments.

Still, the time of death is not consistent with the claim that politics killed the leveraging business. When the effects of each of the court cases, laws, and regulations that are alleged to have hampered the leveraging business are weighed, it is hard to conclude that they did the deed. The Delaware courts showed a fair amount of consistency in allowing managements determined to prevent a takeover to do so; state anti-takeover statutes arrived too early on the scene to explain a change in the market in the late 1980s. Tax changes were too limited to have killed deals wholesale. Bank regulators at most provided the base of information that securities regulators ensured that bank stock investors received; those investors then discouraged banks from making leveraged loans: an informed market at work. In chapter 3, we argued that the 1989 congressional ban on junk bond investment by thrifts was the legal development that most plausibly hurt the leveraging business. But it is hard to push the effect of even this policy too far: The scale of thrifts' junk bond holdings was sufficiently modest that the net supply from that source was no more than the net supply in 1989 from the RJR-Nabisco deal alone. We concede that the full range of legal and regulatory changes taken together could have weighed significantly on the leveraging business. The balance of the evidence, however, suggests that the leveraging business's own excesses did it in.

11.2   Lessons of RJR-Nabisco

Our case study of this deal, which remains at this writing the largest leveraged deal ever, left us hard pressed to say what difference that deal made. To be sure, the original shareholders of RJR-Nabisco did well and the equity investors in KKR's private equity funds did badly, and those who bought later at the public offering did even worse. Taking account of equity and bond holders alike, however, as well as the cash paid out to them, RJR-Nabisco is hard to distinguish from Philip Morris. We found in chapter 4 that after an initial postdeal advantage for RJR-Nabisco, the aggregate market values of the equity, debt, and cumulated cash flows of the two companies ran fairly neck and neck.

It deserves emphasis that the evaluation of the RJR-Nabisco deal depends on when the accounting is taken. Early observers looked at the short-run stock market reactions to the takeover battle. RJR-Nabisco delivered fabulously by this measure, about doubling the money of the prebuyout shareholders. But five years later, none of those involved in RJR-Nabisco, owners and creditors alike, were noticeably ahead of those involved in Philip Morris. Given the fortuitous availability of the latter company as a benchmark, we place more confidence in the five-year result than in the reactions of a stock market driven along by the wildest auction in history.

Other measures of the performance of RJR-Nabisco and Philip Morris yield much the same result. The one exception is in capital spending, where RJR-Nabisco's spending in relation to sales fell considerably after the leveraged buyout. Some observers, citing the techno-extravaganza of RJR's planned investment in Cookieville, would applaud the decline in investment spending. Other observers claim that the same constraint that expressed itself in lower investment spending also kept

RJR-Nabisco from investing abroad in markets that promised fast growth. Overall, we judge the deal to be neither the loser it is now generally thought to be nor the roaring success that early evaluations made it out to be.

In one respect the RJR deal has proven a famous success, generating well in excess of $1 billion in fees for Wall Street. Banks, junk bond underwriters, investment bankers, lawyers, and KKR have done well by the deal. True, KKR has not to date boosted its reputation on the basis of the deal. KKR's acquisition of Borden with most of its RJR-Nabisco shares (owned by KKR's 1987 fund) was widely recognized as a complicated exit strategy from RJR. By late winter 1995, KKR "ended the biggest takeover in history with a whimper, unloading its remaining stock in RJR Nabisco Holdings Co. after six years of dismal returns from the cigarette and food giant."[4] But because KKR was wise enough to raise additional private equity while the RJR-Nabisco deal still looked promising, the buyout firm always had cash on hand to make deals. And by collecting fees of more than $160 million (table 4.4), KKR made sure that it is doing better than the pension funds and university endowments that invested in KKR's 1987 partnership.

Our case study of RJR casts doubt on leverage enthusiasts' broad claims that leveraged deals "created shareholder wealth" over any significant period of time. Most studies purporting to measure the benefits of acquisitions in the 1980s put great faith in short-term stock market reactions. A window of a matter of days or weeks around the announcement of a merger is wide enough for such analyses to conclude that great good was done by a deal because the value of shareholders' stakes rose. As noted above, this measure identifies RJR-Nabisco as a fantastically successful deal, with the near doubling of shareholders' wealth offset only to a minor extent by bondholders' losses.

In this largest leveraged deal ever, the omniscient stock market seems nearsighted, because the initial lead of RJR shareholders and creditors over their counterparts at Philip Morris closed over time. Note that our use of Philip Morris as a benchmark means that this conclusion does not derive from the vagaries of the tobacco business. One way of reading our evidence on RJR-Nabisco is that the deal front-loaded gains that claimants on Philip Morris have enjoyed without the leverage. It might be argued that the frenzied bidding for the largest leveraged deal ever makes it a counterexample with limited power to damage the assumption of market omniscience. But this counterexample gains importance from the widespread criticism of RJR-Nabisco's former management as wasteful and from the firm's decline in capital spending in relation to sales that we describe in chapter 4. In other words, RJR-Nabisco was thought to be a particularly ripe target for an LBO, showed a postbuyout change in behavior consistent with the LBO's having cut back on wasteful investment, and yet fails to provide convincing evidence of medium-term extraordinary gains.

11.3 Corporate Refinancing in the 1990s

In 1988 Ben Bernanke and John Campbell published an article entitled, "Is there a Corporate Debt Crisis?"[5] At the time the answer was clearly no and at this writing the answer is again no. Two questions arise: Did we experience a corporate debt crisis in 1990–91? Could we experience one in the future? We take up the first question now and save the second question for the last part of this chapter.

The answer to the question of whether we had a corporate debt crisis might depend on where you are sitting. From John Reed's chair at Citicorp, it might have seemed a corporate debt crisis. Sometime in 1991 at Citicorp, highly leveraged transactions either written off or still on the books but not yielding regular interest topped $2 billion on a portfolio that peaked at about $10 billion, a substantial problem even for the largest bank in the country. (Only the larger hole in the real estate portfolio put the corporate debt problem in perspective.) From the perspective of any issuer of junk bonds that had planned to refinance or to raise fresh capital for expansion, the closure of the junk bond market might have seemed to define a debt crisis. And the bankruptcy judges in the Customs House in lower Manhattan and in federal buildings across the country might have felt that there was a corporate debt crisis as they exercised authority over dozens of major corporations who had sought protection from their creditors.

If there was no corporate debt crisis,[6] it was not because bankruptcy was privatized, despite claims to the contrary. The claim was that the new structures of debt could handle difficulties in paying interest without resort to bankruptcy. As Jensen asserted, creditors of highly leveraged companies would have a greater incentive collectively to intervene early in badly performing companies.[7] But could the many creditors understand and achieve their collective interest in avoiding the costs of formal bankruptcy? The mid-1980s provided some evidence for an affirmative answer as Drexel was able to provide carrots and sticks to creditors to act consensually to concert their forbearance. But conflicts among classes of creditors of firms with convoluted structures of debt proved hard to resolve, however, particularly after Drexel lost clout and then went bankrupt itself. Creditors' increasingly fractured claims set them one against the other in a manner most productive for the bankruptcy bar. (The development of so-called prepackaged bankruptcies showed the necessity of the coercion that only the court could provide.) The "Chinese paper" of the deal makers, claims bent and folded in an origami of subordination and seniority, cash interest and deferred interest, doomed the privatization of bankruptcy. This notion partook of the fallacy of composition: What was in the interest of creditors as a whole did not move the proliferated classes of creditors, who maneuvered for their own particular advantage. If anyone was responsible for unnecessary bankruptcies, it was the deal makers, not the judges who were mostly following precedents, as we argued in chapter 3.

Bernanke and Campbell predicted a corporate debt crisis under conditions akin to those of the 1973–74 and 1981–82 recessions. Under the conditions of the relatively mild recession of 1990–91, with inter-

est rates having already started to fall a year before the recession's official beginning, their results might err on the side of predicting fewer
bankruptcies than actually experienced. We have argued that the revulsion toward debt started in 1989 and reached an advanced stage
with the defaults in the commercial paper market in late 1989, the
bankruptcy of Campeau and Drexel, and the closure of the junk bond
market in early 1990. The National Bureau of Economic Research ex-
perts put the onset of the recession at August 1990, but by then Allied/
Federated Stores and Drexel had already gone bankrupt, the junk bond
market was closed, and the market for leveraged bank loans had folded
up. The turn in the credit cycle clearly preceded the turn in the business
cycle. From timing alone, it is easier to argue that the collapse of the
leveraging business caused the recession than that the recession caused
the collapse of the leveraging business. Many of the critics of leverage
gave it too much credit and overestimated its staying power in arguing
that a serious recession could lead to a collapse.

Equity to the Rescue

Two factors prevented a spiral of discredit from deepening the recession and leaving wreckage on the scale of the Bernanke and Campbell
scenario, in which a tenth or a fifth of the corporate sector would go
into the tank. We outlined in chapter 4 the first factor: The 180-degree
turn from takeovers' and corporate treasurers' flushing equity out of
the corporate sector to replacing debt with equity limited the damage. The most important step in the return to equity, KKR's injection of equity into the semidistressed RJR-Nabisco, was aided by
fortuitous timing in KKR's fund-raising cycle: The same shareholders
could be tapped to invest in RJR-Nabisco who had invested in the first
instance.

In three years, 1991–93, U.S. corporations raised almost a net $70
billion in equity. This sum did not replace all the equity that takeovers,
cash-financed acquisitions, and repurchases had drained away in the

previous decade. If more than one-half trillion dollars of equity had been retired in the 1980s, something less than an eighth of the damage was undone in these three years.

We examined the particular firms that raised equity in the early 1990s and argued that the connection between the equity raising in the 1990s and the leveraging of the 1980s was not merely temporal succession. Overrepresented among the firms raising equity were highly leveraged firms, like RJR-Nabisco, as well as firms that had leveraged up by building up finance company affiliates and whose losses put them at risk of losing their credit standing, like the auto companies. Firms looking to expand their operations were surprisingly rare among the firms tapping the stock market in the early 1990s.

Shorter Shelf-Life for Fashions in Corporate Structure?

Who foresaw that so much equity could be infused into U.S. corporations so fast? No one. The rapidity with which the theme of the mergers and acquisitions of the 1980s began to play in reverse distinguishes the 1980s from the other postwar burst of acquisition activity in the 1960s.

In the 1960s, Wall Street assembled conglomerate corporations. The theory was that a fast-growing firm, an ITT or Gulf and Western ("Engulf and Devour," according to Mel Brooks), could buy a slow-growing firm and create market value. Why? The high multiple of earnings that the market applied to the highflier, when applied to the earnings of the slowpoke, would raise their joint value in the market. The theory leaned on a variety of flying buttresses, such as the value to investors of smoother earnings as a result of the conglomerate's internal diversification, or the asserted efficiencies of an internal, corporate allocation of capital from mature businesses to new lines of business. The current verdict of the economics profession on the conglomerate wave is that it did not really make much sense and that the structures that it put into place were dismantled by the mergers and acquisitions of the

1980s, which have been dubbed the "return to corporate specialization."[8] As one review of subsequent divestitures of acquisitions put it, "corporate raiders thrive on failed corporate [acquisition] strategy."[9]

For our purpose, what matters is less whether or not the conglomerates made sense, but rather the speed with which they were undone. The conglomerate wave may have peaked in a handful of years, but its undoing came only after a generation. The contrast with the leveraging wave could scarcely be sharper: RJR leveraged in 1989 and hurried to deleverage less than two years later. Today Wall Street can turn on a dime.

Perhaps the contrast between the delayed reversal of the conglomerate wave and the rapid reversal of leveraging reflects the fact that a highly leveraged U.S. firm is more obviously a bad idea than a conglomerate firm. The limitations of leverage become evident quickly, as with holes in the roof, rather than over time, as with termites.

The Role of Short-Term Interest Rates

We calculated with some care in chapter 6 the relative roles of sales of equity and bonds, on the one hand, and the decline of short-term interest rates, on the other, in relieving corporate America of the burden of the debts run up in the previous decade. Our very strong conclusion is that short-term rates did the far heavier lifting.

In this comparison, however, we slight the role of the declines of short-term rates. They must be given credit for some of the decline of long-term rates, even though we have grouped savings on refinanced bonds with sales of equity as two aspects of refinancing. Moreover, the shock of low rates to American savers spurred the households' shift out of bank certificates of deposit into mutual funds in the 1990s. Joe Six-pack couldn't stand 2 percent. From a certain angle, low interest rates ensured willing buyers for the paper that corporate treasurers needed to sell even as lower short-term interest rates bolstered corporate solvency and raised corporate profits directly.

Ongoing Refinancing and the U.S. Stock Market Boom of the 1990s

After the turbulence in the bond market in 1994, when the Federal Reserve raised rates back to normal levels, corporations continued to refinance their outstanding bonds at lower interest rates. The ongoing reduction in the interest costs shifted income from bondholders to stockholders. Our analysis suggests that a significant share of the earnings growth of U.S. nonfinancial corporations in the 1990s derived from this source. Whereas in the early 1990s the availability of equity finance helped to stabilize the bond market, in the latter 1990s the rallying bond market help to provide the earnings that fueled the ascent of stock prices.

We contend, however, that the earnings growth derived from lower bond yields is more nominal than real. That is, bond yields have fallen mostly because inflation has fallen, not because real returns to bondholders have fallen. If this is so, then stock market investors may be suffering from a species of money illusion, confusing lower interest payments with something more substantial like improvements in operating performance.

11.4 The Hot IPO Market

Critics of the leveraging movement underestimated individuals' and institutions' willingness to shift their funds into equity in an environment of low short-term interest rates and falling long-term rates. The oversight was understandable, given the extraordinary strength and length of the hot market for initial public offerings.

Our review of the performance of reverse LBOs in chapter 7 suggests that they did not do badly by their investors. If the shares of deleveraging companies are taken to pose no more than middling risk to their holders, they appeared to remain ahead of the Standard & Poor's 500 after one year, two years, and three years. As we saw with RJR-Nabisco, however, a reverse LBO could leave the newly traded firm with leverage still well above U.S. norms. So investors in reverse LBOs faced greater than average risk from higher interest rates or a slowdown of the economy, risks which proved bearable but for which it is no means clear that the investors were compensated.

Those who ponder the puzzles of IPOs' price performance can learn from our examination of the performance of large reverse LBOs. Underwriters of reverse LBOs in the early 1990s seemed to prop up their share prices when they first started trading with much the same frequency as do underwriters of regular IPOs. Moreover, investors of the time would have been well advised to steer clear of issues that remained at their issue price at the end of the first day of trading, just as they should avoid regular IPOs that do not budge from the offering price on the day of their market debut. As with ordinary IPOs, average short-term performance measures for reverse LBOs can disguise lots of games being played in the market.

Some aspects of the price performance of the 1990s reverse LBOs do set them apart from ordinary IPOs. Guided by knowledgeable former investment bankers, ten times larger than ordinary IPOs, and relatively well known to investors, these "new" shares offered by reverse LBOs showed less of an initial price surge when they hit the market than those of ordinary IPOs. Moreover, their respectable if unspectacular performance as long as three years after issue also sets them apart from the run of IPOs. In these respects, reverse LBOs seem to hit the market more as prodigal friends rather than as new faces.

Thus in buying reverse LBOs in the early 1990s, Main Street bailed out Wall Street with a privately orchestrated and fairly decentralized equity-for-debt swap. Main Street did not do too badly in the process.

We argued in chapter 8 that LBOs in the early 1990s were competing for money in an IPO market that performs a strange function in American capitalism. When the IPO market is hot, innovative companies that are years away from a product or revenues, much less profits, can sell equity to investors looking to make a killing. It is an open question whether an internet bookseller should be worth a multiple of the largest U.S. book retailer, which owns a wholesaler used by the internet firm. The IPO market delivers low average returns to investors but occasionally rewards them by multiplying their investment many times.

In this respect, the U.S. market provides financing for young firms unlike anything to be found in major industrial countries, including Japan. Even at the most vertiginous moment of the Tokyo stock market ascent, nothing like the capital available to new U.S. companies in the 1990s flowed to new companies in Japan.

This financial wonder does not operate as rational Weberian bureaucracy. It is hot when times are getting better, not when times are worst and the need may be greatest. It is as likely to finance steak houses and yuppie soft drinks as "critical" technologies. And to some extent it might have financed the return to equity by the dealmakers of the 1980s instead of young job-creating firms.

11.5 Mergers and Acquisitions in the 1990s

We argued in chapter 9 that the very active mergers and acquisition market of the 1990s remains relatively benign, from the standpoint of its implications for financial robustness at least, if not necessarily for competition. Most of the action remains at writing in share swaps, so that only a minority of deals pose leverage risks. Although megamergers are putting together big firms in telecommunications, media/ entertainment,[10] banking and utilities, spin-offs and carve outs continue to fashion more focused firms. The pockets of equity retirement in the market, including defense and pharmaceuticals, make some sense.

To some extent, institutional investors prepared to speak up in the presence of poor corporate performance have begun to tip the balance from traditionally strong managers toward traditionally weak owners. Thus far, representatives of pension funds for public sector employees have been most active in making their views known; the divided and perhaps conflicted managers of corporate pension funds rarely speak up; whereas managers of mutual funds appear to have spoken up only in isolated instances, as when John Neff weighed in against the reappointment of Lee Iacocca as CEO at Chrysler. The desperate argument that the threat of leveraged takeover is a necessary discipline on managers has lost power.

11.6 Taking Stock: Corporate Leveraging and the Future

Looking back over the 1990s, it is easy to be complacent. Despite the prophesies of disaster, things worked out pretty well. The market showed once again a greater resiliency than its critics foresaw. There is truth in such sentiments, but danger as well.

The market did not arrange, and indeed did not predict, that short-term interest rates would fall to the level of inflation and remain there for some time. What if the bond market had gotten spooked by the interest rate declines at some point and pushed up bond yields in a vote of no confidence in the trend of short-term rates? Under these circumstances, short-term interest rate cuts would have ceased to be passed through to a booming bond and stock market and the capital markets would have turned unreceptive to corporate refinanacing. Similarly, what if the dollar's exchange rate had come under severe pressure at some point when rates were declining? Again, the bond and stock markets could have pulled in the welcome mat for new issues. In short, to say that the market arranged its own Houdini-style escape from high corporate leverage is false, and to assume that the same path of short-term interest rates could have been feasibly set by the Federal Reserve under all circumstances is foolish.

The Risk of Public Recapitalization

Had the private sector recapitalization of U.S. corporations not been possible in the early 1990s, many feared a public recapitalization. We saw in chapter 10 that Benjamin Friedman's predictions that corporate leveraging would hamstring the Federal Reserve did not come to pass. His were by no means the only jeremiads uttered in the direction of the corporate leveraging. Henry Kaufman warned that high leverage would carry the U.S. financial system in the direction of the Continental or Japanese systems that traditionally operated with high leverage:

> The continued rapid growth of debt threatens an amalgamation of business and finance—and that must ultimately lead to a far more intrusive Government and thus corporatized system. . . . A decade from now, we will probably have a variety of financial-industrial combinations similar to those that are now common on the European continent. These combinations are bound to induce a variety of Government intrusions, possibly involving direct Government participation in business, but surely involving bailouts of corporations that fall into severe difficulties.[11]

Albert Wojnilower filled in the steps between leverage and government intervention:

> Now that heavily indebted companies are becoming typical, the risk is already serious that a shock, such as higher interest rates or a recession, could threaten enough household-name companies to form a critical mass. . . . Let me be quick to underline that, . . . the danger of an actual cascade of corporate defaults . . . is slight or nonexistent . . . we may safely assume that public support would be invoked for any important group of corporate debtors in difficulty. The risk we run by tolerating the attrition of equity is not primarily that of economic catastrophe but rather of massive government rescue operations that deeply politicize the economy.[12]

The risk of such rescue operations provided the rationale for Wojnilower's proposal for government regulation of corporate leverage. Low interest rates in the early 1990s allowed a private reintroduction of equity into corporate America that may have proceeded just fast enough to forestall a massive public rescue.

Grounds for Concern

Let us offer four good reasons to worry that the U.S. financial system
has not seen the last of corporate leveraging. First, events in the bond
market in 1992–94 and the growth of hedge funds more generally
show the continuing lure of leverage on Wall Street. Second, short and
selective memories are obscuring the dangers so recently faced. Third,
the money is there to make the leveraged deals. Finally, the trend in
U.S. corporate financing shows a return to the retirement of equity, at
a rate as fast or faster than that of the peak years of the late 1980s.

The Lure of Supercharged Returns: Applying Leverage to Bonds

The surge of bond buying with borrowed money in 1992–93 demonstrated Wall Street's capacity to bring the power of leverage to bear on
any asset class.[13] The securities industry borrows against bonds every
day to some extent as part of its regular operation. Thus every after-
noon Wall Street's inventory of Treasury bonds is pledged for loans
from banks, municipal governments, pension funds, and others. But
with the steep yield curve of the early 1990s—the three percentage
points that separated the cost of such "repo" financing from the yield
on the Treasury paper—and with bond prices rising, leveraged holdings of bonds slipped from financing the business to being the business. Not only did securities firms and banks load up on bonds financed
with overnight or one-month money, but they also put their customers
into what became "the Trade." Just as leveraged buyouts mixed nineteen parts of debt for every one part of equity, ways were devised to
finance vast holdings of bond portfolios not with 10 percent down,
but with 5 percent or less down. When the bond rally ran out of steam
in late 1993 and the market turned nasty in early 1994, the profession-
als liquidated their portfolios of bonds and the slow-footed amateurs,
like the treasurers of several prominent corporations and of Orange
County, California, got nailed by the Trade. The same leverage that
could produce fantastic returns in a benign environment of stable or

falling rates swallowed equity in big bites in an adverse environment.[14] More recently, the bond mania reappeared in a new guise and claimed a new victim, Long-Term Capital Management. Instead of long-term bonds funded with overnight money, bonds of lower quality or liquidity were funded with short positions in high-quality government bonds.

The parallel between the bond mania and the preceding corporate leveraging mania extended beyond the use of leverage to boost returns from a familiar asset even as turbocharging soups up a familiar engine. In addition, a market for private equity emerged to permit outsiders to invest in leveraged assets. Just as private LBO equity funds collected money from pension plans, universities, and other institutional investors to take the equity position in LBOs, so too private funds, persuasively dubbed "hedge funds," collected money from institutional investors to leverage with the Trade. A remarkable structure emerged for the fees the hedge funds charged: 1–2 percent a year up front and 20 percent of the profits.[15] Recall that this structure is precisely that of the LBO funds.

It is no accident that this fee structure has reappeared in the 1990s for a leveraged fund of some variety. The fee structure originated in the oil and gas drilling and venture capital business, where experience and judgment are as necessary as a taste for risk taking. It could be argued that the LBO business required talents as rare as those of venture capitalists or major league ballplayers to identify and negotiate for the right sort of company, although the fact that a leveraged play on the Standard & Poor's 500 would have beat most LBO funds' performance makes one wonder about such an argument. But it is hard to imagine anything more akin to a commodity than government bonds. One way of thinking about the fee structure—a variant on "heads we win, tails you lose"—is that it is so attractive to the Street that "new" products will come to market that will require it. And because there really are no new asset classes to be found, familiar assets will reappear packaged with debt to justify the fee structure.

Memories and the Moral Hazard

Another ground for concern is memory. Plenty of empty space in office buildings kept bankers from financing towers for some time. But the memory of the difficulties experienced with respect to the corporate leveraging business has no such ready reference. Consider the results were Citibank to review the evidence of table 2.4 without anyone present who could recall how close the bank came to larger losses, and how untimely were the difficulties experienced even with a very benign backdrop of interest rates. Corporate planners might well conclude that the bank had not really lost anything, under what could be described (incorrectly, of course) as the worst-case conditions of a freezing up of the junk bond market.

Kevin Phillips's concern that the crisis managers may have done their jobs too well for lessons to have been reliably learned is not without grounds. A crash averted may be risks forgotten and eventually mistakes repeated.

The Availability of Deal Money

At every level of their capital structure, the money became available in the first half of the 1990s again for leveraged deals. As seen in figure 2.1, 1993 was already a good year for fund-raising by leveraged deal makers' private equity funds, and much more has been raised since this has been put to work. As for the mezzanine of debt, as seen in figures 2.2 and 2.3, junk bond issuance and outstandings have grown rapidly in the 1990s. At the level of senior debt, banks had rebuilt capital and were acting hungry for loans by the second half of 1993. According to Loan Pricing Corporation, the typical syndicated loan to a leveraged borrower charged about 2.5 percent over the cost of funding for a loan to a firm carrying a debt load of 4.5 times cash flow in early 1993, much the same price to a firm carrying a debt load of 5.5 times cash flow in late 1993, and much the same price to a firm carrying a debt load of 6.5 times its cash flow in early 1994. Loan conditions continued to ease into the summer of 1998, when the Russian default and the difficulties of Long-Term Capital Management led to a tightening of terms. Before then, Marty Fridson ascribed the recent, "exceptionally low" default rate on junk bonds to "extraordinary forbearance on the part of cash-flush commercial banks. In their eagerness to amend [loan agreements] and extend [maturities], lenders have made it almost impossible for troubled corporations to fail.[16]

Trends in Corporate Financing: Return to the 1980s?

We argued in chapter 9 that the acceleration of mergers and acquisitions in the 1990s did not represent a return to corporate leveraging. Nevertheless some developments point to the possibility of a return to leveraging. 1994 saw Viacom bag Paramount, after a bidding war that offered the Paramount shareholders more cash as the price went up. Thus, as the genteel agreed combinations of the previous several years gave way to contested bids and pitched battles, that old reliable currency, cash, put in an appearance. With the Paramount deal in early 1994, net equity issuance returned to net equity retirement in the aggregate figures, recalling the earlier switch in 1984. In 1998, repurchases and cash acquisitions retired equity at an annual rate of more than $250 billion, an all-time record. At century's end, one force seems to stand in the way of a full-scale return of the leveraging business: high equity prices.

11.7 The Policy Imperative

We argued in chapter 10 that three measures should be adopted to forestall the risks that the corporate leveraging business will swing into high gear once again. Our advice: Reform corporate taxes to make the tax code neutral as between debt and equity. On this policy there is much agreement. Reform corporate governance to encourage institutional investors to hold management accountable. One need not become a proponent of so-called relational investing nor endorse everything done under its banner to recognize its advantage over the threat of raiders bootstrapping their way onto the executive floor with debt.

Our last policy lesson has application well beyond the business of leveraging corporations: Be prepared to set restrictive credit policies, because "delay in making awkward choices among regulatory alternatives can lead to even more unpleasant predicaments in which no choice is left at all as to the nature and scope of intervention."[17] So be prepared to improve disclosure, hoping for help from the capital markets, but if necessary, implement and tighten loan-to-value ratios and capital requirements. At the extreme, consider imposing reserve requirements on credit growth. Just because you have dodged a bullet does not mean that you should stand in the same place.

Notes

Chapter 1

1. *Barbarians at the Gate*, film, Home Box Office, 1993; Christopher Byron, "Drexel's Fall: the Final Days," *New York Magazine*, March 19, 1990, p. 38; George Anders, *Merchants of Debt: KKR and the Mortgaging of American Business* (New York: Basic Books, 1993), pp. 250, 256.

Chapter 2

1. Hyman P. Minsky, *Can "It" Happen Again? Essays in Instability and Finance* (Armonk, NY: M.E. Sharpe, 1982); "Can 'It' Happen Again?" in *Banking and Monetary Studies*, Deane Carson, ed. (Homewood, IL: R.D. Irwin, 1963), pp. 101–111; *Stabilizing an Unstable Economy* (New Haven, CT: Yale University Press, 1986); and Charles P. Kindleberger, *Manias, Panics, and Crashes*, 3rd edition (New York: John Wiley, 1996).

2. Our treatment of the credit developments of the late 1980s builds on the Minskian perspective offered by Richard Cantor and John Wenninger, "Perspective on the Credit Slowdown," Federal Reserve Bank of New York *Quarterly Review*, vol. 18 (Spring 1993), pp. 3–36.

3. Bryan Burrough and John Helyar, *Barbarians at the Gate: The Fall of RJR Nabisco* (New York: Harper & Row, 1990), p. 140. Bruck's account points to the Gibson LBO as a deal that caught the imagination of financiers, but Grant's account highlights the sale of the junk bonds that financed the buyout of Metromedia—although he

does instance the "fabulously successful" Gibson deal as one of the "shining examples of the early leveraged buyouts." Connie Bruck, "The Old Boy and the New Boys," *The New Yorker,* May 8, 1989, pp. 81–96; James Grant, *Money of the Mind* (New York: Farrar, Straus, Giroux, 1992), p. 375.

4. The characterization is that of Joseph L. Rice III of Clayton, Dubilier & Rice, cited in Ron Stodghill II, "Lords of Leverage for the '90s," *Business Week,* November 15, 1993, p. 70. "Clayton, Dubilier & Rice . . . founded in 1978, . . . has since acquired 17 businesses. . . . All but four were divisions of large corporations . . . . " W. Carl Kester and Timothy A. Luehrman, "The LBO Association as a Relational Investment Regime: Clinical Evidence from Clayton, Dubilier & Rice, Inc.," paper presented to Columbia University Law School Institutional Investor Project Conference on Relational Investing, May 1993, p. 17. For evidence of the liberating possibilities of divisional buyouts, see George P. Baker and Karen H. Wruck, "Organizational Changes and Value Creation in Leveraged Buyouts," *Journal of Financial Economics,* vol. 25 (1989), pp. 163–90.

5. George Anders, *Merchants of Debt: KKR and the Mortgaging of American Business* (New York: Basic Books, 1992), pp. 50–56. In a private communication, Charles Kindleberger drew a parallel to the special war loans of Renaissance Florence, which were raised only among the oligarchy. See Michael Veseth, *Mountains of Debt* (Oxford: Oxford University Press, 1990), p. 68. More recently, investment in Long-Term Capital Management had social cachet owing to its hiring of prominent academics.

6. Anders, *Merchants,* pp. 45–53, 223.

7. "Of $122 billion used to finance mergers and acquisitions in 1984, less than 2 percent came from high yield bonds." Statement of G. Chris Anderson, Managing Director, Drexel Burnham Lambert, before the Subcommittee on General Oversight and Investigations, House Committee on Banking, Finance and Urban Affairs, *Issues Relating to High-Yield Securities (Junk Bonds): Hearing,* Ninety-Ninth Congress, First Session, Serial no. 99-47 (September 19, 1985), p. 44.

8. Peter Tufano, "Financing Acquisitions in the Late 1980s: Sources and Forms of Capital," in Margaret M. Blair, ed., *The Deal Decade* (Washington, DC: Brookings Institution, 1993), p. 293.

9. Edward J. Frydl, "Some Issues in Corporate Leverage: An Overview Essay," *Studies in Corporate Leverage* (New York: Federal Reserve Bank of New York, 1990), p. 15.

10. Connie Bruck, *The Predator's Ball* (New York: Simon & Schuster, 1988).

11. David H. Kogut, "Corporate Finance 1985: The Red Hot Year," *Investment Dealers' Digest,* January 13, 1986, p. 27.

12. Glenn A. Kessler, "Big Bucks Belied," *Investment Dealers' Digest,* February 10, 1986, p. 14.

13. Noel Ticky and Ram Charan, "Citicorp Faces the World: An Interview with John Reed," *Harvard Business Review,* November/December 1990, pp. 134–44.

14. Anders, *Merchants,* p. 81.

15. Testimony of Donald N. Boyce, Chief Executive Officer of IDEX, before Subcommittee on Labor-Management Relations, House Committee on Education and Labor, *Oversight Hearings on the Role of Pension Funds in Corporate Takeovers: Hearings,* 101: 1, Serial no. 101-26, March 7, 1989, pp. 371–97.

16. Steven N. Kaplan and Jeremy C. Stein, "The Evolution of Buyout Pricing and Financial Structure in the 1980s," *Quarterly Journal of Economics,* May 1993, pp. 319, 325.

17. Louis Lowenstein, *What's Wrong with Wall Street?* (Reading, MA: Addison-Wesley, 1988), p. 146.

18. Kaplan and Stein, "Evolution," p. 326.

19. Martin S. Fridson, "What Went Wrong with the Highly Leveraged Deals? (Or, All Variety of Agency Costs)," *Continental Bank Journal of Applied Corporate Finance,* vol. 45, no. 3 (Fall 1991), p. 58.

20. "The Cave-In That Never Happened," *Merrill Lynch Extra Credit,* December 1990, p. 19, which reviewed the Wigmore article referred to on figure 2.8.

21. Tufano, "Financing Acquisitions," p. 302.

22. Louis Lowenstein, "Ignorance Isn't Bliss: Lack of Disclosure by Junk-Bond Funds Is Shameful," *Barron's,* May 29, 1989. Lowenstein repeats the argument, substituting Fort Howard Paper Company, to conclude that one dollar was being turned into almost two dollars in *Sense and Nonsense in Corporate Finance* (Reading, MA: Addison-Wesley, 1991), pp. 79–80.

23. William F. Long and David J. Ravenscraft, "Decade of Debt: Lessons from LBOs in the 1980s," in Margaret M. Blair, ed., *The Deal Decade* (Washington, DC: Brookings Institution, 1993), pp. 218–20.

24. Steven N. Kaplan and Jeremy C. Stein. "The Evolution of Buyout and Financial Structure (Or, What Went Wrong) in the 1980s," *Continental Bank Journal of Applied Corporate Finance,* vol. 6, no. 1 (Spring 1993), pp. 72–88.

25. Robert T. Kleiman and Kevin Nathan, "Was Heavy Debt a Good Disciplinarian for Recapped Firms?" *Mergers and Acquisitions,* November/December 1992, p. 25.

Capital spending in relation to sales was adjusted for its change for the Standard and Poor's 500 firms.

26. Bronwyn Hall, "The Impact of Corporate Restructuring on Industrial Research and Development," *Brookings Papers on Economic Activity, Microeconomics,* 1990, pp. 85–124; and "The Effect of Takeover Activity on Corporate Research and Development," in Alan Auerbach, ed., *Corporate Takeovers: Causes and Consequences,* (Chicago: University of Chicago Press, 1988), pp. 69–96. But another study finds no statistical significance to the fall in R & D spending: Frank R. Lichtenberg and Donald Siegel, "The Effects of Leveraged Buyouts on Productivity and Related Aspects of Firm Behavior," *Journal of Financial Economics,* vol 27, no. 1 (September 1990), pp. 187–91.

27. Steven Fazzari, R. Glenn Hubbard, and Bruce Petersen, "Financing Constraints and Corporate Investment," *Brookings Papers on Economic Activity,* 1988:1, pp. 144–95.

28. Richard Cantor, "Effects of Leverage on Corporate Investment and Hiring Decisions," Federal Reserve Bank of New York *Quarterly Review* (Summer 1990), pp. 31–41.

29. Michael C. Jensen, "Agency Costs of Free Cash Flows, Corporate Finance, and Takeovers," *American Economic Review,* vol. 76 (May 1986), pp. 323–9; Margaret M. Blair and Robert Litan, "Corporate Leverage and Leveraged Buyouts in the Eighties," in John B. Shoven and Joel Waldfogel, eds., *Debt, Taxes, and Corporate Restructuring* (Washington, DC: Brookings, 1990), pp. 43–80.

30. Kleiman and Nathan, "Heavy Debt."

31. Steven A. Zimmer, "Event Risk Premia and Bond Market Incentives for Corporate Leverage," Federal Reserve Bank of New York *Quarterly Review,* vol. 15 (Spring 1990), pp. 15–30.

32. John Ryding, "The Rise in Corporate Leveraging in the 1980s," in Edward J. Frydl, ed., *Studies on Corporate Leverage* (New York: Federal Reserve Bank of New York, 1990), pp. 74–79.

33. Andrei Shleifer and Robert W. Vishny, "Liquidation Values and Debt Capacity: A Market Equilibrium Approach," *Journal of Finance,* vol. 47, no. 4 (September 1992), pp. 1343–66.

34. Sanjai Bhagat, Andrei Shleifer, and Robert Vishny, "Hostile Takeovers in the 1980s: The Return to Corporate Specialization," *Brookings Papers in Economic Activity, Microeconomics,* 1990, pp. 1–72.

35. Anders, *Merchants,* p. 297. According to Anders, the sale of assets at Beatrice went well beyond those envisioned in the buyout and was opportunistic. See pp. 199–206.

36. Kaplan and Stein, "The Evolution of Buyout," *Continental Bank Journal, p. 77.*

37. Rebecca Demsetz, "Recent Trends in Commercial Bank Loan Sales," Federal Reserve Bank of New York *Quarterly Review,* vol. 18 (Winter 1993–94), pp. 75–8.

38. Steven A. Zimmer and Robert N. Mccauley, "Bank Cost of Capital and International Competition," Federal Reserve Bank of New York *Quarterly Review,* vol. 15, nos. 3–4 (Winter 1991), pp. 33–59.

39. Claudio E. V. Borio, *Banks' Involvement in Highly Leveraged Transactions,* BIS *Economic Papers* no. 28 (Basle Switzerland: Bank for International Settlements, October 1990), p. 19, citing bank analysts' data on 13 large banks, which showed that HLT exposures at 4 large banks reached more than 200 percent of equity.

40. David Laster and Robert N. McCauley, "Making Sense of the Profits of Foreign Firms in the United States," Federal Reserve Bank of New York *Quarterly Review,* vol. 19, no. 2 (Summer-Fall 1994), pp. 44–75.

41. Robert N. McCauley and Dan P. Eldridge, "The British Invasion: Explaining the Strength of U.K. Acquisitions of U.S. Corporations," in *International Private Capital Flows* (Basle, Switzerland: Bank for International Settlements, 1990), pp. 319–53.

42. Paul Taylor, "Turmoil over the Weinstock Penny," *Financial Times,* December 1, 1993, p. 22; "Manpower, Inc.," Standard and Poor's *Credit Week,* October 26, 1992, pp. 67–8; *International Financing Review,* Issue 1035, June 18, 1994, p. 31.

43. Roger Alcaly, "The Golden Age of Junk Bonds," *New York Review of Books,* vol. 41, no. 10 (May 26, 1994), p. 32. These are flatly "technical charges" to Glenn Yago, "The Credit Crunch: A Regulatory Squeeze on Growth Capital," *Continental Bank Journal of Applied Corporate Finance,* vol. 4 (1991), p. 99.

44. James B. Stewart, *Den of Thieves* (New York: Simon and Schuster, 1991), p. 437.

45. Quoted in Alcaly, "Golden Age," p. 31.

46. Burrough and Helyar, *Barbarians,* p. 513.

47. Allen J. Schneider, "How Top Companies Create Shareholder Value," *Financial Executive,* May-June 1990, p. 38. Precise data from the survey were provided by Schneider.

48. David J. Denis and Diane K. Denis, "Causes of Financial Distress Following Leveraged Recapitalizations," *Journal of Financial Economics,* vol. 37 (1995), pp. 148–9.

49. Lisabeth Weiner and David Neustadt, "UAL Rejection Seen As LBO Turning Point," *American Banker,* October 16, 1989, pp. 1, 46; David Neustadt, "RJR Filing Shows Banks Will Share $325 Million in Fees," *American Banker,* December 8, 1988, p. 2.

50. Denis and Denis, "Causes," pp. 148–9.

51. Weiner and Neustadt, "UAL Rejection," p. 1.

52. Christopher Byron, "Drexel's Fall: The Final Days," *New York Magazine*, March 19, 1990, pp. 32–8.

53. Edward Altman, "Measuring Corporate Bond Mortality and Performance," *Journal of Finance*, 44 (September 1989), pp. 909–22; Paul Asquith, David W. Mullins, Jr., and Eric D. Wolff, "Original Issue High Yield Bonds: Aging Analysis of Defaults, Exchanges and Calls," *Journal of Finance*, 44 (September 1989), pp. 923–52.

54. The numerator, nonfinancial corporate defaults, combines data from two sources: Dun & Bradstreet's *Monthly Business Failures* and First Boston's annual *High Yield Handbook*. Dun & Bradstreet's publication provides data on business failure liabilities (which do not include any long-term, publicly held obligations) by industry. The first component of nonfinancial corporate defaults consists of Dun & Bradstreet's annual total for U.S. failure liabilities less the annual totals for finance, insurance, real estate, and agriculture. The second component of nonfinancial corporate defaults is the difference between the total value of bonds going into default and the defaults of bonds issued by financial firms. First Boston's *Handbook* contains the data for bond defaults. For 1977–88, First Boston provides one default total, covering the entire period, for each business sector. The 1977–88 total for financial sector defaults constituted 5.1 percent of all defaults for the period; therefore, the value of bonds issued by financial firms was estimated as 5.1 percent of the value of bonds going into default each year over this period. After 1988, First Boston gives sector totals on a year-by-year basis. Figure 2.14 shows the sum of the adjusted Dun & Bradstreet and First Boston data as a percentage of the sum of total credit market instruments and total trade debt for nonfinancial corporate business as reported in the flow-of-funds data issued by the Board of Governors of the Federal Reserve System.

55. Robert P. Flood and Peter M. Garber, *Speculative Bubbles, Speculative Attacks, and Policy Switching* (Cambridge: MIT Press, 1994).

56. Charles P. Kindleberger, *A Financial History of Western Europe* (New York: Oxford University Press, 1993), p. 267.

57. John Sabini, *Social Psychology* (New York: Norton, 1993), chaps. 2 and 3.

58. Kaplan and Stein, "The Evolution of Buyout," *Quarterly Journal of Economics*, pp. 344–8.

59. Harlan D. Platt, "Underwriter Effects and the Riskiness of Original-Issue High Yield Bonds," *Continental Bank Journal of Applied Corporate Finance*, vol. 6, no. 1 (Spring 1993), p. 92.

60. Leon Cooperman, *Portfolio Strategy,* Goldman, Sachs & Co., New York, report to clients, September 1987. Ironically, Cooperman, after blowing the whistle on the LBO funds, went on to run a hedge fund.

61. Testimony of Dean LeBaron, Batterymarch Financial Management, before Subcommittee on Labor-Management Relations, *Oversight Hearings,* pp. 183–5.

Chapter 3

1. *Paramount Communications v. Time,* 571 A.2d 1140 (Del. 1989).

2. See Mark J. Roe, "Takeover Politics," in Margaret M. Blair, ed., *The Deal Decade* (1993), pp. 321–80. Roe also suggests that the judges in *Time* were subject to the same political pressures as the legislature.

3. See, for example, Samuel H. Szewczyk and George A. Tsetsekos, "State Intervention in the Market for Corporate Control: The Case of Pennsylvania Senate Bill 1310," *Journal of Financial Economics,* vol. 31, pp. 3–23 (1992), finding statistically significant negative price effects generally, smaller effects for firms with preexisting antitakeover charter amendments, and partial recovery by firms that exempted themselves from the provision. But see also William N. Pugh and John S. Jahera, "State Antitakeover Legislation and Shareholder Wealth," *Journal of Financial Research,* vol. 13, no. 3, pp. 221–31 (1990), finding weak negative market reactions.

4. John Pound, "The Effects of Antitakeover Amendments on Takeover Activity: Some Direct Evidence," *Journal of Law and Economics,* vol. 30 (October 1987), pp. 353–67.

5. Jo Watson Hackl and Rosa Anna Testani, "Second Generation State Takeover Statutes and Shareholder Wealth: An Empirical Study," *Yale Law Journal,* vol. 97, no. 6 (May 1988), pp. 1193–1231.

6. Ibid., p. 1216, Table 2. Robert Comment and G. William Schwert, "Poison or Placebo? Evidence on the Deterrence and Wealth Effects of Modern Antitakeover Measures," *Journal of Financial Economics,* vol. 39 (1995), p. 29, find no decline in response to laws.

7. Merrill Lynch *Mergerstat Review.*

8. Such on interpretation assumes for the sake of argument that Pound's antitakeover amendments can serve as proxies for the full range of modern corporate policies, including ones that need not be approved by the shareholders. Pound's companies used only two types of anti-takeover amendments: staggered board and supermajority amendments.

9. This argument assumes a constant level of hostile activity. Recall from, above, however, that a new equilibrium with fewer bids, with the same probability of success, is conceptually possible.

10. Perhaps an examination of frequency of anti-takeover amendments adopted in the wake of *Time* could give a partial answer to this question.

11. A bond generally has original-issue discount when its periodic coupon payments yield less than interest rates on bonds with similar risk and tax characteristics. As compensation for a reduced interest rate, bondholders are able to buy at less than (at a "discount" to) face value.

12. Sections 163(e)(5) and (i) of the Internal Revenue Code.

13. Under section 1272, an OID bond is generally assumed to have a constant yield to maturity, and for each accrual period, the holder is required to report as income a sufficient portion of the bond's OID to correspond to this yield for the period.

14. In general a bond is covered by these rules if it has a maturity of more than five years, its yield to maturity exceeds comparable U.S. Treasury yields by more than 5 percent, and at some date subsequent to five years after issue, the deferred interest exceeds the first year's interest on the bond.

15. A staff report for the LBO hearings had found that certain foreign tax systems denied interest deductions to debt carrying a spread over government debt wider than a certain threshold. See Joint Committee on Taxation, *Federal Income Tax Aspects of Corporate Financial Structures* (JCS-1-1989), January 18, 1989.

16. Steven N. Kaplan and Jeremy C. Stein, "The Evolution of Buyout Pricing and Financial Structure (or What Went Wrong) in the 1980's," *Continental Bank Journal of Applied Corporate Finance,* Spring 1993, pp. 72–88.

17. Merrill Lynch *Mergerstat Review.*

18. Section 1274(a)(4) of the Internal Revenue Code.

19. The Trust Indenture Act forbids simple majority votes of bondholders to accept reduced interest payments, requiring instead near unanimity of bondholders in the acceptance of a new bond with lower interest. In many cases, however, the distressed issuer lacks current taxable income and may even have net operating loss carry forwards sufficient to reduce income taxes for years to come. Nevertheless, so long as the issuer's effective, or economic, tax rate between the date of the exchange and the maturity of the new debt is greater than 0 (i.e., it has a nonzero probability of using up its net operating loss carry forwards), the change imposes a cost on distressed exchange offers.

20. *In re Chateugay Corp.,* 109 B.R. 51 (Bkrtcy.S.D.N.Y. 1990).

21. Section 502(b)(2) of the U.S. Bankruptcy Code.

22. Michael C. Jensen, "Corporate Control and the Politics of Finance," *Continental Bank Journal of Applied Corporate Finance*, vol. 4, no. 2, Summer 1991, p. 28.

23. Paul Asquith, David W. Mullins, Jr., and Eric D. Wolff, "Original Issue High Yield Bonds: Aging Analysis of Defaults, Exchanges and Calls," *Journal of Finance*, 44 (September 1989), pp. 934–5, found that of fifty-two firms completing exchange offers in 1977–84, twenty-three had entered bankruptcy by 1988; Paul Asquith, Robert Gertner, and David Scharfstein, "Anatomy of Financial Distress: An Examination of Junk-Bond Issuers," *Quarterly Journal of Economics*, vol. 109, no. 3 (August 1994), p. 636, found that of thirty-four firms completing exchange offers, ten subsequently filed for bankruptcy under Chapter 11.

24. These include diversion of management effort, disruption of customer and supplier relations, the freeze on the disposal of business assets, and the stigma associated with bankruptcy. Bankruptcy also has its benefits, however, including the relief of interest burdens and the availability of debtor-in-possession (dip) financing.

25. Jerold B. Warner, "Bankruptcy Costs: Some Evidence," *Journal of Finance*, vol. 26 (May 1977), p. 343.

26. Elizabeth Tashjian, Ronald C. Lease, and John J. McConnell, "Prepacks: An Empirical Analysis of Prepackaged Bankruptcies," *Journal of Financial Economics*, vol. 40 (1996), pp. 135–62.

27. Tashjian, Lease, and McConnell, "Prepacks."

28. "Guidelines for Evaluating Leveraged Buyout Loans," attachment to Federal Reserve Vice-Chairman Preston Martin's testimony before Subcommittee on Telecommunications, Consumer Protection and Finance, House Energy and Commerce Committee, *Corporate Takeovers, Part 1: Hearings*, 99th Congress, 1st Session (Ser. No. 99-99), April 23, 1985, p. 424.

29. Frederic Smoler, "A View from the Fed," *Audacity*, Fall 1994, p. 6. Contrast this eyewitness account with this repetition-makes-it-true statement: "In 1986, the Federal Reserve restricted the use of junk bond financing for takeovers," in Harry DeAngelo, Linda DeAngelo, and Stuart Gilson, "Perceptions and the Politics of Finance: Junk Bonds and the Regulatory Seizure of First Capital Life," *Journal of Financial Economics*, vol. 41 (1996), p. 495. See also Robert A. Taggart, "The Growth of the 'Junk' Bond Market and Its Role in Financing Takeovers," in Alan J. Auerbach, ed., *Mergers and Acquisitions* (Chicago: University of Chicago Press, 1988), p. 14.

30. The balance sheet test—rather than an interest–to–cash flow test—led to complaints that firms with strong cash flows relative to assets, like cable companies, were

unnecessarily treated as high leverage firms. See Gregory J. Millman, "The Invisible Hand of Financial Regulators: Tales of the Credit Crunch," *Continental Bank Journal of Applied Corporate Finance,* vol. 4 (1991), p. 102.

31. Comptroller of the Currency, "Guidelines for Highly Leveraged Transactions," *American Banker,* December 16, 1988, p. 16.

32. Division of Banking Supervision and Regulation, Board of Governors of the Federal Reserve System, "Highly Leveraged Financings," SR 89-5 (FIS), February 16, 1989, attachment, p. 1.

33. Division of Banking Supervision and Regulation, Board of Governors of the Federal Reserve System, "Definition of Highly Leveraged Transaction (HLT)," SR 89–23 (FIS), October 25, 1989.

34. Philip T. Sudo, "Fed Chief Presses Concern over Leveraged Buyouts," *American Banker,* October 27, 1988, p. 3; Anthony Harris, "Congress and SEC to Investigate Buy-Outs," *Financial Times,* December 23, 1988, p. 4.

35. Gerard Meuchner, "SEC Targeting LBOs for Special Reporting Treatment," *Bank Letter,* November 7, 1988, p. 1. One SEC staffer suggested that the agency might proceed by expanding the rule that mandated disclosure of exposures to less-developed countries.

36. "SEC May Hold Off on LBO Reporting," *Bank Letter,* December 19, 1988, p. 5.

37. Citicorp *Annual Report,* 1988, pp. 31–2.

38. Office of the Comptroller of the Currency, Federal Deposit Insurance Corporation, Federal Reserve System, "Highly Leveraged Transactions: Phasing Out of Formal Supervisory Definition of HLTs," *Federal Register,* February 11, 1992, pp. 5040–5045.

39. Jensen, "Corporate Control."

40. Georgette Jasen, "Banks May Suffer from LBO Loans, S&P Report Says," *Wall Street Journal,* December 5, 1988, p. C1.

41. Robert Guenther, "Banks Offer Glimpse at LBO Portfolios Showing That Many Loans Are Re-Sold," *Wall Street Journal,* December 13, 1988, pp. A3, A14.

42. Thomas H. Hanley, John D. Leonard, and Diane B. Glossman, "HLTs: Prospect for Lending in a Deleveraging Economy," *Salomon Brothers Stock Research,* March 1990, pp. 2–3.

43. Claudio E. V. Borio, *Banks' Involvement in Highly Leveraged Transactions,* BIS Economic Papers no. 28 (Basle, Switzerland: Bank for International Settlements, October 1990), p. 49.

44. David. J. Denis and Diane K. Denis, "Causes of Financial Distress Following Le-veraged Recapitalizations," *Journal of Financial Economics,* vol. 37 (1995), p. 147, sug-gests that the difference was substantial. But these authors interpret the collapse of the UAL deal as a "legal and regulatory event" without any justification other than that "shortly after the collapse of the UAL buyout bank regulators imposed new ac-counting standards for loans made in leveraged transactions." The UAL deal col-lapsed on October 16, and the revised HLT definition went out on October 25.

45. Stephen Fidler, "A Deal That Dented Citicorp's Reputation," *Financial Times,* Oc-tober 23, 1989, p. 64; Brian Robins, "Japan Said to Have Urged Lenders to Avoid Buyout," *American Banker,* October 17, 1989, p. 18.

46. 12 U.S.C. 1831e(d)(1).

47. 12 U.S.C. 1831e(d)(4)(A). Note that this provision made a market for "split" rat-ings, in which one of the rating agencies, including the two less well established ones, rate an issue investment grade. See Richard Cantor and Frank Packer, "The Credit Rating Industry," Federal Reserve Bank of New York *Quarterly Review,* vol. 19, no. 2 (1994), pp. 1–26.

48. 12 U.S.C. 1831e(d)(3)(A).

49. 12 U.S.C. 1464(t).

50. 12 C.F.R. 567.8. Core capital generally equals common stock, including retained earnings, plus noncumulative perpetual preferred stock less most intangible assets. S&Ls initially were allowed to include supervisory goodwill up to 1.5 percent of assets in core capital. This percentage was phased out to 0 by the end of 1994.

51. 12 C.F.R. 567.9(a). Tangible capital generally equals common stockholders' eq-uity, including retained earnings, and noncumulative perpetual preferred stock less all intangible assets.

52. 12 C.F.R. 567(a).

53. Specifically, we refer to the "minicrash" of October 1989 and the "Gulf crisis" that began in August 1990 and ended in February 1991.

54. It is generally believed that the yield on junk bonds has two components: a risk-free rate (measured by the Treasury yield) and an equity risk premium. In fact, this notion lies behind the partial disallowance of tax deductions of interest on certain high yield bonds under sections 163(e)(5) and 163(i), discussed above.

55. Compare these figures to the following account: "Because FIRREA came together with the increase in capital requirements, most S&Ls were effectively forced to liqui-date those portfolios [of high-yield bonds] within three months of enactment. This

initiated a further sell-off in an already depressed high-yield market, thus further aggravating the capital problems of S&Ls and creating a downward regulatory spiral in junk bond prices." Glenn Yago, "The Credit Crunch: A Regulatory Squeeze on Growth Capital *"Journal of Applied Corporate Finance,* vol. 4 (1991), p. 97.

56. By the end of 1988, it was clear that that deal was going through, but yields did not react. One response to this criticism, however, is that RJR's new junk bonds were rated single-B, and therefore among the better credits in the high yield market. S&Ls, on the other hand, were faced with the task of unloading all their junk bonds, including the lower-quality credits.

57. Throughout the late 1980s Drexel's market share of new-issue underwriting was consistently about 40 percent. By comparison, the leading underwriters for other types of debt and equity typically have market shares of less than 10 percent.

58. The first proposal to force a liquidation was announced in June 1989.

59. But it is absurd to argue, as does Stephen R. Waite, a one-time employee of the Milken Institute, in "The Eclipse of Growth Capital," *Journal of Applied Corporate Finance,* vol. 4 (1991), pp. 77–85, that the net outflow from junk bond mutual funds in September and October 1989 responded to FIRREA. Congress passed the law in July, yet the striking rise in junk bond redemptions did not occur until September.

60. DeAngelo, DeAngelo, and Gilson, "Perceptions," pp. 476–81.

61. Where a bond is not rated by an agency, as is the case for private placements, the NAIC makes its own classification according to the schedule in table 3.6.

62. Mark Carey, Stephen Prowse, John Rea, and Gregory F. Udell, "The Private Placement Market: Intermediation, Life Insurance Companies and a Credit Crunch," in *Credit Markets in Transition,* Federal Reserve Bank of Chicago (1992), p. 859.

63. Carey, Prowse, Rea, and Udell, "Private Placement Market," p. 859.

64. George W. Fenn and Rebel A. Cole, "Announcements of Asset-Quality Problems and Contagion Effects in the Life Insurance Industry," *Journal of Financial Economics,* vol. 35 (April 1994), pp. 181–98.

65. Harry DeAngelo, Linda DeAngelo, and Stuart Gilson, "The Collapse of First Executive Corporation: Junk Bonds, Adverse Publicity, and the 'Run on the Bank' Phenomenon," *Journal of Financial Economics,* vol. 35 (December 1994), p. 296, shows a rise in liquidity pressure on First Executive in 1989 but does not provide the detail necessary to pinpoint the pressure in the September–November period.

66. Mark J. Roe, *Strong Managers, Weak Owners: The Political Roots of American Corporate Finance* (Princeton, NJ: Princeton University Press, 1994).

67. See David J. Denis and Diane K. Denis, "Causes of Financial Distress."

68. For two reasons, the most important case law explaining these fiduciary duties comes from Delaware. First, Delaware is by far the most popular state of incorporation for public companies in the United States. For example, in the Compustat database, which encompasses substantially all companies listed on exchanges as well as many NASDAQ companies, companies incorporated in Delaware have an asset value totaling over 50 percent of the aggregate. Thus, Delaware law directly affects more large companies than the law of any other state. The second reason, which is a consequence of the first, is that Delaware has the most developed case law, and Delaware judges are perceived as having a special expertise. Thus, Delaware corporate law, like New York's common law of contract, is very influential in other states.

69. Robert Clark, *Corporate Law* (Boston: Little, Brown, 1986), p. 123.

70. *Zapata Corp. v. Mondonado*, 430 A.2d 779, 782 (Del. 1981).

71. See Clark, *Corporate Law*, p. 147.

72. For example, Delaware law provides that where there is a potential conflict, a transaction is not voidable if it (1) was approved by a majority of disinterested directors, or (2) was approved by the shareholders, or (3) is determined by the court to be substantively fair to the corporation. 8 Del. Code Ann. 144 (1974).

73. On the other hand, corporate raiders sometimes structure their tender offers in such a way that individual shareholders are coerced into accepting, even though the transaction actually hurts the shareholders as a group. Common devices used in such offers include two-tiered structures and tight deadlines. Courts recognize this possibility and, as discussed below, the legal standards generally leave fiduciaries the flexibility to address such threats.

74. Some defensive tactics include defensive acquisitions, alignments with "white knights," lockups of key corporate assets (also known as crown-jewel options), avoiding shareholder votes, payment of greenmail to the raider, poison pills, and golden parachutes. These techniques and others are discussed in Clark, *Corporate Law*, pp. 571–77.

75. *Unocal v. Mesa Petroleum Co.*, 493 A.2d 946 (Del. 1985).

76. *Unocal* at 955.

77. *Revlon Inc. v. MacAndrews and Forbes Holdings*, 506 A.2d 173 (Del. 1986).

78. Daniel S. Cahill and Stephen P. Wink, "Time and Time Again the Board Is Paramount: The Evolution of the *Unocal* Standard and the *Revlon* Trigger through *Paramount v. Time*," *Notre Dame Law Review*, vol. 66 (1990), p. 159.

79. *Revlon* at 183.

80. Ronald J. Gilson and Reinier Kraakman, "Delaware's Intermediate Standard for Defensive Tactics: Is There Substance in Proportionality Review?" *The Business Lawyer,* vol. 44 (February 1989), p. 267.

81. Gilson and Kraakman, "Delaware's Intermediate Standard," pp. 254–55.

82. A "lockup" or "crown jewel" option is the right to buy a company's key asset or assets on the occurrence of a "trigger" event, usually a third party's acquisition of a certain percentage of the company's shares.

83. *Revlon* at 183.

84. Gilson and Kraakman, "What Triggers *Revlon*," *Wake Forest Law Review,* vol. 25, no. 1 (1990), pp. 37–59.

85. *Time,* p. 1150.

86. *Time,* p. 1152.

87. Or, in Gilson and Kraakman's terms, the offer was not structurally coercive by engineering a rush for a closing door.

88. *Time,* p. 1153.

89. Nor can it be construed as the first type of threat—the possibility that a hostile offer would preclude a transaction that the shareholders would prefer. In that situation, Gilson and Kraakman seem to contemplate that the shareholders would in fact approve management's alternative in an uncoerced vote. In *Time* there was no such allegation.

90. Gilson and Kraakman, "Delaware's Intermediate Standard," pp. 261–67.

91. In fact, the projected trading ranges generated by *Time*'s own investment bankers (which themselves turned out to be overly optimistic) could not be seen as promising a present value even close to $200.

92. See, for example, Cahill and Wink, "Time and Time Again," p. 206.

93. They could, however, have resulted in a decreased probability of success.

94. For simplicity we ignore the fact that the costs associated with the bid are themselves stochastic. For example, early in the search, the potential bidder might realize that a bid would not be advantageous and discard his plans before hiring financial and legal advisors, and so forth.

95. See, for example, Lucian A. Bebchuk, "The Case For Facilitating Hostile Tender Offers," *Harvard Law Review,* 95 (1982), p. 1028.

96. Bebchuk, "The Case for Facilitating." The debate here was with Easterbrook and Fischel. Although all parties to this debate agreed about the virtues of the market for corporate control, they disagreed on how it should operate. Easterbrook and Fischel argued against auctions, on the ground that bidders would be discouraged if a third party could ultimately benefit from their investments in searches. See Frank H. Easterbrook and Daniel R. Fischel, "The Proper Role of a Target's Management in Responding to a Tender Offer," *Harvard Law Review,* vol. 94 (1981), p. 1161.

97. Delaware Code Annotated, title 8, section 203.

98. Wisconsin Statutes, sections 180.1140–180.1145.

99. The constitutionality of this statute was upheld in *Amanda Acquisitions Corp. v. Universal Foods,* 877 F.2d 496 (7th Cir. 1989).

100. Roberta Romano, "A Guide to Takeovers: Theory, Evidence, and Regulation," *Yale Journal on Regulation,* vol. 9, no. 1, p. 170. The 100 percent tax refers to disgorgement statutes, which require that would-be raiders who subsequently sell their shares disgorge their profits.

101. These are senior loans primarily from banks designed to meet the deal's financing needs from closing until the long-term asset and liability structure is in place.

102. Bebchuk, "The Case for Facilitating."

103. Disgorgement statutes, obviously, get to this result directly and unambiguously.

Chapter 4

1. The $1.4 billion capitalization of U.S. Steel represented 7 percent of gross national product (equivalent to more than $400 billion now). George David Smith and Richard Sylla, "The Transformation of Financial Capitalism: An Essay on the History of American Capital Markets," New York University, typescript, 1993, p. 23. Benjamin M. Friedman, "Risks in Our High-Debt Economy: Depression or Inflation?" in Steven Fazzari and Dimitri B. Papadimitriou, eds., *Financial Conditions and Macroeconomic Performance: Essays in Honor of Hyman P. Minsky* (Armonk, New York: M.E. Sharpe, 1992), p. 65, notes that the RJR-Nabisco buyout represented 0.5 percent of GNP.

2. Bryan Burrough and John Helyar, *Barbarians at the Gate: The Fall of RJR Nabisco* (New York: Harper & Row, 1990), and Hope Lampert, *True Greed: What Really Happened in the Battle for RJR Nabisco* (New York: Plume, 1990).

3. George Anders, *Merchants of Debt: KKR and the Mortgaging of American Business* (New York: Basic Books, 1993).

4. Nancy Mohan and Carl R. Chen, "A Review of the RJR-Nabisco Buyout," *Continental Bank Journal of Applied Corporate Finance*, vol. 3, no. 2 (Summer 1990), p. 108.

5. Michael Jensen, "Corporate Control and the Politics of Finance," *Continental Bank Journal of Applied Corporate Finance*, vol. 4, no. 2 (Summer 1991), p. 14.

6. Randall Smith, "'Deal of the Century'? Not for RJR Investors," *Wall Street Journal*, March 4, 1993, p. C1; Randall Smith and Eben Shapiro, "KKR's Luster Dims as Fall in RJR Stock Hurts Investors' Take," *Wall Street Journal*, April 26, 1993, p. 1; Richard D. Hylton, "How KKR Got Beaten at Its Own Game," *Fortune*, May 2, 1994, p. 105.

7. The back-end paper carried a coupon set at 5.5 percent over the greater of the yield on a three-month Treasury bill, the ten-year Treasury note, or the thirty-year Treasury bond, or 13.7 percent at the end of 1989. RJR-Nabisco's 1989 10-K, p. 63.

8. Prospectus dated May 12, 1989, for RJR Holdings Capital Corp., $525 million 13½ Subordinated Debentures due 2001 and $225 million Subordinated Extendible Reset Debentures, p. 26.

9. Burrough and Helyar, *Barbarians at the Gate*, pp. 441–3.

10. The Moody's analyst noted that "marketing risks are evident." in the light of the events of Marlboro Friday in the spring of 1993, one can regard the analyst's opinion as at worst premature. Anders, *Merchants of Debt*, p. 251.

11. Anders, *Merchants of Debt*, p. 267.

12. "Dear Shareholder," *RJR-Nabisco 1993 Annual Report*, pp. 28–29. Philip Morris's move against budget cigarettes hit RJR where it hurt: "RJRT's domestic cigarette volume of non–full price brands as a percentage of total domestic volume was 44% in 1993, 35% in 1992 and 25% in 1991 versus 37%, 30% and 25%, respectively, for the domestic cigarette market."

13. *RJR Nabisco 1993 Annual Report*, p. 28.

14. Smith, "'Deal of the Century'" p. C1.

15. Smith and Shapiro, "KKR's Luster Dims," p. 1.

16. Hylton, "How KKR Got Beaten," p. 105.

17. Steven N. Kaplan, "Campeau's Acquisition of Federated: Post-Bankruptcy Results," *Journal of Financial Economics*, vol. 35, no. 1 (February 1994), pp. 123–36, and "Campeau's Acquisition of Federated: Value Destroyed or Value Added?" *Journal of Financial Economics*, vol. 25, no. 2 (December 1989), pp. 191–212.

18. Cash moved back and forth between our firms and the capital market, and we track receipts as well as payments. Issuance of securities is just the reverse of payments to equity and bondholders, so we let these cash receipts grow with the appropriate returns and set them against the cumulated cash payments. Thus although we let the $17 billion payment to RJR's shareholders cumulate, so too we let the equal and offsetting receipt of cash from the junk bond buyers and banks that financed the deal cumulate at the appropriate rates. And when RJR purchased some junk bonds with the proceeds of its spring 1991 equity issue, we stop cumulating the cost of that much of the junk bond issue and begin cumulating a receipt from the equity market.

19. Richard B. DuBoff and Edward S. Herman, "The Promotional-Financial Dynamic of Merger Movements: A Historical Perspective," *Journal of Economic Issues,* vol. 23, no. 1 (March 1989), pp. 121, 123.

20. For an earlier comparative analysis of accounting data of highly leveraged and less-leveraged companies within the same industry, see Louis Lowenstein, *Sense and Nonsense in Corporate Finance* (Reading, MA: Addison Wesley, 1991), chap. 2, "The Road to Junk Heaven: A Tale of Three Companies," analyzing May, Allied/Federated, and Macy's. In some ways Philip Morris provides a better foil for RJR-Nabisco than May provides for Allied/Federated and Macy's because May went through its own LBO.

21. Burrough and Helyar, *Barbarians at the Gate* pp. 73–4, 79, 92–3, 165–7, 184–5, 246, and 277.

22. Anders, *Merchants of Debt,* p. 172.

23. These data divide a given year's sales by the average number of persons in the workforce at the end of the previous and current years.

24. Sanjai Bhagat, Andrei Shleifer, and Robert Vishny, "Hostile Takeovers in the 1980s: The Return to Corporate Specialization," *Brookings Papers in Economic Activity, Microeconomics,* 1990, pp. 1–72.

25. Anders, *Merchants of Debt,* pp. 172, 190.

26. Richard Caves and Matthew B. Krepps, "Fat: The Displacement of Nonproduction Workers from U.S. Manufacturing Industries," *Brookings Papers on Economic Activity: Microeconomics,* 2 (1993), pp. 227–88.

27. Measuring layoffs at RJR and Philip Morris over the five years is not a matter of merely opening the annual reports, because the head count reported to shareholders changes with divestitures and acquisitions. The risk in using layoff announcements, as Bhagat, Shleifer, and Vishny acknowledge, is that a firm may reduce its workforce with no public notice, or at least without the event's resulting in a story in the *Wall*

Street Journal. It turns out that both RJR-Nabisco and Philip Morris spoke louder through actions than words: Announced job cuts fell short in both cases of reported downsizing. Still, these stock-flow discrepancies seem not to confound the comparison. RJR-Nabisco was reported to have shrunk its domestic tobacco workforce by 3,500 souls between the buyout and mid-1993 (Eden Shapiro, "Tobacco Unit of RJR to Cut 9% of Its Staff," *Wall Street Journal*, September 15, 1993, p. A4). Announced layoffs or early retirements at RJR fell some 1,000 jobs short of this figure (see the 1989 through 1992 entries for RJR-Nabisco in Table 4.5). On this showing, actual job cutbacks at RJR-Nabisco reached 4–5 percent of the firm's employees in 1989–92, rather than the 3–4 percent its announced figures would indicate. Philip Morris, reduced the head count in its domestic tobacco division by 11 percent over two years, according to a presentation of the senior vice president of that division to financial analysts reported in the above-cited *Journal* article. We are told that in 1993 RJR-Nabisco's domestic tobacco operations employed 8,500 of the firm's 63,000 employees, or 13 percent. Applying this same fraction to Philip Morris's 175,000 employees yields about 23,000 engaged in the production of cigarettes in the United States. If Philip Morris reduced this force by 11 percent, it cashiered about 2,500 employees, or about 1.4 percent plus of its total workforce. The unreported 1,000 RJR-Nabisco employees represented about 1.6 percent of that firm's workforce. Thus, it would appear that each company made unannounced reductions in its domestic tobacco workforce of about 1.5 percent of total employment, so the conclusion drawn from the comparison of reported workforce reductions stands.

28. James R. Schiffman, "RJR to Cut Cigarette-Factory Staff 10% in First Reduction Since KKR Buy-Out," *Wall Street Journal*, March 22, 1989, p. A5.

29. Betsy Morris and Michael J. McCarthy, "RJR, in Long-Awaited Move, to Dismiss about 12% of Workers at Tobacco Unit," *Wall Street Journal*, August 11, 1989, p. A3; "Up in Smoke," *Wall Street Journal*, October 26, 1993, p. 1, citing a study by Wayne Landsman and Douglas Shackelford of the University of North Carolina.

30. Interview with Robert McCauley, June 2, 1994, in New York.

31. It would be a mistake, though, to envision the problem in textbook fashion as one of simply finding the right balance between the disciplinary (and tax) benefits of debt and some stable notion of the costs of possible financial distress and bankruptcy (such as trade creditors demanding cash and counterparties shying away from long-term contracts). As the RJR-Nabisco case illustrates, creditors can pile on debt one year, only to shun indebted firms the next. As the social definition of acceptable debt contracted, a seemingly stretched but manageable capital structure began to threaten distress. RJR-Nabisco after the buyout was like a socialite who buys a whole new wardrobe just before fashion changes: the need to alter all her clothes perforce slows her down socially.

32. Board of Governors of the Federal Reserve System, *Flow of Funds Accounts*, Fourth Quarter 1993 (March 9, 1994), pp. 111–2. Wayne R. Landsman and Douglas A. Shackelford, "The Lock-In of the Capital Gains Taxes:Evidence from the RJR Nabisco Leveraged Buyout," *National Tax Journal*, vol. 48, no. 2 (June 1995), pp. 245–59, have identified the tax status of Tar Heels who held 29.5 million shares of RJR-Nabisco on October 19, 1988, the day before Ross Johnson announced the proposed LBO. Some 22.9 million shares, or almost 80 percent, were held by individuals and corporations, and the balance were held by tax-deferred trusts or tax-exempt organizations.

33. Landsman and Shackelford, "Lock-in of the Capital Gains Taxes," p. 21.

34. Compare our estimate to $3.3 billion reported by Michael Jensen, "The Effects of LBOs and Corporate Debt on the Economy," testimony to the House Ways and Means Committee, *Tax Policy Aspects of Mergers and Acquisitions: Hearings, Part I*, 101st Cong., 1st Sess., Serial no. 101–10 (January 31, February 1, 2, and March 14, 15, 1989), p. 417; and $2.85 billion in Landsman and Shackelford, "Lock-in of the Capital Gains Taxes," p. 25.

Chapter 5

1. This chapter, as well as chapter 6, draws heavily on Eli M. Remolona, Robert N. McCauley, Judith S. Ruud, and Frank Iacono, "Corporate Refinancing in the 1990s," Federal Reserve Bank of New York *Quarterly Review*, vol. 17, no. 4, (Winter 1992–93), pp. 1–27.

2. See Edward J. Frydl, "Overhangs and Hangover: Coping with the Imbalances of the 1980s," Federal Reserve Bank of New York *Seventy-Seventh Annual Report*, 1992; and Edward J. Frydl, ed., *Studies on Corporate Leveraging* (New York: Federal Reserve Bank of New York, September 1991).

3. Michael C. Jensen argued that bankruptcy had been privatized in testimony before the House Ways and Means Committee, *Tax Policy Aspects of Mergers and Acquisitions: Hearings*, 100th Cong., 1st sess. (January 31; February 1, 2; March 14, 15, 1989), pp. 412–14.

4. Tim C. Opler and Sheridan Titman, "Financial Distress and Corporate Performance," *Journal of Finance*, vol. 49 (July 1994), pp. 1015–40.

5. Paul Asquith, Robert Gertner, and David Scharfstein, "Anatomy of Financial Distress: An Examination of Junk-Bond Issuers," *Quarterly Journal of Economics*, vol. 109, no. 3, August 1994, pp. 625–58.

6. Edward I. Altman, *Corporate Financial Distress and Bankruptcy,* 2d ed. (New York: John Wiley & Sons, 1993), p. 105.

7. See Jane D'Arista and Tom Schlesinger, "The Parallel Banking System" in Gary A. Dymski, Gerald Epstein and Robert Pollin, eds., *Transforming the U.S. Financial System: Equity and Efficiency for the 21st Century* (Armonk, N.Y. and London: Sharpe for Economic Policy Institute, 1993), pp. 157–99; and Eli M. Remolona and Kurt Wulfe-kuhler, "Finance Companies, Bank Competition, and Niche Markets," Federal Reserve Bank of New York *Quarterly Review,* vol. 17 (Summer 1992), pp. 25–38.

8. Andrew E. Kimball and Jerome S. Fons, "Coupon Events in 1991," Moody's Investors Service, New York, February 1, 1991.

9. Ronald Johnson, "The Bank Credit 'Crumble,'" Federal Reserve Bank of New York *Quarterly Review,* vol. 16 (Summer 1991), pp. 40–51.

10. See Cara Lown and Ben Bernanke, "The Credit Crunch," *Brookings Papers on Economic Activity,* 1992:2, pp. 205–309, and M. A. Akhtar, ed., *Studies on Causes and Consequences of the 1989–92 Credit Slowdown* (New York: Federal Reserve Bank of New York, 1994), and references contained therein.

11. For a detailed analysis of equity retirements in the 1980s, see Margaret Pickering, "A Review of Recent Corporate Restructuring Activity, 1980–90," Board of Governors of the Federal Reserve System, Staff Study no. 161, May 1991.

12. Pickering, "A Review," p. 2.

13. In addition to less-leveraged deal structures, a shift from whole-company LBOs to division LBOs also tends to reduce the equity retired. An LBO of a division of a company need not result in any equity retirement at all. Although the division's buyers may rely heavily on debt, its seller receives cash with which it retires debt or builds assets. The seller may proceed to repurchase shares with the cash received, but then a repurchase rather than an LBO has retired equity. The LBO of a whole company, by contrast, retires equity in the first instance.

14. Pickering, "A Review," p. 2.

15. Nellie Liang, "Repurchases," Board of Governors of the Federal Reserve System memorandum, 1996.

16. See Louis Lowenstein, *Sense and Nonsense in Corporate Finance* (Reading, MA: Addison-Wesley, 1991).

17. Jean Helwege, "High Yield Bond Returns and Equity Offerings in the Early 1990s," *Financial Management,* forthcoming, estimates that firms with 40 percent of the outstanding junk bonds issued $35 billion in equity, but her junk bond sample excludes convertible bonds.

18. We computed the allocation of proceeds by obtaining from Securities Data Company seven items for each offering—gross proceeds, offering price, underwriting spread, legal expenses, administrative expenses, number of primary shares, and a listing of the use of proceeds. We first determined expenses of the offering by adding legal and administrative expenses to the product of the gross proceeds and the underwriting spread, expressed as a percentage of the offering price. These expenses were assumed to be allocated pro rata among the offering's primary and secondary components. Next, we determined the net primary proceeds by multiplying the number of primary shares by the offering price and subtracting the portion of expenses that was allocated to the primary component. Net secondary proceeds were determined by subtracting expenses and net primary proceeds from gross proceeds. Lastly, we allocated net primary proceeds evenly among the primary uses listed. Therefore, if an offering with net primary proceeds of $100 million had listed "general corporate purposes" and "refinancing bank debt" as uses, $50 million was assumed to be allocated to each, although in actuality any allocation of the $100 million would have been possible. The size of the errors, in percentage terms, produced by this approximation is reduced by the large number of observations and by the fact that almost two-thirds of the offerings listed only one use of proceeds. Offerings that listed no primary use of proceeds were assumed to allocate those proceeds as did other offerings of the same type (IPO, reverse LBO, or other offering).

19. Securities Data Company database.

20. Drawing on the list of the 50 largest finance companies published in the December 11, 1991, issue of the *American Banker,* we examined the profitability of 22 industrial and commercial parents of 23 finance companies (Ford owns two finance companies). We eliminated Macy's both because it sold its credit card affiliate to General Electric and because it entered bankruptcy.

21. The ratio of capital expenditures to fixed assets could have been used, but this ratio would have "normalized" for the capital intensity of operations. The intent was to capture those companies that invested heavily, whether or not they were in capital-intensive industries.

22. However, these companies appear to be no more profitable than average if the ratio of income to market equity is used, except perhaps in 1989. This apparent anomaly arises because the ratio of income to market equity better proxies the cost of capital than book profitability. The explanation would then be that although the largest repurchasers were more profitable, they did not have to meet a higher required rate of return on equity than other companies.

23. Leland E. Crabbe and Jean Helwege, "Alternative Tests of Agency Theories of Callable Corporate Bonds," *Financial Management,* vol. 23, no. 4 (Winter 1994), pp. 3–20.

24. It is dangerous to look at bank lending in isolation. See Bluford H. Putnam, "Regulation and Capital Market Efficiency: Some Evidence from the U.S. Credit Crunch of 1990," *Journal of Applied Corporate Finance*, 4 (1991), pp. 92–5.

25. Benjamin H. Cohen, "Three Essays on Corporate Financial Decisions," Ph.D. dissertation, Massachusetts Institute of Technology, Cambridge, MA, June 1995.

26. Richard A. Brealey and Stewart C. Myers, *Principles of Corporate Finance*, 4th ed. (New York: McGraw-Hill, 1991), p. 328.

27. Tim Loughran and Jay R. Ritter, "The Timing and Subsequent Performance of IPOs: The U.S. and International Evidence," working paper, University of Illinois at Urbana-Champaign, 1993, pp. 21–2.

28. See Deborah J. Lucas and Robert L. McDonald, "Equity Issues and Stock Price Dynamics," *Journal of Finance*, vol. 45, no. 4, (September 1990), pp. 1019–43; Robert A. Korajczyk, Deborah J. Lucas, and Robert L. McDonald, "The Effect of Information Releases on the Pricing and Timing of Equity Issues," *Review of Financial Studies*, vol. 4, no. 4 (1991), pp. 685–708; and the same authors' "Equity Issues with Time-Varying Asymmetric Information," *Journal of Financial and Quantitative Analysis*, vol. 27, no. 3 (September 1992), pp. 397–417.

Chapter 6

1. Benjamin Friedman, *Implications of Increasing Corporate Indebtedness for Monetary Policy*, Group of Thirty, Occasional Paper no. 29 (New York: Group of Thirty, 1990).

2. Testimony by Alan Greenspan, Chairman, Board of Governors of the Federal Reserve System, before the Committee on Banking, Housing, and Urban Affairs, United States Senate, July 20, 1994, *Federal Reserve Bulletin*, vol. 80, no. 9 (September (1994), p. 793.

3. Paul Krugman, *The Age of Diminished Expectations* (Cambridge, MA: MIT Press, 1994), p. 166.

4. Andrea Bryan, "Corporate Credit Quality Erosion Eases," *Standard & Poor's Creditweek*, January 4, 1993, p. 39.

5. Bloomberg database, 153 issues called, January–May 1992.

6. In an unpublished Ph.D. dissertation, Benjamin Cohen found larger savings on investment grade bonds refunded in 1992: 2.37 percent on 7 AAA- and AA-rated bonds called and 1.77 percent on 19 A-rated and BBB-rated bonds. We thank the

author for providing us these data, which are reported as multiyear averages in Benjamin Cohen, "Maturity, Risk and Credit Quality: A Study of Refinancings," in *Three Essays on Corporate Financial Decisions*, Ph.D. dissertation, Massachusetts Institute of Technology, June 1995. Two sources for the difference suggest themselves, quite apart from the different sample sizes, 26 in Cohen's study, and 153 in ours. A small part of the difference can be ascribed to our making an adjustment for the call premium. In addition, Cohen reports simple averages, whereas we calculate weighted averages. If big, well-rated firms pull the trigger sooner, as Cohen's access hypothesis suggests, the weighted average savings may be substantially lower than the unweighted average. Conversely, our savings from junk bond calls of 4.78 percent in 1991 is much larger than Cohen's figure of 1.67 percent, based on a larger sample (13 versus 4). Here it is evident that the 6.5 percent savings on $1.5 billion of RJR Holdings Group's reset bonds bulk large in our result for $3.7 billion of calls. Finally, our savings of 3 percent for junk bonds called in 1992 are much the same as Cohen's 3.14, based on a sizable sample of 28.

7. "Restructurings and refinancings allowed issuers with outstanding debt to achieve higher credit quality. Among high-yield issuers in 1992, there were 98 upgrades totaling $51 billion and 96 downgrades totaling $37 billion. By contrast, in 1991, downgrades almost doubled upgrades. There were 75 upgrades totaling $62 billion and 133 downgrades totaling $81 billion." Diana Vazza, "High-Yield Market Sets Record For Issuance in 1992," *Standard & Poor's Creditweek*, January 25, 1993, p. 33.

8. Sample from First Boston *High Yield Handbook*, (New York: First Boston January 1992), Appendix III.

9. First Boston High Yield Research, *1992 Mid-Year Review*, July 28, 1992, p. 3.

10. Cohen, "Maturity, Risk, and Credit Quality."

11. The difference in underwriting costs makes sense in relation to the risks underwriters run. Junk bonds trade with volatility somewhere between the relatively low levels of bonds and the higher levels of equities. Thus underwriters need to charge junk bond issuers a larger spread to repay underwriters for the risk that the price of the junk will slip below price the underwriters have paid the issuers before the underwriters have unloaded the bonds to end-investors.

12. Net floating-rate or short-term debt is defined in flow-of-funds classifications as the sum of bank loans, commercial paper, and other loans minus all liquid assets except currency and checkable deposits, U.S. government securities, and tax-exempt securities. Net fixed-rate debt is defined as corporate bonds minus U.S. government securities and tax-exempt securities.

U.S. nonfinancial corporations' growing use of interest rate swaps corporations makes balance sheet data less reliable when the analyst tries to gauge the relative importance of fixed- and floating-rate funds. In an interest rate swap, two parties agree to assume interest rate payments for each other on a notional amount of debt. The typical "plain vanilla" swap involves the exchange of floating payments, usually based on LIBOR, for predetermined fixed payments. For example, a corporation that initially has a $100 million LIBOR-based bank loan outstanding enters into a swap whereby it receives LIBOR and pays 8 percent on a $100 million notional value. In so doing, it effectively creates a fixed-rate liability. However, because swaps are off–balance sheet items, the balance sheet (and the flow-of-funds data) would still show an exposure to short-term interest rates. To estimate the effect of interest rate swaps on the composition of debt, one must know U.S. nonfinancial corporations' gross positions in both fixed-to-floating and floating-to-fixed rate swaps. If U.S. nonfinancial corporations are net fixed-rate payers, then the effective ratio of floating-rate to total debt would be somewhat lower than flow-of-funds data indicate, and vice versa. According to the International Swap Dealers Association, the value of interest-rate swaps outstanding stood at more than $3 trillion at the end of 1991, up from about $680 billion just four years earlier. Of this total, U.S. nonfinancial corporations were end users of about $260 billion, up from $76 billion in 1987, according to the Bank for International Settlements. However, conversations with practitioners indicate that this total is more or less evenly divided between fixed-to-floating and floating-to-fixed swaps. If this is true, interest rate swaps have little net effect on the split between fixed-rate and floating-rate debt. To the extent that the split is not fifty-fifty or that the split is changing over time, estimates of interest exposure based on flow-of-funds numbers will be less reliable.

13. One could consider what would have happened if the ratio of debt service to cash flow had stabilized at some level, say that reached at the end of 1993. But in the face of declining interest rates, for interest payments to have mounted as fast as cash flow was growing would have required a massive increase in debt. To use, in effect, another bout of the leveraging business as a baseline would seem strange.

14. Jason Benderly, *The Current Growth of Nonfinancial Profits Is Different—It Has Not Been as Much at the Expense of Labor,* Benderly Associates, Vail, Colorado, November 6, 1997; John V. Duca, "Has Long-Run Profitability Risen in the 1990s?" Federal Reserve Bank of Dallas *Economic Review,* 4th Quarter 1997, pp. 2–14. Olivier Blanchard, "The Medium Term," *Brookings Papers on Economic Activity,* 1997:2, pp. 89–141, finds that the labor share shrank in Europe but not in the United States. See also Dean Baker and Larry Mishel, "Profits Up, Wages Down," Briefing paper, Economic Policy Institute, Washington, D.C. 1995.

15. Franco Modigliani and R. A. Cohn, "Inflation, Rational Valuation and the Market," *Financial Analysts Journal,* March/April 1979, pp. 3–23.

16. The national income account profits exclude foreign profits of US multinational firms and include the US profits of foreign multinational firms. See the warning of

James M. Poterba, "The Rate of Return to Corporate Capital and Factor Shares: New Estimates Using Revised National Income Accounts and Capital Stock Data," National Bureau of Economic Research Working Paper no. 6263, November 1997, p. 26.

17. Poterba, "Rate of Return."

Chapter 7

1. Ministry of International Trade and Industry, *Shin-jidai no Sangyo Kin'yu, Tsusho Sangyo Chosa Kai* [Industrial Finance in a New Age], Report of MITI Research Group, 1994, pp. 37, 65, 67. Citation provided by Mitsuhiro Fukao.

2. David P. Baron, "A Model of the Demand for Investment Banking Advising and Distribution Services for New Issues," *Journal of Finance*, vol. 37 (1982), pp. 955–76.

3. Kevin Rock, "Why New Issues Are Underpriced," *Journal of Financial Economics*, vol. 15 (1986), pp. 187–212.

4. Seha M. Tinic, "Anatomy of Initial Public Offerings of Common Stock," *Journal of Finance*, vol. 43 (1988), pp. 789–822.

5. Franklin Allen and Gerald R. Faulhaber, "Signaling by Underpricing in the IPO Market," *Journal of Financial Economics*, vol. 23 (1989), pp. 303–23; Mark Grinblatt and Chuan Yang Hwang, "Signalling and the Pricing of New Issues," *Journal of Finance*, vol. 44 (1989), pp. 393–420; and Ivo Welch, "Seasoned Offerings, Imitation Costs, and the Underpricing of Initial Public Offerings," *Journal of Finance*, vol. 44 (1989), pp. 421–49.

6. Chris J. Muscarella and Michael R. Vetsuypens, "A Simple Test of Baron's Model of IPO Underpricing," *Journal of Financial Economics*, vol. 24 (1989), pp. 125–35.

7. See note 5.

8. Jean Helwege and Nellie Liang, "Initial Public Offerings in Hot and Cold Markets," Board of Governors of the Federal Reserve, working paper, Washington, D.C., April 1997.

9. Judith S. Ruud, "Underwriter Price Support and the IPO Underpricing Puzzle," *Journal of Financial Economics*, vol. 34 (1993), pp. 135–51.

10. Paul H. Schultz and Mir A. Zaman, "Aftermarket Support and Underpricing of Initial Public Offerings," *Journal of Financial Economics*, vol. 35 (1994), pp. 199–219.

11. Jay R. Ritter, "The Long-Run Performance of Initial Public Offerings," *Journal of Finance*, vol. 46 (1991), pp. 3–27.

12. Tim Loughran and Jay R. Ritter, "The New Issues Puzzle," *Journal of Finance*, vol. 50, no. 1 (March 1995), pp. 23–51.

13. Robert W. Holthausen and David F. Larcker, "The Financial Performance of Reverse Leveraged Buyouts," *Journal of Financial Economics*, vol. 42 (1996), pp. 293–332.

14. "Four Planned Reverse LBOs to Test Reviving Market," *Going Public: The IPO Reporter*, vol. 15, no. 8 (February 25, 1991), p. 2.

15. Phillip L. Zweig, Leah Nathans Spiro, and Michael Schroeder, "Beware the IPO Market—Individual Investors Are at a Big Disadvantage," *Business Week*, April 4, 1994, pp. 84–90. A recent academic study of 38 IPOs by a single underwriter found high but similar allocations of hot and cold IPOs to institutional investors: Kathleen Weiss Hanley and William J. Wilhelm, Jr., "Evidence on the Strategic Allocation of Initial Public Offerings," *Journal of Financial Economics*, 37 (1995), pp. 239–57.

16. Steven N. Kaplan and Jeremy C. Stein, "How Risky Is the Debt in Highly Leveraged Transactions?" *Journal of Financial Economics*, vol. 27, no. 1 (September 1990), pp. 215–45.

17. Kaplan and Stein, "How Risky," p. 220.

18. Kathleen Weiss Hanley and Jay R. Ritter, "Going Public," in Peter Newman, Murray Milgate, and John Eatwell, eds., *The New Palgrave Dictionary of Money and Finance*, vol. 2 (London: Macmillan, 1992), p. 250.

19. Ruud, "Underwriter Price Support," reports log returns, rather than simple returns. Log returns are the natural logarithm of the ratio of the closing price to the offering price. The log return corresponds to a continuously compounded return. Log returns differ only slightly from raw returns over the range of returns observed here. For example, the average first-day log returns of this sample of reverse LBOs is 5.9 percent, whereas the average raw return is 6.54 percent.

20. Ruud, "Underwriter Price Support."

21. Ritter, "Long-Run Performance," and Loughran and Ritter, "New Issues Puzzle."

Chapter 8

1. Statement of Allan Bromley quoted by Senator Donald Riegle, Chairman, Senate Banking Committee, in Subcommittee on International Finance and Monetary Policy of the Senate Banking Committee, *Foreign Acquisitions of U.S. Owned Companies*, 102nd Congress, 2nd Session (1992), p. 4.

2. Statement of Peter Mills, former Chief Administrative Officer, SEMATECH, to Subcommittee on International Finance and Monetary Policy of the Senate Banking Committee, *Foreign Acquisitions of U.S. Owned Companies,* 102nd Congress, 2nd Session, (1992), p. 17.

3. Robert N. McCauley and Steven A. Zimmer, "Cheap Capital as Industrial Policy," *Stanford Law and Policy Review,* vol. 5, no. 1 (Fall 1993), pp. 143–51.

4. Jean Helwege and Nellie Liang, "Initial Public Offerings in Hot and Cold Markets," Board of Governors of the Federal Reserve working paper, April 1997.

5. "SDIO to Issue Target Vehicle Contract to Orbital Sciences," *Aerospace Daily,* vol. 165 (February 11, 1993), p. 241.

6. Thomas N. Cochran, "Offerings in the Offing," *Barron's,* March 26, 1990, p. 50.

7. Cochran, "Offerings," p. 50.

8. Cochran, "Offerings," p. 50.

9. Jonathan R. Laing, "Review and Preview: An Investor's Almanac," *Barron's,* April 2, 1990, p. 7.

10. Daniel Southerland, "Orbital Sciences to Launch Small Satellite System," *Washington Post,* Washington Business Section, April 26, 1993, p. 8.

11. Southerland, "Orbital Sciences," p. 8.

12. Southerland, "Orbital Sciences," p. 8.

13. Computer consultant Tim Bajarin, quoted in Charles McCoy, "Multimedia Start-up 3DO Gets a Vote of Confidence from Investors in IPO," *Wall Street Journal,* May 5, 1993, p. B6.

14. Neil Gross, "A Tsunami of Gizmos," *Business Week,* September 27, 1993, p. 57.

15. Doug Forman, manager of the Putnam OTC Emerging Growth Fund, quoted in Anne Newman, "Shaman's IPO Success Sets Example for Biotech Firms," *Wall Street Journal,* January 28, 1993, p. B2.

16. Alison L. Sprout, "The Rise of Netscape," *Fortune,* July 10, 1995, p. 141.

17. George W. Fenn, Nellie Liang, and Stephen Prowse, "The Private Equity Market: An Overview," *Financial Markets, Institutions and Instruments,* vol. 6, no. 4 (1997), p. 37.

18. Earlier hot IPO markets, marked by heavy issuance, occurred in 1960–62 and 1968–69. See Roger G. Ibbotson and Jeffrey F. Jaffee, "Hot Issue Markets," *Journal of Finance,* vol. 30 (September 1975), p. 1030.

19. Tim Loughran and Jay R. Ritter, "The Timing and Subsequent Performance of IPOs: The U.S. and International Evidence," working paper, University of Illinois at Urbana-Champaign, 1993.

20. Robert N. McCauley and Steven A. Zimmer, "Explaining International Differences in the Cost of Capital," Federal Reserve Bank of New York *Quarterly Review*, 14 (Summer 1989), pp. 7–28; Robert N. McCauley and Steven A. Zimmer, "Exchange Rates and International Differences in the Cost of Capital," in Yakov Amihud and Richard M. Levich, eds., *Exchange Rate Effects on Corporate Financial Performance* (New York: Irwin Professional Publishing, 1994), pp. 119–148; James M. Poterba, "Comparing the Cost of Capital in the United States and Japan: A Survey of Methods," Federal Reserve Bank of New York *Quarterly Review*, vol. 15 (Winter 1991), pp. 20–32; Burton Malkiel, "The Influence of Conditions in Financial Markets on the Time Horizons of Business Managers: An International Comparison," Princeton University typescript, January 1992; Richard Mattione, "A Capital Cost Disadvantage for Japan?" *Journal of International Securities Market*, vol. 6 (Summer 1992), pp. 173–98.

21. Robert Z. Aliber, "A Theory of Direct Foreign Investment," in Charles P. Kindleberger, ed., *The International Corporation: A Symposium* (Cambridge: MIT Press, 1970), pp. 17 and 28.

22. For an econometric analysis of the influence of the cost of equity on foreign acquisitions in the United States, see Davis S. Laster and Robert N. McCauley, "Making Sense of the Profits of Foreign Firms in the United States," Federal Reserve Bank of New York *Quarterly Review*, vol. 19, no. 2 (Summer–Fall, 1994), pp. 46–7.

23. Christopher L. Bach, "U.S. International Transactions, First Quarter 1997," U.S. Department of Commerce *Survey of Current Business*, vol. 77, no. 7, (July 1997), p. 65.

24. Michael Porter, "Capital Disadvantage: America's Failing Capital Investment System," *Harvard Business Review*, vol. 70, September–October 1992, pp. 65–82.

25. See Robert B. Reich and Eric D. Mankin, "Joint Ventures with Japan Give Away Our Future," *Harvard Business Review*, March–April 1986, pp. 78–85; Michael Crichton, *Rising Sun* (New York: Ballentine, 1992), a novel with a three-page bibliography.

26. House of Representatives, *Omnibus Trade and Competitiveness Act of 1988: Conference Report*, 100th Congress, 2nd session, April 20, 1988, pp. 338, 924–28, codified as Section 721 of the Defense Production Act. On the Exon-Florio amendment, see Senate Commerce Committee, *Acquisition by Foreign Companies: Hearing*, 100th Congress, 1st session, June 10, 1987; and Subcommittee on Economic Stabilization of the House Committee on Banking, Finance and Urban Affairs, *Mergers and Acquisitions— Foreign Investment in the United States: Hearing*, 100th Congress, 1st session, October 21, 1987.

27. Linda Spencer, *Foreign Investment in the United States: Unencumbered Access* (Washington, DC: Economic Strategy Institute, 1991).

28. Senator Donald Riegle, Chairman of the Senate Banking Committee, in a statement to the Subcommittee on International Finance and Monetary Policy, Senate Banking Committee, *Foreign Acquisitions of U.S. Owned Companies: Hearing*, 102nd Congress, 2nd Session, S. Hrg. 102–977 (June 4, 1992), p. 4.

29. Laura D'Andrea Tyson, quoted by Senator Donald Riegle, Chairman of the Senate Banking Committee, in a statement to the Subcommittee on International Finance and Monetary Policy, Senate Banking Committee, *Foreign Acquisitions of U.S. Owned Companies: Hearing*, 102nd Congress, 2nd Session, S. Hrg. 102–977 (June 4, 1992), pp. 21, 39, 75. See also Laura D'Andrea Tyson, *Who's Bashing Whom?: Trade Conflict in High Technology Industries* (Washington, DC: Institute for International Economics, 1992), pp. 42–44. Theodore H. Moran has proposed blocking foreign acquisitions that concentrate foreign control of technologies critical to national defense. See Theodore H. Moran, "The Globalization of America's Defense Industries," *International Security* (Summer 1990), pp. 57, 82–83.

30. Dorothy Robyn, "Buying America," *Issues in Science & Technology* (Fall 1989), pp. 88–89, cited by Gregory Tassey, *Technology, Infrastructure and Competitive Position* (Norwell, MA: Kluwer Academic Publishers, 1992), p. 142.

31. Gregory Tassey, *Technology, Infrastructure*, pp. 144, 150.

32. Whereas Edward M. Graham and Paul R. Krugman, in *Foreign Direct Investment in the United States* (Washington, DC: Institute for International Economics, 1989), acquitted foreign firms in the United States of the charge that they do less R&D by reference to data at the level of manufacturing as a whole, Tassey (*Technology, Infrastructure*, pp. 148–49), shows that among industries within manufacturing, only in the chemicals industry do foreign firms conduct about as much R&D, and U.S. firms, and they do less in machinery, electrical equipment, transportation and instruments. The fallacy of composition arises because, as pointed out by Stephen Hymer, *The International Operations of National Firms: A Study of Direct Foreign Investment*, (Cambridge, MA: MIT Press, 1976), foreign direct investment is concentrated in industries with high ratios of R&D and advertising expense. Tassey (pp. 151–2) recognizes that U.S. firms' foreign subsidiaries conduct relatively less R&D abroad than they do at home.

33. Udayan Gupta, "Venture Capital Investment Soars, Reversing Four-Year Slide," *Wall Street Journal*, June 1, 1993, p. B2.

34. See Daniel I. Okimoto, Sheridan M. Tatsuno, E. Floyd Kvamme, Yoshio Nishi, and Edward J. DeWath, *U.S.-Japan Strategic Alliances in the Semiconductor Industry:*

Technology Transfer, Competition and Public Policy, (Washington, D.C.: National Academy Press, 1992).

Chapter 9

1. Houlihan Lokey Howard & Zukin, *Mergerstat,* 4th quarter, January 1998, p. 1. Announced deals are not strictly comparable to the completed deals plotted in figure 3.2, but the year-over-year growth indicates that 1997 was a record year for completed deals as well.

2. Laura Jereski, "Buyout Funds Frustrated by Lack of Deals," *Wall Street Journal* (European edition), April 27, 1995, p. 22, reported that "the funds have huge sums burning holes in their pockets. So far this year, they have raised $5.2 billion of new money, bringing their total available cash to more than $16 billion."

3. KKR's own modus operandi has been adapted to the 1990s in the form of the so-called leveraged buildup. The leveraged buyout partnership acquires a middle-market firm and builds it up through acquisition in a consolidating industry like publishing. See "KKR, Forstmann Adapt Strategies to New Market," *The Private Equity Analyst,* March 1994, cited in George W. Fenn, Nellie Liang, and Stephen Prowse, "The Private Equity Market: An Overview," *Financial Markets, Institutions and Instruments,* vol. 6, no. 4 (July 1997), p. 24.

4. These deals of more than $1 billion were Forstmann Little–Ziff-Davis, KKR-Borden, KKR-Bruno's, GS Capital Partners II–AMF, Forstmann Little–Community Health Systems, and KKR-Amphenol.

5. This structure is somewhat reminiscent of the par refix notes of RJR as discussed in chapter 4.

6. Although table 9.2 only covers deals for which the fees were disclosed, the trends are probably reliable insofar as fees for the largest deals are most often disclosed, and these deals dominate the dollar totals.

7. Personal communication to author by Alexander David, Capital Markets Section, Board of Governors. For 1984–89, David found 3 upgrades and 3 downgrades in stock-swap mergers and 16 upgrades and 38 downgrades in cash-financed mergers; for mid-1994 to mid-1997, he found 25 upgrades and 12 downgrades in stock-swap mergers and 21 upgrades and 24 downgrades in cash-financed mergers.

8. Conglomerates may be valued at less than the sum of their parts, even if profitability is in line with the appropriate blend of "pure play" firms, if Wall Street analysts specialize and thus find it very difficult to build up the value of a conglomerate.

Philip G. Berger and Eli Ofek, "Diversification's Effect on Firm Value," *Journal of Financial Economics,* vol. 37 (January 1995), pp. 3–38, exclude conglomerates with financial services subsidiaries "because applying the valuation methods we use is problematic for such firms. Specifically, many firms in the financial services industry do not have information available on earnings before interest and taxes (EBIT), because such earnings are not meaningful for financial companies." Precisely: It is hard for any one analyst, or even two financial economists, to value a conglomerate.

9. See Anthony Sampson, *The Sovereign State of ITT* (New York: Stein and Day, 1973).

10. This sale lowered Westinghouse's leverage. George Fenn (personal communication with the authors), then on the Board of Governors, found that firms selling divisions in 1991–95 had a median leverage of 32 percent (defined as the ratio of debt to total capital), significantly higher than the 25 percent median leverage for a matched sample of nondivesting firms. Moreover, leverage tended to decline after asset sales.

11. Myron Slovin, Marie E. Sushka, and Steven R. Ferraro, "A Comparison of the Information Conveyed by Equity Carve-outs, Spin-offs and Asset Sell-offs," *Journal of Financial Economics,* vol. 37 (January 1995), pp. 89–104, found that the shares of rivals of spun-off firms rise on the spin-off announcement, whereas the shares of rivals of carved-out firms fall on the carve-out announcement. They interpret this finding as showing that investors conclude that percent managers judge spun-off shares as undervalued and carved-out shares as overvalued.

12. See Ted Fikre, "Equity Carve-outs in Tokyo," Federal Reserve Bank of New York *Quarterly Review,* vol. 15, no. 3–4 (Winter 1991), pp. 60–4.

13. Berger and Ofek, "Diversification's Effect."

14. See Eli Remolona and Kurt Wulfekuhler, "Finance Companies, Bank Competition, and Niche Markets," Federal Reserve Bank of New York *Quarterly Review,* 17 (Summer 1992), pp. 25–38.

15. See Sanjai Bhagat, Andrei Shleifer, and Robert Vishny. "Hostile Takeovers in the 1980s; The Return to Corporate Specialization," *Brookings Papers in Economic Activity, Microeconomics,* 1990, pp. 1–72. Robert Comment and Gregg A. Jarrell, "Corporate Focus and Stock Returns," *Journal of Financial Economics,* vol. 37 (January 1995), pp. 67–87, found that the percentage of Compustat firms with just one segment rose from 36 to 56 percent between 1978 and 1988 and that the average number of segments reported fell from 2.6 to 1.9 in the same years.

16. Joan Harrison, "Going Upstream in Drug Marketing," *Mergers and Acquisitions,* September/October 1994, p. 43.

17. Michael C. Jensen, "The Modern Industrial Revolution, Exit, and the Failure of Internal Control Systems," *Journal of Finance,* vol. 48 (1993), p. 853, cites General Dynamics as a counterexample of a well-functioning internal control system that delivered the goods to shareholders without a takeover threat and without debt. Note that at the aggregate level there was debt associated with General Dynamics payouts in that the buyers drew on cash or lined up new debt to buy the divisions from General Dynamics.

18. The $54 million figure is by the calculation of a by no means hostile pair of observers: Jay Dial and Kevin J. Murphy, "Incentives, Downsizing, and Value Creation at General Dynamics," *Journal of Financial Economics,* vol. 37 (1995), p. 291.

19. See Dial and Murphy, *"Incentives, Downsizing,"* p. 293.

Chapter 10

1. Charles P. Kindleberger, "Asset Inflation and Monetary Policy," Banco Nazionale del Lavoro *Quarterly Review,* no. 192, March 1995, pp. 17–37.

2. John Maynard Keynes, *A Treatise on Money,* vol. 1 (New York: Harcourt Brace, 1930), p. 254.

3. Milton Friedman and Anna J. Schwartz, *A Monetary History of the United States, 1867–1960* (Princeton, NJ: Princeton University Press, 1963), pp. 261–2.

4. Shortly after, Mullins left for the persuasively named investment management firm Long Term Capital, which may turn over its portfolio more than its name suggests.

5. See Bank for International Settlements, *Sixty-Fifth Annual Report, 1995,* (Basle, Switzerland: Bank for International Settlements), p. 90; Andrew Haldane, "Inflation Targets," Bank of England *Quarterly Bulletin,* vol. 35, no. 3 (August 1995), p. 251.

6. See Salomon Brothers, *International Market Roundup* (New York: Salomon Brothers, November 17, 1995), p. 6, setting out a reaction function for the Bundesbank based on John Taylor, "Discretion versus Policy Rules in Practice," *Carnegie-Rochester Conference Series on Public Policy,* vol. 39 (December 1993), pp. 195–214. See also Richard Clarida, Jordi Gali, and Mark Gertler, "Monetary Policy Rules in Practice: Some International Evidence," *European Economic Review,* forthcoming.

7. Kindleberger, "Asset Inflation," pp. 20–3.

8. Even a recent book arguing the thesis that markets have become vastly more powerful than officials cannot deny that Mieno pricked the Tokyo bubble. See Gregory

J. Millman, *The Vandal's Crown*, (New York: Free Press 1995). But that not everyone at the Bank of Japan was convinced is evident from a recent speech by Mieno's successor, Yasuo Matsushita, before the Capital Markets Research Institute in Tokyo on June 14, 1995. Matsushita said: "We believe that it is not appropriate to treat the stability of asset prices, such as those of land and stocks, on the same basis as general price stability, and to include it in the goal of monetary policy." Reprinted in Bank for International Settlements, *BIS Review*, no. 129, August 3, 1995, p. 4.

9. Charles Goodhart, "Price Stability and Financial Stability," in Kuniho Sawamoto, Zenta Nakajima, and Hiroo Taguchi, eds., *Financial Stability in a Changing Environment* (New York: St. Martin's, 1995), pp. 439–97.

10. This is by no means a universal view: "While the non-monetary factors and macroeconomic policy settings contributed to the hike in asset prices, the main reason was obviously the aggressive lending behavior of banks." Zenta Nakajima and Hiroo Taguchi, "Toward a More Stable Financial Framework: Long-term Alternatives—An Overview of Recent Bank Disruption Worldwide," in K. Sawamoto, Z. Nakajima, and H. Taguchi, eds., *Financial Stability*, p. 61.

11. Many treatments blame international cooperation for the Tokyo bubble. "Unlike Germany, Japan allowed itself to be tempted to pursue an unduly expansionary monetary policy geared to the exchange rate. That contributed to the bubble there which has adversely affected the Japanese economy to this day. Viewed in these terms, I am afraid, in those days cooperation was not an unqualified success." Hans Tietmeyer, President of the Deutsche Bundesbank, speech before the Chicago Council on Foreign Relations, Chicago, October 11, 1995, in Bank for International Settlements, *BIS Review*, October 24, 1995, p. 7.

12. Monica Hargraves and Garry J. Schinasi, "Monetary Policy, Financial Liberalization, and Asset Price Inflation," International Monetary Fund *World Economic Outlook*, Annex I (May 1993), p. 81; see also Garry J. Schinasi, "Balance Sheet Constraints and the Sluggishness of the Current Recovery," International Monetary Fund *World Economic Outlook*, Annex I (May 1992), pp. 47–51.

13. See Robert N. McCauley and Steven A. Zimmer, "Explaining International Differences in the Cost of Capital," Federal Reserve Bank of New York *Quarterly Review*, vol. 14 (Summer 1989), pp. 8–10.

14. Armen A. Alchian and Benjamin Klein. "On a Correct Measure of Inflation," *Journal of Money, Credit and Banking*, vol. 5, no. 1, pt. 1 (February 1973), pp. 183–91.

15. By one view, however, higher interest rates might have spurred further corporate leveraging and higher prices for whole companies rather than less activity and lower prices. If high real interest rates created free cash flow (by reducing profitable invest-

ment opportunities more than it raised interest costs) and thereby caused the corpo-rate leveraging of the 1980s, as Margaret Blair and Robert Litan suggest, then still higher rates might have led to still more leveraging. To be fair to these authors, how-ever, note that their preferred policy would have been lower federal deficits to lower bond yields. See Margaret M. Blair and Robert Litan, "Corporate Leverage and Lever-aged Buyouts in the Eightees," in John B. Shoven and Joel Waldfogel, eds., *Debt, Taxes and Corporate Restructuring* (Washington, DC: Brookings, 1990), pp. 43–80.

16. By one measure, real aggregate asset prices rose some 25–30 percent in the United States between 1984 and 1989. See Bank for International Settlements, *Sixty-third Annual Report* (Basle, Switzerland: Bank for International Settlements, 1993), p. 166, and the expansion of the argument in Claudio Borio, Neil Kennedy, and Stephen Prowse, *Exploring Aggregate Price Fluctuations across Countries*, BIS *Economic Papers* no. 40 (Basle, Switzerland: Bank for International Settlements, 1994).

17. See Russell-NCREIF index as plotted in Theodore Fischer and Robert N. McCauley, "Foreign Investors' Losses in U.S. Real Estate," Federal Reserve Bank of New York *Quarterly Review*, vol. 19, no. 2 (Summer–Fall 1994), p. 61.

18. Edward J. Frydl, "Overhangs and Hangovers: Coping with the Imbalances of the 1980s," Federal Reserve Bank of New York *Seventy-Seventh Annual Report* (1992), pp. 5–30.

19. Ronald Johnson, "The Bank Credit 'Crumble,'" Federal Reserve Bank of New York *Quarterly Review*, vol. 16 (Summer 1991), pp. 40–51, and Ronald Johnson and Chun K. Lee, "The Link Between the 1980s Credit Boom and the Recent Bank Credit Slowdown," in M. A. Akhtar, ed., *Federal Reserve Bank of New York Studies on Causes and Consequences of the 1989–92 Credit Slowdown* (New York: Federal Reserve Bank of New York, February 1994), pp. 113–30.

20. Kindleberger, "Asset Inflation," p. 23.

21. Kindleberger, "Asset Inflation," p. 35. Also, see Christopher Kent and Philip Lowe, "Property-price Cycles and Monetary Policy," in *The Role of Assets Prices in the Formulation of Monetary Policy*, BIS *Conference Papers*, vol. 5 (Basle: Bank for Inter-national Settlements, March 1998), pp. 239–263, for a formal argument that an inflation-targeting central bank might need to drive inflation under its target to prick a bubble that threatens financial stability.

22. Alan Greenspan, speech before the American Enterprise Institute, December 1996 (www.bog.frb.fed.us/boardDocs/speeches/1996/19961205.htm).

23. Alan Greenspan, speech at the 15th Anniversary Conference of the Center for Economic Policy Research at Stanford University, Stanford, California, September 5,

1997, as reprinted in Bank for International Settlements, *BIS Review*, no. 79, September 8, 1997, pp. 6–7.

24. "In light of the very large gains in wealth, the impetus to consumption appears to have been smaller than might have been anticipated on the basis of historical relationships." Consumption data were later revised upward. "Monetary Policy Report to Congress," *Federal Reserve Bulletin*, vol. 83, no. 8 (August 1997), p. 645. A year later: "With their incomes and wealth having been on a strong upward track, American consumers remain quite upbeat . . . Reduced prospects for the return to capital . . . could also affect consumption if stock prices adjust to a less optimistic view of earnings prospects." Testimony of Alan Greenspan before the Senate Committee on Banking, Housing and Urban Affairs, July 21, 1998 (www.bog.frb.fed.us/BoardDocs/HH/1998/July/Testimony.htm). A year later: "Consumption growth should slow some, if, as seems most likely, outsized gains in share values are not repeated." Testimony of Alan Greenspan before the House Committee on Banking and Financial Services, July 22, 1999 (www.bog.frb.fed.us/BoardDocs/HH/1999/July/Testimony.htm). For evidence of the instability of the effect of stock prices on spending, see Vincent Raymond Reinhart, "Equity Prices and Monetary Policy in the United States," in *The Role of Assets Prices*, pp. 280–300, and Sydney Ludvigson and Charles Steindel, "How Important Is the Stock Market Effect on Consumption?" Federal Reserve Bank of New York, *Economic Policy Review*, vol. 5, no. 2 (July 1999), pp. 29–51.

25. One popular answer to the observation that the dividend yield on U.S. stocks, at around 2 percent, has been unusually low in the 1990s is to point to share repurchases as tax-efficient dividends. But Kevin Cole, Jean Helwege, and David Laster, "Stock Market Valuation Indicators: Is This Time Different?" *Security Analysts Journal*, May–June 1996, pp. 56–64, have shown that even treating repurchases as dividends leaves the cash yield on U.S. shares at unusually low levels.

26. Benjamin M. Friedman, *Implications of Increasing Corporate Indebtedness for Monetary Policy*, Group of Thirty Occasional Paper no. 29 (New York: Group of Thirty, 1990).

27. In July 1990, Greenspan cited a widening of spreads between banks' cost of funds and rates charged corporate borrowers as evidence of a tightening of credit markets "independent of actions by the Federal Reserve." "Both banks and thrift institutions have cut back on other types of lending that can less easily be rechannelled, however, including construction and nonresidential real estate loans, loans to highly leveraged borrowers, and loans to small and medium-sized businesses. To offset tighter credit market conditions, which could exert undue restraint on aggregate demand, the Federal Reserve has recently adopted a slightly more accommodative stance with regard to reserve provision, fostering a small decline in market interest rates" (Federal Open

Market Committee, "Monetary Report to the Congress," in Board of Governors of the Federal Reserve System, *Seventy-Seventh Annual Report, 1990,* Board of Governors, Washington, DC, p. 64). For the staff work behind Greenspan's conversion to the "credit crunch" or "credit crumble" perspective, see "May STBL [Survey of Terms of Bank Lending] Results," memorandum to Board of Governors from Thomas Brady of June 29, 1990 (available from author). The image of "headwinds" to summarize the drag of banks', corporations', and households' balance sheet restructuring came into vogue later. In July 1993, the Congress was told that "[s]tresses associated with the restructuring of the economy and the earlier buildup of debt linger" (Federal Open Market Committee, "Monetary Policy Report to the Congress," *Federal Reserve Bulletin,* vol. 79, no. 9 (September 1993), p. 841); in February 1994, after the beginning of a cycle of tightening of short-term rates, Congress was told that "[h]ouseholds and businesses were able to take further steps to reduce the burden of servicing debt, and more expansive attitudes toward spending and the use of credit seemed to take hold" (Federal Open Market Committee, "Monetary Policy Report to the Congress," *Federal Reserve Bulletin,* vol. 80, no. 3 (March 1994), p. 199).

28. George Anders, *Merchants, of Debt: KKR and the Mortgaging of American Business* (New York: Basic Books, 1990) p. 274.

29. See Bank for International Settlements, *Sixty-Fifth Annual Report,* pp. 106–7, and *Sixty-Sixth Annual Report* (Basle, Switzerland: Bank for International Settlements, 1996), p. 74; and Claudio E. V. Borio and Robert N. McCauley, *The Economics of Recent Bond Market Volatility,* BIS Economic Papers no. 45 (Basle, Switzerland: Bank for International Settlements, July 1996), pp. 28–31.

30. Charles Calomiris, Anthanasios Orphanides, and Steven A. Sharpe, "Leverage as a State Variable for Employment, Inventory Accumulation, and Fixed Investment," working paper no. 4800, National Bureau of Economic Research, Cambridge, MA. (July 1994).

31. See Edward J. Frydl, "Overhangs and Hangovers": George L. Perry and Charles L. Schultze, "Was This Recession Different? Are They All Different?" *Brookings Papers on Economics Activity,* 1993:1, pp. 145–95; and Charles Steindel and David Brauer, "Credit Supply Constraints on Business Activity, Excluding Construction," in M.A. Akhtar, ed., *Federal Reserve Bank of New York: Studies in the Causes and Consequences of the 1989–92 Credit Slowdown* (New York: Federal Reserve Bank of New York, February 1994).

32. DRI's structural estimates also showed a short-fall of actual against expected investment in producer's durable equipment. See Patricia C. Mosser, "Influence of the Credit Crunch on Aggregate Demand and Implications for Monetary Policy," in M.A. Akhtar, ed., *Federal Reserve Bank of New York, Studies in the Causes and Consequences*

of the 1989–92 Credit Slowdown (New York: Federal Reserve Bank of New York, February 1994), pp. 289, 292.

33. Kevin Phillips, *Arrogant Capital* (Boston: Little Brown, 1994), pp. 94–7. The quotes on the following page of text are from, respectively, pp. 96, 94, 94, 95, 97, and 96. Compare Burton G. Malkiel and J. P. Mei, "Hedge Funds: The New Barbarians at the Gate," *Wall Street Journal*, September 29, 1998, p. 22.

34. See Charles P. Kindleberger, *Manias, Panics, and Crashes*, 3rd edition (New York: John Wiley, 1996), pp. 196–197.

35. See for instance Menahem Prywes, "The Good Work of Financial Crises," *Columbia Journal of World Business*, vol. 27, no. 1 (Spring 1992), pp. 15–21.

36. See Richard Cantor, "Early Signs of Easy Credit," Federal Reserve Bank of New York Pre-FOMC Briefing, December 17, 1993, and "Business Credit: The Demand for C&I Loans," Federal Reserve Bank of New York Pre-FOMC Briefing, June 28, 1994.

37. See Bank for International Settlements, *Sixty-Sixth Annual Report*, pp. 100–102; Robert N. McCauley and Karsten von Kleist, "The Carry Trade Strategy," Bank for International Settlements, *International Banking and Financial Market Developments*, February 1998, pp. 23–24; Bank for International Settlements, *Sixty-Eighth Annual Report* (Basle, Switzerland: Bank for International Settlements, 1998), p. 101; Bank for International Settlements, *Sixty-Ninth Annual Report* (Basle, Switzerland: Bank for International Settlements, 1999), pp. 105–109.

38. See Borio and McCauley, *Economics*, pp. 28–32 and 66–72; Franklin R. Edwards, "Hedge Funds and the Collapse of Long-Term Capital Management," *Journal of Economic Perspectives*, vol. 13, no. 2 (Spring 1999), pp. 189–210; President's Working Group on Financial Markets, *Hedge Funds, Leverage, and the Lessons of Long-Term Capital Management: Report*, April 1999; John Cassidy, "Time Bomb," *The New Yorker*, vol. 75, no. 17 (July 5, 1999), pp. 28–32.

39. Goodhart, "Price Stability," p. 473.

40. See Borio, Kennedy, and Prowse, *Exploring Aggregate Asset Price Fluctuations*, p. 69, for the prescription to strengthen prudential supervision to prevent or mitigate excesses of credit, and as below, to make the tax system more neutral toward debt.

41. This list is by no means exhaustive. It might be worth thinking about the large-exposure directive of the European Community as an instrument for dealing with the credit excesses associated with asset inflation. This directive puts an overall limit on all large exposures in relation to bank capital. Whether such a policy would do any good depends on the size distribution of loans to the bubbly sector.

42. For its application to the much talked about but still obscure business of trading financial derivatives, see Eurocurrency Standing Committee of the Central Banks of

the Group of Ten Countries, *A Discussion Paper on Public Disclosure of Market and Credit Risks by Financial Intermediaries* (the "Fisher Report") Bank for International Settlements, Basle, Switzerland: 1994; and Basle Committee on Banking Supervision and the Technical Committee of the International Organization of Securities Commissions, *Public Disclosure of the Trading and Derivatives Activities of Banks and Securities Firms* Basle, Switzerland: Bank for International Settlement, November 1995.

43. Albert M. Wojnilower, "The Shrinking of Corporate Equity: Good for Each but Not for All," in Richard W. Kopke and Eric S. Rosengren, eds., *Are the Distinctions between Debt and Equity Disappearing? Proceedings of a Federal Reserve Bank of Boston Conference*, October 4–6, 1989, pp. 218–9. The novelty of Wojnilower's proposal resides not least in its imposition on the borrower rather than on the lender.

44. Kerry D. Vandell, Walter Banes, David Hartzell, Dennis Kraft, and William Wendt, "Commercial Mortgage Defaults: Proportional Hazards Estimation Using Individual Loan Histories," *Journal of the American Real Estate and Urban Economics Association*, vol. 21, no. 4 (1993), pp. 451–80.

45. William Sterling, "The Leveraging of Japan," *The International Economy*, vol. 3, no. 3 (May/June 1989), pp. 68–74.

46. Andrew Sheng, "The Linked Exchange Rate System: Review and Prospects," Hong Kong Monetary Authority *Quarterly Bulletin*, no. 3 (May 1995), p. 58 [his italics].

47. Hong Kong Commissioner of Banking, *Annual Report, 1991* (Hong Kong, 1992), p. 20. The authors are indebted to Nelson Man, Acting Head, Banking Department, Hong Kong Monetary Authority, for help in locating this and the following primary records.

48. David Carse, Deputy Chief Executive (Banking) of the Hong Kong Monetary Authority, letter regarding property lending to John Aspden, Chairman, The DTC Association, dated 18 February 1994 (CB/POL/5/21; available from Hong Kong Monetary Authority). See also Simon Holberton, "Fear of Heights Grips HK Property Market," *Financial Times*, March 8, 1994, p. 4; and David Carse, "Market Entry and Asset Quality," Hong Kong Monetary Authority *Quarterly Bulletin*, no. 2 (February 1995), p. 47, in which the 15 percent guidance is coupled with a guidance to keep property loans at no more than 40 percent of all loans.

49. This similarity and the lags involved would not have surprised Homer Hoyt, the author of the 1930s classic, *One Hundred Years of Land Values in Chicago* (Chicago: University of Chicago Press, 1933), which found that property prices fell more slowly than stock prices.

50. "The prudent lending criteria adopted by banks in Hong Kong in their residential mortgage lending, in particular the 70% loan to value ratio, have helped to mitigate

these [liquidity and concentration] risks." David Carse, Deputy Chief Executive (Banking) speech to the Asian Bankers' Association Twelfth General Meeting and Seminar on Risk Management and Information Technology, November 9, 1995, in Manila, reprinted as "Banking Trends in Hong Kong," Hong Kong Monetary Authority *Quarterly Bulletin*, no. 5 (November 1995), pp. 38–9.

51. Sheng, "Linked Exchange Rate System," p. 58.

52. David Carse, Deputy Chief Executive, Hong Kong Monetary Authority, letter regarding criteria for property lending to the Chief Executive, All Authorized Institutions, dated 28 January 1997 (B9/25C; available from Hong Kong Monetary Authority).

53. Basle Committee on Banking Supervision, *Planned Supplement to the Capital Accord to Incorporate Market Risks* (Basle, Switzerland: Bank for International Settlements, 1995), p. 10: "The 'other' category will receive the same specific risk charge as a private-sector borrower under the credit risk requirements, i.e. 8%. However, since this may considerably underestimate the specific risk for high-yield [junk] debt securities, each member country of the Basle Committee will apply a specific risk charge higher than 8% to such securities (the precise charge and the criteria being at national discretion. . .)." In the wake of the Long-Term Capital Management debacle, superweights for exposures to highly leveraged institutions were considered and then a 150% band for high-risk exposures was proposed: Basle Committee on Banking Supervision, *Banks' Interactions Highly Leveraged Institutions*, January 1999, p. 27, and *A New Capital Adequacy Framework: Consultative Paper*, pp. 31–32.

54. Loan-to-value regulation could work through prices rather than prohibitions, too. Thus bank examiners could classify from day 1 loans at high loan-to-value ratios. Banks with ample capital and good earnings could make the loans, put up their loan loss reserves, and simply wait to prove the regulators wrong. Such a measure would amount to a higher capital requirement on the affected loans.

55. Goodhart, "Price Stability," pp. 473–9.

56. Goodhart, "Price Stability," p. 476.

57. Steven A. Zimmer and Robert N. McCauley, "Bank Cost of Capital and International Competition," Federal Reserve Bank of New York *Quarterly Review*, vol. 15, nos. 3–4 (Winter 1991), pp. 39–40. Whether the capital regulation at least strengthened the Japanese banks' ability to withstand the downturn in asset prices is not altogether clear. To be sure, Japanese banks raised massive amounts of equity directly and in the form of convertible bonds. But their realizations of cross-held shares were also massive, and these, because of the tax payments, actually lowered their economic wealth.

58. Hans Tson Soderstrom, "Finland's Economic Crisis: Causes, Present Nature, and Policy Options," in *Three Assessments of Finland's Economic Crisis and Economic Policy* (Helsinki: Bank of Finland, 1993), p 150: "The only serious attempt that was made to cool off the overheated domestic situation was the revaluation of the markka by 4 per cent in March 1989."

59. The "stock adjustment" story was also prominent in Mexico in the late 1980s to justify rapid credit growth.

60. Timo Hamalainen, "Recent Economic and Financial Market Developments," Bank of Finland *Bulletin*, vol. 63, no. 2, February 1989, p. 5.

61. See Sigbjorn Atle Berg, "The Banking Crises in the Scandinavian Countries," in *FDICIA: An Appraisal, Proceedings of the Federal Reserve Bank of Chicago Conference on Bank Structure and Competition* (May 1993), p. 441–9.

62. Many forget that, in the name of monetary control, the Federal Reserve's Euro-dollar reserve requirement (lowered to 0 at the end of 1990) included a reserve on loans originally booked onshore but rebooked offshore. See Robert N. McCauley and Rama Seth, "Bank Credit to U.S. Corporations: the Implications of Offshore Loans," Federal Reserve Bank of New York *Quarterly Review*, vol. 17 (Spring 1992), appendix. Note that a reserve on domestic credit would include credits funded with borrowings from the Euromarket, whereas a reserve against a domestic monetary aggregate would typically exclude liabilities to banks offshore.

63. As indeed the Australian authorities were able to view the losses in 1990–91 of such foreign banks as Citibank and Hong Kong Shanghai in lending to Australian corporations with a fair bit of equanimity.

64. See Ronald J. Gilson, Myron S. Scholes, and Mark A. Wolfson, "Taxation and the Dynamics of Corporate Control: The Uncertain Case for Tax-Motivated Acquisitions," and Alan J. Auerbach and David Reishus, "Taxes in the Merger Decision," both in *Knights, Raiders and Targets: The Impact of the Hostile Takeover*, John C. Coffee, Jr., Louis Lowenstein, and Susan Rose-Ackerman, eds. (New York: Oxford University Press, 1988), pp. 271–99 and 300–13; Alan J. Auerbach, testimony before the Senate Finance Committee, *Leveraged Buyouts and Corporate Debt: Hearing*, 101st Congress, 1st session (S. Hrg. 101-54, pt. 2), January 25, 1989, pp. 52–64.

65. David M. Cutler and Lawrence H. Summers, "The Cost of Conflict Resolution and Financial Distress: Evidence from the Texaco-Pennzoil Litigation," *Rand Journal of Economics*, vol. 19 (Summer 1988), pp. 157–72.

66. Connie Bruck, "The Old Boy and the New Boys," *New Yorker*, May 8, 1989, p. 83.

67. For further discussion of proposals to tax excessive interest, see Robert N. McCauley, "Policies toward Corporate Leveraging," in Edward J. Frydl, ed., *Studies*

on *Corporate Leveraging* (New York: Federal Reserve Bank of New York, 1990), pp. 183–5.

68. See McCauley, "Policies," pp. 185–9.

69. Nicholas Brady, testimony before the Senate Finance Committee, *Leveraged Buyouts and Corporate Debt: Hearing,* 101st Congress, 1st session (S. Hrg. 101–54, pt. 1), January 24, 1989, pp. 16, 18–20. Strangely enough, the Secretary of the Treasury was said to have been persuaded not to testify in favor of the hybrid approach. See Bruck, "Old Boy," pp. 88–93.

70. Martin Feldstein, "Excess Debt and Unbalanced Investment: The Case for a Cashflow Business Tax," statement to the House Ways and Means Committee, *Tax Policy Aspect of Mergers and Acquisitions: Hearings,* 101st Congress, 1st session (Ser. 101–10), January 31, 1989, pp. 214–17.

71. Mervyn A. King, "The Cash Flow Corporate Income Tax," in Martin Feldstein, ed., *The Effects of Taxation on Capital Accumulation,* (Chicago: University of Chicago Press, 1987), pp. 377–96.

72. See Don Fullerton and Andrew B. Lyon, "Tax Neutrality and Intangible Capital," in Lawrence H Summers, ed., *Tax Policy and the Economy,* vol. 2 (Cambridge: MIT Press for the National Bureau of Economic Research, 1988), pp. 63–88.

73. Such an approach was recently urged by a group tasked with lengthening the horizons of corporate managers. See Twentieth Century Fund Task Force on Market Speculation and Corporate Governance, *Report* (New York: Twentieth Century Fund, 1992), pp. 7, 11.

74. Adolph A. Berle and Gardiner Means, *The Modern Corporation and Private Property* (New York: Macmillan, 1933).

75. See Bevis Longstreth, testimony before Subcommittee on Securities, Senate Banking Committee, *Impact of Institutional Investors in Corporate Governance, Takeovers, and Capital Markets: Hearing,* 101st Congress, 1st session (S. Hrg. 101-497), October 3, 1989, pp. 123–50.

76. See review by Bernard S. Black, "The Value of Institutional Investor Monitoring: The Empirical Evidence," *UCLA Law Review,* vol. 39, no. 4 (1992), pp. 898–917.

77. David A. Walker, "Some Perspectives for Pension Fund Managers," Bank of England *Quarterly Bulletin,* vol. 27, no. 2 (May 1987), p. 250.

78. See Twentieth Century Fund Task Force on Market Speculation and Corporate Governance, *Report,* pp. 5–6, 17–20.

79. Mark J. Roe, "The Modern Corporation and Private Pensions," *UCLA Law Review,* vol. 41, no.1 (October 1993), p. 111. See also his *Strong Managers, Weak Owners: The*

Political Roots of American Corporate Finance (Princeton, NJ: Princeton University Press, 1994) for the political basis of fragmented holdings. See letter from Richard H. Koppes, General Counsel, California Public Employees' Retirement System, to Linda C. Quinn, Director, Division of Corporate Finance, Securities and Exchange Commission, November 3, 1989 (available from California Pension Retirement System).

80. See James E. Heard, testimony before Subcommittee on Telecommunications and Finance, House Energy and Commerce Committee, *Corporate Proxy Voting System: Hearing*, 100th Congress, 1st session (August 2, 1989), p. 24.

81. Mark J. Roe, *Strong Managers, Weak Owners: The Political Rights of American Corporate Finance* (Princeton, NJ: Princeton University Press, 1994), p. 274.

82. "Policies favoring privacy and liquidity have led to the system of stock registration in nominee name, creating a labyrinth that makes it all but impossible for shareholders to identify each other, much less contact each other." Robert A. G. Monks, testimony before the Subcommittee on Securities, Senate Banking Committee, *Impact of Institutional Investors in Corporate Governance, Takeovers, and Capital Markets: Hearing*, 100th Congress, 1st session (S. Hrg. 101-497), October 3, 1989, p. 168. Management could be required to disclose the identities of beneficial owners to shareholders under safeguards similar to those pertaining to management at present.

83. This has been suggested in "Rallying the Institutions," *Financial Times*, December 14, 1989, p. 18.

84. James E. Heard and Howard D. Sherman, *Conflicts of Interest in the Proxy Voting System* (Washington, DC: Investor Responsibility Research Center, 1987).

85. Michael Porter, "From Competitive Advantage to Corporate Strategy," *Harvard Business Review*, vol. 65, May–June 1987, pp. 43–59; David J. Ravenscraft and Frank M. Scherer, *Mergers, Sell-offs, and Economic Efficiency* (Washington, DC: Brookings Institution, 1987); and Ellen B. Magenheim and Dennis C. Mueller, "Are Acquiring-Firm Shareholders Better off after an Acquisition?" in *Knights, Raiders, and Targets: The Impact of the Hostile Takeover* (New York: Oxford University Press, 1988), pp. 171–93.

86. See William Nordhaus, "The Vanity of the Takeover Game," *New York Times*, October 2, 1982, Section 3, p. 3; Louis Lowenstein, "Pruning Deadwood in Hostile Takeovers: A Proposal for Legislation," *Columbia Law Review*, 83 (March 1983), pp. 317–34.

87. Louis Lowenstein, *What's Wrong with Wall Street?* (Reading, MA: Addison-Wesley, 1988), pp. 209–11.

88. This proposal should be contrasted with the milder suggestion that substantial shareholders should enjoy the right to include their own nominees for director in the corporation's proxy materials. See Heard, Testimony before Subcommittee, p. 23.

89. Roe, "Modern Corporation."

Chapter 11

1. Unlike the Minsky-Kindleberger view, the rational bubble has no prediction that asset prices play off each other. In fact, manias tend to come in pairs, at least, as with real estate and stock markets in the late 1980s. See C. E. V. Borio, N. Kennedy, and S. D. Prowse, *Exploring Aggregate Asset Price Fluctuations across Countries*, BIS *Economic Papers*, no. 40 (Basle, Switzerland: Bank for International Settlements April 1994).

2. Steven N. Kaplan and Jeremy C. Stein, *Continental Bank Journal of Applied Corporate Finance*, vol. 6, no. 1 (Spring 1993), pp. 72–88, a variant of "The Evolution of Buyout Pricing and Financial Structure in the 1980s," *Quarterly Journal of Economics*, May 1993, pp. 313–57; Martin Fridson, *Continental Bank Journal of Applied Corporate Finance*, vol. 45, no. 3 (Fall 1991).

3. Michael C. Jensen, "Corporate Control and the Politics of Finance," *Continental Bank Journal of Applied Corporate Finance*, vol. 4, no. 2 (Summer 1991), p. 26.

4. Suein L. Hwang and Steven Lipin, "KKR Has Shed Last of Stake in RJR Nabisco," *Wall Street Journal*, March 16, 1995, p. A3. See also "'Barbarians' Revisited: KKR's Buyout of RJR Nabisco Was a Major Fizzle—for Investors," *Business Week*, April 3, 1995, pp. 46–7.

5. *Brookings Papers on Economic Activity*, 1988:1, pp. 83–125; and same authors and Tony M. Whited, "U.S. Corporate Leverage: Developments in 1987 and 1988," *Brookings Papers on Economic Activity*, 1990:1, pp. 255–86.

6. Some analysts have spoken of the "crash that did not happen." See Richard Cantor and John Wenninger, "Perspective on the Credit Slowdown," Federal Reserve Bank of New York *Quarterly Review*, vol. 18 (Spring 1993), pp. 3–36.

7. Michael C. Jensen, "Active Investors, LBOs, and the Privatization of Bankruptcy," *Journal of Applied Corporate Finance* (Spring 1989).

8. Sanjai Bhagat, Andrei Shleifer, and Robert Vishny, "Hostile Takeovers in the 1980s: The Return to Corporate Specialization," *Brookings Papers on Economic Activity, Microeconomics*, 1990, pp. 1–72.

9. Michael Porter, "From Competitive Advantage to Corporate Strategy," *Harvard Business Review*, vol. 65, no. 3 (May–June 1987), p. 43.

10. See Ken Auletta, "American Keiretsu: The Next Corporate Order," *New Yorker*, October 20 and 27, 1997, pp. 225–7.

11. Henry Kaufman, "The 1990s: The Threat to Our Economic Democracy," speech to the Money Marketeers of New York University, November 16, 1989 (available from Henry Kaufman and Company, New York).

12. Albert M. Wojnilower, "The Shrinking of Corporate Equity: Good for Each but Not for All," in Richard W. Kopke and Eric S. Rosengren, eds., *Are the Distinctions between Debt and Equity Disappearing? Proceedings of a Conference Held at Melvin Village*, New Hampshire, October 4–6, 1989, (Boston: Federal Reserve Bank of Boston, 1990) pp. 217–8.

13. See Claudio E. V. Borio and Robert N. McCauley, *The Economics of Recent Bond Yield Volatility*, BIS *Economic Papers* no. 45 (Basle, Switzerland: Bank for International Settlements, July 1996).

14. The "smart money," represented by the hedge funds and their former colleagues on the proprietary trading desks of securities firms and big banks was stung with losses as portfolios of U.S., European, and exotic Latin American bonds headed south. In this case the "smart money" distinguished itself from the "dumb money" represented by Orange County only in figuring out a little faster that the game had changed and that it was no longer safe to finance 10-year bonds with overnight money. See Philippe Jorion, *Big Bets Gone Bad: Derivatives and Bankruptcy in Orange County* (San Diego, CA: Harcourt Brace, 1995).

15. Carl Ackerman, Richard McEnally, and David Ravenscraft, "The Performance of Hedge Funds," *Journal of Finance*, vol. 54, no. 3 (June 1999), p. 844.

16. Merrill Lynch *Extra Credit*, September/October 1997, p. 16.

17. Wojnilower, "Shrinking of Corporate Equity," p. 212.

Index

Bonds. *See also* Junk bonds
below-investment grade, 21
costly extension of maturities, 201,
204–205
debt restructuring through issuance
of, 185–189
interest savings from issuance of,
196–198, 202–203
market timing for issuance of,
189–191
savings on refunded (1992), 370n.6
Borden, 332
Borio, Claudio E. V., 353n.39, 358n.42,
382n.16, 383n.29, 384n.40, 390n.1,
391n.13
Boyce, Donald N., 351n.15
Brademas, John, 325
Brady, Nicholas, 320, 388n.69
B-rated junk bonds, 32–33
Brauer, David, 384n.31
Brealey, Richard A., 370n.26
British Telecom, 269
Bromley, Allan, 374n.1
Bruck, Connie, 350nn.3, 10, 388n.66
Bryan, Andrea, 370n.4
Bryon, Christopher, 349n.1
Bunny bonds, 33, 74
Burn rate, 247
Burrough, Bryan, 349n.3, 353n.46,
363n.2, 364n.9, 365n.21
Bush, George, 93
Business combination freeze statutes,
66–67, 68, 117–118. *See also* Govern-
ment regulations
Byron, Christopher, 354n.52

Caesar's World casinos, 276
Cahill, Daniel S., 361n.78, 362n.92
California's Orange County, 343,
391n.14

California's public employees pension
funds (CALPERS), 324, 325
Calomiris, Charles, 384n.30
Campbell, John, 333, 334, 335
Campeau, Robert, 29, 47, 48, 50, 101,
131, 293, 335
Cantor, Richard, 349n.2, 352n.28,
359n.47, 384n.36, 390n.6
Capital
comparing cost of, 376n.20
components of core, 359n.50
FIRREA establishment of standards
for, 96
increasing requirements for credit,
313–315
Carey, Mark, 360nn.62, 63
Carr-Gottstein Foods, 241
Carse, David, 385n.48, 386nn.50, 52
Carson, Deane, 349n.2
Cash flows
between firms and capital market,
365n.18
B-rated bond interest burden and, 33
changing interest burden on, 212–213
decline in ratio of interest to, 210
determining RJR-Nabisco and Philip
Morris, 135–136
impact of short-term interest rates/
interest burden on, 205–206
ratio of interest to, 194
relieving interest burden on, 209
RJR-Nabisco LBO cumulated, 153–154
Cash flow tax proposal, 320–321
Caves, Richard, 365n.26
CBS, 39
Cessna Aircraft, 283
Chapter 11 bankruptcies, 162–163. *See
also* Bankruptcies; Restructuring
Charan, Ram, 351n.13
Chase Manhattan, 49

effect of buyout on market value,
131–142
Robins, Brian, 359.45
Robinson, Jim, 123
Robyn, Dorothy, 377n.30
Rock, Kevin, 373n.3
Roe, Mark J., 105, 355n.2, 360n.66,
389n.79, 389n.81, 390n.89
Romano, Roberta, 118, 363n.100
Rose-Ackerman, Susan, 387n.64
Rosengren, Eric S., 385n.43, 391n.12
Rubin, Robert, 1
Ruder, David, 89
Ruud, Judith S., 236, 367n.1, 373n.9,
374nn.19, 20
Ryding, John, 352n.32

Sabini, John, 354n.57
Safeway, 232
Salomon Brothers, 22, 23, 153, 200
Sampson, Anthony, 379n.9
Sandoz, 280
Santa Fe Pacific, 39
Savings and loan (S&L) industry
divestitures of junk bonds by, 100
impact of FIRREA on, 93–101,
359n.55
junk bonds holdings by (1985–91), 98
moral hazard of bailout of, 302
Sawamoto Kuniho, 381nn.9, 10
SBC Communications, 267, 273
Schadrack, Fred, 313
Scharfstein, David, 357n.23, 367n.5
Scherer, Frank M., 389n.85
Schiffman, James R., 366n.28
Schinasi, Garry J., 381n.12
Schlesinger, Tom, 368n.7
Schneider, Allen J., 353n.47
Scholes, Myron S., 387n.64
Schroeder, Michael, 374n.15
Schultze, Charles L., 384n.31

Schultz, Paul H., 373n.10
Schwan, Basil, 130
Schwartz, Anna J., 290, 291, 380n.3
Schwert, G. William, 355n.6
SCM Corporation, 41
Scrip, 33
Seagram, 40
Seasoned public offerings. *See also* IPOs
(initial public offerings)
composition of top 50, 178–180
firm issuers of, 176–177
Section 1831e(d) [U.S. Banking Code],
95–101
Securities Act of 1933, 226
Securities Data Company, 229, 369n.
18
Securities and Exchange Commission
(SEC)
California's public employees pension
funds letter to, 324
on leveraged lending, 89–90, 306
Securities firms, 59–60. *See also* Smart
money
Security Pacific, 18
Seth, Rama, 387n.62
Shackelford, Douglas A., 366n.29,
367nn.32, 33, 34
Shaman Pharmaceuticals, 252
Shapiro, Eben, 364n.6, 364n.15
Shareholders. *See also* Stocks
coerced into accepting tender offers,
361n.73
corporate accountability to, 321–323
creating value for, 48
during WorldCom-MCI merger,
269–270
policies facilitating communication
with, 323–325
reserving board seats for nominees of,
325, 390n.88
RJR-Nabisco LBO profits to, 121

Shareholders (cont.)
tax basis of RJR-Nabisco and Philip
    Morris original, 154
Unocal on threats to, 110
Share value. *See also* Stocks
boosting, 48
comparing RJR-Nabisco and Philip
    Morris, 138–142
creating, 48
determining Philip Morris and RJR-
    Nabisco, 133–135
of M&As (1981–96), 69
of Philip Morris and RJR-Nabisco,
    132–133
ratio of Philip Morris and RJR-Nabisco
    debt to, 128
RJR-Nabisco comparative, 132–133
Sharpe, Steven A., 384n.30
Shearson Lehman, 59, 123, 303
Sheng, Andrew, 309, 385n.44, 386n.51
Sheppard, Lee, 77n. 10
Sheraton Hotels, 275
Sherman, Howard D., 389n.84
Shleifer, Andrei, 352n.33, 365nn.24,
    27, 379n.15, 391n.8
Short-term interest rates. *See also* Inter-
    est rates
corporate refinancing and, 206–211
corporate solvency/profits role of, 337
as federal favoritism, 302
interest burden and, 205–213
regression analysis of, 207–208
Shoven, John B., 352n.29, 382n.15
Siegel, Donald, 352n.26
Silicon Graphics, 252
Simon, William, 15, 16
Slovin, Myron, 379n.11
Smart money
banks as, 56–59
distinguished from dumb money,
    391n.14

interpretations of, 55–56
LBO promoters/investors as, 60–61
securities firms as, 59–60
Smith, George David, 363n.1
Smith, Randall, 364nn.6, 14, 15
Smoler, Frederic, 357n.29
Soderstrom, Hans Tson, 387n.58
Sony, 274
Southerland, Daniel, 375nn.10, 11, 12
Space Launch Systems, 283
Speculative trading
during LBOs, 26–28
Kindleberger's model of euphoria on,
    16
Spencer, Linda, 377n.27
Spin-offs, 274–278, 379n.11
Spiro, Leah Nathans, 374n.15
Sprout, Alison L., 375n.16
Stab-in-the-back theory, 329–331
Standard & Poor's, 152, 153, 161
Start-ups. *See* U.S. high technology
    companies
State corporate laws. *See also* Govern-
    ment regulations
anti-takeover statutes and, 66–68,
    117–120, 322, 355n.87
business combination freeze statutes,
    66–67, 68, 117–118
control share acquisition, 67–68,
    118–120
empirical evidence of changes in,
    68–73
fair price statutes, 67, 68, 118
impact of *Time* decision on, 65–66
State insurance regulation, 101–105
Steindel, Charles, 384n.31, 382n.24
Stein, Jeremy C., 79, 351nn.16, 18, 24,
    353n.36, 354n.58, 356n.16,
    374nn.16, 17, 390n.2
Sterling, William, 385n.44
Stewart, James B., 353n.44

Transfer Orbit Stage (TOS) [Orbital Sciences], 250
Treatise on Money (Keynes), 290
Tropicana, 40–41
Trust Indenture Act, 356n.19
Tsetsekos, George A., 355n.3
Tufano, Peter, 350n.8, 351n.21
Tyson, Laura D'Andrea, 260, 377n.29

Udell, Gregory F., 360nn.62, 63
Ulmer Brothers, 255
Underwriting
  differences in costs of, 371n.11
  Drexel market share of new-issue, 360n.57
United Air Lines (UAL), 49, 92, 93, 195, 293, 359n.44
Unocal, 39
Unocal v. Mesa Petroleum Co., 108–109, 111–112, 113–114, 116
U.S. Banking Code, 95–101. *See also* Government regulations
U.S. corporate leveraging. *See* LBOs (leveraged buyouts)
U.S. corporations. *See also* Bankruptcies; Equity; LBOs (leveraged buyouts)
  acquisitions by foreign firms of, 45
  bankruptcies of (1990–92), 52
  comparing accounting data of high/low leveraged, 365n.20
  data on defaults by nonfinancial, 354n.54
  debt restructuring by, 185–189
  foreign investment in high technology, 255–259
  lessons from leveraging by, 7–9
  leverage, profits, investment by equity issuance of nonfinancial, 182–183
  liquidity of assets as stimulant, 40–42
  motives for restructuring by, 159–165

net equity issuance by nonfinancial, 165
  nonfinancial defaults as share of liabilities, 54
  record flotation of new equity by, 172–173
  reform policies governing, 321–323
  return to equity in the 1990s, 2–3, 5–7, 165–185
  share repurchases by nonfinancial, 171
  speculative trading of assets by, 26–28
  Time decision and fiduciary standards of, 107–109
U.S. drug companies, 278–281
U.S. finance companies
  equity issuance by industrial firms with, 181
  examining profitability of (1991), 369n.20
  restructuring by, 163–164
U.S. high technology companies
  foreign investment in, 255–259
  policy debate over foreign acquisitions of, 259–263
U.S. nonfinancial corporations
  bonds calls (1991–93) by, 186
  gross public debt issuance by, 188
  investment spending as GDP percent, 299–300
  leverage, profitability, investment by equity issuance in, 182–183
  net debt issuance by, 187
  net equity issuance by, 165
  share repurchases by, 171
U.S. Steel, 121, 275, 363n.1
U.S. Treasury, 32
USX, 275

Vandell, Kerry D., 385n.44
Vazza, Diana, 371n.7

DATE DUE

DEMCO 38-297